Praise for *Free Speech*

"Jacob Mchangama's history of the world's strangest, best idea is the definitive account we have been waiting for. It teems with valuable insights, lively characters, and the author's passion for the cause he has done so much to advance. Mchangama brings to life the ancient struggles which established free speech and also the modern dangers which embattle it. *Free Speech* is that rare book which will impress scholars as much as it entertains readers, all while telling the world's most improbable success story."

—JONATHAN RAUCH, author of *The Constitution of Knowledge*

"A lot of people now claim that free speech is a danger to democracy or social inclusion. In this vital book, which is as entertaining as it is erudite, Jacob Mchangama shows why that is dead wrong. Drawing on both historical analysis and normative argument, he makes a compelling case for why anyone who cares about liberty or justice must defend free speech."

—YASCHA MOUNK, author of *The Great Experiment: Why Diverse Democracies Fall Apart and How They Can Endure* and associate professor at Johns Hopkins University

"In *Free Speech*, Jacob Mchangama presents a compelling case for the unique, universal, enduring importance of free and equal speech for all people, regardless of their particular identities or ideologies. This fascinating account of magisterial scope demonstrates the constant liberating and equalizing force of free speech throughout history and around the world. It also documents the constant censorial pressures, including many that reflect positive aims, and their inevitable suppression of full and equal human rights."

—NADINE STROSSEN, former national president, American Civil Liberties Union

FREE SPEECH

FREE SPEECH

*A History from
Socrates to Social Media*

JACOB MCHANGAMA

BASIC BOOKS
New York

Basic Books
Hachette Book Group
1290 Avenue of the Americas, New York, NY 10104
www.basicbooks.com

Printed in the United States of America

First Edition: February 2022

Published by Basic Books, an imprint of Perseus Books, LLC, a subsidiary of Hachette Book Group, Inc. The Basic Books name and logo is a trademark of the Hachette Book Group.

The Hachette Speakers Bureau provides a wide range of authors for speaking events. To find out more, go to www.hachettespeakersbureau.com or call (866) 376-6591.

The publisher is not responsible for websites (or their content) that are not owned by the publisher.

Print book interior design by Jeff Williams.

Library of Congress Cataloging-in-Publication Data

Names: Mchangama, Jacob, 1978– author.
Title: Free speech : a history from Socrates to social media / Jacob Mchangama.
Description: First edition. | New York : Basic Books, 2022. | Includes bibliographical references and index.
Identifiers: LCCN 2021034456 | ISBN 9781541600492 (hardcover) | ISBN 9781541620339 (ebook)
Subjects: LCSH: Freedom of speech—History. | Censorship—History. | Internet—Social aspects. | Communication—Political aspects.
Classification: LCC JC591 .M33 2022 | DDC 323.44/3—dc23/eng/20211001
LC record available at https://lccn.loc.gov/2021034456

ISBNs: 9781541600492 (hardcover), 9781541620339 (ebook)

LSC-C

Printing 1, 2021

For Sarah, Leo, and Norma

Contents

Introduction

The commander in chief had had it with the press. He'd spent his time in the highest office of the land trying to do the best for his people, but all the press did was undermine him and endanger the nation. There he was, making the country great again, and what did they write about? His marriages, his divorces, his children, even his weight! It was time the purveyors of fake news paid the price for their slander, sedition, and outright treason. The most powerful man in the country decided it was time to push back, launching a 136-character broadside banning

> writings and books, as well imprinted as other in which such writings and books many open and manifest errors and slanders are contained.[1]

The story of England's mercurial Henry VIII (who else?) sounds contemporary because it is. "Free Speech" is never ultimately won or lost. Ask a college student when the fight for free expression began, and you might get any one of a number of responses. Some Americans would say it started with the ratification of the First Amendment in 1791. A European might point to the 1789 French Declaration of the Rights of Man and of the Citizen. A British person might cite John Milton's *Areopagitica*, published in 1644. Whatever their differences, most would describe freedom of speech as a uniquely Western concept born somewhere around the Enlightenment. The reality is far more complex.

In truth, the roots of free speech are ancient, deep, and sprawling. The Athenian statesman Pericles extolled the democratic values of open debate and tolerance of social dissent in 431 BCE. In the ninth century CE, the irreverent freethinker Ibn al-Rāwandī used the fertile intellectual climate of the ʿAbbāsid Caliphate to question prophecy and holy books. In 1582 the Dutchman Dirck Coornhert insisted that it was "tyrannical to . . . forbid good books in order to squelch the truth."[2] The first legal protection of press freedom was instituted in Sweden in 1766 and Denmark became the first state in the world to abolish any and all censorship in 1770.

Yet, almost invariably the introduction of free speech sets in motion a process of entropy. The leaders of any political system—no matter how enlightened—inevitably convince themselves that *now* freedom of speech has gone too far. Autocratic oligarchs disdainful of sharing power with the masses twice overthrew the ancient Athenian democracy, purging proponents of democracy and dissent along the way. Hardening laws against apostasy and blasphemy curtailed the most daring freethinking in medieval Islam. In the Dutch Republic of the sixteenth century, Dirck Coornhert was exiled and his writings banned on several occasions. Both Sweden's and Denmark's experiments with press freedom were short-lived as absolutist rulers took back control of the printing presses. This phenomenon of free speech entropy is as relevant today as it was 2,500 years ago, and when looking closer, the justifications for limiting free speech in the twenty-first century have more in common with those used many centuries past than perhaps we would like to admit.

The global club of free democracies is shrinking fast. As in ancient Athens, aspirational autocrats—from Viktor Orbán in Hungary to

Narendra Modi in India—view freedom of speech as the first and most important obstacle to be cleared on the path to entrenching their power. In parts of the Islamic world, blasphemy and apostasy are still punishable by death, whether enforced by the state or by jihadist vigilantes. The global free speech recession even extends to liberal democracies, who—not unlike Henry VIII—are fearful of the consequences of disinformation and hostile propaganda spreading uncontrollably among the masses through new technology.

Free speech entropy is not merely political, but deeply rooted in human psychology. The drive to please others, the fear of outgroups, the desire to avoid conflict, and everyday norms of kindness pull us in the direction of wanting to silence uncomfortable speakers, whether on digital platforms, at college campuses, or in cultural institutions. Like a massive body in outer space pulling in all the matter close to it, censorship draws us all in. It is therefore all the more vital to actively foster and maintain a culture of free speech to ensure that this freedom continues. Laws are not enough on their own.

One of the most common and intuitively appealing arguments for limiting tolerance of intolerance—to paraphrase the Austrian philosopher Karl Popper[3]—in modern democracies is the "Weimar fallacy."[4] It argues that if only the Weimar Republic had done more to prohibit totalitarian propaganda, Nazi Germany—and thus the Holocaust—might have been avoided. Therefore modern democracies cannot afford to make the same mistake. As we will see, that is a questionable conclusion for a number of reasons. Not least because there *were* constant attempts to silence both Hitler himself and the National Socialist Party. But those attempts often helped to increase interest in, and sympathy for, the Nazis, turning monsters into martyrs. Perhaps most chillingly, the Nazis used the Weimar Republic's emergency laws to strangle the very democracy the laws were supposed to protect.

After World War II, the imperative of banning Nazi propaganda was cynically exploited by another totalitarian regime. Stalin's Soviet

Union used the Weimar fallacy to successfully lobby for the introduction of hate speech restrictions in international human rights law. This not only helped legitimize the crackdown on dissent in the Soviet bloc, but also provided legal cover under international human rights law to Muslim majority states eager to adopt a global blasphemy ban once communism had been defeated.

Closely related to the Weimar fallacy is a school of thought that insists that a commitment to the equal dignity of all requires banning hate speech in order to protect minorities and vulnerable groups from discrimination and oppression. The digital age has shown that concerns about social media–fanned hate speech should not be taken lightly, and that words that wound can contribute to both psychological and physical harms. The impact of such hate speech tends to impose a disproportionately heavy toll on targeted minorities. However, it does not follow that censorship is an appropriate or efficient remedy in societies committed to both freedom and equality. Protecting the vulnerable from discrimination and oppression while seeking to preserve freedom and equality should and can be mutually reinforcing rather than mutually exclusive.

A global look at the history of free speech suggests that free speech is in fact an indispensable weapon in the fight against oppression. White supremacy, whether in the shape of American slavery and segregation, British colonialism, or South African apartheid, relied heavily on censorship and repression. Conversely, advocates of human equality like Frederick Douglass, Ida B. Wells, Mahatma Gandhi, Martin Luther King Jr., and Nelson Mandela all championed the principle and practice of free speech to great effect and at huge personal cost. Tragically, several countries, not least India, still use hate speech laws with roots stretching back to the era of British colonialism to silence dissent and the minorities these laws were supposed to protect.

The trolling, flaming, and hostile propaganda that we see in the digital age show that speech can get ugly, and that the many benefits of equal and uninhibited discourse come at the price of inevitable abuse, disinformation, and hyperbole. Yet attempts to clamp down on wild-eyed radicals, false information, propaganda, and sedition—from the Reformation to the Enlightenment and even twentieth-century America—suggest that whatever ideas and epithets are deemed beyond the pale according to the prevailing moral norms cannot be effectively eliminated without jeopardizing freedom of speech for all. Even the most well-intentioned attempts to ensure a safe and carefully regulated public sphere will eventually succumb to the phenomenon where erstwhile champions of free speech exclude specific groups or viewpoints, owing to blind spots of intolerance, ideology, or political expediency. Relatedly, the higher someone climbs on the political ladder, the greater the temptation to abandon principles of liberty and impose censorship under the guise of some public-spirited goal. We will see such challenges to the principle of free speech everywhere from John Milton to Voltaire, and from Robespierre to the second US president, John Adams, and his Federalist administration responsible for the Sedition Act of 1798.

Why Elites Fear New Technology

New communication technology is inevitably disruptive and every new advancement—from the printing press to the internet—has been opposed by those whose institutional authority is vulnerable to being undermined by sudden change. In 1525, the great humanist scholar Erasmus of Rotterdam—himself a prodigious writer—complained that printers "fill the world with pamphlets and books . . . foolish, ignorant, malignant, libellous, mad, impious and subversive."[5] In the 1780s, after decades of opposing censorship, the Dutch Enlightenment thinker Elie Luzac categorized as "the pests of society" populist and prodemocratic "Newspaper writers" who publish "everything that surfaces in their raging and sick brains."[6] In 1858, the *New York Times* lamented that the transatlantic telegraph was "Superficial, sudden, unsifted, too fast for the truth."[7] In 1948, even the philosopher and free speech advocate Alexander Meiklejohn argued that "the *radio* as it now operates among us is not free. Nor is it entitled to the protection of the First Amendment," since it "corrupts both our morals and our intelligence."[8] And in November 2020, former US president Barack Obama declared the information architecture of the internet "the single biggest threat to our democracy."[9]

Such outbreaks of "elite panic" may reflect real concerns and dilemmas, but it is notable that they tend to erupt whenever the public sphere is expanded and previously marginalized groups are given a voice. Upon the introduction of new technology that gives access to those previously unheard, the traditional gatekeepers of public opinion fear that the newcomers will manipulate the masses through dangerous ideas and propaganda, threatening the established social and political order. This is particularly true when an expanded public sphere threatens to weaken institutional authority without offering a viable alternative to the apparent chaos and anarchy unleashed by the disruption.

This clash between an egalitarian versus an elitist conception of free speech stretches back to antiquity. It originated in the difference between Athenian democracy, where ordinary (free and male) citizens were given a direct voice in political decision making and freedom to speak frankly in public, and Roman republicanism, which limited free speech to a small elite and distinguished between liberty and licentiousness of the tongue. Yet, while there have always been those who thought of free speech as a luxury only fit to be enjoyed by an educated elite, there have also been those prepared to fight a long and often bloody struggle to expand free speech to include the poor and propertyless, foreigners, women, and religious, racial, ethnic, national, and sexual minorities. All of whom were once thought too credulous, fickle, immoral, ignorant, or dangerous to have a voice in public affairs. So while the history of free expression features an array of martyrs, villains, and cautionary tales, it also includes a number of heroes. Some of them you may know, like the great liberal philosopher John Stuart Mill, the trailblazing Dutch philosopher Baruch Spinoza, the architect of the First Amendment James Madison, and the twentieth-century foe of totalitarianism George Orwell. Others you may not, like the ancient Athenian orator Demosthenes, the ninth-century Persian polymath al-Rāzī, the Dutch freethinker Dirck Coornhert, the irrepressible "Leveller" John Lilburne, the Scottish Whig Thomas Gordon, the eighteenth-century French philosophe Marquis de Condorcet, and his contemporary compatriot, the fearless feminist Olympe de Gouges. And there are still others you have certainly heard of, though not for their contributions to free speech, like the abolitionist Frederick Douglass, the anti-lynching crusader Ida B. Wells, the campaigner for Indian independence Mahatma Gandhi, the godmother of international human rights Eleanor Roosevelt, and the South African prisoner of conscience and statesman Nelson Mandela.

Free Speech, Going Forward

Today, a great number of voices question whether we should continue to consider free speech the "first freedom." In democracies, many have come to see free speech as a tool for the powerful to marginalize minorities and the powerless. Elites in political and media institutions point to unmediated disinformation and hate speech on social media as evidence that free speech is being "weaponized" against democracy itself. Outside democracies, free speech is being crushed by the combination of authoritarian populism, religious fundamentalism, and high-tech policing of the internet.

In addition, the emergence of global tech giants has raised the specter of "moderation without representation" where private corporate behemoths—often relying on opaque algorithmic content moderation—decide the limits of global and domestic debate with little transparency or accountability.

It is true that freedom of speech can be used to amplify division, sow distrust, and inflict serious harm. But the view that the deep challenges to dignity, trust, democracy, and institutions of our splintered age can be overcome by rolling back free speech rests on shaky historical ground. Free speech laws and cultural norms constitute the "great bulwark of liberty," as put by an early eighteenth-century free speech meme that went viral and influenced Enlightenment thinkers in Britain, America, France, and Russia. Over time, the bulwark will break if not maintained, and if history is any guide, without it our future will be less free, democratic, and equal and more ignorant, autocratic, and oppressive. This book is full of examples of countries, leaders, and cultures that thought they could subordinate freedom of speech to other values and preserve a free and just society—and failed. It also tells of others who realized that free speech was all that stood between them and their dreams of absolutist rule. Their examples show us that enforced censorship marks the end of a free society, not its beginning.

To impose silence and call it tolerance does not make it so. Real tolerance requires understanding. Understanding comes from listening. Listening presupposes speech. By connecting past speech controversies with the most pressing contemporary ones, I hope to demonstrate just how much humanity has gained from the gradual spread of free speech—and just how much we stand to lose if we allow its continued erosion in this most recent digital phase of the age-old conflict between authority and free expression.

1

Ancient Beginnings

While free speech has deep and ancient roots, for much of recorded history, speaking truth to power was ill-advised and often dangerous. Judging from surviving law codes and writings, the great ancient civilizations protected the power and authority of their rulers from the speech of their subjects, not the other way around. The Hittite laws, put in place in present-day Turkey around 1650–1500 BCE, decreed that "if anyone rejects a judgment of the king, his house will become a heap of ruins."[1] According to the Hebrew Bible, the punishment for cursing "God and the king" was stoning.[2]

These laws reflected the strict hierarchies that ordered large ancient civilizations, many of which were headed by rulers thought to govern by divine right or even—as in Egypt—to be divine themselves. The Instruction of Ptah-Hotep, an Egyptian collection of maxims from around 2350 BCE, advised against speaking to "a greater man than yourself. . . .Speak when he invites you and your worth will be pleasing."[3] The ancient Chinese philosopher Confucius (551–479 BCE) also stressed the importance of obedience toward superiors and rulers, asserting that "it is unheard of for those who have no taste for defying authority to be keen on initiating rebellion."[4] You would think Confucius's words were sweet music to the ears of China's first emperor, Qin Shi Huang, when he ascended the throne some three centuries later. But in 213 BCE, he ordered Confucian literature and historical records predating his own reign to be burned and banned. In the emperor's own words, as quoted by the ancient historian Sima Qian: "I collected together the writings of all under Heaven and got rid of all which were useless." His chief minister elaborated that studying the literature and records of the past threw people "into confusion" and led them to "reject the laws and teachings. . . .Disagreement they regard as noble, and they encourage all the lower orders to fabricate slander." According to Sima Qian, more than 460 scholars were "buried" for violating the prohibition.[5] (Whether they were buried dead or alive is a matter of debate.)[6] This may have been the first organized mass burning of books in recorded history. It would not be the last.

For slaves and women, speech was especially restricted. The Sumerian Code of Ur-Nammu from around 2050 BCE—the world's oldest surviving law code—decreed that "if a slave woman curses someone acting with the authority of her mistress, they shall scour her mouth with one sila [0.85 liter] of salt."[7] The Babylonian Code of Hammurabi from 1792 to 1750 BCE allowed slave owners to cut off their slaves' ears if they uttered the words "you are not my master." Freeborn women were also punished for overstepping their boundaries. The Middle Assyrian Laws from around 1076 BCE denounced cheeky women who "utter vulgarity or indulge in low talk."[8] Other speech codes were meant to protect the honor of respectable women. According to Hammurabi's Code, the penalty for slandering a married woman or a priestess was public flogging and head shaving.[9]

Still, among the harsh injunctions of the ancient world, we can detect nuggets of religious tolerance. After founding the Achaemenid Persian Empire in the sixth century BCE, Cyrus the Great issued a clay cylinder declaring freedom of worship for the diverse subjects of his sprawling empire. According to the Hebrew Bible, he also delivered the Jews from their exile in Babylon and ordered their desecrated Temple in Jerusalem to be rebuilt.[10] The United Nations have called the Cyrus Cylinder "an ancient declaration of human rights."[11] But even if Cyrus and his successors promoted religious tolerance, they also punished disobedience by burning down temples, cutting off noses and ears, and burying people neck-deep in the desert before leaving them to die in the blistering sun.[12] So much for human rights.

Some three centuries later, the Mauryan emperor Ashoka ordered a declaration of religious tolerance to be inscribed on boulders and pillars erected throughout the Indian subcontinent. Ashoka declared that "all religions should reside everywhere." Yet even this should not be misconstrued as an endorsement of religious expression. The fine print encouraged "restraint in speech, that is, not praising one's own religion, or condemning the religion of others."[13]

We also find strains of what has—perhaps too generously—been called "primitive democracy." Among the Assyrians, Babylonians, Hittites, and Phoenicians there were assemblies, councils, and tribunals that allowed for varying degrees of representativity and political debate.[14] According to Aristotle, the Phoenician city-state of Carthage had a popular assembly, which was consulted whenever the ruling Council of Elders could not reach an agreement, and where "anybody who wishes may speak against the proposal introduced, a right that does not exist under the constitutions of Sparta and Crete."[15] However, this was still far from the idea and practice of free and equal speech that characterized the Greek city-state in which Aristotle did much of his thinking and writing.

Who Wishes to Speak?
Free Speech in Ancient Athens

Not until the fifth century BCE does the fog of ancient history reveal a city-state in which the values of democracy and free speech were formalized and articulated as a source of pride and virtue.

Some form of Athenian democracy lasted from around 507 to 322 BCE, with a number of bloody interruptions, but across the various incarnations of this ancient city-state, democratic government and free speech were inextricably linked. Athens was a direct democracy, in which the citizens themselves proposed, debated, and voted for the laws that governed them. In his famous funeral oration honoring those who died in the Peloponnesian War against Sparta, the eminent Athenian statesman Pericles offered a definition of his city's political system that still serves as a touchstone for democratic governments today: "Our constitution is called a democracy because power is in the hands not of a minority but of the whole people. When it is a question of settling private disputes, everyone is equal before the law."[16]

Yet by modern standards, the Athenian commitment to equality suffered from serious shortcomings. Women, foreigners, and slaves made up the majority of the city's population but were expressly excluded from the democratic process. Even so, the egalitarian nature of Athenian democracy was radical for its time.

For the Athenians, the state did not exist as a separate entity from the people. Free speech was thus an inherent part of the Athenian political system and civic culture, rather than an individual human right protecting one against the state, as we tend to understand it in modern liberal democracies. The Athenians did not have a concept of individual "rights" but rather one of the duties, privileges, and prerogatives of the citizen.

In time, Athens became the dominant Greek city-state, and the most powerful of the Greek forces who repelled the invasions of the Persian Empire between 490 and 479 BCE. The ancient Greek historian Herodotus argued that while living under tyranny the Athenians had been an unremarkable people. They only reached great heights when they were granted equality of speech.[17] Pericles emphasized in his oration that free popular discourse was a key source of Athenian strength: "We Athenians . . . take our decisions on policy or submit them to proper discussions: for . . . the worst thing is to rush into action before the consequences have been properly debated."[18] At least that was the ideal. But as we shall see, reality has a way of mugging ideals.

The Athenians had two distinct but overlapping concepts of free speech. *Isēgoría* referred to equality of public, civic speech, while *parrhēsía* can be translated as "frank" or "uninhibited" speech. *Isēgoría* was exercised in the Athenian Assembly—the *ekklēsia* where each session opened with the question, "who wishes to speak?"[19] *Parrhēsía* allowed the citizens to be bold and honest in expressing their opinions even when outside the assembly and extended to many spheres of Athenian life including philosophy and theater. Central to both *isēgoría* and *parrhēsía* was what scholar Arlene Saxonhouse calls the "egalitarian foundations and participatory principles of the democratic regime of the Athenians."[20] The nineteenth-century English historian and radical member of Parliament George Grote, who did much to rehabilitate the Athenian democracy as a model for liberal reform movements, emphasized "the liberty of thought and action at Athens, not merely from excessive restraint of law, but also from practical intolerance between man and man, and tyranny of the majority over individual dissenters in taste and pursuit."[21] Free speech was not only a political principle but extended to the cultural sphere more broadly.

One of the most noteworthy champions of *parrhēsía* was the famed orator Demosthenes, whose surviving speeches mention the term twenty-six times—more than any other Athenian orator. Rising to prominence in the mid-fourth century BCE, he is viewed as the last defender of Athenian democracy and liberty against the greedy imperial ambitions of Philip II of Macedon—the father of Alexander the Great.

Central to Demosthenes's ideal of democracy and freedom was the principle of open debate.[22] He proclaimed that free speech was what distinguished democratic Athens from her bitter rival, the oligarchic Sparta. In his speech *Against Leptines*, Demosthenes noted with pride that Athenians were allowed to criticize their own constitution and praise the Spartan one, while Spartans could only praise their own.[23] The ability to criticize freely one's own political system is still a litmus test of democracies, both past and present.

Demosthenes valued free speech and political debate because he believed they led to truth. Democracies were superior to oligarchies that "produce fear," since the former "have many noble and just qualities, to which sensible people must be loyal, and in particular freedom of speech, which cannot be prevented from showing the truth."[24] However, to Demosthenes the benefits of free speech depended on both a constitutional framework and civic commitment. He was scornful of Athenians who failed to live up to democratic ideals, such as listening to both sides of an argument during debates in the assembly: "Your duty, men of Athens, when debating such important matters, is, I think, to allow freedom of speech to everyone of your counsellors."[25]

Demosthenes's dogged defenses of liberty and patriotism have had a long afterlife. They inspired Cicero in his fight for the dying Roman Republic and Churchill in his efforts to warn against the threat of Hitler. Demosthenes's insistence that free speech is essential to furthering truth and his emphasis on one's moral obligation to listen to all sides of an argument would become central to later justifications of free speech, including (even if unacknowledged) those of John Milton and John Stuart Mill. While the modern era of social media has demonstrated vividly the naivety of believing that free speech *always* furthers the truth, Demosthenes's arguments still serve as a powerful model for supporters of free and open discourse.

It is, however, important to note that there were limits to free speech in Athens.[26] Those who proposed legislation in the assembly violating established laws were subject to punishment under a legal procedure known as a *graphē paranómōn*, which translates to "indictment against illegal proposals."[27] And while *isēgoría* ensured equality of speech in the assembly, it did not bar the passage of laws limiting what one could say outside the assembly. *Kakēgoría* (serious public verbal insults that we would call defamation) was prohibited. Impiety, called *asébeia*, was another serious offense, punishable by death—as Athens's most daring thinker would eventually discover. Profaning the Eleusinian Mysteries—secret religious rites—or exposing them to the uninitiated was an egregious act of impiety. That said, while it's not clear exactly how often the law against impious speech was enforced, we do know that it was nowhere near as sweeping or harsh as the draconian laws against blasphemy and heresy that would dominate Europe for more than a millennium after the victory of Christianity.

As a practice, *parrhēsía* had a much wider application than *isēgoría*, since it wasn't limited to the political sphere of the assembly. It was *parrhēsía* that allowed the free discussion of politics in the *agora*, the marketplace where (male) citizens mingled freely. There was no public institution of censorship or inquisition to ensure conformity in writing, science, and public discourse. *Parrhēsía* also allowed for a rich intellectual life in Athens and provided both positive and negative confirmation of Demosthenes's (later) point about the virtue of permitting dissent against the very democratic order.

If you were an Athenian citizen in the second half of the fifth century and went to the *agora*, chances are you would run into a man with a peculiar swagger in his walk, bulging eyes, a flat, upturned nose, and large, meaty lips. Always barefoot and unwashed, he never changed his robes despite using them as a blanket during the night. This shabby figure was Socrates, whom many consider the founder of Western philosophy, even though he never wrote a single sentence. Socrates is famous for his dialectic method, which is basically a Q&A session that whittles down a general topic, such as the meaning of virtue or justice, to more precise concepts. Socrates delighted in humiliating his verbal sparring partners by luring them down logical dead ends, forcing even the most prominent of

Athenians to admit their ignorance. Socrates's opponents would start sweating or break down in tears when verbally stripped naked and slowly roasted. Ultimately, the Athenians would abandon tolerance and debate and resort to law and the ultimate punishment to put an end to Socrates's *parrhēsía*. As we'll learn, even modern democracies are prone to repeat such outbreaks of majoritarian intolerance.

The two "rock stars" of Western philosophy, Plato and Aristotle, both set up shop in Athens. Plato, a native Athenian aristocrat, was hostile toward democracy, perhaps inspired by Socrates's disgust that any Athenian, be he a "carpenter, blacksmith, shoemaker, merchant, ship-captain, rich man, poor man, well-born, low-born—it doesn't matter," could speak on public issues in the assembly, "and nobody blast[ed] him for presuming to give counsel without any proper training under a teacher."[28] Plato advocated what some—most famously, the philosopher Karl Popper—have called a totalitarian state. Aristotle, an immigrant noncitizen, had mixed feelings about democracy, and warned lawmakers against "indecency of speech," since "the light utterance of shameful words leads soon to shameful actions."[29] But both Aristotle and Plato were allowed to write, teach, and set up academies in Athens, where they could promote alternative constitutions to the one that ensured their liberty to philosophize freely. Athenian free thought also saw great advancements in science and medicine that might have been impossible under a system of strict political or religious censorship.

Outside of politics, the rich theatrical history of ancient Athens shows just how bold the Athenians were when it came to criticizing their own institutions, culture, and elite. There were some restrictions and restraints on what, and who, could be satirized or abused, but neither the gods nor eminent citizens were spared in the Old Comedies. Aristophanes certainly pulled no punches. He mercilessly trolled Socrates, who is portrayed as a buffoon in *The Clouds*, and cast Cleon, a hawkish politician, as a corrupt slave in *The Knights*.[30]

Even gods like Dionysus, who is made to look a fool in the first half of *The Frogs*, were fair game.

Aristophanes also gave a voice to women who lived under a form of gender apartheid hidden from Athenian public life. In the comedy *Lysistrata*, women on both sides of the great Peloponnesian War effect political change by denying their husbands sex until they end the war between Athens and Sparta. In fact, the artistic freedom that allowed Aristophanes to pen *Lysistrata* in the fifth century BCE surpassed that enjoyed by Americans and Greeks in parts of the nineteenth and twentieth centuries. From 1873 until 1930, the United States prohibited the import and distribution of *Lysistrata* under the anti-obscenity Comstock Laws, and the play was banned during the Greek military dictatorship that lasted from 1967 to 1974.[31]

Unfortunately for the Athenians, the Periclean ideal of free and equal deliberation of public policy serving as a guarantee against rash decisions was vulnerable to exploitation by power-hungry politicians. And the ability of ambitious men to sway the assembly with seductive rhetoric and demagoguery would be a decisive factor in the decay of Athenian power.

The beginning of the end was, as is often the case, an ill-conceived rush to war. In 415 BCE, during the Peloponnesian War, the assembly voted to launch the disastrous Sicilian Expedition against Syracuse, where much of the Athenian army and navy perished. It was the hero-cum-villain Alcibiades, a close friend of Socrates, who—out of selfish ambition for power—managed to persuade the assembly to take that course.

Following the calamitous outcome in Syracuse, Athenians panicked, and many lost faith in democracy, conveniently blaming those who had voted in favor of invasion. How, they asked, could you maintain an empire when the poor and ignorant had as much of a say as the rich and learned? For aristocrats who resented sharing power with common simpletons, this was the perfect time to snuff out democracy and establish rule by the best and wisest—and, of course, the wealthiest.[32]

In 411 BCE, a group of Athenian oligarchs called the Four Hundred overthrew history's first democracy. The Four Hundred assassinated key democrats and browbeat the democratic institutions into serving as the mouthpiece of the new regime, in the words of Thucydides:

> Fear, and the sight of the numbers of the conspirators, closed the mouths of the rest; or if any ventured to rise in opposition, he was presently put to death in some convenient way, . . . the people remained motionless, being so thoroughly cowed that men thought themselves lucky to escape violence, even when they held their tongues.[33]

The coup of the Four Hundred was history's first confirmation that free speech is the premier victim of tyranny and oppression. It would not be the last.

It is a testimony to the strength of the Athenian commitment to democracy that the coup of the Four Hundred lasted for just four months, after internal conflicts doomed the new regime. Eventually, following the eight months in which an intermediate oligarchic regime called the Five Thousand ruled, democracy was restored in 410 BCE. Just a few years later, however, in 404 BCE, the Athenians lost the Peloponnesian War against Sparta, who abolished democracy once again.

The new oligarchic regime soon developed into a bloody dictatorship of the Thirty Tyrants. If your name was not on a list of citizens that was controlled entirely by the Thirty, you could be summarily executed at any time. As many as fifteen hundred Athenian citizens were killed in the antidemocratic purge, while many others were banished or fled.[34] The leader of the most extreme element of the Thirty Tyrants was Critias, a relative of Plato, who, like Alcibiades, had been close to Socrates. Some conspirators protested that the methods of the Thirty were too extreme, but Critias, as reported by the pro-oligarchic Athenian historian Xenophon, dismissed such bleeding-heart concerns:

> If anyone among you thinks that too many people are being put to death, let him consider that where governments change these things have to happen. It is inevitable that those who are changing the government here to an oligarchy should have most numerous enemies . . . because the common folk have been bred and reared in a condition of freedom for the longest time.[35]

Athens managed to overthrow its oligarchic oppressors again the following year, but the two periods of tyranny in close succession left the Athenians anxious to defend their hard-won democracy and less tolerant of dissent. This may also explain why the speech-loving Athenians came to execute their most prolific practitioner of parrhēsía.

Historians have long debated why the Athenians decided to execute Socrates at the ripe age of seventy. He had been speaking in public for decades. Why, then, would Athenian democrats, supposedly committed to uninhibited speech and fresh from surviving two murderous dictatorships, copy the tactics of the hated oligarchs by executing a man for his opinions?

In 399 BCE, a man named Meletus indicted Socrates by a graphē asébeia, which was a public action for impiety. The indictment read: "Socrates is guilty of refusing to recognize the gods recognized by the state, and of introducing other new divinities. He is also guilty of corrupting the youth. The penalty demanded is death."[36]

If we are to believe Plato—and there are reasons to be cautious, as he was Socrates's devoted pupil—Socrates prophesied his fate, knowing that his insistence on pursuing what he saw as truth and justice rubbed many powerful Athenians the wrong way. In Plato's

Gorgias, written almost twenty years after the death of Socrates, Socrates states that he might be dragged into court by "a wicked man," and condemned to death because "the speeches I make . . . do not aim at gratification but at what's best instead of what's most pleasant."[37]

In addition, Socrates often claimed to have an inner voice—his *daimónion*—that prevented him from making choices that were wrong or harmful. This supported Meletus's accusation that Socrates proselytized his own secretive religion, undermining the accepted religious values of the democratic city-state and angering the gods. That was a step too far for the Athenians, for whom religion and politics were not strictly separate. To make matters worse, five of Socrates's friends were convicted of profaning the Eleusinian Mysteries and mutilating sacred religious statues in 415 BCE. All of these factors added weight to the impiety charge, which Cambridge professor Paul Cartledge argues was the decisive element of the trial.[38]

Classicist Mogens Herman Hansen, on the other hand, makes the case that Socrates's trial was politically rather than religiously motivated, and that he was found guilty by association, having developed close relations with Critias, Alcibiades, and a number of other prominent oligarchs who had actively opposed democracy.[39] According to Xenophon, these relationships were brought up by Socrates's accusers during the trial. So too was Socrates's criticism of the way magistrates were chosen by lot rather than by election based on wealth or expertise, which smacked of oligarchy to the Athenians who had only recently rewon democracy at considerable cost.

In Socrates's defense, it should be said that he fought bravely for Athens during the Peloponnesian War and had refused to participate in an extrajudicial execution during the rule of the Thirty Tyrants—who had also prohibited Socrates from philosophizing in public. This was arguably proof that he was not unpatriotic, but it did not prove that he was not an antidemocratic partisan. Socrates was found guilty and sentenced to execution by drinking poisonous hemlock. Thus was born the first recorded martyr for free speech.

We may never be able to determine authoritatively why Socrates was executed. But if we accept that the preceding coups and the fear of resurgent antidemocratic forces spurred Athens to silence permanently a prominent political voice, then the trial of Socrates reveals that the most important of democratic values—free speech—is also the most vulnerable.

Democracies may be as oppressive as oligarchies if the right of the individual to challenge the prevailing ideas and morals of the majority is set aside. Safeguarding speech requires checks and balances that are strong enough to temper the fears and passions of a populace such as that which wielded direct political and judicial power in Athens. Once the civic commitment to *parrhēsía* broke down, the fine line between egalitarian democracy and revanchist mob rule was blurred and those who, like Socrates, offended the deepest convictions of their fellow citizens were at the mercy of popular opinion.

This was one of the chief lessons that James Madison and Alexander Hamilton would later draw from Athenian democracy, which they viewed with deep skepticism. In *Federalist* No. 55, Madison posited, "Had every Athenian citizen been a Socrates, every Athenian assembly would still have been a mob."[40]

Liberty or License?
Free Speech in Ancient Rome

Freedom of speech may have originated in the democracy of ancient Athens, but when Enlightenment thinkers developed justifications for free speech in the early eighteenth century, they generally looked to ancient Rome for precedent. Roman champions of republican values, such as Cicero, Cato the Younger, and the "liberator" Marcus

Brutus, were idealized by French philosophes, English Whigs, and the American Founding Fathers, while Julius Caesar and the first Roman emperors Augustus and Tiberius became synonymous with despotism.

The Roman Republic was established around 509 BCE, when the Romans expelled their last king and swore never to be ruled by a monarch again.[41] Whatever the exact date of its founding, the Roman Republic lasted some five hundred years. When it transformed into an empire, the Western half endured for an additional five hundred years, and the Eastern half for almost a thousand.

The first Roman Republicans were at once thin-skinned and heavy-handed when it came to offensive speech. Around 450 BCE, the basic laws of the early Republic were codified in the Twelve Tables, which touched upon speech. Take the eighth table: "If anyone shall have slandered or libeled another by imputing a wrongful or immoral act to him, he shall be scourged to death."[42] It appears the early Romans had no problem applying sticks and stones to break the bones of name-callers.

Where the Athenian democracy was bottom-up, direct, and egalitarian, the Roman Republic was top-down, hierarchical, and elitist. In the various popular assemblies responsible for approving laws and electing magistrates it was not "one man, one vote." The citizens voted in collective blocs based on tribe or class. In stark contrast to the Greek concept of *isēgoría*, the assemblies were convened and addressed solely by the presiding magistrates. Ordinary citizens did not have the right to speak.[43]

In theory, the popular assemblies held sovereign power. But in practice, the Senate was the most powerful institution in the republic. The Senate could not pass laws, but it would prepare legislation for the popular assemblies with the expectation that it would be ratified. It also controlled finances and foreign affairs.[44] In the Senate, political discussions were free and senators would often attack each other viciously. But freedom of discussion was not equal, seeing that senators spoke in order of rank.[45] Neither was it possible for just anyone to become a senator. Members were usually selected from a small and self-perpetuating elite.[46] In fact, the word "senate" is derived from the Latin word *senex*, meaning "an old man." So a group of old, powerful men presided over Roman politics.

This elitist model was defended by none other than the writer, philosopher, and statesman Cicero—an eloquent, but not always consistent, defender of republican ideals. Cicero loved Greek philosophy and oratory. But Athenian democracy? Not so much. He wrote of Greece:

> That ancient country, which once flourished with riches, and power, and glory, fell owing to that one evil, the immoderate liberty and licentiousness of the popular assemblies. When inexperienced men, ignorant and uninstructed in any description of business whatever, took their seats in the theatre, then they undertook inexpedient wars; then they appointed seditious men to the government of the republic; then they banished from the city the citizens who had deserved best of the state.[47]

Cicero was all in favor of free speech and political liberty, as long as the elite remained in control and tended to the welfare of the republic on behalf of the lower classes. For Cicero, free speech meant, first and foremost, free speech for the "best men" in the Senate, not the plebs, who were "ready to suck the treasury dry," nor the "artisans, shopkeepers and that scum."[48]

Despite the elitist political model of Rome, the idea of liberty, or *libertas*, had a special place in Roman hearts and minds. A free Roman citizen, regardless of rank, was not subject to the arbitrary domination of others. *Libertas* rested on laws that granted Roman citizens civil rights and equality before the law. Citizens could not be executed without a trial and had the right to protest the decisions of magistrates. *Libertas* also included the limited political freedom ordinary citizens enjoyed through voting in the assemblies. And, according to historian P. A. Brunt, "In the late republic freedom of philosophical, religious and even political speculation was unchecked."[49] Perhaps the most striking example was the Epicurean philosopher Lucretius, whose long poem *On the Nature of Things*—a "materialist manifesto" in the words of Philipp Blom—would later inspire radical Enlightenment thinkers with its rejection of religion and embrace of intellectual freedom.[50]

Yet there were no Roman equivalents of the Greek terms *isēgoría* and *parrhēsía*. Roman free speech was first and foremost exercised in the Senate, by magistrates before assemblies, and by orators before the courts, where, as in Athens, political speech would often be interwoven with legal arguments. For men like Cicero and Caesar, oratory was an essential way to further their political careers. Had Caesar not been a brilliant orator, he may not have become a brilliant general—or dictator.

The Romans contrasted *libertas* with *licentia*, or "licentiousness." *Licentia* was essentially an abuse of freedom that was either illegal or very much frowned upon. The ancient Roman historian Tacitus wrote that, in contrast to Rome, with the Greeks "not the freedom only, but even the licentiousness of speech, is unpunished."[51] Whether speech was deemed *libertas* or *licentia* often depended on the wealth and status of the speaker and the person being addressed. Senators and nobles routinely subjected each other to vicious verbal attacks in the courts and assemblies, and no one batted an eyelid if the elite vilified the plebs. But if someone of lower rank turned the tables and went after the rich and famous? Why, then, it was *licentia*! So when in 206 BCE the poet and dramatist Gnaeus Naevius denounced the leading men of Rome, much like Aristophanes had done in Athens, he was first thrown in prison and later exiled. As we will discover throughout this book, the conflict between egalitarian free speech in which every citizen has a say in public affairs, with its roots in democratic Athens, and privileged free speech, limited to a well-educated or wealthy elite, rooted in republican Rome, has never fully been resolved.

In 45 BCE Julius Caesar emerged victorious from the Great Roman Civil War. The following year he declared himself dictator for life. A fairly mild dictator, Caesar did not engage in widespread censorship—only the odd banishment here and there. To display clemency and endure criticism was an important part of his image as a man of the people.[52]

But, according to the later Greco-Roman historian Cassius Dio, Caesar created a martyr-figure for free speech on his way to absolute power. When Caesar had all but won the civil war, the infuriatingly principled senator Cato the Younger committed suicide rather than accept a pardon for opposing Caesar's dictatorship. In his dramatic exit from the stage of history, Cato stabbed himself and pulled out his own intestines, declaring—in the dramatized version of Cassius Dio (writing in Greek)—"I, who have been brought up in freedom, with the right of free speech [*parrhēsia*], cannot in my old age change and learn slavery instead."[53] Caesar's reign was short. On March 15, 44 BCE, he was stabbed to death by a conspiracy of republican senators known as the Liberators led by M. Junius Brutus and G. Cassius Longinus.

Years of bloody and treacherous civil war followed Caesar's death, as Caesar's right-hand man Marc Antony and Caesar's adopted heir Octavian battled the Liberators—and each other—for power. Cicero rather naively threw his support behind the young Octavian as the last best hope for the survival of the republic, and used his rhetorical firepower to hammer away at Marc Antony in a series of speeches known as the *Philippics*, named after speeches Demosthenes had made against Philip II of Macedon.

However, Cicero's attempt to save the republic was doomed when Octavian, Marc Antony, and their junior partner M. Aemilius Lepidus decided to join forces and form a powerful triumvirate. They began purging Rome of opposition once and for all, singling out hundreds of names for execution in lists known as proscriptions. And no opponent loomed larger than Cicero, whose *Philippics* had fired up a murderous rage in Marc Antony. Cicero was hunted down and killed by a death squad in December 43 BCE. His head and hands were cut off and brought back to an ecstatic Marc Antony, who put them on display at the speaker platform in the Forum, where all could see the fate of the head and hands that had spoken and written so forcefully against him.

The following year, the Triumvirate defeated the Liberators at the Battle of Philippi. Cassius Dio dramatically described the battle as one between freedom and autocracy:

> Now as never before liberty and popular government were the issues of the struggle. . . . The one side was trying to lead them to autocracy, the other side to self-government. Hence the people never attained again to absolute freedom of speech, even though vanquished by no foreign nation.[54]

The words of Cicero and Cato would live on, but the republic was mortally wounded.

The Triumvirate was a marriage of convenience that soon broke down. In 31 BCE, Octavian defeated Marc Antony at the Battle of Actium, clearing his way to becoming Augustus—Rome's first emperor in everything but name. (He preferred the title of *princeps civitatis* or "first citizen.") Augustus slowly but steadily narrowed the permissible limits of dissent. He had already cleared much opposition through proscriptions, so he could afford a piecemeal transformation to autocracy, keeping republican institutions but depriving them of much real power. Instead of suppressing his opponents in the Senate directly, he put the proceedings from the senatorial meetings under strict censorship. When anonymous pamphlets against him began circulating in the Senate, he took the high road and refuted his attackers in public instead of taking them to court. But not without introducing a wholesale ban on defamatory anonymous pamphlets.[55]

In 12 BCE, Augustus had himself proclaimed *pontifex maximus*, the high priest of Rome. In that capacity—not as *princeps*—he ordered more than two thousand religious scrolls, pamphlets, and books to be burned.[56] It would not do for fortune tellers to foresee the emperor's death, perhaps tempting some to fulfill the prophecies. Masking this authoritarian move as a religious rather than a political act provided a facade of legitimacy.[57]

A few years later, however, secular writing also came under Augustus's control. Around 6–8 CE, the emperor severely restricted dissent by combining the old Twelve Tables' prohibition of defamation with the *lex maiestatis* or law of treason.[58] Until this point, according to Tacitus, the law of treason had been limited to actions such as "betrayal of an army, inciting the common people to sedition, or generally, maladministration in public office. Actions were prosecuted, words were immune." But the outspoken orator Cassius Severus and his insolent writings against a number of prominent Romans provoked Augustus to widen the scope of the law to include words and writings.[59] Severus was convicted and banished to Crete while his entire writings were burned. But this was merely the beginning of a purge. What historian Frederick H. Cramer has called "literary treason"—purely verbal or written attacks on the government—was now a punishable crime. Charged with this new crime, teachers were taken to court and more writers saw their entire life's work go up in flames.[60] But Augustus did not stop there. The historian Suetonius implies that the Senate made it illegal to own, circulate, or even read the writings of a condemned author.[61]

But things would get worse—much worse—when Augustus died in 14 CE. At first, his successor Tiberius seemed more tolerant of dissent. He initially took no action when mocked in public, stressing the importance of free expression. But when his patience ran out, Tiberius's cruelty far outstripped Augustus's book burnings.[62]

The first victims were members of that most hazardous profession: astrologers and fortune tellers. One was flung to his death from the Tarpeian Rock, a cliff on the Capitoline Hill; another was whipped and beheaded, while the rest of the profession was banished from Italy. The Senate was reined in further, and torture and execution were introduced in cases of literary treason.[63] According to Suetonius, "every crime was treated as capital, even the utterance of a few simple words."[64]

Nothing better illustrates Tiberius's intolerance than the case against the pro-republican historian Aulus Cremutius Cordus in 25 CE. His crime was writing a historical treatise that praised Caesar's assassins Brutus and Cassius and styled the latter as "the last Roman." Charges of literary treason had never before been brought against a historical work. It was, in the words of Tacitus, "a new charge for the first time heard."[65] In Tacitus's dramatized version of the trial, Cordus defended himself, arguing, "The charge, Conscript Fathers, is for my words only; so irreproachable is my conduct." After his speech, he left the Senate and starved himself to death. The senators ordered his books burned, though copies were hidden and spread clandestinely.

Tacitus praised Cordus as a martyr of free speech: "Laughable, indeed, are the delusions of those who fancy that by the exercise of their ephemeral power, posterity can be defrauded of information. On the contrary, through persecution the reputation of the persecuted talents grows stronger."[66] The phenomenon Tacitus articulated would, millennia later, become known as the "Streisand effect," after the American entertainer Barbra Streisand sued a website to remove photos of her home—only to draw massive online attention to the photos.

Tacitus's ideal of free speech was to be long forgotten, until it was revived more than a millennium later by a number of early Enlightenment thinkers who saw clear parallels between the authoritarian tendencies of emperors Augustus and Tiberius and the absolute monarchies of early eighteenth-century Europe.

The Age of Persecution

With Tiberius's authoritarian persecution of "literary treason," political dissent withered away. The next big clash of ideas would be over religion. Had Tiberius not banished the oracles, they might have warned him about another trial that would soon take place in the province of Judaea—one that would define his reputation forever.

Around 30–33 CE, Jesus of Nazareth was sentenced to death by the Roman governor of Judaea, Pontius Pilate. Why was he executed? That depends on whether you believe the Christian Gospels or modern-day scholars. The former stress the Jewish charge of blasphemy;[67] the latter the Roman charge of sedition.[68]

Much like Socrates, Jesus did not leave as much as a letter in his own hand behind. The notion that his teachings would become the state religion of the empire that executed him as a common criminal would have been unimaginable to his contemporaries. But the small Jewish sect of Christians soon spread across the entire Roman Empire, not least due to the indefatigable work of Paul of Tarsus. The man who would be named Saint Paul had initially persecuted Christians for blaspheming against Judaism, but then converted to Christianity himself and dedicated his life to sharing the Christian message.[69] Here was a man who knew how to use what remnants of *libertas* was left to spectacular effect. His lengthy letters providing guidance on Christian theology helped strengthen fledgling Christian communities and became foundational Christian texts, comprising thirteen out of the New Testament's twenty-one epistles.

As Paul would find out the hard way, the Roman Empire was not about to welcome this new cult whose members obstinately refused to worship the Roman gods. Several of his epistles were penned in a Roman prison.[70] Yet, early Christians were not concerned with democratic or republican notions of free and open debate. In fact, Christianity transformed the very meaning of the terms once intimately connected with free speech and democracy. *Parrhēsía* no longer signified uninhibited speech, but instead came to be understood in a more narrowly religious sense, such as referring to the martyr's right and privilege to speak with God. And *ekklēsia* changed from being a political assembly where citizens exercised *isēgoría* by deliberating issues of common concern to an assembly where the faithful worshipped God—a church, hence derivatives like the English word ecclesiastical, French *église*, and Spanish *iglesia*.[71]

In any event, since Athenian democracy and Roman republicanism had long since died, the burning question Christianity raised was not about the limits of political speech but rather the issue of religious tolerance, which would dominate debates over the limits of speech and thought for centuries.

Christians faced periods of sometimes brutal persecution in the empire, starting when Nero blamed them for the Great Fire of Rome in 64 CE.[72] According to Christian tradition, both Peter and Paul were martyred during the Neronian Persecution.[73] The violence culminated with Diocletian's Great Persecution in 303–305, which killed an estimated 3,000 to 3,500 Christians.[74]

Yet Christianity endured, and gained serious traction when it found a champion in the form of Emperor Constantine I.[75] Constantine's first move was to ensure protection and equality for the Christians. In 313, he issued the Edict of Milan—in reality, an agreement between Constantine and his co-emperor Licinius—which held that "the right of open and free observance of their worship for the sake of the peace of our times, that each one may have the free opportunity to worship as he pleases."[76] He then began instituting a number of policies that favored orthodox Christianity over competing Christian sects and traditional Roman paganism.

The persecuted had become the persecutor. The Christian emperor Valens unleashed an outpouring of intolerance in the Eastern half of the empire after pagan diviners tried to predict his death in 369. Suspects accused of magic, including a number of philosophers, were tortured and executed, and heaps of secular works on philosophy and law were burned. According to the historian Ammianus Marcellinus, people frantically burned their whole libraries to avoid accusation.[77]

The steady drip of intolerance turned into a torrent when Theodosius I became emperor in 379 and declared Christianity the official state religion of the empire in 380 via the Edict of Thessalonica. The edict left no doubt about the rights of Christian heretics and non-Christians:

> The rest, however, whom We adjudge demented and insane, shall sustain the infamy of heretical dogmas, their meeting places shall not receive the name of churches, and they shall be smitten first by divine vengeance and secondly by the retribution of Our own initiative, which We shall assume in accordance with the divine judgement.[78]

Indeed, no other Roman emperor issued more laws against pagans and heretics than Theodosius (although the Byzantine emperor Justinian would later give him a run for his money). The Theodosian dynasty's flurry of laws would be compiled in the Theodosian Code from 438, a veritable à la carte menu of religious intolerance, including sixty-six laws against heresy alone.[79]

Heretical literature was targeted around 496, when Pope Gelasius I issued what has been described as history's first "index of forbidden books," singling out sixty books for banishment.[80] The Church would revive and dramatically expand the practice of banning books a millennium later.

The Western Empire disintegrated during the fifth century, but the Eastern half of the Roman Empire, known today as the Byzantine Empire, continued on. The most famous of the Eastern emperors is Justinian I, who ruled from 527 to 565. Among his achievements was the creation of a legal code that still forms the basis for much of European law today.[81]

Perhaps the most infamous act during Justinian's reign was the decision to close the Academy in Athens in 529. The Academy had fostered philosophical teaching for centuries and could trace its intellectual roots back to Plato himself. Even though its intellectual heyday was long past, the closing of the Academy had a hugely symbolic impact as the death knell to the tradition of philosophical inquiry the city had been known for.

But Justinian wanted to purge the empire of pagan ideas, root and branch, and banned all "those infected with the madness of unholy Hellenism" from becoming teachers. Civil rights and property ownership were also limited to those baptized and instructed in the orthodox Christian faith. Anyone found to be making sacrifices or worshipping idols, and any Christians engaged in other pagan practices, could be punished with death.[82] Jews were mentioned thirty-three times in the code, which limited their long-respected religious rights. Restrictions were placed on the construction of synagogues and certain Jewish religious texts were banned.[83] And in 538, Justinian instituted the death penalty for blasphemy lest "God, in His wrath, may destroy the cities and their inhabitants."[84]

———

WHEN THE WESTERN ROMAN EMPIRE FINALLY COLLAPSED, traditional pagan beliefs were already in decline. But the systematic banning, censorship, as well as destruction and neglect of pagan texts and places of worship sped up the process considerably, with grim consequences for the furtherance and development of knowledge, philosophy, and science. As much as 90 percent of the ancient literary works we know of from secondary sources perished.[85] Book burnings and censorship accounted for a small minority of the lost works; most were destroyed by neglect and the closed-mindedness bred by the dogmatic climate. As historian Ramsay MacMullen has put it, "Hostile writings and discarded views were not recopied or passed on, or they were actively suppressed."[86] Church and emperors "allowed the writings of Christianity to pass through but not of Christianity's enemies."[87]

Still, as the next chapter shows, the medieval period was not so dark nor devoid of reason as historians once believed. Despite widespread intolerance, centers of learning, reason, and inquiry managed to survive and even thrive in both European Christendom and the new Islamic lands. These strongholds were critical to the coming of a twelfth-century renaissance in which scientific and philosophic learning flourished and paved the way for the establishment of universities and the rediscovery of the classical learning that had been marginalized during the enforced Christianization of the Roman Empire. With time these ideals also contributed to the revival of republican and ultimately democratic notions of free speech, even if it would take many centuries and struggles for the principles that lay at the heart of Athenian democracy to become dominant once again.

2

The Not-So-Dark Ages

Inquiry and Inquisition
in Medieval Islam and Europe

Until recently, the term "medieval" was synonymous with religious obscurantism and backwardness. According to the
British philosopher A. C. Grayling, the Christianization of the
Roman Empire "plunged Europe into the dark ages for the next
thousand years" with "scarcely any literature or philosophy." Only
with "the rebirth of classical learning" in the Renaissance did Europe
manage to escape "the church's narrow ignorance and oppression."[1]

But medievalists have long recognized the Middle Ages as a period of profound intellectual achievement.[2] True, the general absence
of representative government meant that nothing like the articulated
ideals of free and equal speech, so central to the Athenian democracy, survived. Medieval Europe also saw the construction of what
historian R. I. Moore has called a "machinery of persecution" that
hounded heretics real and perceived.[3] Yet at the same time, crucial
developments paved the way for a culture of curiosity and inquiry
that would challenge orthodoxy and contribute to groundbreaking
philosophical and scientific breakthroughs.

The Caliphate

Perhaps one of the most remarkable and least well-known features of the Middle Ages—at least to many Westerners—is that the Islamic world was home to the most daring freethinkers of the age. In striking contrast to Western Europe, the sprawling ʿAbbāsid Caliphate provided a fruitful environment for the cultivation and dissemination of rationalist philosophy and science. Persecution of philosophers was rare, attempts to root out heresy were often haphazard, and efforts to establish orthodoxy never matched the institutionalized and systematic inquisition launched by the Church in Western Europe.

After the prophet Muhammad died in 632 CE, the new faith of Islam spread out from the Arabian Peninsula and its armies rapidly conquered all before it. Within a century, the Islamic world stretched from the Atlantic Ocean to the Indus River. The ʿAbbāsid Caliphate, which emerged as the most powerful Islamic polity in 750, contributed vastly to expanding the limits of medieval thought and reason and preserving the learning of the ancient world.

From the eighth to tenth centuries, there was a lively theological debate between the four major Sunnī schools of Islamic law. The Ḥanafī, Shāfiʿī, Ḥanbalī, and Mālikī traditions competed among themselves as to who could offer the most persuasive and authoritative interpretation of the Qurʾan and Sunnah, which are the sources of Shariʿah, or canonical, law. Key to each school was the interpretation of Ḥadīth—authoritative accounts of the prophet's example.

The Sunnah includes a number of instances where Muhammad laid down the law with brutal severity. In a famous Ḥadīth, Muhammad condemned those who abandon Islam: "Whoever changes his religion, kill him."[4] According to the prominent modern scholar of Islamic law Mohammad Hashim Kamali, there is strong evidence that the prophet ordered or approved the death penalty in about a dozen cases involving speech and thought crimes like blasphemy, apostasy, treason, and insults against the prophet in satirical writings.[5] In one account, the prophet had two slave girls executed for ridiculing him in poetic songs, which seems to have been a particularly sensitive issue for the prophet and his followers.[6]

As a result, one might think that the death penalty was common. And true enough, all of the four dominant Sunnī schools of Islamic law would eventually regard apostasy as a crime punishable by death.[7] But the Shāfi'ī and Ḥanafī schools that dominated the eastern part of the 'Abbāsid Caliphate stipulated that in order to warrant a death sentence apostasy must be openly declared, and that the apostates must also be given the chance to repent and escape execution. As a result, punishment for apostasy was rare.[8] (That would change in the eleventh century, not least through the influence of the stricter Ḥanbalī school.[9])

Much credit for the Islamic flowering of knowledge and philosophy goes to the second 'Abbāsid caliph, Abū Ja'far al-Manṣūr, who ruled from 754 to 775. It was he who established Baghdad, which soon became a center of scholarship, as his new capital. He was also the founding patron of the Graeco-Arabic translation movement commencing in the middle of the eighth century, which would help catalyze the rediscovery of classical Greek knowledge that would take place in the West after the turn of the millennium.[10] The patronage of al-Manṣūr and his successors enabled the translation of vast amounts of writing, including the works of Greek luminaries such as Galen, Euclid, Ptolemy, Plato, and Aristotle. According to Yale Professor of Graeco-Arabic Dimitri Gutas, "By the end of the tenth century, almost all scientific and philosophical secular Greek works that were available in late antiquity, including such diverse topics as astrology, alchemy, physics, mathematics, medicine, and philosophy, had been translated into Arabic."[11] The result was a sustained and highly influential campaign of cultural and intellectual adaptation that set off long-lasting chain reactions expanding the limits of human reason and knowledge.[12]

Without the active participation of religious minorities, the translation movement could not have taken place. Translations and commentaries on Greek philosophy and science in Syriac and Armenian, the languages of scholarship in Eastern Christian communities, became a crucial bridge between Greek and Arabic scientific culture.[13] Nestorian Christians, an Orthodox sect that originated in Syria but was deemed heretical and driven into Persia, played a key role in translating Greek writings from Syriac into Arabic. Zoroastrian Persians were similarly instrumental in bringing Greek works that already existed in Persian translation into Arabic, and also helped translate Indian works on astronomy and mathematics, written in Sanskrit.[14]

It was Caliph al-Manṣūr and his successors who made the conscious decision to initiate the translation of secular Greek works, but the endeavor also enjoyed broad support and patronage from the elite of ʿAbbāsid society.[15] So highly was this work valued that a team of three full-time translators could make up to five hundred dinars—the equivalent of more than $90,000—per month.[16] Not a bad gig for a Hellenophile bookworm. And when the translation movement came to an end around the tenth century, it was not because of censorship or backlash but because they had simply run out of relevant books to translate.[17]

In one of the few instances of organized top-down persecution during ʿAbbāsid rule, Caliph al-Maʾmūn forbade opposition to the doctrine that the Qurʾan was "created" rather than the uncreated word of God.[18] But paradoxically, this official *miḥna* (a form of inquisition) was aimed at countering traditionalist orthodoxy. The createdness doctrine was a central tenet of the rationalist *Muʿtazilite* school of thought, while the opposing view was championed by traditionalists among the *ulamā*—specialist scholars of religious law.[19] Elevating the Qurʾan to the uncreated word of God would strengthen the role of the *ulamā*, while a more rationalistic approach would allow for religious arguments outside the Qur'an and Sunnah. This meant more wiggle room for the caliph, including his emphasis on pagan Greek learning and *falsafah*—the Islamic term for philosophy. Jurists and theologians were interrogated and forced to swear allegiance to the createdness doctrine. Dissenters were forced to publicly recant or risk imprisonment, flogging, or even execution.[20] Among those tried and punished with prison and flogging was Aḥmad ibn Ḥanbal—prodigious traditionalist jurist, Ḥadīth scholar, and later founder of the strict Ḥanbalī school of Islamic law.[21] Yet, the *miḥna* fizzled out from around 847, having failed to establish rationalist orthodoxy.[22]

The 'Abbāsids' contribution to science and philosophy extended beyond translating the words of others. A long list of truly gifted polymaths made great progress in disciplines such as medicine, astronomy, geography, and philosophy during this period. Many of these Muslim thinkers were ethnically Persian or Central Asian writing in Arabic. When the 'Abbāsid Caliphate began to disintegrate in the early tenth century, the centers of learning spread east beyond Baghdad, to vassal states and territories where 'Abbāsid authority waned to the point where they only ruled in name, if at all. Rather than being the result of positive recognition of freedoms of conscience and expression—notions alien to the absolutist caliphs—it was this lack of centralized religious authority that proved conducive to the emergence of a number of radical freethinkers.

Among them was the enigmatic Ibn al-Rāwandī, born in Khorasan on the border of modern-day Iran and Afghanistan around 815. Though al-Rāwandī is said to have written more than a hundred books, none has survived, so we have to reconstruct his views from the furious—and possibly distorted—attacks of his critics. But even if his critics were only halfway reliable, it seems he gave them ample ammunition by taking an intellectual axe to the very roots of Islam. The Qur'an? An absurd, badly written, and unpersuasive book full of inconsistencies. Prophets? Unnecessary at best, since humans advance by their own intellect, without need of revelation. Cheap frauds at worst—and that included Muhammad. Miracles? Nothing but simple tricks and conspiracies to fool the gullible. The Muslim pilgrimage of the hajj? An exercise in futility—just like prayers! Al-Rāwandī deemed all forms of religious dogma to be irreconcilable with reason.[23]

Like a medieval Tom Paine, he seemingly took delight in the shock and outrage that followed in the wake of his one-man demolition show of revealed religion. He then proclaimed himself blameless of heresy—the words al-Rāwandī used were not his own, you see. He was simply quoting the views of others, such as Indian Brahmins.[24] His critics found this strategy less than convincing, and he was viciously attacked by religious scholars and rationalist philosophers alike.

The fact that al-Rāwandī was able to voice such unorthodox views without being parted from his head indicates that the early Islamic world was remarkably tolerant of intellectual debate. Al-Rāwandī's story offers a stark contrast to the number of Muslims under Islamic rule who face persecution for speech today. On the other hand, the fact that his controversial works have not survived—whether through active destruction or willful neglect—suggests that the appetite for iconoclasm was not without limits.

Another controversial figure was the Persian physician and philosopher Abū Bakr Muḥammad ibn Zakariyyā al-Rāzī (known as Rhazes in the West) who lived from around 850 to around 925. His intellectual output is mind-boggling. In addition to his groundbreaking medical contributions, he is said to have written more than two hundred works on medicine, chemistry, astronomy, mathematics, and philosophy.[25] For al-Rāzī, reason was "the ultimate authority, which should govern and not be governed; should control and not be controlled, should lead and not be led." He was highly critical of the restrictions religious fanaticism placed on free thought:

If the people of [a given] religion are asked about the proof for the soundness of their religion, they flare up, get angry and spill the blood of whoever confronts them with this question. They forbid rational speculation, and strive to kill their adversaries. This is why truth became thoroughly silenced and concealed.[26]

Al-Rāwandī and al-Rāzī were not mainstream in their day, but the boldness of their freethinking—even if exaggerated by their critics and modern admirers—suggests that Islam was uniquely heterodox among the monotheistic faiths of medieval times.[27]

By way of contrast with these two, the majority of great Muslim *falāsifa* (philosophers) of the ninth, tenth, and eleventh centuries focused their efforts on demonstrating Islam's compatibility with reason and philosophy. Al-Kindī (ca. 800–870), the first self-identified Arabic philosopher, used the ideas of Aristotle and Euclid to interpret the Qur'an and defend Islamic doctrines.[28] The philosopher Abū Naṣr al-Fārābī (870–ca. 950) made the political philosophy of Plato compatible with Islamic political thought, promoting the government of a "philosopher prophet ruler" instead of Plato's "philosopher king."[29] Farther east, in the Persian Ghaznavid Empire, the polymath Abū al-Rayḥān al-Bīrūnī (973–ca. 1052) excelled in astronomy, mathematics, history, and geography. He ingeniously defended natural science from the attacks of religious scholars by demonstrating how trigonometry can be used to determine the direction of Mecca.[30]

Yet no Islamic thinker towers above al-Bīrūnī's contemporary polymath Abū ʿAlī ibn Sīnā, better known as Avicenna in the West. Born around 970, he grew up in Bukhara, the capital of the Persian Samanid Empire, where he was allowed access to the magnificent palace library. Reportedly, it was an essay by al-Fārābī that opened his eyes to Aristotle.[31] He became the most influential philosopher of the Islamic world—and perhaps of the medieval world at large—when he developed a sophisticated synthesis of Greek philosophy and Islamic doctrine.[32] When his works were translated into Latin, he became a profound source of inspiration to Western philosophers like Thomas Aquinas, who would strive to bridge Christianity and pagan philosophy in the West in much the same way.

But not everyone was a fan of the kind of freethinking that allowed al-Rāzī, al-Fārābī, and Avicenna to thrive. In the early eleventh century, the ʿAbbāsid caliph al-Qādir was inspired by the austere Ḥanbalī school to enforce strict Sunnī orthodoxy. "Heretics" were purged, and heavy-handed censorship of rationalists and their writings was introduced. Espousing certain beliefs about the nature of the Qurʾan was tantamount to apostasy, punishable by death.[33] Later in the eleventh century, the philosopher and theologian Abū Ḥāmid al-Ghazālī came to play a key role in drawing the new red lines around permissible doctrines in the Muslim world. Born in Persia around 1055, he became an influential intellectual at the courts of both the Seljuq Sultan in Isfahan and the ʿAbbāsid caliph in Baghdad. His work *The Incoherence of the Philosophers* from 1095 blasted Aristotelian *falāsifa* like Avicenna and al-Fārābī. Accordingly, al-Ghazālī is often depicted as a strict opponent of reason and rationalist philosophy, though modern scholars have added nuance to that depiction and showed that al-Ghazālī's thought was much more open to rationalist ideas than previously thought. In fact, part of his criticism of the *falāsifa* was that they did not offer proof of the soundness of their doctrines. What is not disputed is that al-Ghazālī spelled out a number of propositions that amounted to apostasy, including the assertions that the world was not created, and that God is not omniscient. He would later add manifest rejections of monotheism to the list. So dangerous were these ideas, al-Ghazālī believed, that philosophers and theologians who advocated them should be killed without being offered the chance to repent. Al-Ghazālī thus expanded the scope of apostasy laws to heterodox ideas among professing Muslims.[34]

Even though al-Ghazālī reserved the death penalty for a list of specific beliefs, the hardening and widening of apostasy laws continued, with long-term consequences for tolerance and freedom of thought, and an increased focus on a strict literalist understanding of the Qur'an and Sunnah and, consequently, a rejection of non-authoritative sources, such as Aristotelian philosophy.[35] A thirteenth-century compendium of Ḥanbalī jurisprudence defines the following speech crimes as apostasy and thus punishable by death:

> vilifying Allah the Exalted or His Prophet, falsely impugning the honor of the Prophet's Mother, denying the Book of Allah or a part of it, (denying) one of His prophets or one of His books, rejecting a manifest and agreed upon commandment such as the five pillars (of Islam).[36]

These strict injunctions on freedom of thought and speech have had a long half-life. On February 14, 1989, the supreme leader of Iran, Ayatollah Khomeini, issued a fatwa calling on all Muslims—whether Sunnī or Shiʿah—to kill the British author Salman Rushdie for blaspheming against Islam and the prophet Muhammad in his novel *The Satanic Verses*. Khomeini was backed up by religious scholars and organizations spanning the Sunnī/Shiʿah divide. Because Rushdie was born a Muslim, he could be killed as an apostate without a trial or even the opportunity to repent for having vilified the prophet.[37] As of 2020, thirteen Muslim-majority countries formally punished apostasy and/or blasphemy with the death penalty (although actual executions were rare).[38] And in countries like Pakistan, Egypt, Afghanistan, and Jordan significant parts of the population believed that the ultimate penalty was warranted for abandoning Islam.[39] No doubt al-Rāzī would have lamented this development.

The Culture of Poking Around

Historians of the Byzantine Empire have described the seventh and eighth centuries as a "dark age" of stifling orthodoxy and iconoclasm. Science withered away as the treasure trove of Greek secular literature that the Byzantine rulers had inherited was either deemed too irrelevant or "undesirable" to be preserved.[40] More than 90 percent of the Greek titles we know from secondary sources have perished.[41] It was not until the ninth century that an interest in science began to blossom and secular manuscripts were finally copied again. Evidence suggests this renaissance was sparked by Byzantine scholars travelling to the ʿAbbāsid Caliphate and returning with new insights. One of them was the astrologer Stephanus the Philosopher, who argued for the need "to renew this useful science" after he returned from Baghdad in the 790s. A few years later, Byzantine court astrologers began using techniques derived from the caliph's court.[42]

The influence of Arabic translations and their refinement of Greek literature and philosophy would—eventually—be even more pronounced in Western Europe, though the early years of the medieval period were not encouraging. The only institution to survive the collapse of the Western Roman Empire toward the late fifth century was the Church with its network of churches and monasteries subject to the ultimate authority of the pope in Rome. Knowledge of classical Greek was almost completely lost, and likewise it has been estimated that an incredible 99 percent of classical Latin literature titles are forever gone.[43] Fortunately, a small team of dedicated scholars and monks kept classical heritage on life support by copying the few surviving manuscripts within the safe spaces of Christian monasteries. But classical Greek culture was not "rediscovered" in the West until the twelfth and thirteenth centuries, when what had begun as a steady trickle of reclaimed manuscripts in the late eleventh century turned into an outright tsunami, whose different sources included Arabic translations and commentaries from Muslim philosophers. The pioneering works of Muslim scholars such as Avicenna and the renowned twelfth-century philosopher Averroës from al-Andalus in modern-day Spain were eagerly devoured. And while the transmission of classical literature to the West was not solely due to Arab scholarship, Muslim philosophers had become so popular by the twelfth century that the English philosopher Adelard of Bath admitted to often attributing his own thoughts to Arabs just to give them more credit.[44]

These developments coincided with a radical transformation around 1000 to 1300, when Europe experienced a population boom due in part to global warming, increased fertility, and crop production, and new towns and cities sprouted up all over the map.[45] Western medieval intellectuals were children of the cities, where cathedral schools and freelancing educators replaced monasteries as centers of learning.[46] They would soon be upstaged by Europe's first universities, founded in Bologna and Paris around 1200 and at Oxford and Cambridge a few years later. By 1300, the number of universities on the Continent had mushroomed to eighteen.[47] Universities became critical lobes of what evolutionary biologist Joseph Henrich has called "Europe's collective brain."[48]

As philosophical, scientific, and medical works of Greek and Islamic origin were introduced in the West, they became core curriculum at these new universities, radically changing the content of scholarship and challenging traditional Christian preconceptions of the world.[49] Students delved into Plato and Aristotle; Aristotle's influence on European thought became so profound he was simply known as "The Philosopher."[50] Historian of medieval science Edward Grant has argued that, with the introduction of Greek works in general and Aristotelian philosophy in particular, medieval universities institutionalized the use of reason, creating a culture of "poking around" that laid the foundation for later scientific breakthroughs and became emblematic of Western civilization as such.[51] Accordingly, the Middle Ages were just as much an age of reason and inquiry as that of inquisition and superstition, belying the popular misconception of this time as a thousand years of darkness between antiquity and the Renaissance.

Of course for most people in the Middle Ages, actively denying the existence of God may have been as inconceivable as questioning the existence of gravity in our times.[52] This fact clearly influenced the way people thought and were allowed to think, particularly when it came to core Christian doctrine.[53] And as we shall see, the Middle Ages also saw periods of systematic and appalling persecution of "heretics," Jews, and other outsiders. But medieval thought was dominated by "religious dynamics and diversity" rather than strict orthodox regimentation. According to historian Dorothea Weltecke, "not a single theological teaching, be it Jewish, Muslim, or Christian . . . was left unquestioned either by polemics from outside, by opposing groups from inside, or even by those who, with the best of intentions, could not help not to be convinced."[54] In other words, medieval academics expanded the boundaries of permissible inquiry, even if their questions were still posed in an attempt to explain God's eternal truths.

Still, medieval limits to freethinking and the academic pursuit of truth were formidable from a modern perspective. No right to free speech was recognized at this point in history and no one thought or dared to unleash reason entirely from the limits of revelation for several centuries to come. But top-down attempts to curtail academic freedom and inquiry faced pushback and subversion by medieval scholars whose thirst for new knowledge and ideas could not be quenched by papal decrees. So when critics of Aristotelian philosophy thought that the emphasis on reason had become a little too independent and daring, a lengthy conflict broke out between theologians and natural philosophers over the limits between these two disciplines.[55]

The first documented case of academic censure at the University of Paris happened around 1206, when the Aristotelean philosopher and theologist Amalric of Bène was found guilty of false and heretical teachings for advocating pantheism, the belief that God is everything. Condemned by the pope, he was forced to recant his views in front of his academic peers in a medieval version of "self-criticism."[56] In 1210, a provincial council ordered ten of Amalric's followers burned at the stake.

The same council banned Aristotle's natural philosophy, which was becoming increasingly popular at Paris's Faculty of Arts, ruling that "neither the books of Aristotle on natural philosophy nor their commentaries are to be taught at Paris in public or privately."[57] The university chancellor and papal legate Robert of Courçon repeated the ban on Aristotle's books of natural philosophy, their commentaries, and the works of Amalric in his Rules of the University of Paris from 1215.[58] But in spite of the bans, Aristotle's natural philosophy seems to have exerted such a pull on the insatiably curious scholars that it seeped from the Faculty of Arts to the Faculty of Theology. In 1228, Pope Gregory IX addressed an angry letter to the masters of theology, accusing them of "committing adultery with philosophical doctrines." The letter renewed the ban and ordered the theologists to stick to theology.[59]

Competing universities soon realized that they could use Aristotle's forbidden books as bait to lure curious scholars away from Paris. In 1229, teachers and students went on strike and left Paris in great numbers to protest the killing of a number of students after a student riot.[60] Hoping to catch some fish in the troubled waters, the University of Toulouse tempted the Parisian scholars with the promise that "those who wish to scrutinize the bosom of nature to the inmost can hear the books of Aristotle which were forbidden at Paris."[61] Henry III also invited the frustrated scholars to Oxford and Cambridge, where Aristotle's books could still be studied.[62]

Academic freedom and pagan philosophy had become an incentive and competitive advantage in Christendom.

The brain drain put pressure on the pope, who made an attempt to call the Parisian scholars home with a 1231 bull acknowledging the university as the "parent of knowledge" and promising to lift the ban on Aristotle's books once they had "been examined and purged from every suspicion of error" by a theological commission.[63] But the scholars and students were not prepared to settle for a diluted version of their literary stimulants. An anonymous student guide from this period lists several of the banned books on the curriculum for the arts course. Writings of masters of theology from the same period reveal that Aristotle and Avicenna were also studied at the theological faculty.[64] In other words, despite the top-down attempts to limit the reach of Aristotle, networks of scholars thirsty for knowledge resisted and kept sharing these forbidden fruits of philosophy.

One of the theologians at Paris who ignored the ban and immersed himself in Aristotelian philosophy was the Dominican friar Thomas Aquinas. One of his most influential achievements was his attempt to bridge the gap between Aristotelean philosophy and Christian doctrines, rendering the former acceptable to the religious hierarchy.

Aquinas's reconciliation of faith and philosophy was a milestone in the European history of ideas. But not everyone was convinced. In 1277, the pope sent a letter to Paris's Bishop Stephen Tempier, informing him of rumors that heresy had infected the university. Tempier, who was in charge of the Faculty of Arts, reacted by banning a list of 219 philosophical and theological theses. The forbidden propositions concerned issues such as the nature of God, the concept of free will, the world's eternity, and the nature of philosophy and theology. Anyone caught so much as listening to the 219 propositions would be excommunicated, unless they turned themselves in for punishment within seven days. It appears Tempier derived some of his banned propositions from Greek and Arabic thinkers as well as the writings of Aquinas. Many historians have thus interpreted Tempier's condemnation as a response to the creeping advance of pagan philosophy at the Faculty of Arts through the use of Greek and Arabic sources which pitted reason against faith and encouraged philosophical research without concern for Christian orthodoxy.[65] But as we have seen, Aquinas never intended to pit reason against faith.

In spite of strong protests from academics, more bans followed in the fourteenth century. A total of sixteen lists of banned ideas were issued at the University of Paris in the thirteenth and fourteenth centuries.[66] In 1339 and 1340, the masters at the Faculty of Arts issued two statutes banning the "false teachings" of William of Ockham (who is most famous for the problem-solving principle known as "Ockham's razor"). Bachelors of arts were obliged to take an oath swearing that they would "not sustain said [Ockhamist] thought and similar ones in whatever way." In the meantime, the fault lines had changed and, ironically, the bachelors had to swear to sustain "the thought (*scientia*) of Aristotle and his Commentator Averroes and the other ancient commentators and expositors of said Aristotle, except in those cases that are against faith."[67]

Still, these cases of repression should not detract from the overall picture that medieval universities were surprisingly open-minded. And as the repeated bans on Aristotle's natural philosophy show, attempts to keep forbidden knowledge from being studied, taught, and shared often failed miserably. In fact, there are only about fifty known cases of academically related judicial proceedings for erroneous teachings throughout all of the thirteenth and fourteenth centuries.[68] But it was one thing for a small elite of Latin-speaking scholars to probe the resilience of orthodoxy at universities, it was quite another to allow heretical ideas to spread freely among the common people.

The Hounds of God: Medieval Inquisition(s)

Heresy and orthodoxy are two sides of the same coin. Both depend on being defined and enforced by an authority. While laws against heresy stretch all the way back to the Christianization of the Roman Empire, heresy virtually disappeared as a concern in the Latin West from about the seventh to eleventh centuries. But in the eleventh and twelfth centuries, heresy laws returned with a vengeance when a number of ambitious popes—not least Gregory VII—instituted the so-called Papal Revolution, centralizing and vastly enlarging the papacy's temporal power.[69]

In most modern secular and liberal democracies, the freedom to choose one's religion—or no religion at all—is taken for granted. None of the many houses of worship that are welcome to open their doors can compel me to enter, and once I enter, I can freely leave for another or abandon religion altogether. But however natural it might feel today, the idea of having a choice in matters of religious belief has been the exception for much of human history.

Monotheism has been particularly effective in advancing the idea of orthodoxy. The word "heresy" has its roots in the Greek word *haíresis*, which means "choice." In the Middle Ages, heresy was defined as "an opinion chosen by human perception contrary to holy Scripture, publicly avowed and obstinately defended."[70] In other words, it was an active choice to persist with an unsanctioned belief. Stamping out heresy occupied, sometimes obsessively, the minds and policies of ambitious popes and secular rulers as the Middle Ages advanced.

Heresy thus became one of the defining issues of the thirteenth and fourteenth centuries—just as pagan teachings started enjoying a prominent role at the newly emerged universities where reason, inquiry, and science thrived. The quest to eradicate heresy reshaped Western Europe into what British historian R. I. Moore has called a "persecuting society."[71]

Up until the late twelfth century, the first line of defense against heresy was persuasion, rather than persecution.[72] But in the eleventh and twelfth centuries, things started to change. A slow shift toward persecution picked up momentum over the next couple of centuries until, in the words of R. I. Moore,

> Persecution became habitual. That is to say not simply that individuals were subject to violence, but that deliberate and socially sanctioned violence began to be directed, *through established governmental, judicial and social institutions*, against groups of people defined by general characteristics such as race, religion or way of life; and that membership of such groups in itself came to be regarded as justifying these attacks.[73]

The Medieval Inquisition was a key tool in institutionalizing the persecuting society—although it did not function or exist as a monolithic institution. While the inquisitors were appointed by the pope, they nevertheless operated as a loose network of independent tribunals.[74]

To modern eyes the Medieval Inquisition was an oppressive system of thought control, and no doubt ambition and power played a role in constructing the machinery of persecution. But the Church justified it as an attempt to heal, cure, and prevent a deadly infection with devastating consequences. The word religion comes from the Latin *ligare*, meaning to tie or to bind.[75] Christianity was what bound together Western societies in the medieval period. Untie those sacred bonds, and everything would come apart. To the Church, heretical views did not just condemn certain individuals to eternal damnation—they had the power to corrupt and ultimately destroy all of Christian society. If allowed to spread, heresy could even bring the wrath of God down upon Christendom. Accordingly, lust for power and righteous zeal need not be mutually exclusive factors.

The Cathars were a sect centered in the Languedoc region in Southern France. As dualists who believed in the existence of two worlds, a corrupt material world and the world of Heaven, they preached that the Church was the corrupt instrument of an evil God.[76] For much of the twelfth to fourteenth centuries, Cathars bore the brunt of the papal war on heresy and were brutally pursued and decimated. But while they were treated with particular savagery, they were far from being the only group persecuted by the Church. Indeed a torrent of orders and decrees helped further beef up the Church's antiheresy arsenal. In 1184, Pope Lucius III perpetually anathematized "all who presume to think, or to teach . . . otherwise than as the Holy Roman Church teaches and observes." He ordered every bishop to annually comb his parish for heretics and punish them accordingly.[77] In 1199, Pope Innocent III declared heresy to be a crime of treason against God himself—and he treated it as such. Not only were heretics to have their belongings confiscated, even their children were damned to a life of poverty.[78]

The influential Fourth Lateran Council, which Innocent III convened in 1215, issued several decrees regarding heresy. The punishment for unorthodox speech was severe: "We excommunicate and anathematize every heresy that raises against the holy, orthodox and Catholic faith . . . condemning all heretics under whatever names they may be known." Those condemned were to be "handed over to the secular rulers" to be "punished with due justice" and have their property confiscated. As lay preachers opposed to the Church's growing powers started wandering the roads of Europe with messages that contradicted central tenets of the Church, the council also emphasized the prohibition against lay people preaching without prior authorization.[79] This was effectively a system of preventive oral censorship aimed at stopping the spread of unorthodox and heretical ideas. Three centuries later, Gutenberg and Luther would force the Church to update its censorship policy.

The Fourth Lateran Council also took aim at Jews, who were forced to wear distinctive clothing and prohibited from holding public office as well as insulting or blaspheming against Christ. Jewish converts to Christianity, the Church declared, could not continue observing Jewish rituals.[80] These decisions helped formalize the systematic legal persecution of Jews that had already begun in the twelfth century.[81] All in all, the Fourth Lateran Council laid down what Moore has called "a machinery of persecution for Western Christendom."[82]

In 1229 the Council of Toulouse followed up by prohibiting lay persons from the possession of most of the books of the Bible as well as a strict prohibition against translations of Holy Scripture.[83] Given the far-reaching consequences of Luther's translation of the Bible three centuries later these bans were at once equally far-sighted and narrow-minded.

Just prior to the Fourth Lateran Council, even more draconian measures were used against the obstinate Cathars with the launch of the Albigensian Crusade, the first "internal crusade" resulting in the slaughter of tens of thousands of men, women, and children.[84]

The thirteenth century also saw the formation of "mendicant orders"—groups like the Dominicans and Franciscans, whose itinerant members were bound by a vow of poverty. The Dominicans were founded in 1215 to preach a proper understanding of the faith and to combat heresy. Their membership was highly educated and capable, and included Thomas Aquinas among their number. So determined were the Dominicans to do the Lord's work that they were given the nickname *Domini canes*, a pun meaning "the Hounds of God."[85]

In 1231, Pope Gregory IX ordered Dominicans in the German city Regensburg to "seek out diligently those who are heretics or are infamed of heresy," and then dispersed more inquisitors throughout Western Christendom.[86] Although the pope explained that the Inquisition was conducted "not from a zeal for righteous vengeance, but out of love of correcting an erring brother," he demanded that unrepentant heretics pay "the debt of hatred." After 1231, the cost of settling that debt was death at the stake.[87]

Despite Aquinas's enduring efforts to expand the Western mind through his voracious appetite for pagan philosophy, he was fully on board with executing unrepentant and obstinate heretics and blasphemers. In *Summa Theologica* he wrote:

> It is a much graver matter to corrupt the faith . . . than to forge money. . . .Wherefore if forgers of money and other evil-doers are forthwith condemned to death by the secular authority, much more reason is there for heretics . . . to be not only excommunicated but even put to death.[88]

Gregory's new and improved staff needed new and improved tools. Medieval criminal procedure had typically been accusatorial: the accuser initiated a legal procedure against the accused before a court. But the inquisitorial procedure cut out the middleman and empowered a magistrate representing the authority of the emperor—or the pope—to launch investigations and prosecutions on his own initiative. The very magistrate who conducted the investigation was also the one who determined the guilt of the accused.[89]

The inquisitors were nothing if not efficient. In the 1240s, two French inquisitors questioned 5,471 people in just 201 days.[90] The inquisitors helpfully drafted elaborate manuals for others to follow. The legendary Bernard Gui—the Dominican friar portrayed by F. Murray Abraham in the film *The Name of the Rose*—defined his mission clearly in his handbook, *Practice of the Inquisition*:

> The end of the office of the inquisition is the destruction of heresy; this cannot be destroyed unless heretics are destroyed. . . . Heretics are destroyed in a double fashion: first, when they are converted from heresy to the true, Catholic faith . . . secondly, when they are surrendered to the secular jurisdiction to be corporeally burned.[91]

The swift destruction of heresy required streamlined processes. Focusing on an entire community, rather than specific individuals, proved efficient. The inquisitors would publicly announce a grace period during which all were encouraged to confess crimes against the faith and/or denounce others. Those who came forward could often expect to be absolved or let off with light penitence.[92] This method was motivated at least as much by a desire to instill fear and insecurity as it was by mercy.

The definition of heresy developed by canon lawyers and theologians was certainly wide enough to cause anxiety in the communities inquisitors targeted. According to the canon law detailed in the 1234 *Decretals* or *Liber Extra* of Gregory IX,

> He is said to be a heretic . . . who separates himself from the unity of the Church. So is every excommunicated person. So is he who errs in the exposition of Sacred Scripture. So is he who invents a new sect or follows one. So is he who understands the articles of faith differently from the Roman Church. So is he who thinks ill of the sacraments of the Church.[93]

With so much wiggle room, inquisitors used the grace period to put the whole community in a type of prisoner's dilemma. Many might come forward to ingratiate themselves by "confessing" and denouncing others, just to be on the safe side.

The meticulous questioning of entire communities allowed the inquisitors to gather vast amounts of personal information, which they then stored in huge archives and codices. Over time, the Medieval Inquisition amassed an impressive data hub with local archives and indexes that could be used to sift through age-old records to identify patterns and connections, compare statements, and double-check alibis.[94]

For all the horror stories of sadistic cruelty and widespread burnings spread by Protestant partisans, Enlightenment thinkers, and liberal historians in later years, the Medieval Inquisition was less bloody than one might imagine. Torture and execution were not the norm. In fact, the burning of a heretic was considered a failure on the part of the inquisitor. His mission was not to punish so much as to salvage souls and to bring back the wayward to the realm of orthodoxy. The death penalty was reserved for the most obstinate heretics who refused to recant or relapsed into heresy. In his *Book of Sentences*, Bernard Gui listed the punishments for all the heretics he convicted in the early fourteenth century. Out of more than nine hundred sentences, Gui only handed forty-two people (less than 5 percent) over to the authorities to be burned.[95]

Rather than waging a campaign of mass torture and burnings, the Inquisition meted out humiliating and socially shameful punishments. Targets were forced to wear yellow crosses on clothing.[96] Normally, wearing a cross would signal piety. But the yellow crosses were immediately recognizable as symbols of heresy and treason toward the Christian community. They branded the wearer as a very visible member of the out-group while simultaneously defining the in-group by its adherence to orthodoxy. The social cost of unorthodox speech skyrocketed.

Imprisonment was another innovative and effective means of reform. During a nine-month period in the mid-thirteenth century, inquisition prisons in Toulouse held an average of 171 prisoners per week.[97] The inquisitors made extensive use of what we'd call prison on remand, jailing suspected heretics prior to trial. According to James B. Given, this strategy was intended to "create a socially delimited space, in which they could isolate individuals from the outer world and subject them without interruption to an enforced and forcible persuasion. Such a planned and active use of imprisonment for behavior modification was possibly without parallel in medieval Europe."[98] Not surprisingly, inquisitors were enthusiastic about how cooperative and willing to confess suspects became after spending time in prison. Gui tells us, "I have often seen those thus vexed and detained for many years confess not only recent faults but even deeds committed long ago, going back thirty or forty years or more."[99]

Operating as the prosecutor, court, and parole board in one, the inquisitors systematically brought heretics to heel. Those found guilty of contaminating Christendom had only one path to societal reacceptance: religious conformity, as determined by the inquisitors.[100] By the first half of the fourteenth century the Cathar Church had been eliminated from its cradle in Languedoc. It limped on for a couple of decades in Italy before it was snuffed out by the Inquisition in the early fifteenth century.[101] The rule of law and an efficient bureaucracy had succeeded where crusades and mass slaughter had failed.

But in Western Europe, the end of the Cathars by no means meant an end to the war on heresy. Other groups attracted the focus of the Church and secular authorities. Among them were the Beguines—communities of laywomen who combined mysticism with chastity and an apostolic lifestyle outside the cloistered life of monasteries, and therefore beyond clerical control. One such woman was Marguerite Porete, whose book *The Mirror of Simple Souls* was condemned and burned in 1306 on orders from the bishop of Cambrai. He warned her to stop circulating her heretical words and ideas or else. Porete believed that when spiritually united with God, the individual had no need for the laws and sacraments of the Church. To the Church this sounded not only like a repudiation of its authority but also like a manual for sexual license. When Porete defied censorship, she was arrested. After eighteen months behind bars, during which she refused to respond to the inquisitor's questions, she was found guilty of relapsing into heresy. She was burned at the stake on June 1, 1310.[102]

Papal tribunals were not set up everywhere across Western Europe. There were none in England, though the fourteenth and fifteenth centuries still saw ecclesiastical and secular courts following the Inquisition's lead in the pursuit of heretics. Their targets included the so-called Lollards, inspired by the ideas of Oxford scholar and theologian John Wyclif, who rejected the idea of transubstantiation, that is the belief that the consecrated wafer turns into the actual body of Christ during the Eucharist.[103]

The "machinery of persecution" in Western Christendom marks a striking contrast to the Islamic world where—despite outbreaks of persecutions of heretics and blasphemers and systematic discrimination against religious minorities—no comparable institutionalization of authority took hold to enforce orthodoxy in thought or speech. This was not due to any formal recognition or protection of freedom of thought and expression, but rather because there was no central religious and political authority like the Catholic Church.

The Spanish Inquisition

In the fifteenth and sixteenth centuries, the Medieval Inquisition would spawn a Spanish, a Portuguese, a Venetian, and a Roman Inquisition, all recycling and building upon the techniques and practices of their medieval precursor. The two Iberian inquisitions further metastasized to Latin America, India, and as far as the Philippines, reflecting the growing power of the Catholic Church and of the European monarchs who allied themselves with it.[104]

Of all these inquisitions, the Spanish Inquisition of 1478 has become the most infamous, with the early Grand Inquisitor Tomás de Torquemada serving as the archetype of blind religious fanaticism intent on eliminating all opposition to orthodox Catholicism. But the reality of the Spanish Inquisition was more complex. It was not established by the pope but by Isabella and Ferdinand, the *Reyes Católicos* or "Catholic monarchs" of Spain. Initially it mainly targeted *conversos*—Jews who had (supposedly) insincerely converted to Christianity, and who were suspected of "Judaizing" and undermining Christianity. As such the Spanish Inquisition amplified the anti-Semitic aspects of the Medieval Inquisition, adding a racial element to its religious mission.

The intolerance culminated in 1492, when Spanish Jews were given the choice between conversion or expulsion, sparking a mass exodus.[105] The same year, the conquest of Granada, which completed the *Reconquista* of the Iberian Peninsula, added Muslims to the list of persecuted minorities. Still, the Spanish Inquisition was less bloody than often imagined. Historian Henry Kamen offers a cautious estimate of up to two thousand people executed for heresy by all its tribunals by 1520. Up to a thousand more were executed in the next three centuries, until the Spanish Inquisition was finally called off in 1834.[106] Nevertheless, it is misleading—as some apologists have insisted—to speak of a "Black Legend" exaggerating the cruelty of the Inquisition to demonize Spain and Catholicism.[107] According to Kamen the Spanish Inquisition did in fact spark a "reign of terror" in which oral evidence motivated by personal grievances was perfectly admissible, and where people could ultimately be burned on the stake on the basis of neighbors "remembering" how, decades before, someone changed his sheets on a Friday, or nodded his head as if praying in a Jewish manner. Moreover, the use of informers with all sorts of hidden motives for denouncing their victims—financial motives, personal enmity, family problems, or even drunkenness—spread fear and paranoia among a population nowhere near as uniformly committed to strict orthodox beliefs as one might imagine.[108]

In the late sixteenth century, the historian Juan de Mariana described how many ordinary Spaniards initially felt about the "very oppressive" social control caused by some of the Inquisition's methods:

> Because of these secret investigations they were deprived of the liberty to listen and talk freely, since in all the cities, towns and villages there were persons placed to give information of what went on. This was considered by some to be the most wretched slavery and equal to death.[109]

And while relatively few humans were burned, books and man-uscripts were not spared. In 1499 Cardinal Ximénez de Cisneros ran out of patience with recalcitrant Muslims in Granada. He or-dered all Muslim books and manuscripts surrendered and at least five thousand books—some claim as many as two million—went up in smoke in the town's central square, after which the possession of Arabic books was prohibited.[110]

THE MEDIEVAL PERIOD MAY SEEM SO FAR REMOVED FROM modern life that it offers little relevance to people in the twenty-first century in general, and the ideals and practice of free speech in par-ticular. But there are both lessons and warnings that we would do well to heed.

The Arabic translation of ancient Greek literature and its wider dissemination demonstrates vividly that, in the sphere of knowledge and information, cultural cross-fertilization is not only desirable but essential to progress. It provides people separated by culture, geography, and even time the ability to learn from and inspire each other in a positive feedback loop benefitting humankind as a whole. The Western European medieval culture of "poking around" is a powerful reminder of what can be achieved when reason is unshack-led from dogma and intellectual curiosity is allowed to roam free, however unsettling to established belief and authority. But the in-stitution of inquisition in the West and the "closing of the Muslim mind" through the hardening of Islamic law also demonstrate the dangers of imposing orthodoxy by policing thoughts and speech. As such, the Middle Ages provide another lesson of relevance for the wider history of free speech. On the one hand, that centralized authority is important for controlling information and opinion in order to legitimize and sustain the ruling class and its orthodoxy. On the other hand, that decentralized authority can serve as a powerful incubator for new and daring ideas that counter efforts to establish dogma and orthodoxy in the first place.

The machinery of persecution put in place by the Medieval Inquisition has been updated and recycled many times over the centuries, by both religious and secular regimes. Its underlying impulses may well be hardwired into human nature, lying in wait for the right moment to establish new orthodoxies and seek out fresh heretics.

3

The Great Disruption

*Luther, Gutenberg,
and the Viral Reformation*

Few individuals have done as much to change the course of history as the industrious goldsmith Johannes Gutenberg did when he invented a technique for mass producing books around 1450.[1] From Gutenberg's workshop in Mainz, the printing press spread nearly as quickly as the books it churned out. The number of printing workshops exploded from a mere four in 1462 to a whopping 1,700 in 1500, opening up everywhere from Lisbon to Kraków and from Stockholm to Cosenza in southern Italy.[2] European colonizers brought the printing press with them to the New World in the 1530s and the Far East in the 1580s.[3] European printers produced around thirteen million books between 1454 and 1500. In other words, they printed more books in forty-six years than the scribes of Western Europe had produced in a millennium. And that was only the beginning. Production increased to around eighty million books from 1501 to 1550 and jumped to more than 138 million from 1551 to 1600.[4]

As the production of books soared, their price dropped exponentially. In 1424, a manuscript had been worth as much as a farm or a vineyard—which explains why books in cathedral libraries were locked up with chains.[5] By the 1530s, a century and a Gutenberg Revolution later, a pamphlet cost the same as a loaf of bread.[6]

Increasing supply and plummeting prices opened print technology up to a vast new audience. According to a cautious estimate, the literacy rate in Great Britain more than tripled from 5 percent in the late fifteenth century to 16 percent in the sixteenth century. The literacy in France and Germany increased to 16 percent from 6 and 9 percent respectively.[7]

Within decades, the printing press had radically expanded access to knowledge and communication and allowed ideas to spread rapidly both within and across borders, contributing to the sweeping changes of the following centuries.[8] Growth and innovation followed in its wake. A study comparing European cities with and without printing presses by the late 1400s showed that the former grew 60 percent faster than the latter between 1500 and 1600, and that printing presses accounted for between 20 and 80 percent of such growth.[9]

Thanks to the printing press, rare ancient manuscripts were saved from decay and oblivion and disseminated widely, to the joy of a new class of humanist scholars who delighted in the wisdom of the ancients.[10] Rediscovered Roman ideals of oratory and republicanism inspired innovations in political philosophy. The (in)famous sixteenth-century Florentine political philosopher Niccolò Machiavelli wrote an emphatic defense of republican liberty and the importance of public speech and deliberation for safeguarding its values. In his *Discourses on Livy*, Machiavelli longed to "see that golden age" restored in which "every one could hold and defend whatever opinion he pleased."[11] Another great Renaissance thinker, Erasmus of Rotterdam, pointed out the good examples of even "pagan" Roman emperors in his 1516 *Education of a Christian*

Prince—a crash-course manual for princes-to-be, dedicated to the Habsburg prince Charles of Ghent. He concluded his argument with a one-liner from an unspecified emperor: "In a free state, tongues too should be free."[12] We'll see that the young prince did not take the lesson to heart when he ascended to the thrones of Spain, the same year, and the Holy Roman Empire, in 1519, as Charles V.

Though the Islamic world of the Middle Ages had boasted the world's biggest libraries and most daring freethinkers, the first printing press with Arabic characters did not appear in the Ottoman Empire until the 1720s.[13] According to some sources, Sultan Bayezid II and his son Selim I banned Arabic-character printing on pain of death in the 1480s and 1515, respectively.[14] Recent scholarship has raised questions about these specific Sultanic prohibitions.[15] But though the details are murky, it seems clear that printing was suppressed, whether by formal edict or by other means. Several reasons have been offered ranging from religious injunctions to the vested interests of the guild of calligraphers threatened by print technology. Religious concerns may also explain why Jewish, Greek, and Armenian printers were allowed to print in their own languages.[16] And why, after the ban on Arabic print was lifted, it remained illegal to print Islamic texts until 1802.[17] But the Ottomans may also have been persuaded to resist the Gutenberg Revolution after watching the havoc it caused to political and religious authority in Christendom.[18]

Historians continue to debate whether the late arrival of print technology contributed to the Islamic world losing the civilizational leadership it had claimed in the early Middle Ages in terms of literacy, science, philosophy, and the spread of new ideas.[19] It seems intuitively obvious that these developments are connected, given the instrumental role printing presses played in fostering growth and innovation in Europe, and in catalyzing transformative events like the Renaissance, the Reformation, and the Scientific Revolution.[20] To draw a modern parallel, there is a clear correlation between internet penetration and the development status of a nation.[21] Try running an offline university, business, or government, and you'll quickly learn the cost of being outside the digital information loop.

Yet most disruptive technologies bring costs as well as benefits. Printing presses may have eased communication and the dissemination of learning, but they also churned out a steady stream of virulent political and religious propaganda, hate speech, obscene cartoons, and treatises on witchcraft and alchemy.[22] More fundamentally, new ideas spread by printing presses called into question the very assumptions about knowledge, religion, and authority upon which the social order of Europe was based. By 1525, Erasmus had lost faith in the new technology and complained that printers "fill the world with pamphlets and books . . . foolish, ignorant, malignant, libellous, mad, impious and subversive; and such is the flood that even things that might have done some good lose all their goodness."[23]

The printing press also allowed moral panics to go viral, with consequences that were vastly more deadly than those of twenty-first-century Twitter mobs. The *Malleus Maleficarum* or *Hammer of Witches* was a wildly successful witch-hunting manual compiled by two Dominican inquisitors in 1486, which reached its ninth edition within six years.[24] Books like the *Malleus Maleficarum* fanned the flames of witch hunts between the late fifteenth and early eighteenth centuries, in which an estimated forty-five thousand people were executed.[25]

Unlike the Ottoman sultans, Western rulers like the Habsburgs and the Tudors initially welcomed the printing press, endowing printers with lucrative privileges. The Western Church also embraced the printing press as a "divine art."[26] However, it quickly became clear that printing was at least as likely to undermine as it was to consolidate established authority. Sensing the disruptive potential of this new technology, the Church and secular authorities sought to retain their positions as the gatekeepers of knowledge, information, and communication. The archbishop-elector of Gutenberg's hometown of Mainz established a censorship commission for his whole arch-bishopric as early as 1486.[27] Pope Innocent VIII followed suit one year later with a papal bull addressed to the whole of Christendom declaring that "regulation" was necessary to stop "the misuse of the printing press for the distribution of pernicious writing."[28] A second papal bull issued by Leo X in 1515 prohibited printers from pub-lishing anything without prior authorization.[29] But an outspoken, ill-tempered monk from Saxony was about to show both throne and altar that the printing press was more potent and difficult to silence than they could ever have imagined.

Gutenberg and Luther: An Explosive Cocktail

The full revolutionary potential of print technology became apparent only after Martin Luther stepped onto the global stage. On October 31, 1517, he sent his famous list of ninety-five theses boldly criticiz-ing the Church to the new archbishop-elector of Mainz. He cc'd the bishop of Brandenburg and—according to some accounts—nailed a copy to the local church door in Wittenberg.[30] Luther's letter mainly attacked the practice of selling papal indulgences promising time off in Purgatory in exchange for cash—a practice he regarded as a detestable scam. But Luther's censure also veered into much more dangerous territory as he criticized the Church more broadly and questioned its claim to authority.

Luther was not the first to challenge the Church. As early as 1324, the brilliant scholar Marsilius of Padua had denied the tem-poral authority of the Church and argued for popular sovereignty in his book *The Defender of Peace*. This groundbreaking attack on the Church got him excommunicated, but it would not be long before more dissidents raised their voices.[31] In the late fourteenth century, indulgences were criticized by John Wyclif, who also shared Luther's enthusiasm for vernacular translations of the Bible. His re-mains were posthumously condemned and burned for heresy. The

Bohemian reformer Jan Hus questioned the authority of the Church and pope and ignited a local reformation before he was burned alive for heresy in 1415. But neither Marsilius, Wyclif, nor Hus brought about as decisive change as Luther. Born on the wrong side of the Gutenberg Revolution, they lacked the game-changing platform that spread Luther's ideas near and far.[32]

The Church authorities could not say that Luther had not warned them. In his letter to the archbishop, Luther mused darkly that "someone may rise and, by means of publications, silence those preachers" selling indulgences if things were not "quickly remedied."[33] The archbishop (who got a cut of the profits) was not so easily convinced. His failure to react prompted Luther to carry out his threat and publish his theses in pamphlets and broadsheets. German translations soon followed, and before long, the theses had spread like wildfire through Western Christendom.

Even Luther was surprised by the popularity of his dry list of theological propositions, calling it "a mystery" how the theses "were spread to so many places."[34] But he quickly realized that he had a natural talent for religious populism and developed what historian Andrew Pettegree has called "Brand Luther." Instead of Latin, he wrote in an entertaining and colorful German, keeping his messages short and to the point.[35] The layout and design of his writings became increasingly slick, and the punchy text was accompanied by illustrations for the benefit of the illiterate who eagerly shared his anti-Catholic memes.[36]

Luther and Gutenberg proved to be a match made in Heaven (or Hell if you asked the Church). According to one estimate, Luther's thirty publications sold more than three hundred thousand copies between 1517 and 1520.[37] By 1530 his works had been published in more than two thousand editions totaling some two million copies.[38] In Luther's own words, the printing press was "God's highest and extremest act of grace, whereby the business of the Gospel is driven forward."[39] And Luther could back up his claim of divine inspiration with data: the more printing presses operating in a city the more likely the city was to join the Protestant camp.[40]

Too late, both the Church and the secular authorities tried to contain the Reformation. In June 1520, Leo X gave Luther sixty days to recant and "cut off the advance of this plague and cancerous disease so it will not spread any further."[41] But Luther refused to back down, and burned the pope's bull in public.[42] He went on to declare theological war on Rome in three angry treatises, including *The Babylonian Captivity of the Church*, which denounced the popes as "anti-christs" for "seek[ing] to deprive us of this consciousness of our liberty."[43] Luther's subsequent excommunication came as little surprise—and it certainly did not harm his sales. In February 1521, the pope's envoy in Germany complained: "Daily there is a veritable downpour of Lutheran tracts in German and Latin. . . . Nothing is sold here except the tracts of Luther."[44]

The pope's efforts having failed, the Holy Roman emperor Charles V summoned Luther to the imperial diet in Worms in April 1521, demanding that he explain himself. Pointing at a large pile of books, the emperor asked Luther if they were his and if he would recant. Luther was unmovable. He has been quoted as responding, "Here I stand, I can do no other." And even though that particular one-liner is likely apocryphal, his actual words were no less inspiring. The next day he replied:

> Unless I am convinced by scripture and by plain reason (I do not believe in the authority of either popes or councils by themselves, for it is plain that they have often erred and contradicted each other) . . . I cannot and I will not recant anything, for to go against conscience is neither right nor safe. God help me, Amen.[45]

It was a watershed moment in the history of free thought. Charles V promptly issued an edict warning that unless Luther's "detestable and perverse doctrines" were "speedily prevented, the whole

German nation, and later all other nations, will be infected by this same disorder." The edict declared it illegal for "each and all" to even

> dare to buy, sell, read, preserve, copy, print, or cause to be copied or printed, any books of the aforesaid Martin Luther . . . since they are foul, harmful, suspected, and published by a notorious and stiffnecked heretic. Neither shall any dare to approve his opinions, nor to proclaim, defend, or assert them, in any other way that human ingenuity can invent.[46]

Luther and his followers had been declared heretics and thus enemies of both state and church. More bans soon followed in German principalities and neighboring states like the Habsburg Netherlands.[47] The Diet of Speyer in 1529 established prepublication censorship across the Holy Roman Empire.[48] But it was already too late. Not even Luther could stop the Reformation, which had taken on a life of its own.

Instead of backing down, Luther upped the ante when he translated and published the New Testament in German in 1522.[49] For the first time, ordinary Germans had direct access to the word of God, and thanks to Gutenberg's printing press, they could buy their own copy for about as much as a common laborer made in a single day.[50] For everyone to read and understand the Bible was a cornerstone of Luther's Reformation. Of course, that presupposed that everyone was literate in the first place, so Luther often stressed the importance of establishing schools to teach children how to read. In the long term, this had the effect of greatly boosting literacy in Protestant countries. Fast-forward to 1900, and the literacy rates in Britain, the Netherlands, and Sweden approached close to 100 percent, while in Catholic countries like Spain and Italy, on the other hand, the rate was still only about 50 percent.[51]

But Luther could hardly have imagined the consequences in the short term. The democratization of access to the Scriptures gave ordinary people the tools and courage to seek out the Truth on their own. This included German peasants and serfs who had long been treated like chattel. In the pages of Luther's vernacular Bible, they could suddenly read passages like the Letter of James warning their oppressors to "Listen! The wages of the laborers who mowed your fields, which you kept back by fraud, cry out, and the cries of the harvesters have reached the ears of the Lord of hosts."[52] Taking a leaf out of Luther's playbook, peasants staged a massive revolt in 1524–1525, demanding the abolition of serfdom and razing castles and monasteries in the name of the Gospel.[53]

Luther was shocked by the mess he had inspired. He frantically published a new pamphlet, *Against the Robbing and Murdering Hordes of Peasants*, and urged princes to "smite, slay and stab" the rebellious peasants like "mad dogs."[54] Luther's incitement to mass murder found a new readership—this time among the embattled German princes. They took his suggestions to heart, and according to some estimates, as many as a hundred thousand peasants were slaughtered as the princes put the uprising down.[55]

Access to the vernacular Bible also inspired new religious sects. When the Anabaptists concluded that there was no precedent for infant baptism in the Bible, they scrapped the ritual altogether and set about rebaptizing one another as adults. Anabaptists also promoted a form of religious communism and refused to obey both secular and religious authorities. Protestant Zurich cracked down on the sect with brutality, imposing death by drowning on anyone who attended an Anabaptist service.[56]

Though Luther was appalled by the "rebellious and murderous spirits" of the Anabaptists, he was not yet prepared to push for their execution as he had done for the peasant revolt.[57] Writing in 1527, he argued:

> It is not right, and I am deeply troubled that the poor [Anabaptists] are so pitifully put to death, burned, and cruelly slain. Let

everyone believe what he likes. If he is wrong, he will have punishment enough in hell fire. Unless there is sedition, one should oppose them with Scripture and God's Word.[58]

But the stakes were raised when a radical cadre of Anabaptists occupied the city of Münster in northwest Germany in 1534–1535. They erected barricades, burned all books except for the Bible, and made polygamy compulsory.[59] Protestants and Catholics now finally found something to agree upon in their shared revulsion, and the Protestant ruler Philip of Hesse ultimately assisted Münster's Catholic prince-bishop to reclaim the city. Over the following decades, Protestant and Catholic rulers in Germany, Switzerland, and Austria helped each other persecute Anabaptism to the brink of extinction, with Luther's explicit, if reluctant, endorsement.[60]

In retrospect, it was rather naïve of Luther to actively democratize access to the Bible and expect everyone to toe his line. If the *pope* had no divine authority to determine universal Christian truth, why should Christians slavishly follow the theology of some constipated German monk? Luther attempted to put the genie back in the bottle by stressing that good Christians should heed the Bible verses that emphasized the duty to respect secular authorities, like Chapter 13 of the Epistle to the Romans: "Let every person be subject to the governing authorities; for there is no authority except from God, and those authorities that exist have been instituted by God. Therefore whoever resists authority resists what God has appointed, and those who resist will incur judgment."[61] Christian freedom was the certainty that salvation depended on divine grace and faith in God. You might have the freedom to independently interpret Scripture inside your head, but Christian freedom did not grant you license to follow Luther's own example of defying authorities to follow your conscience in speech or practice.

He also resorted to censorship to mute divergent Protestant messages. In 1528, Luther and his colleague Philipp Melanchthon—who both acted as censors as part of their duties at the University of Wittenberg—urged the elector of Saxony to ban the buying and reading of books written by Anabaptists and so-called Sacramentarians, followers of the Protestant reformer Huldrych Zwingli.[62] In 1530, he even promoted the death penalty for sedition and blasphemy.[63] On paper, he did not push for executions for mere "heresy," which the Catholic Church used to persecute Lutherans.[64] But in practice, he considered doctrinal differences, such as rejecting an article of the Apostles' Creed, sufficient to be labeled a blasphemer. For such sinners, Luther was prepared to go Old Testament: "Moses, in his Law, commands that such blasphemers and, indeed, all false teachers, are to be stoned. So, in this case, there ought not to be much disputing, but such open blasphemers should be condemned without a hearing and without defense."[65]

Luther's intolerance became even more extreme in his final years. When he failed to convert Jews to Christianity, he penned the ragingly anti-Semitic pamphlet *The Jews and Their Lies*. It promoted confiscation of Jewish prayer books and Talmudic writings "in which such idolatry, lies, cursing and blasphemy are taught" and advised that "rabbis be forbidden to teach henceforth on pain of loss of life and limb." Luther even encouraged his readers to "set fire to their synagogues or schools."[66] Luther's transformation from the seemingly unmovable champion of freedom of conscience to the persecutor of religious dissenters might seem like a paradox. However, in the early sixteenth century it was an article of faith that no state could subsist without uniformity of belief. Consequently, religious dissent was regarded as akin to what we might call a national security threat today. But as we shall see, Luther was not the last person to appeal to freedom when facing persecution, only to persecute other dissenters once in a position of power and influence.

Luther died in 1546 and Lutheranism was officially recognized in the Holy Roman Empire with the Peace of Augsburg in 1555. But freedom of religion did not carry the day. Instead of giving each individual the freedom to choose his or her own religion, the Peace allowed rulers to choose on behalf of their subjects, introducing the doctrine *cuius regio, eius religio*—whose realm, his religion. Another crucial caveat was that Lutheranism was the only option on the Protestant side of the menu. Reformed Protestantism and other Protestant offshoots were still beyond the pale.[67]

Subject to the authority of kings and princes who became the heads of both state and church, Lutheran churches came to play an important role in enforcing orthodoxy and social control. The Peace of Augsburg also instituted an early modern version of enforced tolerance, which stressed that the social and religious peace of the Holy Roman Empire depended on Catholics and Lutherans refraining from attacking each other's religious doctrines. What constituted "religious invective" was not defined, which provided the authorities wide discretion to censor and punish writings touching on sensitive issues. In fact, according to historian Allyson F. Creasman, the Peace of Augsburg came to "serve as a weapon in the polemical war between the confessions" and a "means to silence opposition and advance political claims."[68]

Luther is often credited with separating religion and politics, yet he effectively made Lutheran churches instruments of the state. In doing so, he unintentionally set Protestant churches on a path of gradually declining influence. For if the king decided to deviate from orthodoxy for economic, geopolitical, or ideological reasons, the church had little authority to resist. Excommunication is not an option when the head of the state is also head of the church. Moreover, the focus on universal literacy meant that people in Protestant lands were empowered to read other publications than the Bible and Luther's interpretation thereof. This prompted many to develop their own thoughts and ideas about the nature of God and man, setting in motion a chain reaction of ever more daring and heterodox thought and connecting new creative centers of Europe's collective brain. And so in the following centuries, novel and more tolerant ideas gradually seeped into Lutheran states until irreconcilable differences ended the marriage of religious orthodoxy and political absolutism.

Today the populations in Lutheran states like Denmark, Sweden, and Norway are among the most secular and liberal in the world. They sharply distinguish between religion and morality, value free speech over religious doctrines, and most of those who identify as Christians don't attach decisive importance to religion nor spend much time in church.[69] It is unlikely that was what Luther intended when he launched the Reformation.

The Splintering of Christendom

Watching the fallout from the Reformation play out across the Channel, England's Henry VIII was determined to keep Lutheranism at bay. He earned the pope's recognition as "Defender of the Faith" in 1521 by penning an anti-Luther pamphlet.[70] He also endeavored to suppress the work of priest and linguist William Tyndale, who translated the New Testament into vernacular English. Tyndale finished and published his translation in Germany between 1526 and 1528. In spite of the English government's efforts to keep it out and destroy all copies, between sixteen and eighteen thousand English Bibles made their way across the Channel to England and Scotland.[71]

Henry attempted to tighten his grip in 1529 and issued an index of forbidden heretical books.[72] The list was drawn up by the king's new chancellor, Thomas More, who is best known for his book *Utopia*, published in 1516. More regarded Protestant writings as a highly infectious disease, warning that "pestiferous" books were "sent to this realm to pervert the people from the true faith of Christ, to stir them to sedition against their princes."[73] More reflected the spirit of the era, a time when religion and politics were joined at the hip, such that religious crimes like blasphemy and heresy were often difficult to separate from political crimes such as sedition and treason.

English agents eventually hunted Tyndale down in the Low Countries. He was handed over to the imperial authorities and strangled and burned in Brussels in 1536.[74] But in the meantime, Henry VIII had changed his mind and joined the Reformation—not because of a sudden epiphany, but because the pope would not let him divorce his wife, Catherine of Aragon, when she failed to provide him with a male heir. One year after Tyndale's execution, the king sanctioned the first official English translation of the hugely influential "Matthew Bible."[75] But Henry's newfound zeal for reform faltered when he saw how popular the vernacular translation became. In 1543, he pressured Parliament to restrict access to the Bible to the upper classes—presumably to prevent the common people from getting funny ideas above their station.[76]

The English Reformation made Henry VIII the supreme head of both state and church and he took full advantage of his new powers. He cracked down on seditious tongues questioning his decision to join the Reformation by declaring it an act of treason to call him "schismatic" or "heretic." Ironically, it was even punishable to call him a "tyrant." His marriages were another touchy subject. After he married his second wife, Anne Boleyn, it became high treason to "do or procure to be done by act or deed or word written or printed, anything to the prejudice of the king against his marriage with Queen Anne."[77]

Neither political dissent nor its suppression were new phenomena. "False News or Tales" scandalizing the king or "the Great Men of the Realm" had been criminalized in England since 1275.[78] But since printing technology facilitated the comparatively easy production and dissemination of fake news at scale, with a much wider reach than oral or handwritten dissent, this threat of punishment was no longer a sufficient deterrent. As we saw in the introduction, the thin-skinned king declared renewed war on fake news in 1536, before instituting prepublication censorship in 1538.[79]

When Henry's devoutly Catholic daughter Mary I took the throne in 1553 she made it her life's goal to reverse her father's reformation of the church. Yet while Mary may have disagreed with her father's rejection of Catholicism, the two were more in tune when it came to cracking down on crimes of conscience, thought, and speech. She revived heresy laws and burned around three hundred heretics at the stake, earning herself the nickname "Bloody Mary."[80] Those who published slanders against the queen had their hands cut off. Following Henry's example, Mary issued a revised index of forbidden literature in 1555. Three years later, it became punishable by death to possess any heretical or treasonable book, whether printed in England or abroad. Prepublication censorship was enforced by the Stationers' Company—the newly established guild of printers. With a complete monopoly on printing and bookselling, the company was given authority to search, confiscate, and burn unlicensed books.[81]

Elizabeth I, who became queen in 1558, was not quite as thin-skinned as her father and half sister, but neither was her government a new regime of permissiveness. Facing the threat of foreign invasion and violent religious upheaval at home, she declared it an act of treason to call her "usurper" and "bastard" and enforced laws against "seditious words and rumors uttered against the Queen's most excellent Majesty."[82] To be fair, the attacks on her were pretty harsh. Not only was she accused of having "abused her body" through "lust," she was also labeled "an incestuous bastard, begotten and born in sin" because the pope had refused to acknowledge her father's marriage to her mother, Anne Boleyn.[83] The consequences for such attacks, which challenged her very legitimacy as queen, were fierce. One man was hanged for writing a seditious letter to the queen declaring her to be "so much an adversary unto us poor men as unto Christ Jesus."[84] Elizabeth also expanded the licensing and printing regime of the Stationers' Company and burned occasional "blasphemous heretics."[85]

There were some in high places who were willing to challenge Elizabeth's crackdown on speech. In 1576, Peter Wentworth, a leading Puritan member of Parliament, gave a rousing speech arguing "that in this House which is termed a place of free Speech, there is nothing so necessary for the preservation of the Prince and State as free Speech, and without it is a scorn and mockery to call it a Parliament House."[86] Yet, to Elizabeth, Parliament's freedom consisted of nothing more than "to saye yea or no to bills" not "to speake . . . of all causes." This reflected the limited powers and representativeness of Parliament, whose members were restricted to wealthy male landowners. Even this tiny elite had little say, as Elizabeth decided when Parliament could meet and what it could discuss, and she specifically banned the touchy subjects of religion and her marital status. Wentworth's praise and practice of free speech, while brave, was premature. He would serve three sentences in the Tower, where he died in 1596.[87]

It might be tempting to equate censorship under the Tudor monarchs with censorship among Catholics and Protestants in Continental Europe. After all, both utilized draconian laws that suppressed speech and lists of banned books. It is also clear that both English and Continental censorship rested on the idea that words and actions are indistinguishable, and that the former can be every bit as harmful and dangerous as the latter.[88]

But there were important differences between the two regions' perceptions of the harms of speech. Most English censorship laws dealt with forms of defamation or libel rather than heresy. And from the age of Elizabeth, this crucial difference between English and Continental censorship became pronounced. According to historian Debora Shuger, Continental—and in particular, Catholic—censorship had a basis in late classical heresy laws like the severe Theodosian and Justinian codes mentioned in Chapter 1. They were ideological in nature and aimed at the wholesale eradication of "thought crimes": wrong ideas that clashed with orthodox doctrine. English defamation and libel laws, on the other hand, were based on older Roman law, such as in the ancient Law of the Twelve Tables that prescribed the death penalty for libelous poems and songs in the Early Republic, and the law of *iniuria* (a form of defamation with no exact equivalent in modern law).[89] English restrictions on speech were adopted piecemeal as a response to specific moral panics or crises rather than as a wholesale attempt to control every word spoken or printed. They typically targeted scandalous and libelous lies and falsehoods undermining the all-important reputation and honor of those in power, or seditious language that might disturb the social peace of the realm by inciting people to violence and rebellion, however tenuous the link between words and deeds. They also stressed the importance of intent and that the most lenient interpretation should be adopted during trials.[90] Accordingly, the English censorship regime was generally mild(er) by sixteenth-century standards, although certainly oppressive by modern ones.

Luther may have started the Reformation, but he was not the only great reformer, nor was he unique in his simultaneous insistence on dismantling Catholic orthodoxy and establishing his own by advocating harsh punishments for religious speech crimes.

One of the most influential branches of Protestantism was established by the French reformer John Calvin. The first bastion of Calvinism was Geneva, where Calvin took control of the church and gradually established a repressive theocracy known as the Republic of Geneva in 1541. Long lists of writers from Ovid to Thomas Aquinas were censored and citizens were instructed to avoid evils such as dancing, singing, talking loudly, reading entertaining books, and wearing bright clothes.[91]

The most famous victim of Calvin's inflexible orthodoxy was the Spanish-born polymath and Renaissance thinker Michael Servetus, whose initial claim to fame was a treatise on medicinal syrups. But thanks to his less than sweet encounter with Calvin he is better known for his controversial theological works *On the Errors of the Trinity* and *The Restoration of Christianity*.[92] As an anti-Trinitarian,

Servetus rejected the divine nature of Christ and insisted that Jesus was merely human.[93] Clearly misjudging the austere Calvin, he mailed him an early draft of *The Restoration* and invited himself to Geneva. Calvin warned him to stay away and forwarded a copy to the inquisitors in Lyon, who were happy to receive kompromat on any heretic, even if the informant himself was a notorious heretic.[94] Servetus was arrested and condemned to death, but escaped from inquisitorial prison by the skin of his teeth. On his way to Zurich he was reckless enough to make a stop in Geneva, where he was recognized and convicted of heresy in a new trial with Calvin serving as first witness. Servetus and his heretical manuscripts were burned at the stake on October 27, 1553.[95]

Servetus's execution proved to be a public-relations disaster for Calvin—one that he exacerbated by continuing to punish sympathetic Genevans. A local book printer was imprisoned for writing that Servetus had been punished at the will and pleasure of Calvin, while a woman was imprisoned for calling Servetus a martyr of Christ.[96] Calvin furiously defended the execution, proclaiming that "perfidious apostates" with their "impure and petulant tongues should not be allowed to lacerate the sacred name of God."[97]

The loudest protest came from the theologian Sebastian Castellio, who had already clashed with Calvin in the past. Castellio had witnessed the execution of heretics in Lyon.[98] When he heard the same horrors were unfolding in Calvin's Geneva, he penned his famous defense of religious toleration, *Concerning Heretics*:

> Men are puffed up with knowledge or with a false opinion of knowledge and look down upon others. Pride is followed by cruelty and persecution so that now scarcely anyone is able to endure another who differs at all from him. Although opinions are almost as numerous as men, nevertheless there is hardly any sect which does not condemn all others and desire to reign alone. Hence arise banishments, chains, imprisonments, stakes, and gallows.

Men would only be "able to dwell together in concord" if everyone learned to check their intolerance and "forbear one another in love, which is the bond of peace." And so, he argued, "every man should be allowed to believe as he will and can, and no one should be constrained."[99] Castellio's response to Calvin's intolerance became a milestone in the long struggle for freedom of conscience in religious matters.

Further bloodshed marked the spread of Calvinism to France, where followers—known as Huguenots—clashed with Catholics in escalating cycles of sectarian violence that turned into outright civil war in March 1562, after the mass slaughter of a congregation of Huguenots caught in the act of illegal worship.[100] The French Wars of Religion raged on, with the loss of an estimated two million lives, until 1598, when the Edict of Nantes granted Huguenots freedom of worship without being "constrained to do anything in respect to religion contrary to their consciences."[101] This uneasy truce lasted less than a century, until the Sun King unleashed a new wave of intolerance, the unintended consequences of which threatened the very authorities it was supposed to protect.

The Counter-Reformation

Having lost both territory and souls to Protestantism, the Catholic Church rallied its troops in the second half of the sixteenth century and launched what is now called the Counter-Reformation. In a series of meetings between 1545 and 1563 known as the Council of Trent, church leaders set out to reform and revitalize the Church by spelling out Catholic doctrine and reinforcing the Church's authority to interpret it, which direct access to Scripture as unleashed by Luther had so undermined. At the Fourth Session, in 1546, the Council warned "petulant spirits" not to interpret the Scripture contrary to "holy mother Church" and forbade the printing and selling of religious books without prior examination and authorization.[102]

The popes also doubled down on censorship and persecution to combat Protestantism. In 1559, Pope Paul IV promulgated a papal Index of Prohibited Books, the infamous *Index Librorum Prohibitorum*, which one historian has labeled "the turning-point for the freedom of enquiry in the Catholic world."[103] The first version banned the entire writings of some 550 authors, including Machiavelli and Erasmus, as well as individual works of other writers.[104] A Congregation of the Index was later established to streamline the censorial process.[105] While its influence drastically diminished over the centuries, the Index was not abandoned until 1966. In the period between 1600 and its final abandonment, it included an estimated 5,200 interdictions.[106] And there is no way of knowing how many authors may have self-censored to avoid inclusion.

At the same instance, the Church restricted access to the Scriptures for the lower classes, who could not read Latin. The same decree that published the first Index of Prohibited Books in 1559 also declared that no vernacular Bibles could be "printed or read or possessed" without written permission from the Roman Inquisition or the so-called Holy Office which governed it.[107] Such restrictions, together with the growing Index, effectively limited reading, with tiny loopholes for the elite who circulated forbidden books clandestinely.[108]

Censorship created the perfect conditions for a booming black market in underground literature. Smugglers would buy forbidden books at the great book fair in Frankfurt and hide them in shipments of officially vetted Catholic literature.[109] Censors patrolled the borders like airport security guards, sniffing out toxic and explosive ideas. But they quickly realized that stopping the printing press was an uphill battle. Since most censors spoke only Italian and Latin, even the most controversial books in German and English often slipped through unnoticed. Moreover, the sheer volume of printed material flooding Christendom rendered the Church's ideal of universal institutional control of the printed word impossible.

As one sixteenth-century censor wistfully wrote, "What we need is a halt to printing, so that the Church can catch up with this deluge of publications."[110]

Such wishful thinking did little to stop the spread of Protestantism in Northern Europe, but the story was different in Spain. The Spanish Inquisition compiled its own index of forbidden books in 1551 and, following the Tudor example, banned all Spanish books printed abroad. To avoid further foreign contamination, it was also forbidden to study abroad.[111] The strategy worked surprisingly well until 1558, when two networks of Lutherans were exposed in Spain. In May 1558, a few months before his death, Charles V called for "a radical cure to this unfortunate situation, punishing the guilty thoroughly to prevent them spreading."[112] On these orders, his son and heir to the Spanish throne Philip II and the Inquisition redirected their focus from Jews and Muslims to Protestants, executing an estimated eighty-three between 1559 and 1563 and effectively insulating Spain from the Reformation that swept across the Continent. Isabella and Ferdinand would have been proud.[113]

As in Spain, papal censorship in Rome went hand in hand with inquisition. Pope Paul III established what is known as the Roman Inquisition in 1542. According to some estimates, it conducted a whopping fifty thousand formal trials and released around 1,250 people to execution by the secular authorities in the first two centuries of operation.[114] One of the most famous victims was the natural philosopher and Dominican friar Giordano Bruno. Historians still debate the exact reason why Bruno was convicted of heresy, but he gave the inquisitors ample ammunition. For one, he promoted the Copernican worldview, which claimed that the sun is the center of the universe around which the earth and other planets revolve. This claim was not simply a matter of astronomy—it was also heretical since it questioned the Bible itself, which clearly states that "the world is firmly established; it shall never be moved."[115] And that was not even Bruno's most controversial idea. He also thought the universe to be infinite and reasoned that, in an infinite universe, Creation must take place indefinitely.

Bruno paid dearly for his radical ideas. In 1600, after spending the better part of a decade behind bars, he was convicted of heresy by the Roman Inquisition. The Inquisition released him to the secular authorities and banished his works to the Index of Forbidden Books. In the early morning of February 17, 1600, Bruno was led to Rome's Campo de' Fiori, stripped naked, and burned alive.[116]

The next famous victim of the Roman Inquisition also drew ire over his promotion of the heliocentric view of the universe. In 1613, after exploring the night sky with the recently invented telescope, the astronomer Galileo concluded "with absolute necessity . . . that Venus revolves around the Sun; around which are moving all the other planets too, as the centre of their revolutions."[117] The Catholic Church declared heliocentrism officially false in 1616, denouncing it as "foolish and absurd in philosophy, and formally heretical since it explicitly contradicts in many places the sense of Holy Scripture."[118] But Galileo was not convinced by dogma. He returned to the discussion in his 1632 *Dialogue Concerning the Two Chief World Systems*. The book was set up as a fictional dialogue between two characters who represented the two competing views of the universe. Galileo made his own position clear by letting the character Simplicio ("Simpleton") represent the Church's geocentric position. This deeply wounded Pope Urban VIII, particularly because he had actually encouraged Galileo to write the book in the first place. Not only was Galileo contradicting the Church by promoting heliocentrism again, he also had the audacity to mock and undermine the authority of the pope. He was summoned to Rome where the Inquisition forced him to recant his false and heretic assertions and sentenced him to perpetual house arrest. When pressured to admit that the earth is unmovable, he supposedly muttered "and yet it moves."[119] The quote is probably apocryphal, but it is emblematic of the Scientific Revolution Galileo pioneered. New knowledge might be inconvenient to established dogmas, but when empirical observations clash with unsubstantiated belief, the latter must yield.

Galileo escaped the death sentence. But many other Europeans accused of heresy were not that lucky. According to a conservative estimate, around five thousand people were executed in Western Europe because of their religious beliefs in the tumultuous period between 1523 and the mid-seventeenth century.[120] To these should be added millions who were killed in wars, mob violence, and related famines fueled by religious intolerance.

The carnage inadvertently unleashed by mixing Gutenberg and Luther culminated in the Thirty Years' War, which began when Bohemian Protestants rebelled against the Catholic Holy Roman Emperor in 1618. Allies were drawn in and the conflict escalated into a Continent-wide power struggle between Catholic and Protestant Europe, killing an estimated eight million people and wiping out a third of the prewar population in Germany and Bohemia.[121] The war formally ended with the Peace of Westphalia in 1648, which elevated the principle of *cuius regio, eius religio* to the international level and added Calvinism to the set menu introduced by the Peace of Augsburg in 1555. However, this did not immediately translate into tolerance and religious freedom, nor into press freedom, as both Protestants and Catholics were eager to shore up the agreed red lines of religious and political authority through censorship, in order to avoid further anarchy and bloodshed. Even so, more and more voices were joining the early pioneers of freedom of conscience, pushing the limits of tolerance and censorship, which had already been probed and extended further to the East.

Eastern Promises

The first state in Europe to formalize religious toleration was the small principality of Transylvania, which became independent from Hungary in 1541. Squeezed between two giants, the Ottoman and the Habsburg Empires, the Transylvanian rulers had no choice but to preserve their independence by gaining the support of their own nobility and religious communities.[122] So, the dowager queen Izabella Jagiellon promised in 1557 that "by our Royal station and office we are obliged to protect all Churches."[123]

Her son, John Sigismund Zápolya II, inherited his mother's pragmatic open-mindedness when he came of age. The young king converted from Catholicism to Lutheranism to Calvinism before finally settling on anti-Trinitarianism, egged on at each step by the persuasive court preacher Ferenc Dávid.[124] King John and the Transylvanian Diet issued the Edict of Torda in 1568, recognizing the legal status of Catholics, Lutherans, Calvinists, and anti-Trinitarians:

> In every place the preachers shall preach and explain the Gospel each according to his understanding of it, and if the congregation like it, well, if not, no one shall compel them . . . no one shall be reviled for his religion by anyone . . . and it is not permitted that anyone should threaten anyone else by imprisonment or by removal from his post for his teaching.[125]

Transylvania was not the only oasis of religious tolerance in Eastern Europe. In the 1570s, the Commonwealth of Poland-Lithuania became another safe haven for religious dissenters and freethinkers—or, in the view of one Polish cardinal, "a place of shelter for heretics."[126] Poland-Lithuania was an elective monarchy, where the king was appointed by the nobility. When Sigismund II Augustus died childless in 1572, the noblemen had to import a member of another European dynasty and settled on Henry Valois, the younger brother of the French king. To prevent the sectarian bloodshed that had enveloped Henry's native France, however, a clause on religious freedom was added to the agreement with the new king in 1573.[127] Known as the Warsaw Confederation, the agreement stated:

> Since there is in our Commonwealth no little disagreement on the subject of religion, in order to prevent any such hurtful strife from beginning among our people . . . we mutually promise for ourselves and our successors forever . . . that we who differ with regard to religion will keep the peace with one another, and will not for a different faith or a change of churches shed blood nor punish one another by confiscation of property, infamy, imprisonment or banishment.[128]

Crucially, the Warsaw Confederation protected the *individual's* freedom of religion—unlike the Peace of Augsburg, which only allowed rulers to choose on behalf of their subjects.[129] It remained in force until the mid-seventeenth century.[130]

Transylvania's Edict of Torda and Poland-Lithuania's Warsaw Confederation together represented a huge leap forward for religious freedom. Each sought to forge social peace in their respective realms based on a mutual understanding of religious plurality. They also protected core elements of religious speech by securing preachers and their adherents the freedom to practice differing rituals and preach differing interpretations of Scripture. This represented a significant departure from neighboring states who still opted for strict uniformity and the doctrine of *cuius regio, eius religio*. But still it's a mistake—however tempting—to regard them as equivalent to modern constitutional guarantees of individual freedom of religion and speech. Both lacked general free speech guarantees—for political speech, for instance—and, when read carefully, their language actually imposed certain *restrictions* on speech. The Edict of Torda stated that "no one shall be reviled for his religion by anyone," and the Warsaw Confederation assured that no one would be subject to "infamy" on the basis of his religion. In other words, religious tolerance under those acts did not include the freedom to engage in what today we might call religious offense. It would also be wrong to read a protection of blasphemy into any of the documents—as the Polish nobleman Iwan Tyszkiewicz learned in 1611, when he had his tongue cut out before being burned for blasphemous heresy, after ditching Catholicism for Socinianism, a branch of anti-Trinitarianism originating in Poland, and stubbornly refusing to swear by the Trinity or on a Crucifix.[131]

Around the same time, while Protestants and Catholics were busy fighting in Western Europe, another great leap forward for religious toleration was being taken in the Mughal Empire of India. In 1556, almost two millennia after the trailblazing tolerance of the Mauryan emperor Ashoka, another charismatic emperor came to rule India. Akbar the Great inherited a Shari'ah state where non-Muslim slaves were converted by force, apostasy was punishable by death, and non-Muslim subjects had to pay a discriminatory *jizyah* tax. In other words, freedom of conscience did not appear to be in the cards. But Akbar came to a sudden realization after a few years on the throne. In his own words, as quoted by his court historian Abu'l-Fażl: "Formerly I persecuted men into conformity with my faith and deemed it Islam. As I grew in knowledge, I was overwhelmed with shame. . . .What constancy is to be expected from proselytes on compulsion?"[132] In the early 1560s, he banned forced conversions and allowed converts to apostatize and return to their old faiths without punishment. He also banned the enslavement of prisoners of war and defied Shari'ah law by permitting non-Muslims to build and repair their temples. Another crowning achievement was to abolish the *jizyah* tax in 1579, to the great frustration of the orthodox Muslim establishment.[133]

Akbar followed a doctrine known as *Sulh-i Kul* or "universal peace." According to Abu'l-Fażl, it represented an attempt to dispel "the darkness of the age by the light of universal toleration."[134] One goal was to prevent sectarian conflicts like the ones that wreaked havoc in Europe. Abu'l-Fażl describes how Akbar would not allow sectarian differences to "raise the dust of strife."[135] But *Sulh-i Kul* also represented a deeper search for a common spiritual ground—leaving dogmatic scripturalism behind and treating all religions as different paths to reach the same God.[136]

To feed his religious curiosity Akbar established a multireligious "House of Worship" in 1575. Philosophers and priests from all corners of the world—Shi'ites, Hindus, Brahmans, Parsis, Jains, Zoroastrians, Christians, and Jews—were invited to this religious "think tank."[137] In the words of Abu'l-Fażl, the whole court "became the home of the inquirers of the seven climes, and the assemblage of the wise of every religion and sect" and "reason was exalted." But the *ulamā*—the body of orthodox religious scholars—were none too pleased. According to Abu'l-Fażl, "the bigoted ulama and lawyers of orthodoxy found their positions difficult to defend."[138] One orthodox scholar complained that Akbar's House of Worship "only settle[d] things with appeal to man's reason."[139]

Akbar also opened a translation bureau and had the holy books of a number of religions translated into Persian, the language of the Mughal court.[140] After exposing himself to the religions of the world, he appears to have left Islam and created his own religion called *Dīn-i Ilāhī* or "Divine Faith"—an eclectic mix of Sufism and Hinduism with a dash of Zoroastrianism and a hint of Catholicism.[141]

While early champions of tolerance like Akbar were far ahead of their time, much like the pioneering Transylvanian and Polish-Lithuanian gestures toward tolerance, we are bound for disappointment if we expect them to live up to modern liberal principles. Even if Akbar promoted religious tolerance, he was also willing to imprison or deport dissenting mullahs who opposed his heterodoxy. And when all is said and done, he was an autocratic warlord who conquered and ruled by the sword. Muslim historians of the time even portrayed Akbar as a tyrant who purged Islamic practices from his court and persecuted orthodox Muslims. But Abu'l-Fażl refuted these accusations and insisted that the enmity of the *ulamā* was only a response to Akbar's "tolerant disposition," because of which he "received all classes of mankind with affection."[142]

Akbar's tolerant attitudes survived under the rule of his son Jahangir. The English traveler Thomas Coryat put the Mughal tolerance to the test in the early seventeenth century by boldly declaring that, if only Muslims knew the truth about their prophet, he was "perswaded thou wouldest spit in the face of thy Alcaron [Qur'an] and trample it under thy feete."[143] At another point, he climbed into a tall building facing a minaret. When the muezzin called out the Islamic prayer, "There is no God but Allah, and Muhammad is his messenger," Coryat heckled him by shouting, "No God but one God, and Christ the Son of God." Even Coryat had to admit that had he "spoken thus much in Turkey or Persia against Mahomet they would have roasted me upon a spit; but in the Mogols dominions a Christian may speake much more freely then hee can in any other Mahometan country in the world."[144] The fact that Coryat got away with mocking and vilifying Allah, the Qur'an, and Muhammad in the open is a great testimony to the tolerance in Mughal India, given the harsh punishments still meted out for those offenses in many countries in the twenty-first century.[145]

After Jahangir's death, the spirit of tolerance ebbed. Akbar's grandson Shah Jahan brought back the Shari'ah-prescribed restrictions against non-Muslim temples in 1633, and his great-grandson Aurangzeb reimposed the *jizyah* tax in 1679.[146] But even if orthodox Islam came to play a much more prominent role, what historian André Wink calls "secular toleration" of non-Muslims remained a "cornerstone of imperial Mughal rule" long after the demise of Akbar and his Universal Peace.[147] This is also the impression we get from the British sea captain Alexander Hamilton, who wrote the following description of the Indian town Surat in the late seventeenth century: "There are above a hundred different Sects . . . but they never have any hot Disputes about their Doctrine or Way of Worship. Everyone is free to serve and worship God their own Way. And Persecutions for Religion's sake are not known among them."[148]

———

THE CULTURAL CRITIC NEIL POSTMAN ONCE NOTED: "IN the year 1500, fifty years after the printing press was invented, we did not have old Europe plus the printing press. We had a different Europe."[149] In that Europe, centuries of settled religious and political authority was suddenly in flux, with violent upheavals and persecution as a consequence. Europeans had not developed the institutions, language, or attitudes necessary to consider religious pluralism—whether in writing or in practice—a strength rather than a threat to both salvation and national security. In fact, censorship and repressive tolerance were key aspects of the settlements that sought to stitch together a bloodied Europe in an uneasy social peace. Yet, out of the chaos would emerge a small but growing number of Europeans calling for freedom of conscience and even of the press as the seventeenth century progressed.

Nor was it a purely European story. As important as the Reformation was, events in Moghul India showed that the idea of tolerance and its institutionalization were not confined to Western culture shaped by the Reformation and its aftermath. Indian tolerance developed along its own distinct path and was both admired and mocked by those who encountered it. Still, Europe would constitute ground zero for the most fruitful and consequential experiments that allowed the freedoms of conscience and speech to spire and grow.

4

The Seeds of Enlightenment

On a Continent embroiled in religious turmoil and persecution, tolerance and free speech found few patches of fertile soil in Western Europe at the dawn of the seventeenth century. The first such patch was the flat and windswept Low Countries on the North Sea coast. During the so-called Dutch Golden Age in the seventeenth century, the Dutch Republic developed a cosmopolitan culture with a comparatively high degree of tolerance and free speech, which contributed to making the Dutch Republic an early modern epicenter of art, learning, publishing, philosophy, and science.

The Dutch Republic was born when the predominantly Protestant northern provinces of the Low Countries launched a series of revolts against the Catholic Spanish Habsburg Empire and finally declared their independence in 1581. After decades of inquisition and relentless persecution, when both heretical books and humans were burned by the Spanish, freedom of conscience was a cornerstone of the Dutch rebellion.[1] And so, the Union of Utrecht of 1579, the birth certificate and informal constitution of the Dutch Republic, guaranteed "that each person shall remain free in his religion and that no one shall be investigated or persecuted because of his religion."[2] Over the following centuries, the republic became a safe haven for persecuted churches and exiled freethinkers like René Descartes, Pierre Bayle, and John Locke and established itself as the printing house of Western Europe.

Between 1600 and 1800 no one read or printed more than the Dutch. An estimated 259 books and pamphlets were consumed per thousand inhabitants annually during the second half of the seventeenth century. The French consumed only seventy books per thousand inhabitants in the same period.[3] But this was not just a nation of readers—as the seeds of the Enlightenment spread across Europe, Dutch printers proved both industrious and daring. Their handiwork spread the latest advances in philosophy and science across the Continent, further connecting the neural circuitry of Europe's collective brain.[4]

Dutch printing served more than just the nation's elites. Amsterdam became the "newspaper hub of early modern Europe" in the early seventeenth century, when weekly newspapers or *corantos* became an addiction for many Dutchmen.[5] This allowed the Dutch to cultivate an egalitarian public sphere or, in the words of Dutch historians Willem Frijhoff and Marijke Spies, "a culture of all-pervasive and unremitting debate in which all segments of society took part."[6] Of course, not everyone welcomed this development. *Corantos* were initially regarded as the seventeenth-century version of social media, and, gripped by elite panic, many wealthier citizens were suspicious of these and other information streams that catered to the common people with little oversight. A prominent member of Amsterdam's upper class scoffed that newspapers had "become so used to lying that they report less than the truth."[7]

Part of the reason for its tolerance was the decentralized nature of the Dutch Republic, with strong local and provincial institutions and a weak political center. The republic's origins in the revolt against the Spanish Habsburgs left the Dutch naturally wary of centralized authority and fiercely protective of local autonomy. Coordinated attempts at censorship were difficult, since writers and printers could skip state and city lines for more tolerant ones if things got too hot. Moreover, local authorities frequently refused to enforce censorship if they thought it too restrictive or hurtful to trade. Urbanization, foreign trade, and openness to foreigners also contributed to a tolerant cosmopolitan culture with an emphasis on the exchange of ideas in cities like Amsterdam.[8] The result was a republic with space for heterodox ideas and daring publications to flourish.

Yet, the famous Dutch tolerance and the freedom of thought and speech that it allowed was based more on pragmatism and necessity than principle. The Dutch Republic was not a secular state with strict separation between religion and politics, so the comparatively high degree of tolerance depended—among other things—on its decentralized political system, and on the large number of different sects inhabiting the same territory.[9] This hindered the establishment of orthodoxy, promoted friction between secular and religious authorities, and led to schisms between hard-liners and pragmatists within the established Reformed Church.[10] Even so, the Reformed Church enjoyed a privileged position, and orthodox hard-liners fought a constant battle to enforce their red lines, in spite of the lofty promises of the Union of Utrecht.[11]

Religious tolerance ebbed and flowed and it could quickly all but evaporate. Minorities like Lutherans, Mennonites, Socinians, and Jews endured various levels of restrictions, while Catholicism was banned in all seven provinces (although the ban was not enforced with the same level of severity everywhere).[12] Yet there were those who literally meant "no one" when they said that no one should be persecuted for their religious ideas.

A Book Forged in Hell: Spinoza and the Radicals of the Dutch Golden Age

The most radical early Dutch champion of tolerance and open debate was the writer, playwright, and classicist Dirck Coornhert. Coornhert was a firm believer in religious freedom for both Catholics and the alphabet soup of Protestant sects. The Dutch revolt should have been a victory for freedom of conscience as guaranteed by the Union of Utrecht.[13] But fearing that the Reformed Church was exploiting the victory by trying to impose its austere version of Calvinism on the rest, Coornhert was determined to fight the encroaching power of the church with the power of the pen and the press.

In 1582, one year after the formal establishment of the Dutch Republic, Coornhert published his *Synod on the Freedom of Conscience*. It consists of a fictional debate between leading historical theologians as well as made-up characters that give voice to Coornhert's own views. In *Synod* Coornhert argued that persecution was both anti-Christian and a danger to peace and stability, and that religious differences should be debated openly, with no secular or religious authorities enforcing doctrines of correct belief. If the goal was "to be left alone by any heretic," he reasoned, "then with God's word, not with the executioner's sword . . . kill not the heretic but the heresy in him." He also made a case against the prohibition of books by letting his alter ego, the "Remonstrant of Leiden," proclaim: "Freedom has always consisted chiefly in the fact that someone is allowed freely to speak his mind. It has been only the mark of tyranny that one was not allowed to speak his thoughts freely. Therefore it is truly tyrannical to . . . forbid good books in order to squelch the truth."

Coornhert did not promote absolute free speech. In the same book, another of his alter egos takes care to exclude from protection "notorious books . . . that incite to sedition."[14] But he was still far ahead of his time. Coornhert's controversial ideas put him on a collision course with the Reformed Church, which had him condemned, censored, and forced into several exiles. His books were the first to be banned in the Dutch Golden Age.[15]

Freedom of the press was not constitutionally protected. The Dutch historian Ingrid Weekhout has compiled a list of 263 publications banned in the Dutch Republic between 1583 and 1700 for crossing various red lines.[16] Few religious dissenters put the practice of Dutch tolerance to the test like the Socinians, whose rejection of the Trinity and the divine nature of Christ united orthodox and moderate Calvinists in horrified revulsion. In 1653, the Reformed Church successfully convinced the States of Holland to issue a law against the "sickness" of Socinianism, banning the creed's books and private religious meetings. The law also became a flexible tool in countering other pernicious theological and philosophical works in the decades to come.[17]

Deciding where to draw the line was not always easy. The mathematician and natural philosopher René Descartes took refuge in the Dutch Republic in 1628, driven out of France as a heretic because of his trademark skeptical method, known as "Cartesian doubt," and his rejection of the now dominant Aristotelian scientific model in favor of a more mechanistic one.[18] Ironically, many theologians accused Cartesianism of undermining Scripture, much like medieval theologians had viewed Aristotelianism as heretical before adopting it as orthodoxy. But Descartes's ideas were too radical even for some influential Dutch thinkers, and Cartesian philosophy was banned from the Universities of Utrecht and Leiden in the 1640s.[19]

Yet, just like the unsuccessful attempts to banish Aristotle at medieval universities, the bans against Cartesianism did little to halt the spread of these new ideas among scholars. In the 1660s, a small group of radical thinkers were ready to take mainstream Cartesianism to the next level. The intellectual leader of this small circle of trailblazing freethinkers was a Jew of Portuguese descent who had already been excommunicated from Amsterdam's Jewish community for his "abominable heresies and monstrous deeds."[20] His name was Baruch Spinoza.

In the 1660s, Spinoza began producing manuscripts that were difficult to square with revealed religion. He chose not to publish them, explaining his reasons for self-censorship in a private letter from 1662: "I fear, of course, that the theologians of our time may be offended and with their usual hatred attack me."[21] And it turned out that Spinoza had good reason to be afraid. The first sign of danger appeared in 1666, when several provinces banned a book by Lodewijk Meyer—a member of Spinoza's circle—for contending that revealed theology was useless and the Scriptures were full of contradictions. Adriaan Koerbagh, another member of Spinoza's circle, fared much worse when he published his controversial *Flowerbed* in 1668, which denied divine revelation, attacking the Reformed Church and the doctrine of the Holy Trinity. Unlike Meyer, Koerbagh was reckless enough to publish the book under his own name and in Dutch.[22] The Reformed consistory in Amsterdam convinced the authorities to ban and seize all copies. Koerbagh went into hiding but was tracked down and sentenced to ten years in prison on the basis of the 1653 anti-Socinian law. He only lasted a few months before he died a broken man.[23]

Historian Jonathan Israel suggests that the fate of Koerbagh may have strongly influenced Spinoza's famous *Theological-Political Treatise*, published in 1670, a counterattack against religious fanaticism.[24] It certainly makes sense that Spinoza would seek to disarm the theological intolerance of the Reformed Church that had instigated the suppression of his friends and driven him to self-censor. He did so by cleverly undermining the authority of Scripture and revealed religion, which he thought bred superstition, hatred, and persecution. He also promoted *Libertas Philosophandi* ("the freedom to philosophize") and free speech as necessary preconditions for peace, prosperity, and progress. He famously argued that "in a free state everyone is at liberty to think as he pleases, and to say what he thinks." Any regime that violated this "natural right" was "tyrannical." Spinoza also made the very modern distinction between actions and speech. Only the former were subject to government control.

In fact, many of Spinoza's ideas remain strikingly relevant today. To Spinoza, "the end and aim of the state, in fact, is LIBERTY." Centuries before the current debate regarding the tensions between free speech and tolerance in diverse societies, he asserted that freedom of expression is indispensable for peaceful coexistence between members of different faiths and backgrounds. He held up as an example seventeenth-century Amsterdam "where the fruits of this liberty of thought and opinion are seen in its wonderful increase and testified to by the admiration of every people. In this most flourishing republic and noble city, men of every nation, and creed, and sect live together in the utmost harmony." He contrasted this happy state of affairs with the attempts by Reformed hard-liners to impose strict limits on freedom of religion and thought of dissenters, which, according to Spinoza, did not "arise from the anxious study of truth" but rather "from the lust of dominion."

It's important to note that like so many others before him, Spinoza's free speech doctrine was not all-encompassing. He too had his "buts," since unlimited free speech "would be most baneful." He put a premium on calm and reasoned intellectual debate and distinguished between criticism of laws based on (permissible) "good sense" and (impermissible) sedition—a problematic distinction, open to abuse, that undermined his otherwise robust "overt acts" theory and raised the thorny question of who gets to determine what constitutes "good sense" and "sedition." Still, at this point in history, very few shared Spinoza's degree of commitment to the idea that free speech is a precondition rather than a danger to social peace.[25]

Spinoza probably expected some controversy after the Koerbagh case, so unlike his friend, he published the *Treatise* anonymously and in Latin to limit its circulation to the learned elite. He even listed Hamburg as the book's place of publication. But despite this literary camouflage, the *Treatise* became one of the most hated and suppressed works of its time—not only in the Dutch Republic but all across the Continent. It even united Protestants and Catholics, as the Treatise was put on the Index of Prohibited Books in 1679.[26]

Spinoza's rejection of Christian doctrines that were accepted by most as Truth earned him a reputation as a dangerous and destructive radical. One outraged pamphleteer described the *Treatise* as a work "forged in Hell by a renegade Jew and the Devil."[27] The Reformed Church immediately moved to have it banned, while the South Holland synod condemned it as a book "as vile and blasphemous as any that are known of, or that the world has ever seen." Copies of the work were confiscated from bookshops in Leiden as early as 1670 because of its "godless passages." Even Dutch Cartesians saw red. A professor encouraged colleagues to "attack and destroy this utterly pestilential book."[28] The States of Holland caved in to ecclesiastical pressure and banned the book in 1674. In June 1678—just over a year after Spinoza's death—they banned his entire works, since they "contain very many profane, blasphemous and atheistic propositions."[29] The prohibition included the owning, reading, distribution, copying, and restating of Spinoza's books, and even the reworking of his fundamental ideas.[30] But an early "samizdat" of underground printers managed to spread Spinoza's scandalous work far and wide, to the horror of most and the inspiration of a growing number of European freethinkers.

The French freethinker Pierre Bayle sought shelter in the Dutch Republic in 1681 as a result of Louis XIV's increasingly anti-Huguenot policies.[31] In 1682, Bayle used his new safe haven to publish *Letter on the Comet*, a book that had previously been rejected by French censors. Retitled *Various Thoughts on the Occasion of a Comet* in 1683, it amounted to a frontal attack on religious superstition, claiming that beliefs resting on tradition and the "unanimous consent of mankind" were unreliable guides to truth, which required the use of reason and critical examination.[32] Divorcing morality from religion, Bayle even claimed that atheists could be *more* virtuous than Christians and that a society of atheists would not necessarily lead to moral corruption.[33] This was hardly orthodox Calvinism. Just about everyone in Europe at this time agreed that atheism was uniquely pernicious and disastrous for any state.

But Bayle was only just getting started. In 1684, he founded and edited the weekly journal *News from the Republic of Letters*. The journal included book reviews and learned commentary and became the seventeenth-century version of a listserv for European intellectuals eager to share and comment upon new and daring ideas sprouting up around the Continent. It helped establish the Dutch Republic as a European hub not only for newspapers but also for books and journals, many of which were clandestinely smuggled into countries with much stricter censorship.[34] In the very first edition, Bayle praised the Dutch freedom of the press as "an advantage found in no other country."[35] He also defended this liberty in 1685 with an article in which he argued that permitting heretical books was not the same as accepting heretical ideas—rather, press freedom was necessary to refute heresy.[36]

The following year, Bayle published the first volume of his famous defense of freedom of conscience, *Philosophical Commentary*.[37] It was written in response to the culmination of Louis XIV's burst of intolerance: his decision in 1685 to shore up more firmly the marriage between the monarchy and the Catholic Church and revoke the Edict of Nantes.[38] This move sent shockwaves through Europe, dispersing around two hundred thousand religious refugees to Protestant countries like the Dutch Republic and England.[39] Bayle insisted that reason and philosophy, not theology and religious doctrine, were the proper instruments to determine questions of conscience and toleration.[40] In effect, he expressed a theory of universal toleration that rejected the validity of theological arguments in questions of individual freedom of conscience. His critics objected—rightfully—that one could never distinguish between Truth and heresy in such a system. It was perhaps inevitable that Bayle's irreverence and intellectual curiosity would land him in trouble, and these heterodox views saw him fall out even with his fellow Huguenot exiles, who fretted that Bayle would use his position as professor at the University of Rotterdam to undermine the Reformed Church and corrupt the youth. A very public and nasty debate culminated in 1693 when Dutch and French Reformed consistories condemned Bayle's "highly offensive and dangerous positions" and prodded the city government of Rotterdam into action. Bayle was stripped of his professorship and banned from teaching students in private.[41]

But Bayle was far from beaten. Freed from his academic duties, he embarked on a new endeavor. His 1697 *Historical and Critical Dictionary* was a hugely influential encyclopedia, with articles on various subjects and persons accompanied by extensive commentaries and annotations infused with a spirit of skepticism. "Liberty is what reigns in the Republic of Letters," he declared in the *Dictionary*. "This Republic is an extremely free state. In it the only empire is that of truth and reason."[42] No wonder the French censors banned the *Dictionary*.[43] Yet Bayle's dictionary would provide inspiration for the even more ambitious and influential eighteenth-century *Encyclopédie*, edited by the French philosophe Denis Diderot. The relative press freedom of the Dutch Republic may have had its limits, but it was already sowing the seeds of the French Radical Enlightenment.

England's Forgotten Martyrs of Free Speech

The Dutch Republic may only have been separated from England by a narrow stretch of the North Sea, but it was more than a century after the adoption of the Union of Utrecht before England formally recognized a similar protection of freedom of conscience. And unlike the Dutch, the English operated with various versions of centralized pre- and postpublication censorship for most of the seventeenth century. Still, during that time England became another hotbed of radical arguments about freedom of speech and religion. Following a familiar pattern, religious dissenters were among the trailblazers. As early as 1611/1612, the Baptist Thomas Helwys called for complete and universal freedom of conscience—even for "heretics, Turks, Jews, or whatsoever"—in his book *A Short Declaration of the Mystery of Iniquity*.[44] Before publication, he made the daring move of sending James I a copy with a personal message: "The King is a mortall man and not God," he argued, "therefore [he] hath no Power over the immortall soules of his subjects to make lawes and ordinances for them and to set spirituall Lords over them."[45] Helwys's audacity landed him behind bars where he died around 1616.[46] Another Baptist named John Murton soon pushed the agenda of absolute tolerance even further. Even though Murton believed that blasphemy was an abhorrent sin, he denied the right of worldly powers to punish blasphemers.[47] Sadly, it turned out that James I rather liked exercising his worldly powers and Murton spent the last thirteen years of his life in Newgate Prison.[48]

There were also calls for political freedom of speech among the elite. Peter Wentworth's lonely voice for free speech in Parliament under Elizabeth had now gained greater resonance among MPs. But James was no more inclined to suffer criticism and debate than Elizabeth. In 1621, he claimed his right to punish any member for "insolent Behavior." In response, Parliament issued a protestation penned by the great jurist and politician Sir Edward Coke insisting that "every Member of the House of Parliament hath, and, of Right, ought to have Freedom of Speech."[49] Yet even this "Roman" conception of free speech limited to the upper elite was rejected. For now.

The climate of suppression did not end when James I died in 1625. Charles I and his chief enforcer William Laud, the archbishop of Canterbury, demonstrated a ruthless willingness to impose religious and political uniformity, demanding that their subjects adopt the *Book of Common Prayer* and the Thirty-nine Articles that defined Anglicanism. When the religiously austere Puritans protested that these measures smelled suspiciously of popery, Charles and Laud responded with a string of proclamations further tightening religious censorship.[50]

Tired of bickering over taxes and religion, Charles dissolved Parliament in 1629, instituting eleven years of personal rule. During this period, the infamous Star Chamber, a dreaded court of law, became nearly synonymous with the Inquisition among Charles's detractors.[51] In 1634, the Puritan writer William Prynne was put on trial because of his book *Histrio-mastix*, a thinly veiled attack on the king and his Catholic queen, Henrietta Maria. Prynne was found guilty of seditious libel and sentenced to having his ears cropped, the pillory, imprisonment, and the burning of his books.[52] Prynne found himself in a new sadistic drama in 1637, when he was put on trial again, this time for "divers scandalous bookes & libels, against the whole clergie of the kingdome, & against the Government of the Church of England," and once more sentenced to have his ears cut off.[53] Since they had already been reduced to stumps, he also had the letters "S. L." (for "Seditious Libeller") burned into his cheeks. Prynne, in a rare display of humor, quipped that the letters stood for *Stigmata Laudis*, "marks of praise" or "marks of Laud"—a play on the archbishop's name.[54] One historian argues that Prynne turned his torture and humiliation "into a triumph of propaganda," which did much to strengthen the Puritan cause and blacken the policies and religious agenda of Charles I and Laud.[55]

In an effort to crack down on Puritan dissenters like Prynne, a 1637 Star Chamber decree prohibited the print, import, and sale of "any Seditious, Schismaticall, or offensive Books or Pamphlets" on pains of "severe Punishment, either by Fine, Imprisonment, or other Corporal Punishment."[56] The decree ensured that printers toed the line of licensing, and the number of unlicensed publications slowed considerably in the following years.[57] When another Puritan, John Lilburne (or "Free-Born John"), was caught smuggling "seditious books" from Amsterdam in 1638, he was tied to a cart, whipped through the streets of London, and placed in the pillory. But just as with Prynne, the crowd was on Lilburne's side, cheering rather than jeering, a warning sign that Charles's crackdown on devout English Protestants was undermining his popularity.[58]

In desperate need of funds to wage war against the religiously intransigent Scots, Charles reinstated Parliament in 1640, yet the MPs were determined not to become Charles's willing tools.[59] One of the first decisions of the "Long Parliament" was to abolish the Star Chamber and the prepublication licensing system in 1641, though this was not the result of a principled commitment to free speech. The Root and Branch Petition, signed by some fifteen thousand Londoners and presented to Parliament in December 1640, complained first that licensing had been responsible for "the hindering of godly Books to be printed, [and] the blotting out or perverting those which they suffer." So far, so liberal. But in the very next paragraph, the petition protested "the publishing and venting of popish, arminian, and other dangerous books and tenets."[60] In other words, the problem wasn't censorship as such—it was that Charles and Laud had been censoring the wrong kind of books.

Nevertheless, the decision sparked a huge increase in publications. 1641 broke the English record of most published titles in one year, with 2,177 cataloged titles. 1642 broke the record again with a staggering 4,188 titles.[61] That record would not be beaten until the eighteenth century, however, as in 1643, Parliament reintroduced licensing, targeting "false, forged, scandalous, seditious, libellous, and unlicensed Papers, Pamphlets, and Books to the great defamation of Religion and Government."[62] Parliament even forbade the publication of the orders and declarations of either House of Parliament without prior approval.[63] The monopoly of the Stationers' Company was back in business, this time serving Parliament rather than the king and Laud.

This return to prepublication censorship in 1643 prompted the poet John Milton to pen *Areopagitica*, a plea for press freedom that was published—unlicensed—the following year.[64] Milton's central argument was that censorship led to "the discouragement of all learning, and the stop of truth, not only by disexercising and blunting our abilities, in what we know already, but by hindering and cropping the discovery that might be yet further made, both in religious and civil wisdom." In a memorable passage that has lost none of its potency over the centuries, he declared, "Give me the liberty to know, to utter and to argue freely according to conscience, above all liberties."

Milton's defense of press freedom invoked both ancient Athenian and Roman precedents. It was prefaced by a quotation from the Athenian tragedian Euripides's play *The Suppliant Women*: "This is true Liberty when free born men / Having to advise the public may speak free. . . .What can be juster in a State than this?" The title *Areopagitica* refers to a pamphlet by another Athenian, the speechwriter Isocrates. Milton cleverly portrayed book censorship as an invention of the Catholic Church and the Inquisition—one previously unknown to Protestant countries. This was revisionist, anti-Catholic propaganda on the part of Milton, since Protestant states had long engaged in censorship, with the blessing of reformers like Luther and Calvin, but Milton was far from neutral when it came to Catholicism.

In fact, Milton stressed that, with press freedom, "I mean not tolerated popery, and open superstition, which as it extirpates all religions and civil supremacies, so itself should be extirpate." Nor did Milton wish to provide shelter to ideas that were "impious or evil . . . against faith or manners." If "mischievous and libellous" books were printed nonetheless, Milton's remedy was "the fire and the executioner" (i.e., book burnings). His chief goal was the open discussion of "those neighbouring differences, or rather indifferences" that saw various Reformed Protestant sects at each other's throats, not free and equal speech for all.[65]

Milton would double down on his anti-Catholic intolerance in the following decades. He also praised the enactment of an additional blasphemy ban in 1650.[66] Eventually Milton even joined the corps of licensors.[67] That Milton—the scourge of censors—would become a licensor himself is indeed one of the great ironies of the history of free speech. "Milton's Curse"—the selective and unprincipled defense of free speech—would afflict many other great champions of free speech in the centuries to come, and remains a recurrent theme today. At any rate, *Areopagitica* was largely ignored at the time. It was later revived by Whigs, who cited the work during the debates that culminated with the end of licensing in 1695, and was also part of the canon when American revolutionaries made the case for free speech.[68]

In the meantime, the relationship between Charles and Parliament continued to deteriorate. In 1642, irreconcilable differences triggered the First English Civil War, which lasted until 1646, when Charles surrendered after a string of defeats by the Parliamentarians' New Model Army. The late-seventeenth-century royalist historian John Nalson laid the blame for the Civil War on printing:

> I know not any one thing that more hurt the late King then the Paper Bullets of the Press; it was the Scandalous and Calumniating Ink of the Faction that from thence blackned him, and represented all his Words and Actions to the misguided People, who would difficultly have been perswaded to such a horrid Rebellion, if they had not been first prepossessed by the Tongues and the Pens of the Faction.[69]

But God knows that Charles tried to silence the printing presses that bled him of support one paper cut at a time.

Nevertheless, the famous political philosopher Thomas Hobbes reached much the same conclusion as Nalson and consequently adopted an extreme position on censorship. In his 1651 book *Leviathan*, he argued that the king held "the Soveraign Power, to be Judge, or constitute all Judges of Opinions and Doctrines, as a thing necessary to Peace; thereby to prevent Discord and Civill Warre."[70]

And Hobbes was not one to forgive and forget those who crossed the red lines of acceptable speech. In another work he stressed that "words can be a crime, and can be punished without injury with whatever punishments the legislators wish—indeed, with the ultimate penalty. If blasphemy against the king can be punished by death, much more can blasphemy against God."[71] Ironically, several of Hobbes's books were later banned as blasphemous, and *Leviathan* was burned at the University of Oxford.[72]

Despite their victory over the king, the Parliamentarian side was sharply divided between the Presbyterian hard-liners on the one hand, and Independents on the other, who were in favor of varying degrees of religious tolerance. They also had to contend with a loose group of people in favor of radical tolerance, press freedom, equality before the law, and representative government based on full male suffrage. Their opponents called them the Levellers—a smear suggesting that they meant to level all distinctions between the high and the low.

The most prominent Levellers were Richard Overton, William Walwyn, and (Free-Born) John Lilburne—the Puritan who was whipped and pilloried in 1638. Between them, they published almost 250 pamphlets from 1645 to 1649—many of which were written from prison when their ideals and notions about liberty of conscience became too radical to tolerate.[73] Interestingly, William Walwyn explicitly invoked the Dutch Republic as evidence of how religious freedom furthered prosperity and social peace.[74] Crucially, the Levellers used the language of individual and natural rights, with Lilburne often appealing to the rights of "free-born Englishmen."

A few months before Milton's *Areopagitica* was published, William Walwyn defended both freedom of speech and the press. He complained that Parliament and ministers

> stop all mens mouthes from speaking, and prohibit the Printing of any thing that might be produced in way of defence

and vindication; and if any thing bee attempted, spoken or published without authority or licence, Pursuivants, fines and imprisonments, are sure to wait the Authors, Printers and publishers.[75]

In 1645, Lilburne was jailed after denouncing members of Parliament for living the good life while soldiers bled and died for the Parliamentarian cause.[76] To offer his support, Walwyn wrote a public letter to Lilburne called *England's Lamentable Slaverie*, in which he accused Parliament not only of violating ancient rights in the Magna Carta—a royal charter of rights from 1215—but also of acting as oppressively as the very king and court of the Star Chamber.[77] Overton followed up in 1646 with the pamphlet *A Remonstrance of Many Thousand Citizens*, which set out Leveller arguments for popular rather than parliamentary sovereignty, liberty of conscience, and freedom of the press. He demanded that the government "let the imprisoned Presses at liberty, that all mens understandings may be more conveniently informed."[78] But for Overton, the immediate effect of the remonstrance was a substantial loss of liberty. Like Lilburne, he was arrested and put behind bars.

Ambitious Leveller ideas for constitutional reform were set out in manifestos such as the three versions of the *Agreement of the People* and discussed at the famous Putney Debates in 1647, where the Leveller Colonel Thomas Rainsborough made the case for universal suffrage and democracy:

I think that the poorest he that is in England hath a life to live as the greatest he; and therefore truly, sir, I think it's clear, that every man that is to live under a government ought first by his own consent to put himself under that government. And I do think that the poorest man in England is not at all bound in a strict sense to that government that he hath not had a voice to put himself under.[79]

It would take more than two centuries for Rainsborough's ideas to go from radical fringe to mainstream British democratic ideals.

Precisely where the Levellers drew the red line when it came to free speech and tolerance is difficult to say. They were neither of one mind nor entirely consistent, though at times they appeared to be almost free speech absolutists. Facing severe attack in 1649, the Levellers complained that censorship had "ever ushered in a tyranny; men's mouth being to be kept from making noise, whilst they are robbed of their liberties." And so, even "the least restraint upon the press" must be removed, since the people cannot enjoy liberty if stopped from "speaking, writing, printing, and publishing their minds freely."[80] Another Leveller pamphlet used the very modern argument that more speech was the best weapon against bad speech, and that censorship was injurious to the common good and a threat to the liberties of the people.[81] This was a rejection not only of licensing but also of subsequent restrictions on free speech. Crucially, we even find Levellers explicitly arguing for the importance of being principled and defending the freedoms of both friend and foe, lest the temptation to use the law selectively end up "overwhelming your own liberties."[82]

But in the 1649 version of their proposed constitution, *An Agreement of the Free People of England*, the Levellers adopted a more pragmatic stance. Perhaps sensing impending defeat in their struggle against the commander of the New Model Army, Oliver Cromwell, who they (rightly) suspected was creating a military dictatorship, they opened the door for excluding intransigent Catholics from holding public office.[83] Lilburne even pressed for stricter licensing of royalist books that might contribute to "the ruine of the Kingdome."[84]

The Leveller ideas of democracy and almost limitless free speech remained a pipe dream. The Army Grandees rejected the Levellers' demands in both theory and practice. In 1648, Parliament made "Heresie and Blasphemy" punishable by imprisonment and even death in case of obstinacy.[85] The following year, Charles I was executed and the monarchy abolished in favor of a republican Commonwealth. Parliament gave the Council of State under Cromwell's chairmanship draconian powers to arrest, interrogate, and imprison those who opposed the new regime. The new standing army was given authority to enforce licensing laws, which included destroying illicit printing presses and flogging those who sold unlicensed pamphlets. Naturally, the Levellers protested vehemently. In the 1649 pamphlet *England's New Chains Discovered*, they blamed Parliament for "the stopping of our mouths from Printing" and "dealing with us as the Bishops of old did with the honest Puritan."[86] Running out of patience, Parliament had Walwyn, Overton, and Lilburne arrested for treason.

Lilburne was acquitted, but convicted and exiled for criminal libel in 1652 after accusing Cromwell of treason in pamphlets. When he defied his exile, he was promptly arrested and threatened with execution for breaking an order of Parliament. Cromwell, who was appointed Lord Protector and the de facto ruler of Great Britain in 1653, kept Lilburne behind bars or on parole until he died in 1657.[87]

It is surely one of the injustices of the history of free speech that Milton—for all his importance and eloquence—should be remembered as *the* great seventeenth-century champion of free speech, while most have forgotten the names Lilburne, Overton, and Walwyn.

Oliver Cromwell died suddenly in 1658. After much disarray, Parliament invited Charles II home from his exile in Holland and offered him the throne in 1660. In return, the reinstated king promised religious freedom and "Freedom of Conversation."[88] But Parliament had other ideas. The next eighteen years became known as England's Great Persecution, as the Anglican majority in Parliament spat out a steady flow of discriminatory statutes against Catholics and Protestant dissenters. Up to sixty thousand people suffered some sort of consequence, such as imprisonment for "non-conformism," between 1660 and 1688.[89]

The unorthodox and often querulous Quakers were particularly hard-hit because they were seen as a threat to the religious, social, and political order. The victims included William Penn, who served several prison terms for his tireless calls for liberty of conscience before founding the Pennsylvania Colony as a safe haven for his church in 1681. An estimated 450 Quakers died behind bars during Charles II's regency.[90]

In 1662, Charles II and Parliament introduced the so-called Licensing Act, which effectively set the clock back to 1637 and the Star Chamber decree. The act reintroduced prepublication censorship and declared it illegal to print, publish, sell, or import "any heretical seditious schismatical or offensive Bookes or Pamphlets wherein any Doctrine or Opinion shall be asserted or maintained which is contrary to Christian Faith or the Doctrine or Discipline of the Church of England."[91] The chief enforcer of the Licensing Act was Roger L'Estrange, the infamous Surveyor of the Imprimery and Licenser of the Press. In 1664, L'Estrange boasted that he had seized no less than thirty-one thousand unlicensed pamphlets from booksellers.[92] These were indeed dark days for the rights of freeborn Englishmen.

Catholics were the next victims of persecution. Rumors of a "Popish plot" to assassinate Charles II and place his Catholic brother James on the throne sparked a wave of persecution in the late 1670s and early 1680s. At least twenty-four Catholics were executed for treason, and a faction of Whig MPs headed by the Earl of Shaftesbury pressed to exclude Catholics from Parliament and keep James from the throne by law.[93] But Charles resisted and forced Shaftesbury and his secretary, the philosopher John Locke, to flee to the Dutch Republic in 1683.

In exile, Locke penned his famous *Letter Concerning Toleration* in 1685. It was first published anonymously in Latin in Gouda in 1689, with a subsequent English translation published in London. The Dutch air had a radicalizing effect on Locke, whose views developed from an almost Hobbesian position arguing for religious unity as essential for social peace to asserting in his *Letter* that "neither *Pagan*, nor *Mahumetan*, nor *Jew*, ought to be excluded from the Civil Rights of the Commonwealth, because of his Religion." But even though Locke's famous treatise is often hailed for its eloquence and influence, it was not nearly as radical—or as concerned with free speech—as the texts of Bayle, Spinoza, the Levellers, or even Coornhert. Locke was reluctant to tolerate Catholics and outright hostile to atheists. Still infused with the anti-Catholic paranoia of his time, he argued that Catholics should be excluded because they themselves did not "own and teach the Duty of tolerating All men in matters of meer Religion." He also insisted that "those that are Seditious" as well as "Slanderers," ought to be "punished and suppressed."[94]

Dramatic events in England meant an abrupt reversal of fortune for Locke, who was able to return triumphantly to England in 1689 and provide Whiggish legitimacy to the so-called Glorious Revolution. The seeds of the revolution had been sown when Charles II died suddenly in 1685 and his brother prevailed in spite of all the efforts to keep him off the throne. As king, James II actually made various attempts to repeal discriminatory laws and introduce liberty of conscience, not only for his fellow Catholics but also for Protestant dissenters.[95] But with the ascension of a Catholic king, the anti-Catholic conspiracy theories reached fever pitch. After all, everyone knew that Catholics were loyal to the "anti-Christ" in Rome and that popery yielded an unholy alliance of political and religious tyranny. It did not help James's PR when Louis XIV revoked the Edict of Nantes and flooded England with Protestant refugees. While British Protestants might have tolerated one papist king, the birth of James's heir in 1688 raised the specter of a Catholic dynasty. Whigs and Tories joined forces and convinced the Dutch ruler William of Orange to depose James. He invaded England to ascend the throne as William III in 1689, carrying out what supporters were quick to brand as the "Glorious Revolution."[96] This revolution (or invasion, depending on the point of view) is often hailed as a defeat of absolutism, a landmark victory for liberty and representative government, and the precursor of the American Revolution. But from the perspective of freedom of thought, speech, and religion, the story was a little more complicated.

The passage of the Toleration Act of 1689 freed most Protestant dissenters from the restrictions imposed during the Great Persecution.[97] Presbyterians, Baptists, Quakers, and Congregationalists heaved a sigh of relief.[98] But the Toleration Act is a bit of a misnomer. It did not repeal all discriminatory laws or establish religious tolerance as a constitutional principle; it merely exempted specific groups from persecution.[99] Catholics, Jews, Deists, and anti-Trinitarians were still beyond the pale.[100]

The Act may not have satisfied the principles of Spinoza, Bayle, or even Locke, but it still weakened the dominance of the Church of England. A full 3,901 dissenters' places of worship were licensed between 1689 and 1710.[101] Buttressed by the later publication of Locke's *Letter Concerning Toleration*, the Act was part of a general European movement toward wider religious tolerance at the end of the seventeenth century. William III also had to accept a Bill of Rights in late 1689. While it was a far cry from modern bills of rights or the Levellers' demands from forty years earlier, it did secure "freedom of speech and debates or proceedings in Parliament." Finally, the struggles of Wentworth and Coke had borne fruit, although this newly recognized right did not extend to the people that Parliament was supposed to represent.[102] It was an important step in the long march toward codifying free speech as a fundamental right for all, but egalitarian free speech was still a step too far.

———

IRONICALLY, PARLIAMENT'S GREATEST BOOST TO FREE SPEECH was not ensuring this freedom for itself but rather a momentous display of inaction. In 1695, Parliament let lapse the Licensing Act and its system of prepublication censorship.

John Locke may not have been as radical as John Lilburne, but he played an important role in ending licensing by lobbying a friend in Parliament with arguments against the Licensing Act. Locke focused primarily on the pragmatic argument that the monopoly of "a lazy, ignorant Company of Stationers" drove book prices up and quality down. But he also advanced more principled arguments against censorship:

> I know not why a man should not have liberty to print whatever he would speak; . . . gagging a man, for fear he should talk heresy or sedition, has no other ground than such as will make gyves necessary, for fear a man should use violence if his hands were free, and must at last end in the imprisonment of all who you will suspect may be guilty of treason or misdemeanor.[103]

Walwyn and Milton had landed the first punches against licensing some fifty years earlier, but it was Locke who dealt the killer blow.

The death of the Licensing Act in 1695 resulted in a marked increase of pamphlets, newspapers, and books. From 1691 to 1694, when the Act was still in force, the average number of titles printed in Britain was 1,600 per year. After the Act expired, the average spiked to 2,074 titles per year from 1695 to 1700.[104] In 1695, the secretary of state bitterly complained that "London swarmes with seditious Pamphletts."[105] A flurry of anonymous anti-Trinitarian publications prompted Parliament to strike back in 1697 with the so-called Blasphemy Act, which banned anyone educated or employed in the Church from denying the Trinity, the trueness of Christianity, or the authority of the Scriptures.[106] Prior censorship was gone but subsequent punishment for speech crimes was very much alive.

Earlier that year in Scotland, Thomas Aikenhead, a twenty-year-old freethinking medical student, was hanged for irreverent comments mocking religion. The Scottish "Act against the cryme of blasphemie" from 1661 made it punishable by death to "rail upon or curse God or any of the persons of the Blessed Trinity."[107] Aikenhead became the last person to be executed for blasphemy in Great Britain, closing a dark chapter in its history.[108] Though the fight over how rigorously to police opinion had only just begun.

5

Enlightenment Now

Historians are not now, nor have they ever been, in agreement about how to define the Enlightenment or its legacy. But if there is one central theme underlying the Enlightenment, it's the emphasis on rationality and demystification at the expense of dogmatic theology and unquestioned tradition.[1] Before 1650, the major fault line dividing Europeans was confessional—adherence to a particular denomination's beliefs. But the devastating effects of the Thirty Years' War, the advent of Cartesian philosophy, Newtonian science, and Spinozist audacity, as well as the enlargement of Europe's collective brain through the emergence of an active public sphere all contributed to a changed Continent.

Europe emerged from these events infused with the spirit of skepticism. Most people still believed in God and atheism was widely condemned as immoral and (both individually and communally) destructive. But many began holding up dogma to the skeptical light of rational investigation—and some went even further. Radicals "started by criticizing the abuses of theocratic clergy and absolutist kings, and then they did not know where to stop."[2] In the Age of Enlightenment, the question was no longer which orthodoxy to believe, but whether to believe in (any) orthodoxy at all. As an unnerved English publicist lamented in 1713, "Now religion in general is the question; religion is the thing stabb'd at; the controversie now is, whether there ought to be any form of religion on earth, or whether there be any God in Heaven."[3]

The gradual growth of a more secularist and humanist-rationalist outlook was key to rising religious tolerance in the eighteenth century. From the early Enlightenment onward, Western states became less obsessed with militantly enforcing strict confessionalism. Even in Spain, there was a marked drop in the already declining number of arrests and executions by the Inquisition from the 1740s.[4] Of course, the tolerance of that time still seems distinctly intolerant from a modern perspective. Catholics, Jews, and Socinians were exempted from the Toleration Act in England, and the comparatively lenient Dutch Republic did not welcome Socinianism either. But in most countries, cleansing the land of heresy and ensuring strict religious orthodoxy fell out of fashion.

Permitting differing religious ideas, however, did not automatically mean broader acceptance of new political ideas or the open challenge of institutional authority. The most striking development in the practice of censorship in the late seventeenth and early eighteenth centuries was that it passed from the church to the secular hands of the state, whose censors redirected their attention from heresy to corrosive philosophy, political dissent, and obscenity.[5]

Still, the eighteenth century also saw a gradual advancement of the *principle* of free speech and its expansion beyond abstract philosophical musings. The *practice* of free speech played a vital role in this development. Sharp increases in book production and consumption in the eighteenth century helped lay the groundwork for revolutionary dissent. European printers produced an estimated 355 million books and pamphlets in the first half of the eighteenth century. That number almost doubled to 629 million in the second half of the century.[6] This explosion of books, pamphlets, newspapers, and underground literature made it possible for ideas to spread, gain momentum, and—ultimately—topple dogma, kings, and empires.

The Expanding Republic of Letters

The proliferation of print was most profound in the states where press freedom was most pronounced. We have already seen how the Dutch Republic dwarfed every other nation in terms of per capita consumption of literature. Moreover, the rate of literacy in the Dutch Republic reached an incredible 85 percent in the eighteenth century—almost three times greater than that of France. As predicted by John Locke, Great Britain benefitted when prepublication censorship was abolished in 1695, becoming the world's leading producer of books and taking second place in terms of per capita consumption and literacy between 1651 and 1750.[7]

The flood of print created an irresistible urge to share and discuss the news and novel ideas in the many new venues of Europe's emerging public sphere.[8] Coffee houses became the eighteenth-century version of social media, where pamphlets, newspapers, and books were shared and discussed. The number of coffee houses in London swelled from 83 in 1663 to 550 at the turn of the century.[9] In Paris, these venues surged in number from 280 in 1720 to 900 at the dawn of the French Revolution in 1789.[10] London coffee houses were egalitarian in nature. What mattered was the intellectual input you brought to the table—not the size of your wallet nor the purity of your bloodline. They became known as "penny universities," because anyone could enter an informal institution of knowledge for just one penny—the price of a cup of coffee. Not coincidentally, they were also a favored haunt of "coffee-house radicals" of the Radical Whig sort, who wanted further republican reforms and whose ideas would soon travel westward. The emerging public sphere also made it easier for women to mingle, participate in public debate, and enjoy "conversational freedom," paving the way for towering figures like Olympe de Gouges and Mary Wollstonecraft, whose writings on women's rights made vital contributions to Enlightenment thought, as we will see later on.[11]

Despite the harsh crackdown on Spinozist ideas by Dutch authorities in the 1670s, a pandora's box of materialist thinking had been opened that authorities could not fully contain. As the Dutch Republic strengthened its role as an epicenter of print, illegal books were steadily smuggled over the walls of censorship erected in most European countries. Clandestine Dutch printing presses and networks of print diffusion were regarded much like the Dark Web of the twenty-first century: a lawless black hole of filth, crime, and sedition that undermined and corrupted the essential foundations of society.

By 1700, the publisher given the fictional title "Pierre Marteau"—an imprint invented by anonymous French radicals in the Dutch Republic—had published upwards of three hundred books totaling some 150,000 copies. These books criticized Catholicism and the Sun King, and evolved into ever more daring naturalistic philosophy and erotica.[12] One of the Dutch Dark Web's most outrageous texts was the *Treatise of the Three Imposters*. Falsely attributed to Spinoza to increase its shock effect, the work shows how radical freethinking had become by the time the treatise began circulating in the early eighteenth century.[13] It explicitly rejected the existence of God, the Devil, Heaven, Hell, and souls, and attacked Moses, Jesus, and Muhammad as "the greatest impostures which anyone has been able to hatch, & which you should flee if you love the truth."[14] Censors across the Continent fought vigorously to search and destroy this odious atheist screed, and only a few contemporary copies survive.

"Pierre Marteau" and other iconoclastic Dutch printers took full advantage of the republic's press freedom. But as we've seen, this liberty was a matter of conventional practice and did not rest on any positive law, and postpublication censorship was far from uncommon. At least 254 books were officially banned in Amsterdam between 1747 and 1797, including works by French philosophes such as Voltaire and Rousseau.[15] All hell broke loose when the French materialist Julien Offray de La Mettrie published his anonymous *Man a Machine* in 1747. By "machine," La Mettrie meant that man is a soulless animal guided by the blind and uncreated laws of nature.[16] The book was banned and burned across Europe, including in the Dutch Republic. Its publisher, Elie Luzac, was incensed by Dutch authorities' oppressive response. Not because Luzac was a materialist like Le Mettrie—he was a pious, if liberal, Calvinist repulsed by atheism—but because he strongly believed that atheism should be countered by open debate.[17] This was a radical position at a time when the denial of central Christian tenets was banned even in the Dutch Republic and England.

Luzac provided pious Christians (which at that time could fairly describe the vast majority of Europeans) a justification for tolerating impious speech at a time when such tolerance was rejected out of hand even by liberals. His truly groundbreaking contribution to the history of free speech was his defense of the right to publish a book containing ideas widely deemed utterly loathsome, even by himself. Luzac thus helped pave the way for the idea and practice that social peace, harmony, and truth could all be furthered, despite deep and fundamental philosophical and religious differences, if settled or accommodated through open debate rather than policed through force.

Luzac developed this defense of dangerous ideas in his 1749 *Essay on Freedom of Expression*, anticipating John Stuart Mill by more than a century:

> I am convinced that the three angles of a triangle are equal to two right angles. As evident as this proposition is to me, if someone claimed to me to have arguments which demolished this truth, I

wonder if in conscience I could say that I was fully convinced, as long as I had not seen the falseness of these arguments. It follows from this that we cannot take pride in the power of persuasion of the most important truths, as long as we prevent atheists, free-thinkers, and others of that ilk from brandishing their pen.

Yet, Luzac limited his free speech concept to highbrow intellectual debate among a learned elite. He specifically exempted "novels, lampoons," and "insulting or indecent expressions."[18] There's no way that Luzac would have termed a Twitter feud an exercise of a natural right. But the fact that Luzac—like Dirck Coornhert and the Levellers—has largely faded from the history of free speech is a travesty, given the trailblazing nature of his arguments.

Twenty years later, Luzac took up the good fight yet again. In 1769, the Court of Holland proposed to introduce prepublication censorship of ideas that "undermined the foundations of Christian religion or Holy Scripture."[19] Luzac penned a fiercely critical rebuttal. The plan, he argued, was unworkable, unconstitutional, unnatural, and—close to heart for the Dutch merchant state—harmful to trade. Eventually, the authorities quietly abandoned the idea.[20]

Even though England had abolished prepublication censorship, English press freedom did not protect against postpublication punishment for speech crimes like blasphemy and sedition, which remained part and parcel of British common law. With the shadow of the bloody Civil War of the 1640s still lingering, deference to properly constituted authority was widely considered the precondition for liberty. Anonymous Tory writers echoed Thomas Hobbes when they warned that seditious libelers were the "very Assassins of all Government," or that "a Civil War began with Ink may end in Blood."[21]

Lord Chief Justice John Holt explained the deeply elitist rationale for the crime of seditious libel in 1704: "If people should not be called to account for possessing the people with an ill opinion of the government, no government can subsist."[22] Moreover, since a Star Chamber case from 1606, truth did not constitute a defense for libelers of the government.[23]

This view developed into the "Blackstonian" model of press freedom, named after the eighteenth-century conservative judge and politician Sir William Blackstone. In his hugely influential *Commentaries on the Laws of England* from the late 1760s, he argued that press freedom was "essential to the nature of a free state." But this only entailed a protection against prepublication censorship, not against subsequent punishments: "Every freeman has an undoubted right to lay what sentiments he pleases before the public: to forbid this, is to destroy the freedom of the press: but if he publishes what is improper, mischievous, or illegal, he must take the consequence of his own temerity."[24] This left authorities free to punish authors of publications whose "bad tendencies" were thought to threaten the social and political order, even in the absence of any incitement to unlawful action. Accordingly, criminal law remained a very real threat to seditious pens and tongues. Blackstonianism would continue to exert a restrictive influence over the limits of free speech in both Britain and the US into the twentieth century.

But there were also those who saw deference to liberty as the foundation of legitimate authority. Britain was home to some of the most influential free speech theorists of the eighteenth century— although their ideas would find the most fertile ground across the Atlantic. One of the clearest voices was that of the Deist freethinker Matthew Tindal, who had insisted in his 1698 *Letter to a Member of Parliament* that "Men have the same right to communicate their Thoughts, as to think themselves."[25] In 1704, Tindal anonymously published *Reasons Against Restraining the Press* (sometimes attributed to John Toland). In it, he asserted that everyone had "a natural Right in all matters of Learning and Knowledge." Neither religion nor government was exempt from discussion. Tindal also held that "the liberty of the Press must keep a Ministry within some tolerable Bounds, by exposing their ill Designs to the People." He even attacked parliamentary privilege, asking why Parliament, which enjoyed freedom of the press, should also "deny those they Represent the same Liberty?"[26] Unsurprisingly, the works of Tindal were burned in 1710 on orders from the House of Commons.[27]

Yet the most influential argument for free speech was a series of letters published in the *London Journal* between 1720 and 1723. Known as *Cato's Letters*, they were authored by the Radical Whigs John Trenchard and Thomas Gordon, who took their pseudonym from the Roman senator Cato the Younger, who had become a martyr for republicanism and free speech under Caesar.[28] Like their ancient role model, Trenchard and Gordon stressed individual and political freedom and warned against the despotic tendencies of un-limited and arbitrary government. Letter No. 15 was dedicated to the issue of free speech. Written by Gordon, it opened with this stir-ring salvo: "Without freedom of thought, there can be no such thing as wisdom; and no such thing as publick liberty, without freedom of speech." A few paragraphs later, Gordon wrote the now-iconic words: "Freedom of speech is the great bulwark of liberty; they pros-per and die together: And it is the terror of traitors and oppressors, and a barrier against them." He used historical precedents to demon-strate the intimate link between freedom of speech and liberty and pointed to Charles I's heavy-handed censorship, for instance, as clear evidence that despotism and suppression went hand in hand. But Gordon drew his chief historical lessons from Tacitus's account of how the fall of the Roman Republic restricted *libertas* of the tongue. Letter No. 15 is therefore a secular, rational, and political defense of freedom of speech.[29]

Gordon's argument was for free speech in its Roman tradition, as "the bulwark of liberty" that protected the natural liberty of the individual against arbitrary abuse of power, rather than a call for egalitarian and democratic free speech, as in its Athenian version.

It was undoubtedly an idealized and Whiggish account of Roman free speech. But what *Cato's Letters* might have lacked in historical accuracy they made up for in historical impact.

Cato's Letters also tackled the difficult question of how far speech protections should extend. Trenchard and Gordon wrote three letters—Nos. 32, 100, and 101—that specifically addressed the question of libel, slander, and scandalous rumors. They conceded that libelous statements against the government were "always base and unlawful." But—unlike what followed from common law precedent—truthful statements were not to be punished. More fundamentally, Gordon argued that libel was an unavoidable consequence of press freedom—"an evil arising out of a much greater good." The only way to avoid libels altogether would be to return to the bad old days of licensing and Star Chamber justice. And so, "I must own, that I would rather many libels should escape, than the liberty of the press should be infringed."[30] *Cato's Letters* also warned of the vague and arbitrary nature of the crime of seditious libel. Words could always be interpreted in several ways. If the government could prosecute any writer for literary crimes, real or imagined, even when the wording and intentions were unclear, then no pen would be safe.[31]

Cato's Letters became wildly successful, especially in colonial America. "From Boston to Savannah" it became nearly impossible to open a newspaper without encountering reprints, quotations, or discussions of the essays.[32] The metaphor of free speech as the "great bulwark of liberty" found its way into Virginia's famous Declaration of Rights, James Madison's initial draft of the First Amendment, speeches of French revolutionaries, and even the writings of Russian radicals.[33]

Yet no one tested the limits of British press freedom like the notorious jester and MP John Wilkes. His satirical newspaper, the *North Briton*, mocked George III and his government relentlessly. Naturally, its very first issue paraphrased *Cato's Letters*, and its insistence that freedom of the press is the "bulwark" of all other liberties. The *North Briton*'s articles spread rumors that the prime minister was sleeping with the king's mother and called the secretary of the treasury "the most treacherous, base, selfish, mean, abject, low-lived and dirty fellow, that ever *wriggled* himself into a secretaryship."[34] When a French official asked him how far press freedom extended in England, he replied, "I cannot tell, but I am trying to know."[35] In April 1763, he collided with the limits head on, after releasing the infamous *North Briton* No. 45, which not only lampooned the king and his ministers but also flirted with open calls for rebellion.[36] Wilkes spent a week in the Tower, and the House of Commons ordered his newspaper burnt for its seditious libels. Wilkes sought escape by going into exile in France, but was found guilty of seditious and obscene libels in absentia. When debt forced him to return to England in 1768, he gave himself up to the authorities and received two years in prison.[37]

Wilkes had tested the limits of the law and paid the price, creating a divisive example for other thinkers. David Hume was apparently so appalled by *l'affaire* Wilkes that he toned down his own hitherto enthusiastic defense of free speech and cautioned against the dangers of the "unbounded liberty of the press," though he still insisted that censorship was worse than suffering hyperbole.[38] Across the Atlantic, on the other hand, Wilkes's crusade for British *parrhēsia* resonated deeply with American Patriots who adopted "Wilkes and Liberty" and the number 45 as rallying cries on the eve of the Revolutionary War.[39]

Censorship and Subversion in Old Regime France

France, or rather Paris, became the capital of the High Enlightenment in the mid-eighteenth century. The movement was spearheaded by philosophes, like the indefatigable Voltaire, and the more radical

Encyclopedists, who congregated (their enemies would say conspired) at Baron d'Holbach's salon. Most prominent among them was the chief editor of the *Encyclopédie*, Denis Diderot.

French censorship had relaxed considerably after Louis XIV died in 1715 and the relatively freethinking Duke of Orléans took over the reins. French publishers soon began printing more controversial books on philosophy, science, and even theology. By 1732, one could even publish Bayle's controversial *Dictionary* in Paris.[40] But despite this relative relaxation, censorship was still very much in play, and proved to be a formidable obstacle to writers who wished to openly challenge monarchical and religious authority.

The Old Regime used a bewildering patchwork of pre- and post-publication censorship to root out dangerous ideas.[41] The first line of defense against such material were the royal censors working under the authority of the *directeur de la Librairie*.[42] The royal censors' job was to prevent writings "against religion, service to the king, the good of the state, the purity of customs," and—not least—"the honor and reputation of families and of individuals."[43] Books accepted by the royal censors were given a *privilège* or "permission." Technically, this was the only legal way to enter the book market.[44] In theory, the system of prepublication censorship and a monopolized book trade should have provided the Old Regime with an iron grip on print material. But in practice, the book trade only had the resources to impose a literary lockdown on Paris. Owing to lax enforcement outside the capital, provincial printer-booksellers were effectively exempt from the many regulations and could get away with printing things that might have been banned in Paris.[45]

There's also a basic rule in economics that whenever you ban something for which there is a large demand, black markets thrive. According to one estimate, France had 3,000 book dealers in the 1770s. Only 1,004 were officially listed.[46] Prohibited books were also readily available from printers in neighboring countries, who were happy to supply French readers with addictive literary uppers and downers. That was where the second line of defense came into play. The police had special *inspecteurs de la Librairie* to infiltrate clandestine networks and sniff out bad books.[47] Around 17 percent of the inmates in the Bastille prison between 1659 and 1789 were convicted of literary crimes, and among those who spent time there were Voltaire and the notorious pornographer Marquis de Sade.[48]

Newspapers suffered under the Old Regime as well. The only legal news outlets were heavily censored governmental newspapers like the *Gazette de France*.[49] But this only forced news-hungry readers to get creative, passing snippets of gossip from hand to hand or exchanging information orally.[50] As Paris's despairing chief of police complained, "the Parisians had more of a propensity to believe the malicious rumors and *libelles* that circulated clandestinely than the facts printed and published by order or with the permission of the government."[51]

In 1750, the new *directeur de la Librairie*, Chrétien Guillaume de Lamoignon de Malesherbes, realized that a more pragmatic approach was needed to prevent the legal book trade from bleeding revenue to black markets and foreign publishers. Draconian censorship had become a competitive disadvantage in Enlightenment Europe. His solution was to increase the use of "tacit permissions"—a form of gentleman's agreement that allowed books lacking a censor's approval and privilege to be sold openly.[52] But Malesherbes was also sympathetic to enlightened ideas, admitting that "a man who reads only books that originally appeared with the explicit sanction of the government . . . would be behind his contemporaries by nearly a century."[53] He even grew friendly with many philosophes who would previously have used the "VPN" of the day, having their works published anonymously abroad and then smuggled into France, rather than ask permission from the very state whose foundations they were accused of undermining. Malesherbes's literary glasnost contributed to a rapid growth of books. The number of printed titles in France more than doubled from 73.6 million in the first half of the eighteenth century to more than 157 million in the second half of the century.[54]

The most prominent—or, to traditionalists, utterly repugnant—work to receive Malesherbes's stamp of approval was the *Encyclopédie* edited by Diderot and Jean le Rond d'Alembert. Their ambition was nothing less than compiling all of the knowledge in the world.[55] The main contributors to the *Encyclopédie* met at Baron d'Holbach's salon in rue Royale to discuss new texts, philosophy, politics, and the latest news. These "Sheikhs of the rue Royale" included a who's who of French Enlightenment thinkers like Marmontel, Raynal, Turgot, and Rousseau, as well as visiting foreigners like Cesare Beccaria, Adam Smith, Edward Gibbon, and David Hume. Irreverent conversation abounded at d'Holbach's salon. Hume, unsettled by their frankness, once told d'Holbach that he had never met an atheist and did not believe they even existed. The baron pointed to the eighteen people present and replied: "Monsieur, count how many of us are here. . . .It is a good start to be able to show you fifteen straight away. The other three haven't yet made up their minds."[56]

Naturally, the Encyclopedists were controversial figures. In 1749, Diderot spent three months in prison for writing a religiously subversive book.[57] Upon release, he compiled the first volume of the *Encyclopédie*. Covering A to AZYMITES, it was granted a privilege and published in 1751. But the *Encyclopédie*'s articles were filled with subtle and not-so-subtle challenges to the twin authority of the Catholic Church and the French absolute monarchy, and it did not take long for the authorities to recognize what was afoot.

The first volume alone was packed with subversive asides. Diderot supplemented the entry on the soul (*âme*) with an article asking uncomfortable questions like where the soul connects to the body. In the brain? The nervous system? Or the heart?[58] All but inviting the curious reader to ask the more fundamental question of whether the soul exists at all. Whether intended mockingly or not, the entry on cannibals (*anthropophages*) famously contained the cross reference "See EUCHARIST, COMMUNION, ALTAR."[59] The entry on political authority was not exactly deferential to royal absolutism when asserting that "no man has received from nature the right to command others. Liberty is a gift from heaven."[60] By the time the second volume was published in 1752, the *Encyclopédie* was officially condemned by the King's Council, although it was not prohibited—yet. However, this slap on the wrist proved to be a gigantic self-defeat. In an Enlightenment version of the Streisand effect, the condemnation only helped boost the *Encyclopédie*'s sales. The number of subscriptions surged to four thousand, bringing in a total of 1,120,000 livres—almost five million present-day USD. In fact, it would become one of the most profitable works in eighteenth-century France.[61]

But the faction of traditionalist anti-philosophes did not take their humiliating defeat lying down. Starting in 1755, the Church put the "poisonous" writings of the "so-called philosophes" on the agenda.[62] Most anti-philosophes were deeply opposed to freedom of thought and the press. They felt the enemies of religion and monarchy had been given free reign; the royal censors were doling out privileges left and right to dangerous books, while the police sat idly by as illegal literature flooded France, sweeping away all that was good and sacred. At the center of anti-philosophes ideology was the essential marriage between Catholicism and monarchy—Throne and Altar. They viewed philosophes as coconspirators engaged in literary terrorism, since "impiety and heresy have in all times been as much enemies of kings as of the Church."[63]

The anti-philosophes campaign put pressure on Malesherbes to reconcile irreconcilable ideologies. And when one of his censors fell asleep at the wheel, the anti-philosophes were quick to pounce. In 1757, a royal censor recommended a privilege for Claude-Adrien Helvétius's *De l'esprit* ("On the Mind") after lightly skimming through it.[64] But the book should have raised a number of red flags, especially for its radical egalitarianism and its attacks on the Christian view of morality.[65] According to the Faculty of Theology at the Sorbonne, Helvétius's arguments tended to "destroy the very foundations of political authority."[66] *De l'esprit* may not have been the most radical book of its time, but it was certainly one of the most radical books to obtain a royal privilege when released in 1758. And it came at the worst possible time. After an assassination attempt on Louis XV in January 1757, the government had issued a decree threatening to execute writers, printers, and sellers of works attacking the state or Church. Moreover, the daring and provocative seventh volume of the *Encyclopédie* had just hit the streets in November 1757, generating so much controversy that Diderot's coeditor d'Alembert and many of the contributors withdrew from the project. Helvétius was sacked from his prestigious job at the royal court and told to publicly disavow the book—or else. But the *parlement* of Paris did not stop there. Egged on by the Church, it declared collective war on the philosophes. In 1759, *De l'esprit* and seven other works by prominent Enlightenment authors, including Voltaire and Diderot, were publicly burned.[67]

The *Encyclopédie* escaped the flames. But on March 8, the King's Council withdrew the privilege for the first seven volumes, condemning the work as a "vehicle for disseminating *pernicious maxims* damaging to religion and morality."[68] The Catholic Church followed suit and placed the seven volumes on the Index of Prohibited Books.[69] The path was finally clear to destroy the *Encyclopédie*. The police burst into Diderot's office to seize the contraband, but found only an empty desk. Diderot had been tipped off—by none other than Malesherbes, who even offered his own home as a safe haven, knowing that Diderot had nowhere to hide his enormous piles of paper on such short notice. Tens of thousands of hours of work were securely stashed with the chief censor formally tasked with destroying it.[70]

Thanks to the hard work of Diderot, the remaining contributors, and his guardian angel Malesherbes, the last ten volumes of the

Encyclopédie were published together in 1765. The seventeen-volume set contained 17,818 articles on eighteen thousand pages, totaling more than twenty million words all in all.[71] The work was given a tacit permission on the condition that it was not sold or imported into Paris or Versailles.[72] The Encyclopedists had triumphed to the great benefit of religious tolerance, open debate, and diffusion of ideas. Yet the positive effects of the *Encyclopédie* were not limited to politics and religion. Science and progress also benefitted from the audacious attempt to map and disseminate all human knowledge. A century after the first publication, the French cities with most subscribers to the *Encyclopédie* were also the most innovative and prosperous.[73]

By the end of the 1770s, the philosophes had inserted themselves into the institutions of prestige and power, and many of their ideas were gradually accepted. The Enlightenment rebels had become part of the establishment. As in Britain, the discussion of free speech and religious tolerance in France moved from the fringes of radical freethinkers to the mainstream of French intellectual life from the mid-eighteenth century. According to historian Charles Walton, however, "there was no coherent campaign for press freedom in the French Enlightenment," nor agreement on where the boundary lines of free speech should be drawn.[74]

There were of course French thinkers who addressed free speech and tested the limits of the Old Regime's censorship. In his famous *Spirit of Laws* from 1748, Baron Montesquieu revived Tacitus's ancient separation of words from treasonable acts and viewed diversity of opinion as an advantage, not a danger, to the state. Yet Montesquieu stopped short of explicitly demanding the abolition of censorship.[75]

The ubiquitous Voltaire has become famous for the—apocryphal—words "I disapprove of what you say, but I will defend to the death your right to say it."[76] Though the real Voltaire might

not have been willing to die to defend the free speech of his enemies, he did spend time in the Bastille and in exile because of his
writings, which included several canonical arguments for freedom
of speech and conscience. His highly influential *Treatise on Tolerance*
from 1763, penned in protest of the bigoted execution of the protestant Jean Calas, declared religious intolerance "absurd and barbaric"
and against the laws of nature.[77] The essay was promptly banned.[78]
His *Philosophical Dictionary* from 1764 contained an entry on "Liberty of the Press," advancing the familiar Enlightenment trope that
books never cause harm. To Voltaire, the solution to offensive material was straightforward: "Does a book displease you? refute it.
Does it tire you? read it not."[79] Unfortunately, the authorities did
not share Voltaire's views on press freedom and the anonymously
published dictionary was banned as "false philosophy."[80]

Voltaire's writings were not only perilous to himself. In the summer of 1766, the nineteen-year-old François-Jean de la Barre was
arrested after spurious statements from locals incriminated him in
the vandalizing of a crucifix. A search of the young nobleman's house
unveiled a copy of Voltaire's prohibited *Philosophical Dictionary* and
two erotic novels. That was enough for a conviction. After a humiliating public penance, la Barre was beheaded and then burned along
with a copy of the dictionary that sealed his fate.[81]

Still, Voltaire was far from a free speech absolutist. His inspiration
was England, where press freedom meant the right to publish without prior censorship, but not without subsequent punishments—in
his own words, the "right to make use of our pens as our language,
at our own peril."[82] He even tried to game the system of French
censorship in order to advance his own writings and suppress those
of his foes, whom he simultaneously blackened in his writings.[83] He
also viewed free speech as a privilege for the enlightened few. Much
like Cicero, holding the unwashed mob and their opinions in contempt, Voltaire remarked that it was "a very great question . . . up to

what degree the people, that is, nine tenth of the human race, must be treated as monkeys."[84] On free speech, Voltaire was more Roman than Athenian.

Nonetheless, Voltaire's arguments would play a key role in advancing the cause of free speech in eighteenth-century Europe—and beyond. In 2015, Voltaire's *Treatise on Tolerance* became a best-seller in a France shocked by the murderous attack on the satirical magazine *Charlie Hebdo*.[85] That a book once banned as dangerous by religious hard-liners is now seen as the antidote to murderous fanaticism is a powerful testament to the enduring legacy of Voltaire's ideas.

Denis Diderot was philosophically more radical than both Montesquieu and Voltaire. And given the systematic intolerance, censorship, and suppression to which he was subjected, one might have assumed Diderot to be a free speech absolutist. But historian Edoardo Tortarolo notes that Diderot, while strongly in favor of relaxing censorship, never advanced the idea of "unrestrained legal printing in France . . . as a feasible and desirable goal."[86] In fact, Diderot too was struck with Milton's Curse and called for censorship in 1772 when a philosophe defector lobbed a literary grenade at the Encyclopedists and their works. Instead of writing a reply, Diderot and d'Alembert—now members of the elite rather than embattled renegades—went straight to the lieutenant general of the police and implored him to suppress the work for impugning their honor.[87]

Diderot's failure to condemn censorship outright may have stemmed from his close relationship with Malesherbes—who did, after all, risk his job, prestige, and possibly his freedom to ensure the survival of the *Encyclopédie*. Attacking the institution of censorship headed by your most influential protector might have seemed not only awkward but also counterproductive and outright dangerous. And the *Encyclopédie* did include a strong defense of press freedom in Volume 13, though the article was written by the prolific Protestant nobleman Louis de Jaucourt, and not Diderot himself.[88]

Diderot's real contribution to freedom of speech was his often lonely and desperate fight to keep writing, editing, and publishing the *Encyclopédie* against all odds, surviving vicious abuse and intimidation, mass defection by his contributors, heavy official suppression, and the very real threat of prison and worse. Whereas Diderot's theoretical defense of free speech fell short, his practice of freedom of inquiry and expression was a human triumph that would reverberate around the world and down the ages.

One of the friends Diderot lost along the way was Jean-Jacques Rousseau, who became the sworn enemy of the philosophes he had once hung out with in rue Royale. Their differences were both personal and philosophical. For one, Rousseau had grown increasingly paranoid and was convinced that his former friends were conspiring against him behind his back.[89] But he also had a very different conception of liberty than most philosophes. As early as 1750, Rousseau had written about "the horrible disorders that printing has already produced in Europe" and how states should "banish this awful art."[90] And though Rousseau had cultivated a relationship with Malesherbes and received a tacit permission for his book *La Nouvelle Héloïse*, he felt deeply wounded when one of Malesherbes's censors hacked and slashed his way through the manuscript, deleting a full twenty-five pages before giving the thumbs up to the mutilated leftovers. So when Rousseau published his novel *Émile*, he opted to go Dutch. Rather foolhardily, he chose to have his name splashed across the cover. The book was promptly condemned by both the archbishop and the Paris *parlement*, which ordered an effigy of Rousseau to be burned along with his book. Rousseau himself managed to escape the Bastille only because he had fled after being warned by—you guessed it—Malesherbes.[91]

While Rousseau bravely continued to publish in his own name, he did not champion any coherent idea of free speech. In his most famous work *The Social Contract*, published in 1762, he asserted that in order to ensure the general will—or common good—"each individual will be forced to be free." Moreover, to create "good citizen[s]" and "faithful subject[s]" all men must believe in a civil religion established by the sovereign. Rousseau's perfect utopia had a grim fate in store for those who spurned the civil religious creed:

> While it can't compel anyone to believe them, it can banish from the state anyone who doesn't believe them—banishing him not for impiety but for being anti-social, incapable of truly loving the laws and justice, and if necessary sacrificing his life to his duty. If anyone publicly recognises these dogmas and then behaves as if he doesn't believe them, let him be punished by death.[92]

The free speech doctrines of Voltaire and Diderot might have been imperfect and inconsistent, but both argued for relaxing rather than tightening censorship. Rousseau essentially argued for the establishment of a new orthodoxy with no room for heretics. A position ominously close to that which would justify the Terror, once the Revolution spiraled out of control three decades later.

No doubt the Revolution would have become less murderously intolerant if the prevailing attitude toward political disagreement had taken fewer cues from Rousseau and more from the Marquis de Condorcet, perhaps the most radical proponent of free speech in the period immediately leading up to the Revolution. In his 1776 *Fragments Concerning Freedom of the Press*, he forcefully opposed both prepublication censorship and the system of suffocating privileges and monopolies that regulated the French printing industry. Condorcet also invoked the language of human rights to stress the importance of free speech, stating that censorship "violates my rights as a man and as a citizen."[93] Thirteen years later, Condorcet would have his wish granted—almost verbatim. Article 11 of the French Declaration of the Rights of Man guaranteed that "the free communication of thoughts and opinions is one of the most precious of the rights of man."[94]

Condorcet's free speech radicalism may eventually have been enshrined in law but there were still significant loopholes. A product of the culture of honor that permeated French society, Condorcet excluded calumny, defamation, insults, and vague accusations from his otherwise radical free speech doctrine, leaving it vulnerable to arbitrariness of interpretation and other abuse. In a sense, this failure to buttress his conception of free speech doctrine properly was a sign of things to come when the Declaration of the Rights of Man was adopted. Article 11's exception of "abuse" as "defined by law" would divide the revolutionaries bitterly. In fact, the failure to properly articulate the how and why of free speech would become the crux of the ultimately lethal debate over the proper role and limits of press freedom once prepublication censorship was abolished.

Enlightened Absolutism

As Enlightenment ideals gained strength throughout the eighteenth century, monarchs took notice. For some, free expression became a central part of so-called Enlightened Absolutism, in which benevolent (though still all-powerful) monarchs worked to improve society based on new rationalist and secular ideas. Philosophes like Voltaire and Montesquieu showered praise on Prussia's Frederick the Great and Russia's Catherine the Great for encouraging this spirit of openness.[95]

Catherine was steeped in Enlightenment ideals. She corresponded enthusiastically with Voltaire, Diderot, and d'Alembert, brainstorming with the philosophes on how best to carry out her grand designs of progressive social engineering. According to historian K. A. Papmehl, Catherine was "the first ruler in Russian history who was conscious of the concept of freedom of expression and of its positive value." Under the first years of her reign, Russia experienced a "very considerable liberalization . . . of freedom of expression."[96] One of her first decisions was to permit—and even fund—the publication of Diderot's *Encyclopédie* at a time when the work was still banned in France. The watershed moment for freedom of speech in Russia was Catherine's hugely ambitious idea to summon a Great Commission to revise and codify a new legal code in 1767. She prepared a so-called Great Instruction to the deputies to explain her own suggestions in great detail. According to Papmehl, this instruction was "the first articulate statement of the principles of this aspect of freedom [of speech], conceived as one of the civil liberties, in the history of Russia."[97] Half of the articles in Catherine's draft legal code were copied and pasted from the works of Enlightenment thinkers like Beccaria and Montesquieu, such as the latter's warning against punishing words in themselves as treason. She also went on to liberalize access to printing presses, creating a small public sphere of intellectual debate.

But Catherine was still an absolutist monarch at heart, and her reign included crackdowns on sedition, libel, and those who "tarnish the Glory of their Sovereign."[98] In 1767, the very year she issued her great liberal instruction, she also issued a decree demanding "absolute obedience in all matters" from serfs and peasants and punishing anyone "who dare[d] to incite serfs and peasants to disobey their landlords." Petitioning the empress with unlawful complaints about landlords was rewarded with the whip and lifelong penal labor in Siberia.[99] Diderot tried in vain to convince Catherine to abolish serfdom on a visit to Russia. She replied, "You work only on paper which accepts anything, is smooth and flexible and offers no obstacle either to your imagination or your pen, while I, poor empress, work on human skin, which is far more sensitive and touchy."[100] Catherine's liberal ideals came with strings attached, and she was willing to yank hard when those ideals threatened her authority.

Catherine was not the only eighteenth-century autocrat to be hailed as an Enlightened monarch. Frederick the Great assumed the Prussian throne in 1740. The self-proclaimed "philosopher king" launched a blitzkrieg of Enlightenment reforms that included academic freedom, religious tolerance, and the easing of censorship.[101] Frederick delighted in offering refuge to some of the most controversial writers of the time, including Voltaire and La Mettrie, who had become wanted all over Europe after the publication of *Man a Machine*. Frederick's reforms led to a comparatively open public sphere, at least among the elite. The Scotsman John Moore wrote the following account of his visit to Berlin in 1775:

> Nothing surprised me more, when I first came to Berlin, than the freedom with which many people spoke of the measures of government, and the conduct of the king. I have heard political topics, and others which I should have thought still more ticklish, discussed here with as little ceremony as at a London coffeehouse.[102]

But like Catherine, Frederick was an absolutist who ran an autocratic and highly militarized society and maintained a firm grip on political censorship. In a letter to d'Alembert, the philosopher king admitted "that restrictive measures are absolutely necessary, because freedom is invariably abused." He established a prepublication censorship committee in 1749 to weed out works "contrary to the principles of religion, as well as to moral and social order."[103] Writings on foreign policy and overt calls for political reform were off limits, as were "scandalous" and "offensive" books imported from abroad, including Rousseau's *Émile*.[104]

As in Paris and London, the Prussian Enlightenment was boosted by an emerging public sphere. New ideas were exchanged and discussed in the many bookshops, reading societies, and masonic lodges that mushroomed throughout Prussia after 1750.[105] But the Prussian public sphere was nothing like London's egalitarian "penny universities." It put a premium on civility and consisted of elites who debated publicly on the pages of the *Berlinische Monatsschrift* ("Berlin Monthly") and privately in the Wednesday Club, a society dedicated to the advancement of enlightenment.[106] The goal of this enlightened circle—most of whom were civil servants—was not to use Enlightenment principles to subvert absolutism, but to ensure a more perfect union between the two.[107] Thus, they promoted an elitist (one might call it "Ciceronian" or "Voltairean") conception of free speech. An influential lawyer summed it up nicely: "I advocate unrestricted freedom of publication for works intended only for that part of the nation which is already enlightened." For the common people, on the other hand, he insisted that "a highly vigilant censorship is needed."[108] The exception was the German-Jewish philosopher Moses Mendelssohn, who stressed that he could find no historical examples in which "unrestricted freedom to express one's opinion in particular has actually been detrimental to the general happiness."[109]

The December 1783 issue of the *Berlin Monthly* included one of the most influential footnotes in the history of political thought. It asked the question, "What is Enlightenment?" Many attempted to answer, including the soon-to-be-famous philosopher Immanuel Kant, who published the following reply in December 1784:

Enlightenment is mankind's exit from its self-incurred immaturity. Immaturity is the inability to make use of one's own understanding without the guidance of another. *Self-incurred* is the inability if its cause lies not in the lack of understanding but rather in the lack of the resolution and the courage to use it without the guidance of another. *Sapere aude!* [dare to know!] Have the courage to use your *own* understanding! is thus the motto of enlightenment.

Kant's discussion of man's self-imposed immaturity referred chiefly to religion. But he also wrote that an enlightened ruler should allow "his subjects to make *public* use of their reason and to lay publicly before the world their thoughts about a better formulation of this legislation as well as a candid criticism of laws already given."

In other words, true enlightenment required freedom of political, as well as philosophical and religious, speech.

One might think that Kant's insistence on free political expression would see him clash with Frederick. But Kant was no revolutionary. He stressed that "this age is the age of enlightenment or the century of *Frederick*"—whose ideas of Enlightened absolutism Kant approvingly summed up as the dictum of "*Argue,* as much as you want and about whatever you want, but *obey!*"[110] Rather fancifully—at least from a modern perspective—Kant thought that as the dissemination of Enlightenment values led to the freeing of common people's minds, the interests and values of the enlightened ruler and his newly enlightened subjects would converge. This view of free speech was certainly more expansive than that of the civil servants in the Wednesday Club. Sadly, and as we shall see, Kant soon learned that his optimism about the potential of Enlightened Absolutism was deeply unrealistic.

Northern Lights

For all the groundbreaking developments in the Dutch Republic, Britain, and France (not to mention America), it was ultimately Scandinavia that became the first region in the world to provide legal protection for free speech and abolish any and all forms of censorship. After the death of Charles XII in 1718, the Swedish Diet, or Parliament, gained the upper hand at the expense of the weakened monarchy.[111] Around 60 percent of the male population was granted a direct or indirect vote in elections, which made it, in the words of Swedish historian Jonas Nordin, "by far the most widely participatory political system anywhere in Europe."[112] This period of Swedish history is known as the Age of Liberty.[113] That liberty consisted of collective political freedom from absolute monarchy, but did not encompass individual freedom to think, speak, and write as you wished—at least not yet.

From around the 1750s, educational reforms and Enlightenment ideas had sown powerful seeds among Swedish intellectuals. In his 1759 pamphlet *Thoughts on Civil Liberty* the philosopher Peter Forsskål wrote, "the life and strength of civil liberty consist in limited Government and unlimited freedom of the written word."[114] These ideas would soon be elevated from theory to practice.

The Diet first put press freedom on the agenda in 1760. The most influential proponent of press freedom in the Diet was the priest and prolific writer Anders Chydenius. In 1766 he drafted a Diet committee report on press freedom in which he first outlined the arguments against abolishing censorship and then systematically dismantled them. Chydenius's report concluded that "the freedom of the nation is always proportional to the freedom of printing it possesses, so that neither can exist without the other."[115]

The report persuaded the Diet of the need to protect both freedom of the press and of information. In December 1766, "His Majesty's Gracious Ordinance Regarding the Freedom of Writing and of the Press," also known as the Freedom of the Press Act, was adopted. The act stressed the "great benefits a legal freedom of writing and of the press will bring to the public."[116] It was legally binding in nature, abolished preventive censorship—except for theological writings—and was based on the principle that only those topics specifically exempted in the act could be punished: the evangelical faith, the constitution, the royal family, and obscene literature were off limits.[117] Everything else, however, could be written and printed.[118]

The Swedish Freedom of the Press Act was a watershed moment in the history of free speech. Such a firm protection of free speech did not exist anywhere else on earth. For all their liberality, neither the Dutch Republic nor Britain had adopted specific laws that positively protected freedom of speech. Another groundbreaking feature of the act was that it protected freedom of information—extensively so. Most documents and minutes from the courts, public authorities, Diet, and even the executive were now accessible to the public.

Following the passage of the act, helped along by a policy aimed at increasing literacy, print production and consumption skyrocketed. The eight years from 1766 to 1774 account for 75 percent of the political pamphlets published between 1700 and 1809.[119] Sweden's annual per capita consumption of literature more than doubled between the first and the second half of the eighteenth century, making the Swedes the second most avid consumers of literature in Europe.[120]

This policy of openness only prevailed for eight years. A royal coup in 1772 ended Sweden's Age of Liberty, and with it the extensive protection of freedom of speech and information. But even within that short time, Sweden's neighbors and bitter rivals endeavored to outdo them in radical free speech reforms.

The Kingdom of Denmark-Norway was both highly absolutist and strictly Lutheran in nature; consequently, censorship had long been a pervasive force. But in 1768, the German physician and Spinozist Johann Friedrich Struensee was appointed the personal physician of the mentally ill King Christian VII. Struensee quickly took advantage of the king's instability to further his own ambitions (which included sleeping with the queen). In 1770, he became de facto ruler of the realm.

Struensee's reign was short but intense. In about sixteen months, he issued some 1,800 decrees, many of which may as well have been cribbed straight from "Enlightenment Principles for Dummies." With Struensee pulling the strings, the king published the following rescript on September 14, 1770:

> [It] is as harmful to the impartial search for truth as it is to the discovery of obsolete errors and prejudices, if upright patriots, zealous for the common good and what is genuinely best for their fellow citizens, because they are frightened by reputation, orders, and preconceived opinions, are hindered from being free to write according to their insight, conscience, and conviction, attacking

abuses and uncovering prejudices . . . thus . . . we have decided to permit in our kingdoms and lands in general an unlimited freedom of the press of such a form, that from now on no one shall be required and obliged to submit books and writings that he wants to bring to the press to the previously required censorship and approval.[121]

And with that, Denmark exceeded the Swedes, becoming the first and only state in the world to formally and explicitly abolish any and all censorship of the press.[122] Unlike the Swedish Freedom of the Press Act, the Danish rescript contained no "buts" or exceptions. The rescript was widely reported in newspapers around Europe, and Voltaire even wrote a long poem praising Christian VII for it.[123]

In effect, Struensee had promoted Danes from being passive subjects to "citizens" and "patriots." They were now free to voice their opinion on all the matters that concerned them. A radical experiment of egalitarian free speech in a strictly absolutist state, where hitherto information had been jealously controlled by a small elite serving the narrow interest of king and church. But as Frederick and Catherine the Great would surely have warned Struensee, this was an explosive mix.

The inhabitants of Denmark-Norway enthusiastically used their new liberty to comment on current affairs. Around a thousand pamphlets were published from 1770 to 1772 on everything from the economy to religion, sex, and the merits of free speech. Unsurprisingly, egalitarian free speech also opened the floodgates of literary filth, lies, and vituperations. And many Danes used the freedom Struensee had granted them to express contempt and ridicule rather than gratitude and praise for the man behind the throne.[124] Few shared the more hedonistic Enlightenment ideals that this German usurper and adulterer tried to ram down the throats of ordinary, God-fearing Danes. Sensing his already precarious position being undermined by the very "patriots" whose pens he had set free,

Struensee issued a rescript in October 1771 warning that "libels, lampoons and rebellious publications" were still subject to postpublication punishment.[125]

No amount of backpedaling could save Struensee from the PR disaster he had brought upon himself. He was arrested and charged with high treason and lèse majesté in January 1772. Struensee mounted the scaffold on April 28. His right hand was chopped off, he was beheaded, his corpse was drawn and quartered, and the severed head and dismembered body parts were exhibited publicly.[126]

The new regime flooded the public with anti-Struensee propaganda, but it took almost two years to strangle press freedom by prohibiting the publication of matters concerning "state and government" as well as "town rumors" and "made-up tales" of an "offensive or indecent" nature.[127] However, it is notable that the new regime did not formally reintroduce prepublication censorship. So even though Struensee's age of absolute free speech was short, intense, and its conclusion nasty and brutish, a crucial aspect of his Enlightenment ideals limped on.

———

STRUENSEE'S FALL, THE INHERENT CONTRADICTIONS OF Enlightened Absolutism, the British tendency to value order over liberty, and the informal protection of press freedom in the Dutch Republic suggested that no form of government had yet been devised in which egalitarian free speech could truly thrive. Establishing such a state of affairs would require a political as well as a cultural revolution, and it just so happened that revolutionary dissent was germinating in colonial America. Indeed, free speech would soon become an indispensable rallying cry for would-be revolutionaries on both sides of the Atlantic. But once press freedom had lit the revolutionary fuse, many of those who had fanned the blazing flame of freedom scampered to douse the fire for fear of being burned.

6

Constructing the Bulwark of Liberty

I n 1671, Virginia's governor William Berkeley summed up the prevailing attitude to free speech and education among many colonial elites: "I thank God, there are no free schools nor *printing*, and I hope we shall not have these hundred years; for *learning* has brought disobedience, and heresy, and sects into the world, and *printing* has divulged them, and libels against the best government. God keep us from both."[1] Fast-forward to the twenty-first century and—in the words of Columbia University president and free speech scholar Lee Bollinger—the US is "the most speech protective of any nation on Earth, now or throughout history."[2] Along the path to the current state of American "free speech exceptionalism," the United States Supreme Court has entirely inverted Governor Berkeley's doctrine of deferential obedience to political and religious authority by holding that "if there is any fixed star in our constitutional constellation, it is that no official, high or petty, can prescribe what shall be orthodox in politics, nationalism, religion, or other matters of opinion, or force citizens to confess by word or act their faith therein."[3]

But in seventeenth-century colonial America there were few signs of such commitment to robust and uninhibited speech. Early Enlightenment ideals were slow to make their way across the

Atlantic from Europe, but once Americans got a taste for printing, pamphlets, and punchy writing, the inhabitants of the New World quickly made up ground and ultimately surpassed the liberality of the Old World.

Puritanical Restrictions

Printing came late to the colonies, and when it finally arrived, it was heavily regulated. Set up in Cambridge, Massachusetts, in 1638, America's first printing press came under the ownership of Harvard College. As the colony swiftly established a board of censors with the power to exercise prior censorship, however, it hardly opened the floodgates to unbridled publications.[4]

In the years that followed, British common law and colonial laws were used to punish seditious loudmouths lampooning governments and officials and spreading false news.[5] Scholar Larry Eldridge has identified at least 1,244 "seditious speech prosecutions" from seventeenth-century colonial America, although these were inconsistently applied and let much seditious speech go unpunished.[6]

Freedom of conscience was decidedly not on the menu either when the first colonists settled the East Coast in the early seventeenth century. They imposed harsh and austere religious laws, and most colonies had established churches and punished dissent. One scholar has identified 147 prosecutions for religious crimes from 1620 to 1700 (excluding county and local records), including fifty prosecutions for sacrilegious speech, thirty for profanity/swearing, twenty for blasphemy, and five for heresy.[7]

Nowhere was as unforgiving as Puritan New England. The—sometimes violent—religious intolerance of Charles I had driven many Puritans to leave the motherland and settle New England in the 1620s and '30s. But once they reached America, they had little sympathy for what one leading Puritan called "the lawlessness of liberty of conscience."[8] Religious dissenters were subject to brutal punishments including flogging, maiming, fire branding, and even the death penalty.[9]

As in England, Quakers were specifically targeted. Their religious enthusiasm led some of them to walk around naked, swear, disrupt church services, and "quake at the name of God," and their belief in the equality of all before God led them to condemn church authorities and government. So, Quakers—both men and women—were frequently the target of persecution such as this, meted out in Connecticut:

> The Drum was Beat, the People gather'd, Norton was fetch'd and stripp'd to the Waste, and set with his back to the Magistrates, and given in their View Thirty-six cruel Stripes with a knotted cord, and his hand made fast in the Stocks where they had set his Body before, and burn'd very deep with a Red-hot Iron with H. for Heresie.[10]

Between 1659 and 1661, four obstinate Quakers were even executed in the Massachusetts Bay Colony.[11]

But some colonists yearned for the freedom to follow their own conscience in matters of religion. The first colony to establish freedom of religion was Rhode Island, founded by the renegade Puritan Roger Williams in 1636 after he was kicked out of Massachusetts for spreading "newe & dangerous opinions."[12] Ahead of his time, Williams went so far as to argue that "a permission of the most Paganish, Jewish, Turkish or anti-Christian consciences and worship" should "be granted to all men, in all nations and countries."[13] His colony quickly attracted like-minded religious contrarians and became informally known as "Rogue Island." When Charles II granted the colony a Royal Charter in 1663, the king stressed the colonists' wish "to hold forth a lively experiment, that a most flourishing civil state may stand and best be maintained . . . with a full liberty in religious concernments."[14]

Similar experiments characterized a number of other colonies. Maryland was formed in 1632 as a safe space for persecuted Catholics and named in honor of Charles I's Catholic wife, Queen Henrietta Maria. To ensure peace between Protestants and Catholics, the colony adopted the Maryland Toleration Act in 1649, including language that would later be repeated in the free exercise clause of the First Amendment.[15] Religious freedom was also formalized in Pennsylvania, founded by the Quaker William Penn in 1681 as a refuge for his church. Pennsylvania's Act for Freedom of Conscience from 1682 declared:

No person . . . who shall confess and acknowledge one almighty God to be the creator . . . and who professes him or herself obliged in conscience to live peaceably and quietly under the civil government, shall in any case be molested or prejudiced for his or her conscientious persuasion or practice."[16]

These codifications of tolerance were signs of real progress. The mere coexistence of Protestants and Catholics under equal protection of the law was a big achievement. So was the creation of thriving pluralist alternatives to the religious fundamentalism and uniformity of New England, which undermined the claim that strict religious uniformity was necessary for a well-functioning polity. As the Dutch Republic had shown in the Old World, decentralized authority is fertile soil for the cultivation of tolerance.

But freedom of religion did not immediately translate into unbridled freedom of speech. Both Pennsylvania and Maryland punished blasphemous speech and what we today might call "religious hatred" aimed at other sects. Blasphemy, including the denial of the Trinity, was a capital offense in Maryland. According to the Maryland Toleration

Act, it was also illegal to insult another person or group with religious slurs like "heretick," "Roundhead," and "popish priest."[17] Pennsylvania's Act for Freedom of Conscience punished anyone who abused or ridiculed another person for her religion as a disturber of the peace.[18] In the words of political theorist Teresa Bejan, the "similarity" of these colonial laws "to modern-day (European) religious insult laws—and their contrast with the First Amendment—is striking."[19]

Neither did religious tolerance translate into political freedom of speech. Marylanders were required to "honor, respect and obey" the colony's proprietor Lord Baltimore. In Rhode Island, it was a crime to "use words of contempt against a chief officer, especially in the execution of his office." The colony went further, punishing open criticism of its assembly's acts and orders with a fine, thirty lashes, or up to a year in jail.[20] Not even William Penn, a former prisoner of conscience, welcomed political dissent. He instituted prepublication censorship, and Pennsylvania's Frame of Government from 1682 punished "all scandalous and malicious reporters, backbiters, defamers and spreaders of false news."[21] And these were not empty threats. At a 1683 council presided over by Penn himself, an Anthony Weston was sentenced to thirty whip lashes at the marketplace in Philadelphia for displaying "great presumption and contempt of this government and authority."[22] As the seventeenth century progressed, punishments for seditious speech became rarer and milder, but it was not until the following century that radical ideas from the motherland mass-converted Americans to the idea that free speech is the great bulwark of liberty.

Under these conditions, America's first generation of journalists had to walk a tightrope to avoid offending the authorities. *Publick Occurrences*, the very first newspaper published in colonial America, printed a grand total of one issue before folding in 1690. Slamming Britain's Native American allies and intimating that Louis XIV "used to lie with the Son's Wife" provoked the government of the

Massachusetts Bay Colony to shut down the paper and burn all un-sold copies.[23] To prevent similar problems from arising, the governor released a public order "strictly forbidding any person or persons for the future to Set forth any thing in Print without Licence."[24]

Journalism remained a risky business in early eighteenth-century America. The Boston-based *New-England Courant* drew official ire in June 1722 when its editor James Franklin published a satirical remark on the government's lethargic attempts to battle piracy. The infuriated authorities sent him to jail for three weeks. Luckily, James's sixteen-year-old brother Benjamin was ready to step in while James was in prison. Benjamin Franklin worked as an apprentice, but he had already published several essays in the *Courant* without his brother's knowledge under the pseudonym Silence Dogood. He protested James's imprisonment by reprinting the 1721 essay from the *London Journal* that later became known as *Cato's Letter* No. 15, including the passage, "Without Freedom of Thought, there can be no such Thing as Wisdom; and no such Thing as publick Liberty, without Freedom of Speech."[25]

A new scandal erupted in 1723 when James published a let-ter in the *Courant* insulting the powerful minister Cotton Mather. This time he was warned by the government that he was no lon-ger allowed to print anything without preapproval. True to form, James disregarded the order and printed an unlicensed edition of the *Courant*, then went into hiding and let Benjamin run the show again. James finally gave up and let the *Courant* fold in 1726.[26] In the meantime, Benjamin had struck out on his own and relocated to the City of Brotherly Love, where he established the *Pennsylvania Gazette* in 1728. In November 1737, Franklin published an article, "On Freedom of Speech and the Press," in which he argued, "Free-dom of speech is a principal pillar of a free government; when this support is taken away, the constitution of a free society is dissolved, and tyranny is erected on its ruins."[27] But as we shall soon see, even Franklin wasn't always prepared to practice what he preached.

Perhaps the most prominent free speech clash in early American journalism was the Zenger case in New York. It took place in 1735, two years after a circle of prominent political figures founded the *New-York Weekly Journal* as a platform for criticizing the new governor, William Cosby. They had plenty of reasons to attack Cosby. Not only was he greedy, petty, corrupt, unprincipled, and vindictive, but he also controlled New York's sole newspaper—the *New York Gazette*—which functioned a bit like an eighteenth-century version of *Pravda*, praising "Cosby the mild, the happy, good and great."[28] Cosby's enemies decided to give the governor a taste of his own medicine and set up America's first opposition newspaper.[29]

The *Journal* savagely attacked the governor with mockery and hard-hitting pieces published anonymously or under pseudonyms like the increasingly popular "Cato." Cosby was accused of endangering the "liberties and properties" of the people with "slavery." One satirical hit piece warned that "a Monkey of the larger sort . . . has lately broke his Chain, and run into the Country" and promised that "whosoever shall take this little mischievous Animal, and send him back to his Master, so that he may be chained up again, shall have for his Reward a Thousand thanks."[30] Everyone knew Cosby was the ape in question. The hit pieces were mixed with a heavy dose of *Cato's Letters*, whose radical message was tailor-made for the anti-Cosby faction. Cato showed that free speech was not only a natural right, but also the bulwark of liberty trumping the good name of governors who set aside their role as the people's representatives for personal gain and arbitrary power. Since most New Yorkers thought Cosby a petty tyrant, the newspaper's anonymous editor James Alexander bet that popular opinion would be swayed by Cato's principles. So if and when Cosby retaliated, the people would see it as confirmation that "only the wicked governors of men dread what is said of them."[31]

Cosby was not exactly famous for his sense of humor or thick skin. He soon ran out of patience with "those insolent and scandalous papers"[32] and had his chief justice request a grand jury to try the paper for seditious libel. But the jurors refused to indict because of the anonymity of the authors.[33] Cosby and the Governor's Council took matters into their own hands and ordered four libelous editions of the *Journal* burned.[34] Though the obstinate grand jury may have stymied Cosby temporarily, he had another avenue in legislative privilege, which allowed provincial assemblies to summarily imprison seditious writers for "contempt," since the people's representatives were not to be second-guessed for their official actions outside the assembly.[35] This process bypassed the judicial system and thus the complications of due process. But both the provincial and the city legislatures rejected Cosby's advances, citing the need to preserve "liberty of the press."[36] So Cosby turned to the instrument of an "information," which allowed a prosecution to circumvent the need for a grand jury indictment. Consequently, the *Journal*'s official publisher, the poor German immigrant John Peter Zenger, a mere surrogate pawn for the paper's real editor, Alexander, and the anti-Cosby conspirators, was charged with seditious libel and sent to prison on remand.[37] With a biased judge, an intimidated jury, a court-appointed defense attorney, and the law firmly against him, Zenger looked doomed.

But then the case took a twist worthy of a Hollywood drama. On the first day of the trial, a certain Andrew Hamilton walked into a full courtroom in New York City Hall and identified himself as Zenger's new defense counsel. Hamilton was one of the best and most experienced trial lawyers in the colonies.[38] Hamilton deployed a high-risk, all-or-nothing strategy. To the gasping courtroom's surprise, he admitted that Zenger was responsible for publishing the impugned articles. The prosecutor could not believe his luck. He immediately moved to declare the case closed since the job of the jury was to determine only whether Zenger had published the articles, not whether the content was seditious. But Hamilton was far from done. He appealed to the jury, asking them whether the allegations against Cosby weren't "notoriously known to be true"—a point that the *Journal* had already hammered home in advance. Taking a page out of *Cato's Letters*, he argued that "the Words themselves must be libelous, that is, *false, scandalous and seditious*, or else we are not guilty." He also disputed that "the just Complaints of a Number of Men, who suffer under a bad Administration, is libelling that Administration," and cleverly compared the prosecution of those who spoke truth to corrupted power to the notorious Star Chamber trials. In other words, Hamilton asked the jury to disregard established common law and declare truth a defense to seditious libel.

Hamilton delivered a closing statement that elevated the case from petty political dispute to a principled question about the nature of American liberty. Hamilton appealed directly to the jurors:

> I make no Doubt but that your upright Conduct, this Day, will not only entitle you to the Love and Esteem of your Fellow-Citizens; but every Man who prefers Freedom to a Life of Slavery will bless and honour You, as Men who have baffled the Attempt of Tyranny; and by an impartial and uncorrupt Verdict, have laid a noble Foundation for securing to ourselves, our Posterity, and our Neighbors, That, to which Nature and the Laws of our Country have given us a Right—the Liberty—both of exposing and opposing arbitrary Power . . . by speaking and writing Truth.

The attorney general and chief justice scrambled to control the damage. They reminded the jury that truth did not make it legal to smear the governor with poisonous writings whose bad tendencies threaten public order. But Hamilton's words appealed to jurors who he knew had read and discussed the *Journal's* punchy free speech advocacy lifted from *Cato*. After brief deliberations, the jury chose to acquit Zenger—"Upon which there were three Huzzas in the Hall, which was crowded with People."[39]

The verdict was a milestone for press freedom in America. Legally, the common-law crime of seditious libel stood intact, with no defense of truth. But in practice, the act of jury nullification all but ended seditious libel prosecutions in colonial courts. The Zenger case was publicized all over America and cited with every new free-press controversy, and in its wake, popular opinion swung so far in favor of an expanded right to freedom of speech that colonial governors could no longer rely on juries to punish dissent.[40] The Zenger case was crucial to the creation of a culture of free speech in the New World that would prove decisive in future battles over the limits of dissent after American independence.

Unfortunately for the colonial loudmouths, the Zenger case did little to rein in the odious concept of legislative privilege. In the 1750s, the New York Assembly still jailed writers and printers who had maligned its "Honour, Justice and Authority." In fact, the mere printing of the proceedings and speeches of the assemblies was a punishable breach of the privilege.[41]

A particularly egregious example of legislative privilege took place in Pennsylvania in 1758, during the Seven Years' War between Britain and France. The Anglican judge William Moore had long been unpopular with the Quaker-dominated assembly because of his outspoken opposition to their pacifist principles. In an open letter to the governor published in the *Pennsylvania Gazette* in late 1757, the assembly demanded Moore's removal from office on ground of corruption. Insisting on his innocence, Moore had a rebuttal published in several newspapers, including a paper cofounded by the reverend William Smith. Another prominent Anglican, Smith had also made himself unpopular with the Quaker majority by vocally promoting a more aggressive stance against the French. When a newly elected assembly met in 1758, it took the opportunity to silence its detractors and arrested both of them. Moore was found guilty of "false, scandalous, virulent and seditious Libel" against the House, government, and constitution of Pennsylvania. His publications were ordered to be burned and he was ordered to be held in jail indefinitely with no possibility of bail or "any writ of *Habeas Corpus.*" The assembly then declared Smith "guilty of promoting and publishing Moore's libel"—a week before the trial was due to start. Like his partner in crime, Smith was sent to prison indefinitely without habeas corpus. When the two prisoners were released after three months, the assembly ordered them reimprisoned, but Moore had gone into hiding and Smith absconded to England where he petitioned the Privy Council for relief.[42]

Unfortunately for Smith, his petition was opposed by the official agent of Pennsylvania's assembly in London: Benjamin Franklin, the same Silence Dogood who had once argued that "freedom of speech is a principal pillar of a free government" without which a "free society dissolves" and "tyranny is erected on its ruins." Struck by Milton's Curse, he was now vigorously defending legislative privilege in a case that historian Leonard Levy denounced as a "mock trial before a kangaroo court" worse than Star Chamber justice.[43] Franklin insisted that the assembly, which was the representative of the people, needed legislative privilege, because "without such power no Authority or decency can be preserved." Moreover, Smith was but "a common Scribbler of Libels and false abusive Papers."[44] Fortunately for Smith, the Privy Council thought the assembly had gone too far and found in his favor, effectively overturning the arrest warrant in 1759.[45]

So why would a man like Franklin support a practice that silenced the people? The answer lies in a—by modern standards—idiosyncratic conception of popular sovereignty. The assemblies saw themselves as both the people's representatives and defenders against the executive. Consequently, undermining the assemblies undermined the freedom of the people.[46] The idea that the bulwark of liberty also had to protect the people from their own representatives had not yet clearly crystallized among American colonialists. They were influenced by *Cato's Letters*, which chiefly warned against the executive and ministerial plots rather than overzealous parliaments. Independence was what forced Americans—finally free to regulate themselves—to consider where they should draw the line between collective and individual freedom.

A Revolution of the Mind

In 1815, eighty-year-old John Adams reflected on the American Revolution in a letter to his old friend and sometimes bitter rival, Thomas Jefferson:

> What do we mean by the Revolution? The war? That was no part of the Revolution; it was only an effect and consequence of it. The Revolution was in the minds of the people, and this was effected, from 1760 to 1775, in the course of fifteen years before a drop of blood was shed at Lexington.[47]

To Adams, the decisive battlegrounds of the Revolution had not been Lexington or Yorktown, but newspapers and pamphlets. The battles had not been fought with guns and steel, but with pens and paper. And the main prize had not been enemy territory, but public opinion. More than four hundred pamphlets discussed the souring relationship between Britain and the American colonies between 1750 and 1776. In 1783, the number swelled to 1,500.[48] Similarly, the number of British-American newspapers more than doubled from around twenty in 1760 to around fifty in 1775.[49]

Print technology had democratized America's public sphere. Here's how a contemporary observer described Americans in 1774:

> They are a well-informed, reasoning commonalty, too, perhaps the most of any on earth, because of the free intercourse between man and man that prevails in America . . . together with the freedom

and general circulation of newspapers, and the eagerness and leisure of the people to read them, or to listen to those who do.[50]

But you'll be disappointed if you imagine pamphleteering as polite debate among learned individuals adhering to a strict code of reasoned argumentation. "Pamphlet wars" often *started out* with reason and arguments. But they quickly descended into an eighteenth-century version of flaming, trolling, name-calling, motivated reasoning, and butchering of straw men in chains of pamphlets responding to each other in increasingly shrill language.[51] Political tribalism—then called factionalism—was alive and kicking in the eighteenth century. And the reasonable and well-informed Americans could become rowdy and rebellious, particularly when imbibing. One Loyalist complained that people met "at taverns, where they talk politicks, get drunk, damn King, Ministers and Taxes; and *vow* they will follow any measures proposed to them by their demagogues, however repugnant to religion, reason and common sense."[52] One such rowdy tavern was the Green Dragon in Boston, where Paul Revere, Samuel Adams, John Hancock, and other members of the Sons of Liberty—a secretive group of American colonists resisting British colonial overreach—would hatch their secret plans on a potent mixture of coffee, rum, and *Cato's Letters*.[53]

Add to this that the principles of *Cato's Letter* No. 15 had fatally wounded the enforcement of seditious libel laws, as witnessed by the Zenger case. It was not surprising that when the chain reaction leading to war and independence erupted in 1765, the British authorities were powerless to stop the onslaught of patriotic sentiment.

The first real rupture in American-British relations occurred in 1765, when the British government announced the Stamp Act, a new tax that required paper to be bought from and stamped by a governmental agent.[54] A virtual tsunami of dissent soon broke out in pamphlets, broadsides, and newspapers across the American colonies, with the printing press functioning as "the engine moving the protest forward," cementing both the principle and practice of free speech as a central pillar of colonial American identity.[55]

To the American colonists, taxation without representation was nothing short of slavery—an outrageous claim given the very real enslavement of Black Africans by leading colonists, but one that nonetheless came to be repeated in newspapers across the colonies. An issue of the radical newspaper the *Constitutional Courant* that went viral in the streets of New York in September 1765 warned its audience against "the vile minions of tyranny" and "the chains of abject slavery just ready to be riveted about our necks." The anonymous writers encouraged readers to "never . . . pay one farthing of this tax."[56] The lieutenant governor of New York warned headquarters in London that the colonial newspapers were filled with "every falsehood" and seditiously stirring up the people to disobey not only the authority of Parliament to tax the colonies but even the very authority of Parliament over the colonies as such.[57]

No one undermined the Stamp Act more systematically than Benjamin Edes and John Gill, the irascible editors of the *Boston Gazette*.[58] When the Stamp Act crisis unfolded, they launched an unapologetic crusade against the Act, calling its supporters "dirty Sycophants," "ministerial Hacks," "detestable Villains," and "insatiable Vultures."[59] They also published critical essays by writers like James Otis, James Warren, and John and Samuel Adams. In an article printed in the *Boston Gazette*, John Adams attacked the Stamp Act as a calculated attack on the colonists' freedom of speech and information. It seemed "very manifest from the [Stamp Act] itself, that a design is form'd to strip us in a great measure of the means of knowledge, by loading the Press, the Colleges, and even an Almanack and a News-Paper, with restraints and duties."[60]

The Patriots even resorted to spreading some genuine fake news. In May 1765, the great orator and firebrand Patrick Henry proposed a series of resolves against the Stamp Act in Virginia's assembly, the House of Burgesses. The most radical resolves more than flirted with rebellion, insisting that colonists were free to ignore tax laws not imposed by their own representatives. After fierce debate in the assembly, Henry's famous oratory genius managed to browbeat a slim majority into passing five of the resolutions, while two were rejected as too extreme. But the next day, the legislators got cold feet and dropped the fifth (and most radical) resolution. That did not stop Northern newspapers from printing *all* the Virginia Resolves—including the ones that were defeated or rescinded. Instead of the watered-down prescription for polite dialogue that Virginia's assembly had actually enacted, newspaper readers were presented with Henry's undiluted recipe for confrontational resistance[61] The fake resolutions quickly spread to other newspapers, with very real consequences. Henry's undiluted Virginia Resolves soon turned from fiction into fact, as eight colonies passed similar resolutions.[62]

But rousing the chattering classes who read pamphlets and newspapers was not enough to produce real change. The Patriots had to get the lowly commoners on board, too. To do so, they made effective use of symbolic speech in the form of parades, flags, political cartoons, emblems, liberty trees, and liberty poles—wooden poles erected as a symbolic protest against tyranny. Some even resorted to hanging effigies of public officials.[63] This combination of eloquent commentary, fake news, propaganda, symbolic speech, and naked intimidation did the job.[64] Parliament repealed the Stamp Act in the spring of 1766. But it was only a tactical retreat. The repeal was accompanied by a Declaratory Act, in which Parliament insisted it had the rightful authority to pass binding laws on the American colonies "in all cases whatsoever."[65] And just to show the American rebels who really wore the pants, it passed the so-called Townshend Duties on commodities like glass, paper, and tea in 1767. The levies sparked a new burst of angry pamphlets and essays.[66] In his highly influential *Letters from a Farmer in Pennsylvania*, John Dickinson ominously warned the English government, "If at length it becomes UNDOUBTED that an inveterate resolution is formed to annihilate the liberties of the governed, the *English* history affords frequent examples of resistance by force."[67]

The Patriots also fired paper bullets at their local officials. Massachusetts's governor, Sir Francis Bernard, and his lieutenant-governor and chief justice, Thomas Hutchinson, were frequent targets of merciless attacks, especially from the *Boston Gazette*. By 1767, Hutchinson had had enough. He refused to be "treated in the most abusive Manner, and vilified beyond all Bounds."[68] To shut up the bullies, he made several appeals to a grand jury to indict the editors of the *Boston Gazette* for seditious libel. Formally, the case was a no-brainer. The newspaper's attacks on Hutchinson and Bernard were textbook examples of seditious libel. But Hutchinson was in for a rude awakening when his appeals were rejected. Bostonians had no appetite for prosecuting their own and had come to regard even fierce criticism of their rulers as legitimate. Next, Governor Bernard turned to the popular assembly, which could bypass the grand jury system and punish offensive writers by way of its legislative privilege. But, as in the Zenger case, the House turned him down flat with a humiliating lecture on the principles of *Cato's Letters*: "The Liberty of the Press is a great Bulwark of the Liberty of the People: It is, therefore, the incumbent Duty of those who are constituted the Guardians of the People's Rights to defend them and maintain it."[69] Samuel Adams, writing under the pseudonym Populus, rubbed salt in the wounds in his column in the *Boston Gazette*: "THERE is nothing so *fretting* and *vexatious*; nothing so justly TERRIBLE to tyrants, and their tools and abettors, as a FREE PRESS," he sneered, adding that a free press was "*the bulwark of the People's Liberties.*"[70]

The outcry over the Townshend Acts had barely subsided before the British government was hit by a third wave of angry pamphlets and articles in March 1770, this one triggered by an incident now known as the Boston Massacre, in which British troops opened fire on an angry and physically abusive mob and killed five protestors. The renewed backlash contributed to the repeal of the Townshend Acts in April 1770. The heated writings tapered off in response, and for a while it looked like the British government might manage to appease the Patriots. But in 1773, Parliament made the fatal mistake of granting the failing East India Company a monopoly on the importation and sale of tea to the colonies.

The colonists, who had been purchasing smuggled tea to avoid Townshend taxes, complained bitterly about yet more taxation without representation, which a Patriot group denounced as "a violent attack upon the liberties of America."[71] The new flurry of protests culminated in the iconic Boston Tea Party on December 16, 1773. A group of angry colonists, reportedly linked to the Sons of Liberty, dressed up as Native Americans and dumped 342 chests of precious tea into Boston Harbor. The furious British government struck back in the spring of 1774 with a series of Coercive Acts—which the Patriots renamed as the Intolerable Acts—designed to bring Massachusetts to heel and serve as a warning to the rest of the colonies.

In the words of John Adams, this was when the British government "threw off the mask" and revealed its true tyranny.[72] The time for action had come. Twelve colonies (Georgia sat this one out) sent delegates to the First Continental Congress in Philadelphia in the fall of 1774 to discuss the next move, setting themselves on a path that would ultimately lead to war the following year.

Those who supported the Crown made use of the press as well. The years 1774 and 1775 saw a marked increase in Tory pamphlets arguing against the brewing revolutionary dissent. Like those of the Patriots, Loyalist pamphlets were a mashup of reasoned arguments, propaganda, and personal abuse, including accusations that George Washington was romantically involved with a washer's daughter.[73]

As hostilities with England intensified, the same Patriots who had called for freedom of speech began using systematic intimidation tactics to silence Loyalist printers and newspapers, applying what author Robert W. T. Martin calls "an active program of threats, public exposure, financial sanctions, and, ultimately, physical violence." We might call it a "Patriot's Veto." The most prominent Loyalist newspaper was the *New-York Gazetteer*, printed by James Rivington. Shortly after the Revolutionary War broke out, Rivington's print shop was vandalized by seventy-five men on horseback. He tried to continue publishing, but not for long. A few months later, a mob marched all the way from New Haven to New York to destroy Rivington's print shop and confiscate his type. The gutting of the *New-York Gazetteer* was effectively the end of the loyalist Tory press.[74]

Few on the Patriot side saw the intimidation of Loyalists as a problem. Even James Madison was on board with the Patriot's Veto: "I wish most heartily we had Rivington & his ministerial Gazetteers for 24. hours in this place," he wrote in a private letter. "Execrable as their designs are, they would meet with adequate punishment."[75] Like many throughout history, in a time of national crisis, Patriots reserved the great bulwark of liberty for friends, not foes.

The conflict between England and colonial America escalated into full-blown war in April 1775. To quote John Adams, "the Instruments of Warfare" had changed "from the Pen to the Sword." Yet the Patriots still hadn't decided if their goal was independence or, as Adams put it, "only to keep their old privileges."[76] Clearly, the fence sitters needed an injection of common sense; in early January 1776, a new anonymous pamphlet delivered it.

Common Sense made an unapologetic case for independence, savaging the institution of hereditary monarchy and calling for popular sovereignty and equality.[77] Its author was soon revealed to be Thomas Paine, a British corset maker who had arrived in America in 1774. According to one member of the Continental Congress, the pamphlet was "greedily bought up and read by all ranks of people."[78] It may have sold up to seventy-five thousand copies,[79] helping push indecisive Americans toward independence. In April of 1776,

George Washington told a friend, "by private Letters which I have lately received from Virginia, I find common sense is working a wonderful change there in the Minds of many Men."[80] A perhaps slightly jealous John Adams admitted in a letter to Thomas Jefferson many years later that "history is to ascribe the American Revolution to Thomas Paine."[81]

On July 4, 1776, the Congress approved Jefferson's amended draft of the Declaration of Independence, which proclaimed that liberty and the unalienable rights of man were self-evident truths—without saying exactly what those rights entailed. However, several states were writing their own constitutions and bills of rights. Three of them—Virginia, Pennsylvania, and Delaware—explicitly protected freedom of speech, press, religion, or all three.

The Virginia Declaration of Rights was ratified on June 12—almost a month before the Declaration of Independence. Section 12 elevated *Cato's Letters* to state law: "That the freedom of the press is one of the great bulwarks of liberty, and can never be restrained but by despotic governments."[82] Pennsylvania's constitution went even further. It included a declaration of rights asserting "that the people have a right to freedom of speech, and of writing, and publishing their sentiments; therefore the freedom of the press ought not to be restrained."[83] This language secured both freedom of speech and freedom of the press—a significant improvement over the censorious governance established by William Penn.

———

ON NOVEMBER 15, 1777, THE CONTINENTAL CONGRESS adopted the Articles of Confederation that served as the first constitution of the loosely United States when finally ratified by all thirteen states in 1781. By 1787, many saw the need to replace the articles with a new constitution—one that created a republic with a stronger federal government empowered to adopt laws binding on all states and citizens. Moreover, while the Articles of Confederation had guaranteed freedom of speech and debate, this applied only to members of Congress, much like the English Bill of Rights from 1689.[84] This raised the question of whether the time was ripe for a federal bulwark of liberty protecting Americans from all branches of the government.

The new Constitution was signed in Philadelphia on September 17, 1787, after what John Adams called "the greatest single effort of national deliberation that the world has ever seen."[85] In the words of constitutional scholar Akhil Reed Amar, "Americans *in the enactment process itself* exercised and exemplified an amazingly vigorous freedom of expression. Sharp-elbowed political maneuvering there was aplenty; widespread punishment of exuberant expression there was not."[86]

It is hardly surprising, then, that much of the deliberation centered on protecting the right of the people to speak freely. The Constitution itself barely touched upon the subject, apart from limiting the crime of treason to "overt acts" and providing members of Congress immunity from any "Speech or Debate in either House."[87] This lack of fundamental rights—especially free speech—was one of the main arguments a group who became known as the Anti-Federalists used to oppose the ratification of the Constitution. Once it was adopted, the Anti-Federalists turned their efforts to the passage of the Bill of Rights. Free speech was essential, not only for liberty as such, but also for the self-governance and self-improvement of all members of society, high and low. As one Anti-Federalist wrote: "The most illiterate may now discern the usefulness of the press in a free state. It gives all the people an opportunity to learn to be wise, to choose or refuse, in an important affair."[88]

The Federalists dismissed the idea of a bill of rights. For one thing, nothing in the Constitution gave the federal government any authority to control speech or the press. "Why for instance," asked Alexander Hamilton, "should it be said, that the liberty of the press shall not be restrained, when no power is given by which restrictions may be imposed?"[89] Madison pointed out "the inefficacy of a bill of rights," proven by "repeated violations of these parchment barriers," though he would soon change his mind.[90]

The Anti-Federalists were not convinced. Their distrust was further fed by the fact that Anti-Federalist publications—already vastly outnumbered by Federalist writings—were sometimes stopped from wider circulation by the postmaster general.[91] Most importantly, Anti-Federalists detected elitist and illiberal attitudes among more conservative Federalists who seemed to think of press freedom in Blackstonian terms and recoil at the idea of "the bulk of the people" participating actively in public affairs, which were better left to their elite representatives. Benjamin Workman, writing under the pen name Philadelphiensis, gave voice to Anti-Federalist fears of Federalist designs and machinations in a bitterly sarcastic—and, as it turned out, eerily prophetic—article in the *Independent Gazetteer* in 1787:

> I wonder that our *well born* should allow such mean fellows to write against this their *government*; such base wretches ought not to live in the same country with gentlemen. . . . Ah! what glorious days are coming; how I anticipate the brilliancy of the American court! . . . here is the president going in state to the senate house to confirm the law for the abolition of the liberty of the press. Men and brethren will not these things be so?[92]

You might say that the Anti-Federalists favored an egalitarian model of free speech—along the lines of the Levellers—with (unacknowledged) roots in the Athenian concepts of *isēgoría* and *parrhēsía*, while the more conservative Federalists favored a more narrow and elitist conception of free speech with roots in the Roman republican ideal of *libertas*.

But there were also those who supported both the new constitution and a bill of rights, not least among them Thomas Jefferson. Eventually, Madison joined their ranks. In June 1789, the former skeptic introduced a number of draft amendments for a bill of rights in which freedom of speech and the press was included. Madison explained the need for a bill of rights by contrasting America with Britain, where the 1689 Bill of Rights protected against encroachment by the executive, not Parliament. Nor did the British Bill of Rights secure free speech for the people represented by Parliament. But in America, the people—not Congress—were ultimately sovereign; members of Congress were the servants, not the masters, of those who elected them. From this, it followed that the people had a right to scrutinize and criticize those who exercised power on their behalf.[93] A bill of rights would raise "barriers against power in all forms and departments of government."[94] Madison's draft of what would become the First Amendment fused the idea that egalitarian free speech is necessary for a sovereign people to rule itself with *Cato's* assertion that free speech is the bulwark of liberty. Free speech would be safe both from democratic majorities intent on administering hemlock to new Socrateses and from designs to thwart dissent by the newly empowered federal government—or so he intended.

The draft had the following wording: "The people shall not be deprived or abridged of their right to speak, to write, or to publish their sentiments; and the freedom of the press, as one of the great bulwarks of liberty, shall be inviolable."[95] The reference to *Cato* did not survive the ratification process, but Madison's intent was preserved in the First Amendment as ratified in 1791: "Congress shall make no law . . . abridging the freedom of speech, or of the press."[96] Crucially, Madison also proposed that "no state shall violate the equal rights of conscience, or the freedom of the press."[97] This mirrored Madison's fear that state governments would be the worst offenders against free speech, given that these—not the federal government—would be those whose laws and authority Americans were most frequently subjected to. In fact, Madison believed this to be "the most valuable amendment on the whole list."[98] Alas, it was rejected—with fateful consequences for free speech in America.

Still, with the ratification of the First Amendment, Madison was satisfied that "the right of freedom of speech is secured; the liberty of the press is expressly declared to be beyond the reach of this Government."[99] One might therefore have thought that the British legacy of Blackstonian press freedom and seditious libel had been laid to rest for good, and that the egalitarian free speech ideals of the Levellers had finally been given their (unacknowledged) due. But Blackstonianism and sedition would rise again like zombies to torment Americans challenging the established order well into the twentieth century. In fact, less than a decade after ratification of the First Amendment, Philadelphiensis's sarcastic warning about the federal government's impending assault on the liberty of the press would become all too real.

7

Revolution and Reaction

When revolutionary fever crossed the Atlantic from America back to the Old World, the Dutch were the first to catch it. The result was what historian Jonathan Israel calls "Europe's first avowedly democratic movement."[1]

While other European states' systems of centralized censorship stifled discussion of the American Revolution, the decentralized Dutch press had a head start.[2] A central figure in this development was the politician Joan Derk van der Capellen tot den Pol, who translated American arguments for free speech and dissent. In his anonymous 1781 pamphlet *To the people of the Netherlands*, he accused the regime of conspiring with the British to suppress ancient Dutch liberties, just as George III had done in the American colonies.[3] Echoing *Cato's Letters*, he stressed the importance of a free press:

> Take care of the liberty of the press, for that is the only support of your national liberty. If we have no liberty to speak freely to our fellow-citizens, or to give them timely advice, it will be very easy for our oppressors to act their sinister parts; and it is for that reason that those, who cannot bear to hear their conduct enquired

into, are always exclaiming against the liberty of speech and of the press, and could wish that nothing was printed or sold without permission.[4]

The estates proved his point by promptly banning the pamphlet. But it was already too late.[5]

As copies spread throughout the Netherlands, so too did cells of revolutionary *Patriotten* (inspired by American Patriots). In newspapers and pamphlets, they portrayed the stadtholder—the chief magistrate—as a corrupt and drunken fool, demanded democratic self-government, and repeated Van der Capellen's call for freedom of the press. According to one Patriot, "there would not remain a trace or shadow of liberty" without press freedom.[6] The authorities responded by issuing fines and occasionally jailing the editors of the Patriot newspapers.[7] But the embattled revolutionaries received no support from veteran champion of Dutch press freedom Elie Luzac. He had previously defended the free speech of atheists and defeated attempts at introducing prior religious censorship, but Luzac was no fan of democracy, nor of appeals to the political instincts of the masses. "Newspaper writers, who turn their liberty to relate the news into the impertinence of publishing everything that surfaces in their raging and sick brains, are a disgrace to nature and the pests of society," he groused in the early 1780s.[8]

The pests were undeterred. The Dutch Patriots organized themselves into American-style militias after 1783. Armed conflicts broke out and the Patriots took control of major cities like Amsterdam and The Hague, where the stadtholder fled his palace. The republic was on the brink of civil war. The king of Prussia, whose sister was married to the Dutch stadtholder, intervened in the fall of 1787. He crushed the Patriots, dissolved their militias, banned political meetings, and censored the radical press. Tens of thousands of Patriots found refuge in France, where Louis XVI welcomed them, oblivious to the rising dangers at home—just as the Dutch had welcomed

French Protestants fleeing France after Louis XIV revoked the Edict of Nantes a century before.[9] Soon, Louis would wish that he had been able to deal with revolutionaries as effectively as the Prussians had done.

Free Speech and Political Heresy in Revolutionary France

Revolutionaries found more success in France, where decades of expensive wars, overspending, and bad fiscal policies had drained the royal coffers. In 1787, Louis XVI tried to push through a number of reforms, including a new uniform land tax—even for the nobility and clergy who used to be tax exempt. Unsurprisingly, the proposal was poorly received by the prelates and noblemen. They demanded a convention of the Estates-General (the three estates representing the clergy, the nobility, and the commoners) before they would approve anything. To make the financial and political situation even worse, the country was seething with unrest after two decades of bad harvests and soaring bread prices. By 1788, France was a powder keg waiting to explode.[10]

The king blinked first and summoned the Estates-General to a crisis meeting in Versailles in 1789. Before the assembly, the estates were invited to voice their grievances in lists known as *cahiers de doléances*. This request was interpreted as a de facto abolishment of the byzantine system of censorship that had caused so much grief for philosophes like Diderot and Voltaire in previous decades. Once the floodgates of speech were open, a sea of pamphlets called for more or less radical reform of the Old Regime. More than 80 percent of the *cahiers* demanded press freedom. But the three estates did not agree on the limits of free speech. The clergy, who were the most censorious, objected to attacks on religion. The nobility focused on protecting honor, while the Third Estate was most concerned with protecting morality or *mœurs*. Their clashes revealed how little common ground existed between the different elements of French society on the question of what exactly free speech entailed, with each faction unwilling to compromise on the issues they held most dear.[11]

The Estates-General was unable to cure the deep-seated divisions within the Old Regime. On June 17, 1789, after endless squabbling, the commoners of the Third Estate and a few of their sympathizers in the clergy and nobility proclaimed themselves the National Assembly and claimed sovereignty in the name of the French Nation. Three days later, in an indoor tennis court near the palace, they vowed not to disperse until they had a constitution. Riots erupted. On July 14, an armed mob broke into the Bastille prison—a notorious symbol of Old Regime repression, although by then largely empty of political prisoners. The French Revolution was in motion.

The National Assembly immediately set to work reforming the Old Regime. Unlike the Americans, who added the Bill of Rights after ratifying their constitution, the French focused on tackling principles first with a declaration of rights. The initial version was drafted by the Marquis de Lafayette with assistance from Thomas Jefferson, who served as American ambassador to France. The Declaration of the Rights of Man and of the Citizen was adopted by the National Assembly on August 26, 1789, and signed by Louis XVI on October 5. The landmark document protected freedom of expression, freedom of religion, and equality before the law—with some rather significant caveats.

The Declaration famously declared that "men are born and remain free and equal in rights."[12] But what did the term "men" mean? Did it include Protestants? Jews? Slaves? The non-propertied? Women? The universal language of the Declaration provoked a heretofore inconceivable public discussion of first principles relating to social, racial, religious, and gender equality, both in the National Assembly and in the press. One of the most radically egalitarian members of the National Assembly was the Marquis de Condorcet, who in 1788 was one of the cofounders of the abolitionist Society of the Friends of the Blacks. Condorcet promoted truly universal rights for people of both genders and all colors. He also argued against the punishment of homosexuality and other crimes that did not harm or violate the rights of others.[13]

But while Assembly members were largely open to change, the extraordinary range of Condorcet's proposals went beyond what most were willing to tolerate. Protestants were readily accepted as citizens despite reservations among some Catholics. The subject of Jews was more controversial, but they too received citizenship in September 1791. Over the next couple of years, the newly dubbed deputies also removed property qualifications for voting and extended citizenship to free Blacks, even—temporarily—abolishing slavery in the colonies.[14]

But the National Assembly was much less progressive on gender equality, even as an increasing number of French women began to demand equal rights, join political clubs, and take part in the public debate. Thousands of women had marched on Versailles in October 1789 and pressured Louis XVI to sign the Declaration—thereby helping secure the king's signature on a bill of rights that did not even recognize them as equal citizens. The playwright and protofeminist Olympe de Gouges had already raised a storm of controversy when she attacked slavery in her 1788 abolitionist play *The Slavery of the Blacks*, which was forced off stage by proslavery hecklers after three performances in 1790.[15] In 1791, she penned a Declaration of the Rights of Woman, insisting, "Woman is born free and remains equal to man in rights." These rights included the rights to free speech and freedom of opinion. "Woman has the right to mount the scaffold," she argued, "so she should have the right equally to mount the tribune."[16] As we will see, her point was all too tragically proven during the Reign of Terror only two years later. Condorcet also argued forcefully for the equality of women: "If we agree that men have rights simply by virtue of being capable of reason and moral ideas, then women should have precisely the same rights. Yet never in any so-called free constitution have women had the right of citizenship."[17] These arguments did not sway the National Convention (as the parliament was renamed after 1792). It banned women from forming and participating in political clubs on October 30, 1793, since they were "hardly capable of lofty conceptions and serious cogitations."[18]

Freedom of expression and print were granted, up to a point. Article 11 of the Declaration held that "the free communication of thoughts and opinions is one of the most precious of the rights of man. Every citizen may therefore speak, write, and print freely, if he accepts his own responsibility for any abuse of this liberty in the cases set by the law."[19] Everyone agreed that prepublication censorship was dead. But the definition of "abuse" was still to be determined, and the lack of agreement so apparent in the *cahiers* of the three estates remained strong. Lafayette proposed a draft with no limits on free speech based on American state constitutions, including Virginia's Bill of Rights with its *Cato*-inspired principles.[20] Ultimately, however, apprehensions about unlimited free speech led to the passage of an "abuse clause" that lacked a definition of the term itself, leaving the new "precious right" vulnerable to the pull of Milton's Curse and free speech entropy.[21]

Writers quickly learned that speech was still subject to repercussions, especially if it opposed the new political landscape or lingering notions of personal honor. As the debate about the legal limits of censorship grew increasingly toxic, radicals enforced their own "Revolutionary's Veto." In May 1790, several royalist newspapers were attacked by violent crowds who burned the newspapers in the streets. The Revolution had altered the fault lines; the speech crime of lèse majesté was now the speech crime of lèse nation. Officials routinely seized seditious pamphlets and arrested and intimidated journalists who criticized the National Assembly, despite having no legal grounds for their actions. Insults against the nation were suddenly subsumed under a sweeping blanket category of inflammatory speech against the government, its members, and its laws.[22]

The radical journalist Jean-Paul Marat protested that the act of writing, in and of itself, could not be seditious. But Marat's definition of press freedom was violently factionist. According to Marat, the "real criminals" of lèse nation were the counterrevolutionaries, and they should be crushed mercilessly.[23] A July 1790 article in his newspaper the *Friend of the People* argued, "Five or six hundred heads cut off would have assured your repose, freedom, and happiness."[24] In September 1792, he fanned the flames yet further and invited provincial radicals to join the bloodshed when mobs broke into the overflowing prisons of Paris and slaughtered up to 1,400, including priests who had refused to take an oath to the Revolution and other political prisoners.[25] Despite the government's many attempts to arrest Marat, his pen was only silenced when he was assassinated in his bathtub in 1793.

Ironically, given how events would unfold, the biggest advocates for free speech—initially—were the radicals known as Jacobins, including Maximilien Robespierre, who at this point argued that only actions, not words, could constitute sedition.[26] Another Jacobin, François Xavier Lanthenas, called for the "complete abrogation of all Old Regime laws concerning injurious speech, calumny, blasphemy, religious cults, the theater, and the press." These were to be replaced with "guidelines that consecrate the most unlimited freedom to communicate ideas."[27] But the Jacobins—then a minority—lost out.

In July 1791, the legislators passed a decree against "seditious speech," with the result that several journalists and printers were arrested in what historians like Charles Walton have dubbed the *petite terreur*. Robespierre objected loudly and referred to the language of Article 12 of Virginia's Bill of Rights: "The freedom of the press, one of the greatest avenues of liberty, can only be limited by despotic governments" (which had, in turn, been lifted from *Cato's Letters*).[28] Paying no heed to Robespierre, the National Assembly adopted a constitution and penal code in September 1791, officially defining the legal limits of free speech.

By June 1792, France was at war with Austria and Prussia, further radicalizing the revolutionaries who swiftly moved to abolish the monarchy in September 1792. As is often the case, a crisis of national security meant that tolerance for dissent reduced markedly. The parliament—renamed the National Convention—used a combination of laws and emergency decrees to target ever-wider categories of speech crimes. Anyone who opposed its laws could be arrested and punished for sedition.[29] And in this atmosphere, warring political factions weaponized the limits of free speech to serve as a sword with which to cut down their opponents, rather than as a shield to ensure the peaceful exchange of ideas necessary to viable political compromise. The National Convention set up a Revolutionary Tribunal to deal with enemies of the people. But attempts to define these enemies became mired in political tribalism, with the anti-Parisian and relatively moderate Girondins pitted against the ultraradical Montagnards.[30] The stakes were raised after Louis XVI was sent to the guillotine on January 21, 1793. While the republic was at war with a growing international coalition, a Catholic and royalist counterrevolution erupted on the home front to reestablish the authority of Throne and Altar.[31] An emergency Committee of Public Safety assumed provisional government of the republic, including the Revolutionary Tribunal, in April.

By now even Tom Paine, who had become a member of the National Convention, was beginning to panic. In a letter to the president of the Committee of Public Safety, the Montagnard Georges Danton, he voiced his fear that, if the toxic atmosphere continued, "all authority" would "be destroyed."[32] Paine was ready to compromise free speech to avoid such a disaster: "Calumny is a species of Treachery that ought to be punished as well as any other kind of Treachery."[33] Startling words from a man who had narrowly escaped the harsh sedition laws of England the previous year, as we will see.

Condorcet and the Girondins—with input from Tom Paine—had proposed a new constitution and a revised set of rights in February 1793, expanding the freedoms of speech and the press without the limitations of the 1789 Declaration of Rights.[34] But before it could be ratified, the Montagnards won the power struggle. The Girondins were brutally purged from the National Convention and arrested in early June. Ironically, that did not stop the Convention from adopting its own constitution later that month, with strong speech protections and without the 1789 abuse clause, although both the spirit and the letter were systematically disregarded once the Montagnards were safely in power with no intention of tolerating dissent.[35]

Soon the Terror was unleashed. The infamous Law of Suspects of September 17, 1793, called for the arrest of "those who, by their conduct, associations, comments, or writings have shown themselves partisans of tyranny and enemies of liberty."[36] The Girondin deputies who had been arrested in June were sent to the guillotine on October 31. Olympe de Gouges, who had objected to Louis XVI's execution and supported the Girondins, stood trial two days later. Her crime was to write and publish a pamphlet titled *The Three Urns, or the Welfare of the Motherland*, pleading for "a decent government" and "a stop to assassinations and the suffering . . . for merely holding opposing views."[37] A rushed mock trial found her guilty of the capital crime of composing and publishing "writings which provoke the dissolution of the national representation, the reestablishment of royalty, or of any other power attacking the sovereignty of the people."[38] De Gouges was guillotined on November 3, 1793, tragically proving her own point that women only enjoyed equality in the right to mount the scaffold. Free speech had become another victim of the Terror.

Freedom of religion was also sacrificed on the altar of Revolution. In November 1790, members of the clergy had been forced to take an oath of obedience to "the nation, the king, and the law."

Nearly half of the clergy refused, and many more withdrew their oath after the pope condemned the Revolution in 1791.[39] From that point onward, the Catholic church became the focal point of the simmering counterrevolution. In response, the revolutionaries attempted to "dechristianize" the country by vandalizing Catholic images and churches.[40] In October 1793, the National Convention banned clerical clothing in Paris and declared that any priest who was condemned for lack of *civisme* would be deported on pain of death. Nearly twenty-five thousand—almost a sixth of the whole clergy—were deported or emigrated, and up to a thousand priests were condemned to death in the Terror.[41]

A de facto dictatorship was established on December 4, 1793, under the leadership of Robespierre, the Montagnards, and the Committee of Public Safety, which controlled the military and the Revolutionary Tribunal. The Law of 14 Frimaire (December 4) imposed the death penalty on those proposing to reestablish the monarchy or threatening the sovereignty of the people.[42] In a speech to the National Convention in February 1794, Robespierre stressed the need to terrorize "the enemies of liberty," including "mercenary libellists paid to dishonor the cause of the people, to smother public virtue, to fan the flame of civil discord, and bring about a political counter revolution."[43] The man who had been a protolibertarian in 1791 now grew paranoid and began executing potential rivals. The infamous Law of 22 Prairial (June 10, 1794), also known as the law of the Great Terror, condemned to death "enemies of the people" who were found guilty of "disparaging the National Convention and the republican government"; "calumniating patriotism"; "spreading false news"; "misleading public opinion"; "corrupting the public conscience"; and "impairing the energy and purity of revolutionary and republican principles."[44] In other words, any dissent, real or perceived, was enough to send you to the guillotine. Trials under the law had only two outcomes: either you were acquitted or you were executed. An estimated 16,594 people were condemned to death during the Reign of Terror.[45] The Revolutionary Tribunal in Paris alone passed 2,639 indictments, and 988, or 37.5 percent, of those were for speech crimes.[46] In the words of Donald Greer: "In Paris . . . the home of the purest Jacobinism, there was no quarter for political heresy."[47]

The Old Regime Strikes Back

The Terror came to an end when Robespierre was toppled by a conspiracy of deputies who all feared they were next in line for the guillotine. He was executed—without trial—on July 28, 1794.[48] The more reactionary Thermidorians took control of the Convention and the landmark achievements of the French Revolution were quickly rolled back. The revised and retitled Declaration of Rights and Duties of Man and Citizen that accompanied the new Constitution of 1795 was much more conservative than its predecessor. Not only did it omit Article 11 and its protection of free speech, it actively restricted freedom of expression by declaring that "those who incite, promote, sign, execute, or cause to be executed arbitrary acts are guilty and ought to be punished."[49] The press was hit with a new stamp tax and a new license was required to publish newspapers. When Napoléon Bonaparte established his autocracy in 1799, he reintroduced draconian control of the press, shutting down sixty newspapers and limiting the total number of papers in Paris to thirteen—all of them subject to surveillance and strict limits on permissible speech.[50]

France was not the only country to experience a reactionary backlash after the French Revolution. And one of the first victims of the counterrevolution was the hard-won expansion of free speech, which to most rulers now seemed like a recipe for radicalism and anarchy rather than enlightenment and progress.

The so-called Enlightened Absolutists were quick to realize that the ideas they had allowed to spread in their own realms could easily turn against them. According to Catherine the Great, "the affairs of France were the concern of all crowned heads."[51] And to ensure that her crowned head remained fixed to her neck, she ditched all liberal sensibilities. In May 1790, less than a year after the eruption of the French Revolution, the Russian author Alexander Radishchev published *Journey from St. Petersburg to Moscow*, which boldly criticized the social and political conditions in Catherine's Russia and even flirted with incitement to regicide. Since no publisher dared to touch it, Radishchev published it anonymously on his own printing press. It sold out immediately.[52]

Catherine was angry and terrified that the French Revolution would metastasize to Russia—where the serfs had plenty of reasons to rebel. She thought *Journey from St. Petersburg to Moscow* was "infected and full of the French madness" and "trying in every possible way to break down respect for authority and . . . to stir up in the people indignation against their superiors and against the government."[53] The book was banned and Radishchev, who was quickly identified as the author, was sentenced to death by beheading for insulting the honor of the ruler, among other crimes. In an act of "mercy," Catherine changed the sentence to ten years of exile in Siberia.[54] The ban on the book wasn't officially lifted until 1868. According to one biographer, "no book in Russia or Europe was so long and so thoroughly suppressed."[55]

What makes *Journey from St. Petersburg to Moscow* interesting from a free speech perspective isn't just the fierce repression it provoked. The book also contains a radical and uncompromising argument for free speech, which includes the now-familiar notion that "freedom of the press is the greatest bulwark of liberty." The greatest free speech meme of the eighteenth century, which had spread from *Cato's Letter* No. 15 in London to the American colonies, had made its way to Russia. To Radishchev, Catherine's liberal reforms did not a great bulwark make, and he complained that censorship kept the Russian people in a state of perpetual intellectual infancy: "Censorship has become the nursemaid of reason, wit, imagination, of everything great and enlightened. But where there are guardians, there are minors and immature minds unable to take care of themselves."

Radishchev's criticism was also overtly political, condemning absolutist power and its censorship of dissent:

> In prohibiting freedom of the press, timid governments are not afraid of blasphemy, but of criticism of themselves. . . . The free-thinker who has been stirred to his depths will stretch forth his audacious but mighty and fearless arm against the idol of power, will tear off his mask and veil, and lay bare its true character."[56]

But what must really have stung Catherine was Radishchev's surgically precise indictment of the incompatibility of "enlightened monarchs" and freedom of speech. In what may have been an uncomfortably accurate psychological profile of Catherine's state of mind he wrote, "In whose head can there be more incongruities than in that of a tsar?"[57] Truth hurts.

Catherine moved decisively away from her previous liberal stance. A directive from 1791 instructed the newspaper *St. Petersburg News* to avoid any potentially offensive news about the court, Russia's allies, and the royal families of Europe. Editors were also ordered to portray events in France in the most unfavorable light.[58] The intellectuals who had benefited from the empress's initial tolerance were banished. Even the French philosophes whose ideas she had once favored were now seen as dangerous. The fact that she banned the complete works of her greatest fan, Voltaire, as "harmful and filled with demoralisation" speaks volumes of Catherine's complete volte-face. She cemented her backlash against free speech with an edict in October 1796 that established censors' offices in major towns, closed all private printing presses, and banned the writing, translation, and importation of books without prior licensing. Catherine had been the first ruler in Russian history to champion freedom of speech and the press. She was now also the first ruler in Russian history to erect an official and systematic regime of censorship.[59]

In Prussia, the Counter-Enlightenment began just before the French Revolution took hold, when Frederick William II succeeded his uncle Frederick the Great as ruler in 1786. On July 9, 1788, the new and deeply conservative minister of culture, Johann Christoph von Wöllner, engineered a "Religious Edict" with the intent of stopping skepticism and rationalism from undermining the traditional tenets of faith, which he believed held together the social fabric of Prussian society. Proclaiming that "**enlightenment**"—printed in bold letters—had gone too far, it imposed doctrinal censorship on the curriculum in schools and universities.[60]

When pamphlets and articles criticized the new measures, the king complained that "*Pressfreiheit*" (press freedom) had degraded into "*Pressfrechheit*" (press insolence).[61] Wöllner followed up with a new and beefed up censorship edict that included imprisonment as a penalty in December 1788. The new regime also followed through on its intent to rein in subversive ideas as witnessed by a steep increase in the number of books banned and confiscated.[62] The new red lines precipitated a marked decline in the number of independent printing presses in the following years.[63] A new Royal Examining Commission was established to root out nonconformists in the church and schools.[64] Among its targets was none other than Immanuel Kant.

Kant had had such high hopes for the potential for freedoms of thought and speech under Frederick the Great. But in 1792, the new censorship regime rejected an essay of his on religion.[65] The following year, he smuggled the prohibited essay into a volume of essays on

Religion Within the Boundaries of Mere Reason. This defiance was not appreciated, and in 1794 the philosopher received a warning from the king, signed by Wöllner, accusing him of "misus[ing his] philosophy to distort and disparage many of the cardinal and foundational teachings of the Holy Scriptures and of Christianity." Kant was told that he would incur the king's "highest disfavor" were he to pull a similar stunt ever again.[66] He protested politely, but promised to "refrain altogether from discoursing publicly, in lectures or writings, on religion, whether natural or revealed."[67]

The Revolution Controversy:
Burke vs. Paine and Pitt's Reign of Terror

In Britain, the French Revolution and its fresh new principles of human rights highlighted age-old tensions between order and liberty. Many Britons were reconsidering whether the balance had become skewed in favor of crown, nobility, established religion, and property at the expense of democracy, tolerance, freedom, and equality. Nothing better symbolizes the battle of ideas that would shake British society to its core than the pamphlet war known as the Revolution Controversy and its aftermath.

The controversy began on November 4, 1789, some four months after the Storming of the Bastille. The London Revolutionary Society was celebrating the centenary of the Glorious Revolution. On this occasion, the Welsh dissenter Reverend Richard Price delivered a sermon comparing the Glorious and American Revolutions with the events unfolding in Paris, which he believed were foreshadowing a new era:

> I see the ardor for liberty catching and spreading, . . . the dominion of kings changed for the dominion of laws, and the dominion of priests giving way to the dominion of reason and conscience.

. . . Behold, the light you have struck out, after setting America free, reflected to France and there kindled into a blaze that lays despotism in ashes and warms and illuminates Europe![68]

Published under the title *A Discourse on the Love of Our Country*, copies of the speech were soon circulating in America, Dublin, and Paris.[69] The loudest among many responses came one year later from the Whig MP Edmund Burke. His stinging *Reflections on the Revolution in France* of November 1790 has become synonymous with conservative antipathy against the Revolution and its lofty Declaration of the Rights of Man. Burke did not object to the ideals of liberty as such; he had after all shown sympathy toward the grievances of American colonists. What fueled his disgust for the French Revolution was his deep opposition to the philosophical premise of abstract human rights. In a speech to the House of Commons in February 1790, he called the Declaration of the Rights of Man a "digest of anarchy."[70]

To Burke, institutions and rights had to evolve gradually and reflect the traditions, experience, and wisdom of past generations. The Glorious Revolution of 1688 preserved "*ancient* rights and liberties" stretching back to the Magna Carta of 1215. The French Revolution was a very different beast, constructed solely on the shifting sand of pure human reason. Burke's rejection of the French Revolution included a grave warning: "Massacre, torture, hanging! These are your rights of men! These are the fruits of metaphysic declarations wantonly made!" Burke also defended the strict social and political hierarchy of Old Regime France and warned that without elite gatekeepers "learning will be cast into the mire, and trodden down under the hoofs of a swinish multitude." French freedom of speech and conscience had already produced "an insolent irreligion in opinions." In contrast Burke praised the "cold sluggishness" of the British national character: "We are not the converts of Rousseau; we are not the disciples of Voltaire; Helvetius has made no progress amongst us. Atheists are not our preachers; madmen are not our lawgivers."[71]

Burke's *Reflections* sold an impressive thirty-thousand copies in two years and provoked an outpouring of responses.[72] The first published response to Burke's counterrevolutionary tract was *A Vindication of the Rights of Men* by the protofeminist Mary Wollstonecraft. Published anonymously in November 1790, it attacked Burke's "tyrannic principles" and contended that "property in England is much more secure than liberty."[73] In *A Vindication of the Rights of Woman*, published two years later, Wollstonecraft made a forceful case for why women must enjoy the equal protection of the natural rights promised by the French Revolution and its foundational Declaration.

The prominent scientist, political philosopher, and renegade preacher Joseph Priestley was also provoked to write a response to Burke's *Reflections*. In his 1791 *Letters to the Right Honourable Edmund Burke*, he declared that the American and French Revolutions had ushered in a "wonderful, and important, æra in the history of mankind."[74] As a founding father of the English Unitarian Church, Priestley was a personal victim of laws discriminating against dissenters. In spite of his scientific prowess, he was barred from public offices and prestigious universities like Oxford and Cambridge.[75] Accordingly, Priestley demanded above all else "the free discussion of everything relating to religion."[76] In July 1791, on the second anniversary of the Storming of the Bastille, a mob dedicated to "Church and King" destroyed Priestley's Birmingham home, library, and laboratory, forcing him to flee first to London and from there to Pennsylvania.[77]

Yet the most influential reaction to Burke's barrage was Thomas Paine's *Rights of Man*, the first part of which was released in 1791. Paine fully supported the French Revolution and the Declaration of the Rights of Man and denounced Burke's *Reflections* as a hyperbolic defense of despotic absolutism and obscurantist religion. He also argued that all men are created equal with "natural rights," including the "liberty of speech," and that the sole purpose of governments was to safeguard those freedoms.

Paine thrust a brilliant rhetorical dagger into the very heart of the British political system, describing its aristocracy as having "a tendency to degenerate the human species." He found the very "idea of hereditary legislators . . . as absurd as an hereditary mathematician, or an hereditary wise man," since the soundness of arguments, not birth or pedigree, should be the yardstick of democratic decision making.[78] Burke versus Paine was a lesson in the practice and principle of elitist versus egalitarian free speech, reflecting the former's commitment to ordered liberty respecting the existing social, political, and religious hierarchy, and the latter's radical democratic-republican ideals supported by free and equal speech.

Burke refused to reply directly to the substance of Paine's arguments: "I will not attempt in the smallest degree to refute them. This will probably be done (if such writings shall be thought to deserve any other than the refutation of criminal justice) by others."[79] Burke had predicted that the French Revolution would descend into anarchy and violence, and now he intimated that Paine would be dealt with by the criminal justice system. He was prophetic on both counts.

The government was initially reluctant to make Paine a martyr like John Wilkes. Besides, the authorities hoped that the relatively high price of the book would prevent it from spreading to and inciting radical ideas among the lower classes. But Paine became impossible to ignore in February 1792, when he followed up with the even more radical *Rights of Man, Part the Second*. In it, he famously argued: "Freedom had been hunted round the globe; reason was considered as rebellion; and the slavery of fear had made men afraid to think. But such is the irresistible nature of truth, that all it asks, and all it wants, is the liberty of appearing." Significantly, he praised the Athenian democracy as a model and seriously upped the seditious ante by taking aim at the "ridiculous" institution of hereditary monarchy.[80] That would include George III (or his "Madjesty," as he impertinently dubbed the mentally unstable monarch in an open letter to the home secretary).[81] Paine had written another best seller. According to a conservative estimate, *Rights of Man* sold between one and two hundred thousand copies in the first three years after its publication.[82] If Burke was Cliff Richard, Paine was the Beatles. These incredible numbers were further enhanced by Paine using the money he received to publish new and cheaper versions, so that everyone from the street prostitute to the coal miner would be able to quote from his work.[83]

Paine's sensational book gave powerful ammunition to the many corresponding and constitutional societies that had sprung up since 1790 to strengthen democracy and work for toleration. These societies increasingly targeted the middle and lower classes of society to foster popular support for their demands, which deeply worried the government.[84] Paine even united reform- and independent-minded Protestants and Catholics in Ireland, where the book also became a sensation.

As Paine's ideas went viral, government toleration of Paine's insolent propaganda quickly ran out. Prime Minister William Pitt the Younger struck back at Paine with a one-two punch in the form of a personal criminal charge for seditious libel as well as a general Royal Proclamation Against Seditious Writings and Publications. Calling upon magistrates from across Great Britain to hunt down "the Authors and Printers of such wicked and seditious Writings," it led to a flurry of arrests and around two hundred prosecutions for seditious libel in the 1790s.[85] Paine biographer John Keane provides a vivid description of the extent and intensity of the anti-Paineite crusade:

Government spies were assigned to the popular societies to monitor and obstruct their activities. Billstickers were imprisoned for posting notices in favor of Paineite reforms. Bookshops selling *Rights of Man* were visited and harassed by agents of the book police, and sometimes arrested, prosecuted, fined, or imprisoned.[86]

The government even sponsored writers to drag Paine's name through the gutter with lurid accounts of his private life and allegedly suspect business dealings. Newspapers thundered against "Mad Tom" in articles and demonizing cartoons. Most unnerving were the organized campaigns of symbolic murderous violence that took place in hundreds of towns all over the country, as described in a January 1793 edition of the *Newcastle Chronicle*: "Paine's effigy has been burnt, shot, hanged, and undergone the greatest marks of popular resentment in most towns and villages in this part of the country."[87] Paine himself was followed by government spies wherever he went, which—given the incitement against him—must have been intimidating to say the least.[88]

When things got too hot for Paine, he managed to escape across the Channel to revolutionary France, where he received a hero's welcome and a seat in the National Convention. But Britain wasn't about to let Paine off the hook, so he was tried in absentia. The attorney general highlighted some of Paine's most inflammatory remarks and accused him of rousing "the lower classes of the people" and addressing his dangerous positions "to the ignorant, the credulous, and the desperate." Paine's lawyer responded with a four-hour-long speech in which he argued against the Blackstonian conception of press freedom, which only protected against prepublication censorship, not against subsequent punishments for criminal writings. He promoted a different standard: "Every man is protected in his opinions, it is only his conduct that makes guilt."[89] When the attorney general got up to reply, the foreman of the jury told him he needn't bother: the jury—handpicked from among the upper classes—had already reached their verdict. Paine was guilty as charged. Egalitarian free speech was (still) a bridge too far for the hierarchical British society, which valued order over liberty when those values appeared to clash.

But Paine would get his revenge. His person might have been exiled, but his ideas could not be quarantined. Having already hacked away at the monarchy, he now turned his fire on another sensitive target. In *The Age of Reason* (published in two parts in 1793 and 1795), Paine launched an incendiary attack on another pillar of British society: Christianity. "What is it the Bible teaches us?" he asked. "Rapine, cruelty, and murder." It got worse. "What is it the Testament teaches us?—to believe that the Almighty committed debauchery with a woman engaged to be married; and the belief of this debauchery is called faith."[90] No other book has been so frequently prosecuted for blasphemy in England.[91] Yet nineteenth-century English radicals found much to admire in Paine's ideas. In combination with Deism—the belief in a noninterventionist Supreme Being and the supremacy of reason over superstition—they delivered a two-pronged attack against the conservative foundations of English society, which justified the discrimination of dissenters and the exclusion of the lower classes from political influence.

Pitt's crackdown on Paine was only the first in a long series of increasingly drastic measures to contain revolutionary sentiment. In late 1792, after the French abolished the monarchy and promised armed support for fellow European revolutionaries, rumors spread of an imminent uprising in England.[92] The government responded by calling hundreds of troops to London and issuing another Proclamation Against Seditious Writings.[93] The stakes became even higher after the French declared war on February 1, 1793. Pitt tried to weed out so-called English Jacobins in the reform movement by monitoring and infiltrating British corresponding societies with spies.[94] In a speech to the House of Commons, he expressed concern that "the Motion for a reform was nothing more than the preliminary to overthrow of the whole system of our present government. And if they succeeded, they would overthrow . . . the best constitution that was ever formed on the habitable globe."[95] But how much of the best constitution on the habitable globe was Pitt willing to sacrifice in order to protect it?

In May 1794, Pitt moved to temporarily suspend the right of habeas corpus guaranteed in the Habeas Corpus Act of 1679 and with roots stretching back to the Magna Carta. Based on the seized proceedings and documents of two corresponding societies, as well as some questionable intelligence from governments spies, Pitt had convinced himself that "a plan had been formed, and was in forwardness, to assemble a convention of the people; which was to assume the character and powers of a national representation, and to supersede the authority of parliament." But that was not all. These corresponding societies were in contact with French Jacobins and, following their precedent, they aimed "to arrive at the same degree of power." Elite panic had now firmly gripped the government, which feared an English revolution. Several MPs furiously protested Pitt's attack on English liberties. Pitt's nemesis, the Whig MP Charles James Fox, accused the prime minister of wanting "to invest the executive power with absolute authority over every subject in the kingdom"—a measure "incompatible with that manly freedom of thought and speech, without which no liberty could exist." The Earl of Lauderdale, another prominent opponent, warned that the government's crackdown risked establishing "that system of terror which we so much reprobated in France." But most MPs were convinced that the threat was real. This included Edmund Burke, who held that Pitt's proposal to suspend habeas corpus was "far from being an oppressive measure."[96] When it came to opposing abstract human rights, Burke had no qualms about suspending those "ancient liberties" that he thought superior to the Rights of Man. Pitt had his way and suspected enemies of the state could now be detained without trial.

In 1795, Parliament also rushed through the two so-called Gagging Acts, which severely limited the freedoms of assembly and speech, even if only temporarily. The Treasonable and Seditious Practices Act made verbal or written attacks on the king and his ministers treasonable offenses punishable by death. It also punished offenders who brought the king, government, or constitution into contempt "by writing, printing, preaching, or other speaking."[97] The Seditious Meetings Act made it illegal for more than fifty persons to meet without a permit from a government official. But Pitt wasn't done. He also slapped a steep tax on all printed matter in 1797. What couldn't be outright banned could be taxed so as to limit circulation of writings to the better classes.[98] This was the final straw for Charles James Fox who condemned Pitt's "reign of terror" and quit his position in Parliament in protest.[99]

Pitt's clampdown on revolutionaries was even more heavy-handed in the rest of the British Empire. In the West Indies, the French Revolution's provision of equal rights to free Blacks and subsequent liberation of all slaves spread hopes of racial equality and the abolishment of slavery in British dominions. When the Redcoats put down an armed rebellion in Grenada in 1796, around seven thousand slaves were slaughtered and thirty-eight free Black rebels hanged. Closer to home, armed rebellion broke out in Ireland in 1798, where between twenty-five and thirty thousand people were killed. Another 1,450 Irishmen were convicted for insurrection, a third of which were sentenced to death.[100]

One year later, the so-called Unlawful Societies Act "utterly suppressed and prohibited" a number of radical societies throughout Great Britain, including the United Irishmen, which had led the Irish Rebellion, as well as the London Corresponding Society.[101] Having closed the last safe spaces for reform and radicalism, Pitt could now claim that his resolute action had prevented the danger of revolution, whether real or perceived. Historian Jennifer Mori has argued that Pitt and his government actually strove to balance liberty against order so as not to overreact. Some of the most draconian proposals were scrapped, and at any rate, the independence of local magistrates and juries ensured that there were counterweights to Pitt's crackdown.[102] But even if Pitt's Reign of Terror was nothing like the Terror unleashed in France, and permitted more dissent than in Russia and Prussia, it still amounted to an orchestrated and systematic campaign against political opposition. And when compared to simultaneous events in America, the British commitment to free speech looked decidedly ragged and tattered.

John Adams's Temptation

America may have been separated from Europe by the vast Atlantic Ocean, but the new republic could not insulate itself from the spillover effects of the French Revolution. Events in France polarized an already bitterly divided political landscape, with Federalists and their Democratic-Republican rivals clashing over first principles. Federalists—including Washington, Hamilton, and Adams—favored a strong national government, were pro-British, and felt increasingly fearful that French revolutionary principles would export the Terror to America. Republicans—including Jefferson and Madison—saw great danger in further centralizing the powers of the federal government and (Jefferson in particular) had strong French sympathies.[103]

The rancorous spirit of factionalism was amplified by hyperpartisan newspapers serving as the attack dogs of the warring parties. Nearing the end of his presidential term in 1796, George Washington complained bitterly about newspapers that described him "in such exaggerated, and indecent terms as could scarcely be applied to a Nero; a notorious defaulter, or even to a common pickpocket." John Adams faced similar treatment when he assumed the presidency. He was called "blind, bald, crippled, toothless, [and] querulous" in the fiercely Republican newspaper *Aurora*, published by Benjamin Franklin Bache, who delighted in portraying Federalists as closet-royalists intent on reestablishing the monarchy with themselves at the top and the people downtrodden. Federalist newspapers were just as vicious, and vastly outnumbered Republican ones. When French privateers captured American commercial vessels and the French government arrogantly dismissed American diplomatic efforts at détente, the papers described Republicans as "American Jacobins" preparing the ground for an impending French armed invasion and consequent bloodbath (which never happened). Alexander Hamilton further fanned the flames of division by referring to Republicans as "the French Faction" and accusing them of harboring treasonous tendencies.[104]

In this toxic atmosphere, Federalists decided that the young American republic could not withstand the combination of a looming war with France and concerted efforts to undermine public trust in the duly elected government. In May 1798, Madison had warned Jefferson, "Perhaps it is a universal truth that the loss of liberty at home is to be charged to provisions agst. danger real or pretended from abroad."[105]

A month later, on June 26, 1798, Madison's premonitions were confirmed, when an arrest warrant was issued for Bache. He was charged with libeling the president and the government "in a manner tending to excite sedition."[106] The common-law crime of seditious libel, so odious to Patriots during British rule, had become a tool for enforced patriotism as defined by the Federalists.

Bache's arrest was just the prelude to a much more concerted effort to silence the insolent and disloyal Republican agitators. In July 1798, Congress passed the Sedition Act, which made it a crime to:

> write, print, utter or publish . . . any false, scandalous and malicious writing or writings against the government of the United States, or either house of the Congress of the United States, or the President of the United States, with intent to defame . . . or

to bring them . . . into contempt or disrepute; or to excite against them . . . the hatred of the good people of the United States.[107]

The extremely broad and subjective wording of the Sedition Act made it, in the words of legal historian Wendell Bird, "a crime, in effect, to criticize the president, Congress, the federal government as a whole, or its measures, whether by press or speech."[108] The fiercely partisan nature of the act was demonstrated by its omission of the vice president. That office was held by Thomas Jefferson, whom Federalists had no inclination to shield against the coordinated smear campaign in the Federalist press, where he was accused of atheism, being drunk with subversive French philosophy, and moral corruption.[109]

A mere seven years after the adoption of the Bill of Rights and the First Amendment's promise that "Congress shall make no law . . . abridging the freedom of speech, or of the press," Congress had done just that. The Sedition Act paved the way for the prosecution and imprisonment of journalists, editors, and politicians, including a sitting congressman, engaging in political speech and satire—just as Philadelphiensis had predicted eleven years earlier.

Even if leading Federalists, including Hamilton, Adams, and Washington, were not among the Sedition Act's architects, it commanded their tacit or direct support.[110] In a letter in late June 1798, a few weeks before the Act's passage, Hamilton had warned that the bill should be amended so as not to "establish a tyranny" and that by "push[ing] things to an extreme we shall then give to faction *body & solidarity*."[111] But in 1799 he argued for further restrictions on press freedom in order to protect any "Officers of the General Government" from "malicious and unfounded slanders." He also argued for the mass expulsion of "Renegade Aliens" who were behind most of the "incendiary presses" in America, where in "contempt and defiance of the laws they are permitted to continue their destructive labours."[112]

Federalists defended the Sedition Act's constitutionality by reverting to Blackstonianism. Free speech meant nothing but the protection against prior restraints; scurrilous pens and tongues could be held to account once their words had been published, since sedition was punishable under common law. Thus, no law abridging the freedoms of speech and the press had actually been passed. It was a startling switch for men who had justified their revolutionary dissent by claiming that free speech was the great bulwark of liberty that protected the people against common-law prosecutions for seditious libel by the British.

Republicans, on the other hand, were aghast at what they saw as a concerted attempt to subvert the constitution and entrench unopposed Federalist rule. The Virginian lawyer George Hay wrote *An Essay on the Liberty of the Press* addressed "to the President of the United States." It provided a detailed legal argument for why the Sedition Act was unconstitutional. But it also included a forceful attack on the elitist British conception of free speech with which Federalists sought to protect their authority. The inherent uncertainty involved in determining the limits between liberty and licentiousness, so characteristic of seditious libel under English common law, was natural in Britain "where privilege and monopoly form the basis of the government" but, according to Hay, "in the United States it is disgraceful." To the argument that press freedom meant nothing more than Blackstonian protection from prepublication censorship, Hay retorted, "In Britain, a legislative control over the press, is, perhaps essential to the preservation of the 'present order of things;' but it does not follow, that such control is essential here." To Hay, free speech in its American sense was close to absolute, and he thus provided a truly radical defense of free and equal speech, which right included "*speaking* against the government matters that are false, scandalous, and malicious."

Hay did not approve of such speech, but a legislative remedy to counter it would inevitably result in "a power fatal to the liberty of the people." Indeed, "the licentiousness of the press, though an evil, was a less evil than that resulting from any law to restrain it." And so, Hay concluded:

> The freedom of the press, therefore, means the total exemption of the press from any kind of legislative control, and consequently the sedition bill, which is an act of legislative control, is an abridgment of its liberty, and expressly forbidden by the constitution.[113]

Madison and Jefferson rallied the opposition and drafted resolutions passed by the legislatures of Virginia and Kentucky in 1798 declaring the Sedition Act a manifestly unconstitutional attack on the "right of freely examining public characters and measures, and of free communication thereon, which has ever been justly deemed the only effectual guardian of every other right."[114] Jefferson wrote of Federalists that "they have brought into the lower house a sedition bill . . . so palpably in the teeth of the constitution as to shew they mean to pay no respect to it."[115]

Madison followed up with Virginia's Report of 1800, which included a devastating philosophical and legal analysis of why the Sedition Act violated not only the letter but also the spirit and rationale of the First Amendment. It stressed that Congress had no power to control the press—in fact, the First Amendment explicitly forbade such laws as the Sedition Act. To Madison, the English common-law restrictions on free speech were inapplicable to the United States, where ultimate sovereignty rested with the people and not Parliament. As opposed to the common-law crime of seditious libel, the Sedition Act allowed truth as a defense. But to Madison this was no effective safeguard against violations of press freedom:

> It must be obvious to the plainest minds, that opinions, and inferences, and conjectural observations, are not only in many cases

inseparable from the facts, but may often be more the objects of
the prosecution than the facts themselves; or may even be altogether abstracted from particular facts; and . . . cannot be subjects
of that kind of proof which appertains to facts, before a court
of law.

As we shall see, the actual prosecutions under the Sedition Act
supported Madison's principled point, given that many were prosecuted merely for voicing negative opinions about President Adams
and/or his administration.

Madison also appealed to the very recent founding history of
the United States and how the colonists had attacked the British
government and its authority in the press. If back then Sedition Acts
had prohibited "every publication that might bring the constituted
agents into contempt or disrepute, or that might excite the hatred
of the people against the authors of unjust or pernicious measures,"
the United States might still be "miserable colonies, groaning under
a foreign yoke."

Madison did not deny that the public sphere could be toxic and
that newspapers filtering the truth through partisan glasses contributed to the fraught atmosphere. But he warned that punishing
hyperbole and bad faith presented greater dangers:

> Some degree of abuse is inseparable from the proper use of every
> thing; and in no instance is this more true, than in that of the
> press. It has accordingly been decided by the practice of the states,
> that it is better to leave a few of its noxious branches, to their lux-
> uriant growth, than by pruning them away, to injure the vigor of
> those yielding the proper fruits.[116]

The consequences of the Sedition Act were nowhere near as
severe as the Terror in France or Pitt's anti-Paineite crackdown in

Great Britain, nor did it compare to the antirevolutionary crackdowns in absolutist states like Russia and Prussia. But a recent study by Wendell Bird has significantly revised the number of prosecutions under the Sedition Act from fourteen to fifty-one cases affecting 126 defendants, including fourteen newspaper editors and various politicians. Some were sent to prison, others were bankrupted, and several newspapers were forced to fold. One man was fined and jailed for making a drunken joke about John Adams's "arse" when the President passed through Newark in a carriage, another for erecting a liberty pole, and many others for criticizing President Adams in newspaper articles. This included the fiery Republican member of Congress Matthew Lyon, who had accused Adams and his administration of disregarding "every consideration of the public welfare . . . in a continual grasp for power, in an unbounded thirst for ridiculous pomp, foolish adulation, and selfish avarice."[117] In reality, the merit of the charges depended largely on subjective political opinion, not any clear set of facts. That did not help Lyon, who was sentenced to four months in prison and a fine of $1,000, thus providing a case in point for Madison's intellectual denunciation of the Sedition Act.[118]

Even Vice President Jefferson was investigated for violating the Act and had his mail intercepted, though no indictment was made. With very few exceptions, all those targeted by the Act were Republicans or opposed to Federalist policies, while Federalist newspapers were generally free to use hyperbole and invectives against Republicans—including, of course, Thomas Jefferson.[119] Equally shameless was the fact that the Sedition Act was set to expire on March 3, 1801, which coincided with the inauguration of the next president and Congress. In other words, Federalists were not willing to become the potential targets rather than the enforcers of the Sedition Act should they lose political power.[120]

The partisan nature of the Sedition Act was a perfect weapon in the hands of its most enthusiastic supporter, the equally vindictive and paranoid Secretary of State Timothy Pickering. He coordinated the efforts of targeting political enemies by sifting through evidence received from a network of informers who sent him newspaper clippings and correspondence with "seditious" material.[121] Pickering would then forward the material to the relevant state attorney with the expectation that the offender be indicted. In August 1799, George Washington wrote approvingly to Pickering asserting that newspapers like the *Aurora* worked to "destroy all confidence, that the People might, and . . . ought, to have in their government; thereby dissolving it, and producing a disunion of the States."[122] The man who had led a revolutionary army against the "tyranny" of England's King George now sounded like an American echo of King George's Prime Minister Pitt.

Still, the Sedition Act did not succeed in quelling dissent. In the two and a half years it was in force, the number of Republican newspapers more than doubled.[123] Before his untimely death in September 1798, Benjamin Franklin Bache wrote defiantly that his prosecution for seditious libel had only boosted his sales.[124] And the Federalists were utterly trounced in the elections of 1800, losing the presidency—with Jefferson defeating Adams—and both houses of Congress to their Democratic-Republican opponents, not least because of popular backlash against the heavy-handed methods of the Sedition Act. In the words of Wendell Bird, "Federalists sought to crush Republican newspapers and the Republican party, and instead they multiplied both."[125]

Instead of owning the Feds, Jefferson resisted the alluring pull of censorship and struck a unifying and bipartisan note in his first inaugural address:

> We are all republicans: we are all federalists. If there be any among us who would wish to dissolve this Union, or to change its republican form, let them stand undisturbed as monuments of the safety with which error of opinion may be tolerated, where reason is left free to combat it.[126]

It was a powerful appeal to unity that views free speech as the precondition for social peace rather than a vehicle for treason and strife.

Like Washington and Adams before him, President Jefferson quickly found himself the target of newspaper smear campaigns. In a private letter he complained that Federalist newspapers undermined press freedom "by pushing it's licentiousness and it's lying to such a degree of prostitution as to deprive it of all credit. . . . A few prosecutions of the most eminent offenders would have a wholesome effect in restoring the integrity of the presses."[127] There were even a few libel cases in which defendants were prosecuted for defaming Jefferson under state laws—some initiated with a nod and a wink from Jefferson himself.[128]

But he let the Sedition Act lapse and made no concerted efforts to target political enemies with sedition charges, and the efforts of Madison, Jefferson, Hay, and other critics undoubtedly helped to develop a robust commitment to First Amendment ideals as well as to deepen the understanding of what that constitutional provision meant in both principle and practice. Yet, the culture of free speech was not yet sufficiently robust for the bulwark of liberty to resist the force of free speech entropy, once the issue of slavery became too toxic to ignore in the nineteenth century.

———

IN A CERTAIN SENSE, THE CLASH OVER THE SEDITION ACT was a reenactment of the debate between Federalists and Anti-Federalists over the Bill of Rights. And the parallels between Pitt's Reign of Terror and the Sedition Act are also obvious in that they sought to protect the established authorities against radical ideas identified with the French Revolution at a time when Britain was at war, and America on the brink of war, with France. All of these controversies represented a deeper clash between an elitist and an egalitarian conception of free speech. As we have seen, that fundamental conflict has been a recurrent theme since antiquity.

In America this conflict ended with a—temporary—triumph for egalitarian free speech, while in Britain the power of hierarchy and tradition managed to hold fast and limit the public sphere to the elite.

It is interesting to compare the very different trajectory of free speech in France and America, where, unlike in Britain, revolutions toppled old regimes and enshrined free speech as a fundamental human right of the new order. Comparing events in France after 1789 and in America after 1798 raises the question of what truly ensures the entrenchment of free speech as a principle. Is the key to its endurance the wording of constitutions or declarations? Or is it a nation's commitment to a culture of free speech and the tolerance of the controversies, offensive ideas, and very public disagreement about fundamental values that inevitably arise from this freedom? A possible answer to why free speech fared so differently could be that in 1789, the French—after centuries of absolutism—had comparatively little experience with a wide and uninhibited public sphere outside more abstract philosophical circles. And with the collapse of the Old Regime, they no longer had a natural seat of authority to draw the red line. As Old Regime concepts of honor and morals survived, the principle of free speech soon became weaponized by warring factions who could not imagine "living and letting live" with political rivals. It did not help that Article 11 of the Declaration of Rights allowed for punishing "abuse" of the freedom to speak, write, and print, without any definition or agreement on the meaning of the term.

In contrast, a critical mass of Americans had internalized the idea of dissent as natural and beneficial by 1798. Not least because they had in effect wrestled away the British colonial authorities' ability to punish seditious libel in the previous decades. Americans had thus become accustomed to a much more vibrant public sphere, where different views clashed openly in taverns and on the pages of pamphlets and newspapers, as reflected in the uncompromising language of the First Amendment. Accordingly, the attempt to punish as seditious American patriots whose political opinions differed from Federalist ideals backfired spectacularly, even if the passing of the Sedition Act demonstrated that American acceptance of free speech was far from universal. If there is any merit in this interpretation, the difference between the uncompromising wording of the First Amendment and the equivocal nature of Article 11 of the French Declaration might have been less decisive for the different free speech climates than the popular attitudes toward free speech that these differences reflected. The contrast between France and America thus lends credence to the words of the influential twentieth-century judge and scholar Learned Hand: "Liberty lies in the hearts of men and women; when it dies there, no constitution, no law, no court can even do much to help it. While it lies there it needs no constitution, no law, no court to save it."[129]

8

The Quiet Continent

The War on Free Speech in Nineteenth-Century Europe

The entry on "Press" in the *Encyclopédie*, one of the greatest triumphs of the Enlightenment, concluded exuberantly:

> It is asked whether liberty of the *press* is advantageous or detrimental to a state. The response is not difficult. It is of the greatest importance to preserve this practice in all states founded on liberty. I say more: the drawbacks of this liberty are so trivial compared with its advantages that it ought to be the common right of the world, and that it is proper to authorize it under all governments.[1]

Yet, for all its landmark achievements, the eighteenth century ended with free speech in full retreat from the advancing forces of counterrevolution.

Moreover, following the defeats of Napoleon in 1814 and 1815, conservatives and monarchs resumed the reins of power in Europe with no intention of ever letting wild-eyed radicals seduce the people with lofty principles and propaganda again. In order to rebuild a stable Europe with respect for authority and tradition, freedom of speech had to be reined in and treated as the harbinger of chaos and anarchy rather than progress and virtue. The Continent's new conservative order was sewn up at the Congress of Vienna from 1814 to 1815, dominated by Austria, Prussia, Russia, and Great Britain, which had defeated Napoleon. The leading powers, later known as the Concert of Europe, agreed to defend the political status quo and crush uprisings in states like Italy in 1820 and Spain in 1822.[2]

Despite their best efforts, however, Enlightenment values lived on. Writers, thinkers, academics (many exiled), and even some statesmen continuously challenged the new reactionary order with revolutionary fervor. Nor were all European states committed to taking the Counter-Enlightenment's agenda of restoring the might and glory of Throne and Altar, and its repudiation of the freedoms of conscience and speech, to the extremes of the "Holy Alliance" of Russia, Austria, and Prussia. Remnants of (moderate) Enlightenment values and cautious press freedom still remained—though precariously so—in Britain, post-Napoleonic France, Scandinavia, and the Netherlands.[3]

The Post-Napoleonic Repression

In Britain, William Pitt had managed to suffocate revolutionary tendencies with a slew of repressive laws and proclamations. Pitt's demise in 1806 did not improve things for Britons demanding fair political representation or decent working conditions. With the exception of a brief interim in 1806 and 1807, the Tories occupied Downing Street until 1830. Most of Pitt's successors in this period belonged to his faction—the Pittites—including Lord Liverpool, who served as PM from 1812 to 1827. They would use the matrix molded by Pitt to clamp down on radical speech and action.

The most trusted tool of Liverpool's government was the good old crime of seditious libel. There were no less than 167 prosecutions for blasphemous and seditious libel in the eight years from 1817 to 1824 alone.[4] Publishers and printers bore the brunt of the prosecutions rather than writers, much as today's governments target the choke point of social media platforms rather than the individual users. However, the law of seditious libel sometimes backfired. In 1792 the role of juries had been strengthened, and they did not always prove to be reliable government stooges—even though they were often cherry-picked with a biased judge presiding. On average, sedition trials resulted in convictions and jail time in only around 38 percent of the cases brought before the King's Bench Court in the most repressive years from 1817 to 1822.[5]

Still, the relatively low rate of convictions does not capture the most pernicious effects of seditious libel proceedings. Defendants faced extreme uncertainty of outcome, opaque legal procedure, and significant financial distress. This took its toll on their physical and mental health—not to mention their wallets —and made many others think twice about publishing controversial ideas.[6]

After the Napoleonic wars, Britain was struck hard by an economic downturn known as the post-Napoleonic depression, resulting in heavy unemployment and lower wages for the mass of factory workers with little voice in public affairs.[7] Hardest hit by the postwar slump was the new industrial powerhouse and textile hub of Manchester. Since 1773, Manchester had grown from a small town of some twenty-four thousand to more than a hundred thousand souls, many living in horrid conditions of grinding poverty.[8] When the government ignored their petitions for a minimum wage and affordable bread, the workers of Manchester concluded that their biggest problem was lack of representation in Parliament. A full third of British MPs had been elected by fewer than a hundred voters in the so-called rotten boroughs, while Manchester's large population had no representation at all.

As the movement for parliamentary reform gained momentum, the press joined in the crusade. In 1818, the weekly *Manchester*

Observer began amplifying the voice of the movement and quickly became one of the leading radical papers in Britain. Magistrates complained that "the unbounded liberty of the press" was one of the principal causes "of the evil which we apprehend." So the government turned to its manual on responding to political dissent and repeatedly indicted the *Observer*'s chief editor, the radical activist James Wroe, for seditious publication, succeeding twice.[9] Not to be outdone, the *Manchester Observer* and the radicals behind it responded to the crackdown by calling an enormous public demonstration to demand parliamentary reform in August 1819 that would later become known as the Peterloo Massacre.[10]

Two years earlier, the government had revived Pitt's Gagging Acts, clamped down on seditious libel, and banned unlicensed public meetings of more than fifty people. But on August 16, around sixty thousand protesters marched into St Peter's Field in central Manchester, shouting slogans and waving banners with demands of "Equal Representation or Death."[11] The magistrates were convinced that such a large public meeting could only end in rioting. Just as the radical orator Henry Hunt was about to speak, troops moved in to arrest him. Panic spread among the crowd and then to the soldiers, who drew their swords and began to swing at the protesters. In little more than ten minutes, those who could get clear of the field had fled, leaving eleven dead civilians and more than four hundred injured behind.[12] To add insult to injury the government prosecuted Hunt and other key players at Peterloo for unlawful assembly.[13]

The Peterloo Massacre became a powerful symbol of oppression for democratic reformers throughout the country. The event inspired Percy B. Shelley to write one of his most famous poems, *The Masque of Anarchy*. Its rallying cry to the "Men of England" echoed Pericles's definition of the ancient Athenian democracy: "ye are many—they are few."[14] The radical press concurred, and steadily increased its circulation in the wake of the tragedy. A government official lamented that "odious and blasphemous publications poured forth throughout the country" because of the massacre.[15]

The government concluded that its own conduct was beyond reproach and that the "most efficient cause" of "the present critical state of the country" was "the audacious licentiousness of the press."[16] Its response was the "Six Acts" of 1819, which imposed even stiffer punishments for seditious libel, limited freedom of association, and—most effectively—increased stamp duties to a level that made newspapers unaffordable for the poor. Facing a loss of up to 80 percent of their circulation, much of the radical press was swiftly squeezed out of existence.[17] The government finally succeeded in shutting down the *Manchester Observer* in 1821 with charges of seditious libel. But a new paper was founded in the ashes of Peterloo—the paper we know today as the *Guardian*.[18]

The government also pulled out another weapon from its arsenal of repressive tricks. A 1676 court case had made blasphemous libel part of the common law based on the premise that reviling Christianity was not only an offense to God but also a crime against the laws, state, and government.[19] In 1819, during the government's post-Peterloo offensive, the number of prosecutions for blasphemous and seditious libel soared to a national total of seventy-five, constituting what historian E. P. Thompson has called "the most sustained campaign of prosecutions in the courts in British history."[20]

One of the government's favorite targets was the journalist and publisher Richard Carlile, who spent a total of ten years in prison, including six for blasphemy.[21] Carlile covered the Peterloo Massacre in his newspaper the *Republican* with an incendiary article urging "every man in Manchester" to "never go unarmed."[22] To make matters worse, Carlile was also a prolific blasphemer publishing and peddling Deist publications like Tom Paine's *The Age of Reason* to the lower classes. In October 1819, Carlile was tried for blasphemy and seditious libel, and the attorney general pulled no punches. He denounced *The Age of Reason* as "one of the most abominable, disgusting, and wicked attacks on religion and its author, that has ever appeared in the world." But it was not God or religion that needed protection. It was the established order of the British class-based society. According to the attorney general, prosecuting Carlile was necessary for

> protecting the lower and illiterate classes from having their faith sapped and their minds divested from those principles of morality, which are so powerfully inculcated by the Christian religion. . . .When such terrible productions . . . are put . . . into the hands of those who unlike the rich, the informed, and the powerful, are unable to draw distinctions between ingenious though mischievous arguments, and divine truth—the consequences are too frightful to be contemplated.[23]

The presiding judge refused Carlile the right to defend his statements by demonstrating inconsistencies in the Bible, since it was against the law to revile Christianity, and he was sentenced to three years in prison.[24] There he would soon be joined by his equally radical wife, Jane, and his sister, Mary Anne Carlile, both of whom helped Richard Carlile continue his impious republican crusade.[25] When Jane and Mary Anne had been convicted, another fiery woman, Susannah Wright, volunteered to run the Carlile family's radical bookshop "at all risk." She too was soon arrested and tried for blasphemy. Insisting on defending herself, she had to request a break to breastfeed her infant child in the middle of one of her trials. The spectacle attracted a lot of attention. Wright quickly gained notoriety as the "She-Champion of Impiety" and was sentenced to eighteen months.[26] Yet Wright's and the Carliles' time behind bars was not in vain.

The rough treatment of Carlile, Wright, and other radicals prompted serious discussion about the value of the free press and captured the attention of leading philosophers such as James Mill. His 1825 article on "Liberty of the Press" for the *Encyclopedia Britannica* made a detailed case for why it was essential that governments had no power to limit even indecent, false, and hateful criticism of their conduct, and that press freedom must extend to both politics and religion.[27] Yet Mill's greatest contribution to free speech was fathering the wunderkind John Stuart Mill. He learned Greek at age three, Latin at eight, and most of the classical canon and algebra by twelve.[28] And at the ripe age of eighteen, the young Mill published an essay, "On Religious Persecution," which used Carlile's case to show that blasphemy prosecutions were both indefensible and counterproductive. He estimated that the prosecutions of Carlile had increased the reach of Paine's *Age of Reason* by some twenty-thousand copies and a hundred thousand readers.[29] If reading about Deism was safe only for the well-educated classes, then the solution was not to prosecute but to educate the lower classes.

The indefatigable efforts of radicals such as Carlile and the intellectual efforts of Messrs. Mill and Mill seemed to work. After a string of convictions in 1824, the constant barrage of seditious and blasphemous libel prosecutions shrank to a mere sixteen in the period between 1825 and 1834. The rising uproar over oppressive restrictions on freedom of speech played a part, as did a dawning recognition that the prosecutions were indeed counterproductive, as defendants like Wright and the Carliles used the publicity of trials to read out the offending material and generate sympathy among the masses. As the attorney general later noted, "a libeller thirsted for nothing more than the valuable advertisement of a public trial in a Court of Justice." Indeed, when Carlile was prosecuted, the circulation of the *Republican* grew by as much as 50 percent.[30]

The government had won battle after battle in the courts but lost the wider war against blasphemy. And as an unintended consequence, it had entrenched the idea of press freedom, extending it to both political and religious ideas and to the consumption of ideas by the masses. There would still be prosecutions for blasphemy in subsequent decades, but it had become an increasingly outdated measure.

With the swift drop in blasphemous libel prosecutions after 1825, Deist publications including *Age of Reason* could suddenly be sold freely. However, the authorities were not about to simply turn a blind eye to the radical press. Instead, they restricted the access of the lower classes by increasing newspaper stamp duties and taxes on paper and advertisement, or "Taxes on Knowledge" as they were later described by a parliamentary campaign.[31] The predictable result was a growing clandestine "unstamped press," which by 1836 commanded a readership of more than two million in London—exceeding the readership of the (officially approved) stamped press.[32]

On Liberty: Toward Free and Equal Speech in Britain

In a parallel development, the press was successfully amplifying the calls for parliamentary reform, stoking a growing movement for change. As the High Tory Sir Walter Scott lamented, "The whole daily press seems to me to have embraced democratical opinions without exception."[33] The 1830 election of a Whig government with a platform of comprehensive reform was at least a recognition of the need for progress, and marked the beginning of the end of seditious libel as an instrument to punish public opinion in Britain, even though it was only formally removed as a crime in 2009.[34]

The Great Reform Act of 1832 got rid of most of the rotten boroughs and substantially expanded the electorate. And, most importantly from the perspective of the press, stamp duty was reduced by 75 percent in 1836. This reform is often hailed as a landmark in the history of press freedom in Britain, but the government had ulterior motives. In fact, professor James Curran goes so far as to suggest it was "manifestly repressive both in intention and in effect."[35] He argues it was not driven by ideals of press freedom as much as the need to "put down the unstamped papers," as the chancellor of the exchequer explained to the House of Commons.[36] The massive unstamped press had virtually broken down the system of information control, and the "strategic concession" of reducing the stamp duty went hand in hand with increased repressive measures to search for and confiscate unstamped newspapers, and to ramp up penalties for possessing them.[37]

Still, the combination of tax reductions and the rapid mechanization of the press seems to have had a profound effect. After the stamp duty was reduced in 1836, annual newspaper sales increased dramatically from 25.5 million to over 53 million in just two years.[38] From 1835 to 1850, the number of stamped newspapers grew from 35 million to almost 100 million.[39] Further reforms were enacted in the 1850s and early 1860s, eliminating the "knowledge taxes" on advertisement, stamp, and paper.[40] When the stamp duty was repealed in 1855, six new provincial dailies popped up in a single day.[41]

As early as 1848, John Stuart Mill declared the reforms successful. He triumphantly concluded that the working classes had as good as thrown off the yoke of the "patriarchal or paternal system of government . . . when they were taught to read, and allowed access to newspapers and political tracts." He likewise highlighted the beneficial effects of "dissenting preachers" finally being allowed to spread heterodox religious ideas among the common man thus encouraging the working classes to think for themselves and to "seek a share in the government."[42]

Egalitarian free speech had been secured by the indefatigable practice of uninhibited speech and was won by growing popular demand rather than granted as a fundamental right. And in Britain, the freedom of the press had come to stay as, in the realm of political speech (as opposed to "obscenity"), the government increasingly focused on threats to public order rather than dangerous ideas.[43]

This was in part due to the emergence of a liberal political movement inspired by what classicist Mogens Herman Hansen calls "the Athenian view of liberty and equality as the basic democratic values."[44] Key to the rehabilitation of Athenian democracy was George Grote, whom we met in Chapter 1. Grote was a friend of both James and John Stuart Mill. In his classic work *A History of Greece*, Grote praised Pericles's Funeral Oration and "the picture of generous tolerance towards social dissent, and spontaneity of individual taste" that it painted of Athenian culture. To Grote, Periclean democracy compared favorably to that of contemporary nineteenth-century societies where "the intolerance of the national opinion cuts down individual character."[45]

Still, in 1859, John Stuart Mill could open one of the most famous chapters in the history of political liberalism on a positive note:

> The time, it is to be hoped, is gone by when any defence would be necessary of the "liberty of the press" as one of the securities against corrupt or tyrannical government. No argument, we may suppose, can now be needed, against permitting a legislature or an executive, not identified in interest with the people, to prescribe opinions to them, and determine what doctrines or what arguments they shall be allowed to hear.

Chapter 2 of Mill's *On Liberty* is hailed by many as *the* foundational text on the importance of free speech. Of course, several of Mill's arguments had been made much earlier. This includes his famous dictum that restricting free speech prevents people from the great benefit of "exchanging error for truth" as well as "the clearer perception and livelier impression of truth, produced by its collision with error." We find traces of that idea all the way back to Demosthenes in ancient Athens and a very clear precedent in Elie Luzac's 1749 defense of atheist publications.

But the forcefulness of Mill's argument is undeniable. Take this quote: "If all mankind minus one, were of one opinion, and only one person were of the contrary opinion, mankind would be no more justified in silencing that one person, than he, if he had the power, would be justified in silencing mankind." Or this encouragement of intellectual humility to the partisans of orthodoxy, whether religious or secular: "We can never be sure that the opinion we are endeavouring to stifle is a false opinion; and if we were sure, stifling it would be an evil still." Mill also took issue with free speech "butism." He found it strange "that men should admit the validity of the arguments for free discussion, but object to their being 'pushed to an extreme;' not seeing that unless the reasons are good for an extreme case, they are not good for any case."

While Mill (diplomatically) presented the British government as being reasonably tolerant of dissent, he expressed grave concern about the stifling effects of the social norms that pervaded Victorian England. He warned not only against the "tyranny of the magistrate" but also the "tyranny of the prevailing opinion and feeling" and society's tendency to "impose, by other means than civil penalties, its own ideas and practices as rules of conduct on those who dissent from them."[46] It was a powerful endorsement of the importance of establishing a culture of free speech permeating both law and civil society, mirroring his friend George Grote's Periclean ideals and his concerns about society's receptiveness to them.

Mill's fears about the private threats to the culture of free speech were well-founded. Onerous legal impediments to press freedom may have been on the decline, but powerful new informal ones were taking their place. Wealthy businessmen assumed ownership and control of the press from the working classes, whose radical presses more or less disappeared in the second half of the century. Unlike the radical press, which had been forced to seek sources of finance beyond advertising, this new press model became increasingly dependent on advertisements, and subsidies from proprietors and political parties, which effectively restricted its independence and muted radical voices.[47]

The Quiet Concert of Europe

Despite the harsh repression of Carlile and his fellow radicals, seen from across the Channel, Britain surely seemed like a paradise of tolerance and free debate, even at the height of Tory repression. The mood among Continental European hard-liners after the final fall of Napoleon in 1815 was best expressed by Austria's top diplomat and secretary to the Congress of Vienna, Friedrich von Gentz, writing in 1819: "As a preventive measure against the abuses of the press, absolutely nothing should be printed for years. . . .With this maxim as a rule, we should in a short time get back to God and the Truth."[48]

Most states realized that halting all printing presses would be unrealistic. But the Congress did commit the member states of the new German Confederation to adopt a common law regarding the press. The powerful Austrian chancellor Klemens von Metternich believed press freedom to be the "Scourge of the World."[49] With the aid of Prussia, Metternich succeeded in finally establishing a common press law for all German states under the notorious Carlsbad Decrees of 1819, centralizing prepublication censorship and establishing an investigation commission—a secular inquisition vested with sniffing out "revolutionary machinations."[50]

Metternich and like-minded reactionaries across Europe saw the reintroduction of censorship as a necessary tool to guarantee social order. Or, in the words of a leading French conservative, a "sanitary precaution to protect society from the contagion of false doctrines, just like measures taken to prevent the spread of the plague."[51] In France, this sanitary precaution came in the form of an 1814 press law, which required all publications, printers, and booksellers to obtain royal sanction from the newly restored monarchy.[52]

There were, however, corners of Europe where the end of the Napoleonic Wars led to more press freedom and less censorship. Norway, which had been ruled by Denmark on and off since 1380, grabbed the chance to break free in 1814, after Denmark bet on the wrong horse and sided with Napoleon. Promising "entire liberty of the press," Article 100 of the Norwegian Eidsvoll Constitution allowed "everybody freely to deliver his opinions of government or any other subject."[53] But Sweden, which had chosen the winning side, soon invaded and ruled Norway until 1905, though the Swedes promised to uphold the Eidsvoll Constitution, which still forms the basis of the current Norwegian constitution.[54]

Press freedom also limped on in its old heartland. The Dutch Republic had fallen into the orbit of revolutionary France in 1795, becoming first the Batavian Republic, then a puppet kingdom under Napoleon's brother, and finally a province in Napoleon's empire. William I, who assumed the throne of the independent Kingdom of the Netherlands in 1815, ignored the urgings of Austria and Prussia and initially pursued a fairly liberal policy of press freedom and religious toleration, though eventually William too would rein in the press of this former free speech haven.[55]

Beneath the conservative restoration, Enlightenment values also smoldered among the networks of intransigent radicals and intellectuals who bided their time in small oases of intellectual freedom scattered around Switzerland, Belgium, and Paris. They diffused their ideas through reading groups and universities, where Europe's collective brain fought to withstand the lobotomizing efforts of Counter-Enlightenment forces.[56] The Carlsbad Decrees of 1819 sought to mitigate this threat by severely restricting academic freedom and purging teachers and students who expressed subversive or supposedly immoral opinions.[57]

The reactionary backlash against free speech was forcefully refuted by the Swiss-French political theorist Benjamin Constant in one of the most important but underrated contributions to free speech doctrine of its time. During Napoleon's short and ill-fated comeback in 1815, Constant was asked to draft a new and more liberal constitution for France. The work inspired him to finish and publish his *Principles of Politics Applicable to All Governments*. Constant came to the opposite conclusion of the prevailing conservative wisdom of the day: It was not press freedom that had led to the French Revolution and its horrors. Instead, the Revolution had been caused—partly—by the systematic denial of press freedom, which had allowed the French state and its finances to degenerate and its abuses to go unchecked by any public scrutiny. Moreover, censorship and repression had made the French people too "credulous, anxious, and ignorant" to know the real value and meaning of freedom once it was suddenly thrust upon them. In fact, he argued, free speech was the guardian of all civil and political liberty, and censorship was tantamount to "restrain[ing] the human race's intellectual freedom."[58]

Like Spinoza, Madison, and *Cato's Letters*, Constant argued that the advantages of a free press far surpassed the uncertain gains of censorship, which would always be liable to abuse. Consequently, restrictions on free speech had to be narrow and limited to overt acts. At a perilous time for free speech, Constant's ideas wielded influence among liberals both in and outside of France, though they would remain distant ideals for decades.

As in Britain, Continental rulers were also worried about the effect of the radical press on the lower classes. By the 1840s, literacy rates had climbed to around 60 percent of the adult population in France and 75 percent in Britain and the German states. As many as 90 percent of Scandinavians could read and write. The spread of literacy gave a far larger group of people the opportunity to participate in public discussions previously reserved for the elite.[59] Rapid urbanization meant that the lower classes were clustered together in cities, making rulers even more fearful of their exposure to dangerous ideas. If the lower classes were seduced by seditious publications, they could easily mobilize and riot.[60] An effective way of keeping newspapers out of the hands of the poor was to make them unaffordable, so a number of European states imposed various stamp taxes and/or expensive licensing requirements for newspaper ownership.[61]

The first real cracks in the reactionary armor appeared in France in 1822, when French liberals succeeded in pressuring the government to give up prior censorship of the press. Though a severe postpublication censorship apparatus still remained in place, this relaxation permitted the liberal press in Paris to explode in popularity, reaching a combined circulation of fifty thousand subscribers by 1826—more than three times that of its conservative rivals.[62]

This horrified King Charles X, who blamed the press for destabilizing the government, depressing the army, and subverting religion. In July 1830, Charles suspended press freedom, and tried to silence all liberal newspapers by seizing their presses and arresting their editors.[63] But instead of acceptance from a pliant press, Charles found himself with a revolution on his hands. Journalists and printers refused to comply with the emergency laws, bolted the doors of their print shops, and began publishing calls for resistance.[64] The working people of Paris heeded their calls, and—in what has since become a symbol of revolution itself—put up barricades in the streets. Within "Three Glorious Days," the king had been deposed, and power was in the hands of a provisional government ruled by liberals. A constitutional monarchy known as the July Monarchy was established under the liberally inclined Louis Philippe I, who was crowned in August 1830. Article 7 of the new constitution declared: "Frenchmen have the right to publish and to have printed their opinions, while conforming with the laws. The censorship can never be re-established."[65]

The July Revolution sent waves of joy and relief to embattled liberals throughout the Western world. Could the long conservative winter finally be thawing? Famous reformers and free speech enthusiasts flocked to France, including John Stuart Mill and the German journalist and poet Heinrich Heine.[66] Heine had famously—and, it would turn out, prophetically—predicted, "Where they burn books, they will also burn people in the end."[67] He had also shown his disdain for censorship in a satirical poem titled "The German Censors":

The German censors ——

————————

————————

————————

————————

——————*Idiots*——

————————

————————

————————

————————[68]

The reports coming out of Paris from writers like Heine had repercussions in Germany, where popular unrest swelled and several states were pressured into creating constitutions. In the small state of Baden, a powerful reform movement succeeded in passing a libertarian press law that removed censorship.[69] Its leader, Karl von Rotteck, believed that a free press "assures certain victory for truth and justice, without force, solely through the divine judgment of unfettered public opinion, through the directing authority of human reason."[70] Everywhere, associations working toward freedom of the press emerged, culminating in a large public demonstration in Hambach in 1832, where national liberals denounced the German governments and called for freedom of the press to an audience of more than thirty thousand people.[71]

But the powerful Prussian and Austrian rulers refused to let the specter of "Re-Enlightenment" gain a foothold. In 1832, the German Confederation reacted by passing the Six Articles, holding that "the limits of free expression cannot . . . be exceeded in a manner that endangers the peace of an individual Confederal state or that of Germany as a whole."[72] A few days later, it passed the Ten Articles, forcing individual states to enforce censorship. The starry-eyed liberals of Baden were forced to retract the permissive press law. Its author, Rotteck, was put on a list of suspected subversives, and more than two thousand people were investigated throughout Germany.[73] In 1835, a full-scale ban was placed on all works by Heine and the other writers associated with the liberal "Young Germany" movement.[74]

Back in France, the new king was having second thoughts about press freedom. Louis Philippe was increasingly annoyed at the critical press and stinging caricatures of him that popped up everywhere. Only a couple of months after the Three Glorious Days, the first exceptions to freedom of speech were introduced.[75] The political press was targeted by the notorious September Laws of 1835—dubbed a "reign of terror for ideas" by the liberal poet Alphonse de Lamartine.[76] Caricatures were outright banned, as was the use of the word "republic."[77] Heavy financial obligations were also placed upon newspapers. A leading writer commented, "During the French Revolution, one cut journalists' heads; under Napoleon one silenced them; under the Restoration one jailed them; under the July Monarchy one ruined them financially."[78] In the span of a couple of years, the liberal dream had died once more in France, and the European continent was yet again under the thumb of monarchical censors.

Russia was also affected by the revolutionary wave sweeping across Europe. Shortly after Nicholas I's assumption of the throne in December 1825, a secret society of officers marched into the streets of Saint Petersburg backed by around three thousand soldiers, refusing to recognize the new tsar and demanding representative democracy. Nicholas crushed the Decembrist revolt and tightened his grip on the press. A huge apparatus of more than twelve different censorship units placed almost comically strict limits on what could be published and imported, including among "subversive works" the fairy tales of Hans Christian Andersen and a cookbook that referred to the "free air" in an oven.[79] A Russian censor complained that the workload reached such "incredible dimensions" that the "poor clerks got calluses on their hands from this Sisyphean labor day and night."[80] Throughout the nineteenth century a pantheon of great Russian authors including Pushkin, Dostoyevsky, and Tolstoy were imprisoned, exiled, and/or censored for their writings. Long books, however, were often exempt from prepublication censorship, as these were thought to be read only by scholars and not the general population. Among the scholarly works given the thumbs up by tsarist Russia in the 1870s was Karl Marx's *Das Kapital*. The censors concluded that few people would "read it and even fewer will understand it" anyway. Surely, no one would read such a "colossal mass of abstruse, somewhat obscure politico-economic argumentation."[81]

If things were better in parts of Germany, it was mostly because of a comparative lack of central coordination of censorship, even though the Carlsbad Decrees of 1819 had gone some way to establish a common print policy. German writers often dodged the censors by crossing the many state borders. Newspaper articles and books censored in Hamburg, for example, were often simply published in the Danish-administered state of Holstein and swiftly reimported. But the annual number of books published in Germany also doubled from around seven thousand to almost fourteen thousand between 1830 and 1846, so German censors were often too buried under the sheer volume of work to catch all the offending material.[82]

Still, things were not easy for writers of a liberal—much less radical—inclination. One of them was the young revolutionary Karl Marx. Because of the appalling free speech record of socialist countries, few realize that the young Marx was a vocal defender of press freedom. In 1842, at the age of twenty-four, he kickstarted his career with a series of articles for the *Rheinische Zeitung*, a newly established reformist newspaper in Prussia. Focusing on the intellectually ruinous consequences of state censorship, he wrote:

The free press is the ubiquitous vigilant eye of a people's soul, the embodiment of a people's faith in itself, the eloquent link that connects the individual with the state and the world, the embodied culture that transforms material struggles into intellectual struggles and idealises their crude material form.[83]

Marx soon became the editor of the *Rheinische Zeitung* and radicalized its editorial line. The growing fame of Marx's writings inevitably attracted the censors, and the paper was forced to shut down in March 1843 after a complaint from the Russian tsar.[84]

Faced by the growing zeal of the censors, Marx went into exile in Paris where he met and befriended Heinrich Heine. In the years that followed, with the censors constantly looking over his shoulder, he moved to Brussels, then back to Germany, and then to Paris again, before he ended up in London in 1849—by now the last refuge for radical European writers.[85]

False Spring: The Revolutions of 1848

Throughout the 1830s and early 1840s the repressive measures imposed by European monarchs and governments mostly succeeded in keeping liberal ideas at bay. But continuous growth in literacy rates and the volume of publications, along with the social changes accompanying the emerging industrialization of Europe, made popular discontent harder and harder to control. In 1847, the Prussian diplomat Christian Karl Josias, Baron von Bunsen, dramatically expressed what was at stake: "The freedom of the press . . . is the political question of life and death in our time, the question that wrecks governments and reduces kingdoms to death, or gives them the strength to rise. The fight for the freedom of the press is a holy war, the holy war of the nineteenth century."[86]

The tightening system of censorship had become a pressure cooker and, in the spring of 1848, finally burst. After an Italian prelude, the fuse was—as always—lit in Paris, where growing disillusionment with the July Monarchy found its expression in the so-called Banquet Campaign. Because freedom of assembly was suppressed, political meetings were thinly disguised as a series of public banquets. When the French government responded by forbidding the banquets, all hell broke loose. People flooded into the streets, erected the obligatory barricades, and in a matter of days forced Louis Philippe to abdicate and go into exile. In his place, a Second Republic was declared. The republican leadership immediately introduced universal suffrage and abolished censorship, asserting that "the Republic lives by liberty and discussion."[87]

In a matter of weeks, the revolution spread through the European continent in what has become known as the Springtime of the Peoples. In Germany, the notorious Carlsbad system of federal censorship controls was demolished. In the electorate of Hesse-Kassel, the police chief responded to demonstrators clamoring for press freedom by shouting, "Yes, just write, just write; everything you write will be printed!"[88] By the end of March, censorship had fallen throughout Germany, and conservatives were in fast retreat.[89] In Denmark, popular demonstrations organized in part by the Society for the Proper Use of Freedom of the Press brought censorship to a halt and led to the peaceful introduction of a constitutional monarchy.[90] In Austria-Hungary, a popular uprising forced Chancellor Metternich to flee into exile, and ended restrictions on the press. The only major powers that escaped the conflagration were the already comparatively liberal United Kingdom and the extremely repressive Russian Empire.

The collapse of censorship in Western and Central Europe resulted in a boom in political journalism. In Paris, the combined circulation of newspapers jumped from fifty thousand before the revolution to four hundred thousand by May 1848. In three districts of the Prussian Rhine Province, the number of different newspapers doubled almost overnight. And in the Austrian Empire, the nineteen newspapers permitted to cover political affairs suddenly had to compete with 287 new publications discussing politics.[91] But the substance of political journalism changed as much as the quantity. Publications had traditionally been written in a dense style and aimed at a well-educated audience. Now, papers for the working man entered the public sphere. Helped by the gradual introduction of the steam press in the 1840s, newspapers were on the way to becoming the first truly mass media in history.[92]

But as we have seen countless times, the march of history rarely follows a straight line. Revolutions are often followed by counter-revolutions, and 1848 was no exception. For all the hope inspired, the pendulum quickly swung back toward autocracy and repression. As early as August 1848, the republican regime in France had begun reintroducing mild forms of press controls. In December, the French—perhaps having snoozed through classes on their republican history—elected Napoleon's nephew, Louis-Napoléon Bonaparte, as the first president of the Republic of France.

To his contemporaries within French high society, Louis did not strike a very impressive figure, and he was often the subject of public ridicule. But ridiculing the president was no laughing matter, and Louis began clamping down on the liberal press with a template familiar to the illiberal populists of the twenty-first century. He prohibited insulting the president and "maliciously affirming erroneous facts likely to disturb the peace," though for him "erroneous" more often meant "inconvenient" rather than "false."[93] The president gradually tightened the screws of press censorship in the following two years until he finally let his mask fully drop in December 1851. He mounted a coup d'état, proclaiming himself Napoleon III, Emperor of France. The last remains of the free press were buried alongside the Second Republic.[94]

The radical idea and practice of a free press did not survive for long in Austria, either. Censorship crept back in Vienna after the revolutionaries were defeated in October 1848. By 1852, a new press decree banned all writings "of an orientation that was hostile to the throne, the monarchy, the unity and integrity of the empire, monarchical principles, religion, public morals, or the overall foundations of the state's society, or of an orientation that was incompatible with maintenance of public law and order." The ridiculously broad scope of the law essentially empowered the state to ban everything it did not like, with the threat of punishment hanging over the heads of journalists and writers like the Sword of Damocles. It's hardly surprising that the number of publications fell to less than a third of what it had been at the high point of the revolution.[95]

In Prussia and the rest of the German lands, the return of censorship followed the same track as in Austria. Although prior censorship was not reinstated, a repressive postpublication regime was enforced everywhere by the early 1850s. The lack of prepublication censorship was not an ideological victory; rather, the governments no longer viewed it as a practical way of controlling public discourse. The persistent growth in the number of publications made prior censorship ever more difficult and expensive. It was simply more effective to outsource the task to the publishers and writers themselves, who were intimidated into self-censorship by the constant threat of heavy punishment.[96]

Denmark stood out as something of a pragmatic exception, as the constitutional monarchy established in 1848 and 1849 proved to be resilient. Still, whereas under Struensee in 1770, Denmark became a trailblazer, the Danish constitution of 1849 remained very modest and conservative. It abolished prepublication censorship but provided no protection against postpublication penalties or restrictions. It was essentially a rehash of the Blackstonian model of free speech implemented more than 150 years after prepublication restrictions had been abolished in England. While it allowed much freer public debate, it provided scant protection when the nascent socialist movement was persecuted by democratically elected governments in the 1870s. Press freedom was also part of the Dutch constitution of 1848, which too survived the reactionary backlash and set the Netherlands on the path to parliamentary democracy.

Outside the few pockets of relatively free speech on the European continent, repression continued to be the rule in the decades following 1848. The newly restored French imperial government was among the harshest censors. The countless restrictive laws passed after Napoleon III's coup created a veritable maze of regulation. At least six different handbooks were published to guide both censors and journalists through the Kafkaesque red lines.[97] Hundreds of prosecutions were brought against publishers and writers, and more than sixty newspapers were suppressed or suspended, along with countless books, pamphlets, plays, and more. "In France there is only one journalist and that is the Emperor," complained a liberal parliamentarian.[98]

The chaotic year of 1870 provided a brief respite from censorship, when the catastrophic military defeat to Prussia caused the French imperial regime to collapse, and censorship with it. Radicals made a bid for power during the Paris Commune—the city's short-lived independent government through the spring of 1871—but the new Third Republic made short work of them. The national government reimposed censorship and enforced it even more harshly than the empire had. In the closely contested election year of 1877, the repression reached epic proportions, with more than twenty-five hundred prosecutions brought against the press in the span of six months.[99]

Despite the massive crackdown, liberal factions won the elections—and promptly turned the weapons of censorship on the conservative papers. But this game of back-and-forth oppression did not continue for long. In 1881, the liberal government issued a new press law, which essentially freed the press from the most odious restrictions. France had again, for the fourth time in a century, established freedom of the press. But this time, it was there to stay.

The new press law fed a boom in publications and ushered in a golden age of the French press.[100] Between 1881 and 1892, the number of newspapers rose from thirty-eight hundred to six thousand.[101] The press law of 1881 still forms the basis of France's current press regime, though quite a few exceptions have been added over time.

The Iron Chancellor and the Social Democratic Press

Events in Germany took a similar course, though with a somewhat less liberal end point. Even though German states refrained from reintroducing prior censorship after 1849, a repressive apparatus of postpublication censorship continued. And cooperation between the different states was strengthened by the creation of a secret Pan-German police association in 1851, which coordinated repression of publications deemed dangerous to the state. This was accomplished with enough success that an 1854 report happily concluded, "A revolutionary press as it was to be found in 1848 . . . no longer exists; in the whole of Germany at this time there is not a single newspaper that would dare to preach open revolt."[102]

Press suppression initially declined after the Prussian statesman Otto von Bismarck created a unified German Empire under Prussian dominance in 1871. The Imperial Press Law of 1874, which replaced the various state laws, cemented the abolition of prior censorship and removed all licensing requirements for publishers, ensuring a much more vibrant media environment than before. The most dramatic difference was that every infringement on freedom of the press now had to go through the courts, where the government was far from certain to secure conviction.[103] But there were still limits. It was a crime "to knowingly fabricate or distort facts"—to write false news, in other words—"in order to incite in others contempt for state institutions or the law." It was also illegal "to slander or libel officials, clergymen, or members of the armed forces who were carrying out their professional duties."[104] Free and equal speech this was not. With ample room to clamp down on troublemakers, the state brought no less than twenty-five hundred legal charges against the press in the first three years of the new law.[105]

There's a reason why Bismarck was called the Iron Chancellor, as political dissenters and Catholics learned. During the so-called Kulturkampf from 1871 to 1878, the government harshly suppressed Catholic newspapers, journalists, and members of the clergy with discriminatory laws, as Catholicism was deemed a threat to the nation.[106] But to Bismarck, Catholics were not the only danger to national security. By the 1870s, the recently founded Social Democratic Labor Party of Germany (SDAP) was growing popular enough to become a threat. If the liberal press became more free in the last half of the nineteenth century, it was because the German state recognized a new and even more dangerous enemy on the Left. Socialists and Social Democrats represented the worst fear of the old conservative guard: an organized working class taking active part in society, with crazy ideas about abolishing private property and upending the social order.

To Bismarck, the Social Democratic party was "an enemy against whom the state and society are bound to defend themselves." As the old saying goes, the best defense is a good offense. After Emperor Wilhelm I was the target of two failed assassination attempts, Bismarck pounced. In 1878, he forced through an Anti-Socialist Law allowing the government to ban any organization or publication "featuring social democratic, socialist or communist efforts to overthrow the existing social order in a manner endangering public peace, and especially the harmony of the different social classes." The measure was highly effective; in less than two months, the socialist press was essentially gone. Over the following twelve years, 1,299 publications were banned, many associations were banned, countless works of art suspected of socialist influence were prohibited, and this period also saw at least 3,287 press trials covering 5,975 separate offenses. Astonishingly, libels of Bismarck alone made up more than 16 percent of those cases.[107]

The Iron Chancellor resigned in 1890 because of disagreements with the new emperor Wilhelm II. The Anti-Socialist Law lapsed and the now-legalized Social Democrats regrouped under their present-day name, the Social Democratic Party of Germany (SPD). As a result of the new and more permissive media environment there were no less than 3,405 newspapers in circulation by 1898.[108] But the Social Democratic press continued to be severely repressed. For many conservatives, the very idea of social democracy was tantamount to lèse majesté. Countless charges of incitement to contempt of the social order were leveled against socialist writers and publishers.[109] The papers did their best to fight back. In 1910, the *Hamburger Echo* wrote, "In waging our war, we do not throw bombs. Instead we throw our newspapers amongst the masses of the working people. Printing ink is our explosive."[110] But it was an uphill battle, as the socialists controlled neither the means of production nor the monopoly on the use of force. In the first half of 1913 alone, 104 Social Democratic journalists were sentenced to a combined forty years of prison and crippling fines.[111] The full arsenal of reactionary repression was put to the task of suppressing the Social Democratic press all the way up to the end of World War I.

———

DESPITE THE DRAMATIC BACKLASH OF THE EARLY NINE-teenth century and the lengthy back-and-forth between liberal reforms and reactionary crackdowns, free speech and press freedom (with limitations, of course) had come to stay in Europe by the end of nineteenth century. Prepublication censorship was all but dead and the public sphere gave room to much more diverse points of view than when the likes of Lord Liverpool and Metternich were in charge.

In 1912, the British historian J. B. Bury summed up the state of free speech at the beginning of the twentieth century:

> At present, in most civilized countries, freedom of speech is taken as a matter of course and seems a perfectly simple thing. We are so accustomed to it that we look on it as a natural right. But this right has been acquired only in recent times, and the way to its attainment has lain through lakes of blood.[112]

A mere two years later—and a century after the Congress of Vienna—the Great War would carve out new lakes of blood that were deeper than any before in human history, and would bring massive repression of dissent, censorship, and surveillance of global communications. The emergence of totalitarian ideologies and another cataclysmic world war, immediately followed by a cold one, dashed Bury's hope that free speech would continue its victory march uninhibited in the twentieth century.

9

White Man's Burden

Slavery, Colonialism, and Racial (In)Justice

One of the few Western nations to avoid the top-down reactionary pushback of the nineteenth century was the United States. In his famous treatise on *Democracy in America*, Alexis de Tocqueville claimed that "not a single individual of the twelve millions who inhabit the territory of the United States has as yet dared to propose any restrictions to the liberty of the press." Indeed, once press freedom had been unleashed from the shackles of the Sedition Act, America stood apart from the crowd.

Yet Tocqueville was a cautious rather than an enthusiastic supporter of American free speech. He saw a direct relationship between a free and open American press and the idea of popular sovereignty underpinning American democracy, and mused that, as a consequence, "censorship of the press and universal suffrage are two things which are irreconcilably opposed, and which cannot long be retained among the institutions of the same people." At the same time, like Mill, he found that the dominance of majority opinion carried its own set of dangers since "it represses not only all contest, but all controversy."

In fact, Tocqueville knew of "no country in which there is so little true independence of mind and freedom of discussion as in America." Only the "excessive dissemination" of newspapers, the number of which "surpasses belief," prevented the power of public opinion from subverting American freedom and democracy. Because of the decentralized nature of the American press, "neither discipline nor unity of design can be communicated to so multifarious a host," and therefore, "they cannot succeed in forming those great currents of opinion which overwhelm the most solid obstacles."[1]

No doubt, Tocqueville painted an overly rosy picture of American press freedom. There were still the occasional seditious libel and blasphemy prosecutions under state laws, and mobs sometimes took their own actions against printers who offended the feelings of their local community. And then there was a particularly glaring exception to the ideal of egalitarian free speech: the Bill of Rights did not extend to the states, much less the cotton fields where the slave owner ruled supreme and obedience was enforced by the whip.

The Slaver's Veto

While the Northern states gradually abolished slavery after the War of Independence, the practice thrived and spread in the South, which was "home" to about four million slaves—roughly one-third of the Southern population at large—by 1860, at the dawn of the Civil War.[2]

The depravity of slavery in a nation founded on the ideal of freedom and equality became too much for a growing number of white Americans and free Blacks to bear, and a movement to end slavery stirred. Given that most Southern state constitutions protected press freedom and/or free speech, the institution of slavery should in principle have been open to debate. But Southern legislators, congressmen, and mobs enforced a "Slaver's Veto," adopting some of the most draconian laws against free speech in American history.

The trend was kicked off in 1829 when David Walker—a free Black man—mailed his recently published antislavery pamphlet *Appeal to the Colored Citizens of the World* to the South. The legislature in Georgia responded by imposing the death penalty for the "circulation of pamphlets of evil tendency among our domestics."[3] The battle escalated after the American Anti-Slavery Society (AASS) was established in 1833. By 1837, more than a thousand groups worked for abolition through peaceful means such as meetings, publications, and petitions. In 1835, abolitionists began an organized campaign of targeting Southerners—including women and children—with antislavery literature in the mail. In response, more Southern states followed Georgia and adopted or doubled down on existing laws banning "incendiary" literature, with punishments including flogging and even death.[4]

The rank hypocrisy of such laws was striking. In 1776, Virginia had approved the first and most famous state declaration of rights affirming that press freedom was restrained only by "despotic governments." Virginia had also led the fight against the Sedition Act. But a sweeping Virginia law from 1836 criminalized publications intent on "persuading persons of colour . . . to rebel, or denying the right of masters to property in their slaves, and inculcating the duty of resistance to such right."[5] In Alabama, a grand jury indicted a newspaper publisher who had written that "God commands, and all nature cries out, that man should not be held as property."[6]

But Southern politicians were not content with simply keeping a lid on abolitionist writings in Dixie. They demanded that Northern states follow suit. In fact, some sought federal action to keep "incendiary publications" out of the South.[7] Amos Kendall, President Andrew Jackson's postmaster general, lamented his lack of "legal authority to exclude newspapers from the mail . . . on account of their character or tendency." Unable to intervene himself, he looked the other way when Southern postmasters withheld antislavery publications, considering it "patriotism to disregard" the law in this situation.[8] Sympathetic to slaveholders' concerns, President Jackson proposed a bill in December 1835 to "prohibit, under severe penalties, the circulation in the southern States, through the mail, of incendiary publications intended to instigate the slaves to insurrection."[9] It was a form of "intermediary liability"—not unlike how some states today oblige (private) social media platforms to delete undesirable user content. However, there was broad agreement that the First Amendment prohibited Jackson's direct federal control of the press by prohibiting the circulation of antislavery tracts in the South. Instead, Senator John Calhoun of South Carolina proposed prohibiting deputy postmasters from receiving and mailing or delivering any and all publications "touching the subject of slavery, directed to any person or post office, where, by the laws thereof, their circulation is prohibited."[10] That way, postmasters would enforce state rather than federal law.

These various initiatives ignited a debate over first principles. Southerners used a number of different justifications for the censorship of "fanatic" and "incendiary" abolitionist speech. Ironically, this included the idea of group libel—a progenitor of modern "hate speech" laws, which protected specific groups from defamatory statements. Senator Calhoun complained that the abolitionist petitions "contained reflections injurious to the feelings" of Southerners who were being "deeply, basely and maliciously slandered."[11] Southern politicians also argued that the "bad tendency" of abolitionist speech—the mere possibility of adverse effects at some future point—was sufficient reason to punish and prevent abolitionist ideas from spreading. As one commentator wrote, "The unavoidable consequences of [abolitionist] sentiments is to stir up discontent, hatred, and sedition among the slaves."[12] Southern bad tendency laws essentially prohibited antislavery opinion in the South. As the AASS pointed out, even certain writings of Jefferson would "undoubtedly be regarded . . . insurrectionary."[13] (Jefferson had acknowledged the "moral and political depravity" of slavery despite profiting from it himself.)[14]

Most Northerners were opposed to slavery, but at the same time denounced abolitionists as "fanatics" who jeopardized the commercial interests of Northerners, and indeed the very Union, by provoking Southern fears of slave revolts.[15] Yet the Southern campaign to essentially ban the discussion of slavery across the nation was rejected on principle, rather than sympathy for the abolitionist cause. Northerners feared that once an exception to free expression had been made to suppress abolitionist speech, the list of exceptions to free speech might quickly grow very long indeed.[16]

In his pamphlet *Freedom's Defence*, the pseudonymous writer "Cincinnatus" provided a detailed discussion of free speech and exposed the inequity of the Southern position, which he likened to the doctrine that:

> they who have the power in this country have an undoubted RIGHT to abuse that power; and, lest the oppressed classes, should, by using the freedom of the press, assert their rights, those powerful men, who have already so much control over the press, ought to seize on more power that they may be more secure in holding what . . . has been unjustly obtained.[17]

Free speech belonged to neither the federal nor state governments, but to the people. Hence, Cincinnatus took the principled high ground and invited the Southern press to publish their "most violent and incendiary publications" so long as "we may be free to repel the attack by truth and manly argument through the press and the mail."[18] Free speech for me and for thee alike.

In their willingness to allow the circulation of proslavery writings in the North, even as Southern states banned abolitionist writings, Northerners put Southerners on the defensive. This suggested that the Slaver's Veto was in effect an admission that the very concept of slavery could not withstand public scrutiny, nor be defended in a free and open debate.

The First Amendment might legally have been nothing more than a "parchment barrier," to use James Madison's phrase, but the ideals it embodied were very much alive. President Jackson's mail censorship bill tanked in 1836, and despite the urgings of the South, no nonslaveholding states adopted laws prohibiting antiabolitionist publications.[19] Proslavery congressmen had more success curbing their own free speech with the 1836 "gag rule," which restricted the presentation and discussion of antislavery petitions in the House—but even that ended in 1844.[20] The commitment to the underlying values of the First Amendment constituted an effective firewall against the spread of censorious antiabolitionist laws from South to North, just as a culture of free speech had ultimately defeated the Sedition Act. And as seen again and again throughout this book, the lack of centralized (in this case federal) authority over the means of communication encouraged lively debate and undermined the effectiveness of local speech restrictions.

In the meantime, abolitionist writings grew in number, with women playing an instrumental role in spreading the gospel of freedom. Angelina Grimké was the daughter of a South Carolina slave owner but viewed slavery as inconsistent with her Christian beliefs. In 1837, she and her sister Sarah toured Massachusetts. In twenty-three weeks, they spoke at eighty-eight meetings in sixty-seven towns, directly reaching an estimated forty thousand people and persuading some twenty thousand women to sign antislavery petitions. Grimké became the first woman in America to address a legislative body when she spoke against slavery at the Massachusetts State House in February 1838. In her speech, she ingeniously combined advocacy of both abolition and women's rights. Grimké noted that women were told that slavery was a political issue, and thus off limits. She then eloquently destroyed such logic: "American women have to do with this subject, not only because it is moral and religious, but because it is political, inasmuch as we are citizens of this republic and as such our honor, happiness and well-being are bound up in its politics, governments and laws."[21]

More generally, print enabled women to wage war against slavery in a political battlefield normally reserved for men. In 1852, Harriet Beecher Stowe's *Uncle Tom's Cabin* became a sensation. It sold ten thousand copies within a week, three hundred thousand copies within a year, and two million copies by 1857 (it had been translated into more than twenty languages by then).[22] The book was said to have caused several slaveholders to emancipate their slaves, and to have inspired many slaves to flee. Unsurprisingly, the book was banned in Southern states, with fierce penalties for violators. In one instance, a free Black man in Maryland was sentenced to ten years in prison for possessing abolitionist literature that included *Uncle Tom's Cabin*.[23]

Outside the law, mobs—both in the South and in the North—took it into their own hands to muzzle the abolitionist movement by intimidation tactics, public burnings of abolitionist literature, and worse.[24] Elijah Lovejoy, editor of the abolitionist *Alton Observer* in Illinois, paid the ultimate price for his convictions. His printing press was attacked four times, until a mob destroyed it and killed Lovejoy while he desperately fought to defend it.[25] Southern newspapers invoked the Slaver's Veto and blamed Lovejoy for his own death, since he had "utterly disregarded the sentiments and feeling of a large majority of the people of that place." But in the North, the murder of Lovejoy did much to swing the public mood in favor of abolitionists. The *Brooklyn Gazette* spoke for many Northern newspapers when it commented that Lovejoy "was exercising a natural right, a right guaranteed to him by the Constitution of his country. He fell a martyr to the freedom of speech and of the press."[26]

Still, mobs in the North continued to disrupt abolitionist meetings, sometimes with the help of city officials. On May 16, 1838,

Angelina Grimké gave a speech at the newly opened Pennsylvania Hall in Philadelphia, which had been constructed by abolitionists to provide a public platform for discussing antislavery ideas. The combination of abolitionist speeches and Blacks and whites freely mingling greatly offended many Philadelphians; Grimké was heckled and the windows were pelted with stones.[27] Despite the attempts to intimidate her, Grimké insisted, "Every man and every woman present may do something by showing that we fear not a mob, and, in the midst of threatenings and revilings, by opening our mouths for the dumb and pleading the cause of those who are ready to perish."[28] The next day, an estimated ten thousand people attacked and burned Pennsylvania Hall to the ground, while the police and fire brigade stood idly by.[29]

Among the foremost voices in the abolitionist movement was Frederick Douglass. A runaway slave, Douglass became one of the nation's leading orators as well as a prominent writer and journalist, whose speeches and articles delivered devastating blows to the legitimacy of slavery. For Douglass, free speech was a decisive weapon. In an 1854 speech, he declared that he spoke on behalf of the enslaved who were "dumb in their chains! To utter one groan, or scream, for freedom in the presence of the Southern advocate of Popular Sovereignty, is to bring down the frightful lash upon their quivering flesh." Douglass, having tasted that very lash, made a compelling case for "why [he] should speak and speak freely," since "the right of speech is a very precious one, especially to the oppressed."[30]

Douglass became another target of mob action when a group of well-to-do Bostonians and their acolytes disrupted an abolitionist meeting in 1860. He responded with his short article "A Plea for Free Speech in Boston," delivered at a lecture at Boston's Music Hall. In it, Douglass called free speech "the dread of tyrants," without which "liberty is meaningless." All oppressive systems, he argued, were built on the denial of the right to think and speak freely, and slavery was no exception: "Slavery cannot tolerate free speech. Five years of its exercise would banish the auction block and break every chain in the South." Free speech served as a "moral renovator," but the full potential of this right rested on both the right to speak and to listen. Accordingly, "To suppress free speech is a double wrong. It violates the rights of the hearer as well as those of the speaker."

Douglass concluded by insisting, "A man's right to speak does not depend upon where he was born or upon his color. The simple quality of manhood is the solid basis of the right—and there let it rest forever."[31] Douglass's underlying idea that free speech is a core component of racial equality would resonate with the civil rights movement a century later.

Free speech on the subject of slavery became a key issue for the new Republican Party, which listed opposition to slavery as one of its central platforms when founded in 1854.[32] In the 1856 presidential election, Republicans campaigned for their nominee, John C. Frémont, with the slogan "Free Speech, Free Press, Free Men, Free Labor, Free Territory, and Frémont."[33] The Republican antislavery platform was furiously opposed by a Slaver's Veto. In 1856, an editorial in the *North Carolina Standard* responded to rumors of Frémont supporters in the state by declaring that "the expression of black Republican opinions in our midst, is incompatible with our honor and safety as a people."[34] An anonymous reply to the editorial claimed that a professor at the University of North Carolina was a Frémont supporter. Benjamin Hedrick, a professor of chemistry at the university, penned his own response to the editor, in which he openly declared that he was the Frémont supporter in question and explained in detail the reasons for his political opinions.

The reaction was fast and furious. Hendrick was condemned by the school's students, faculty, and trustees. He was even burned in effigy on campus. Local newspapers thundered against him. Under intense pressure, the university decided to terminate Hedrick's employment. The *Standard* wrote triumphantly: "Our object was to rid the University and the State of an avowed Fremont man; and we have succeeded. . . . No man who is avowedly for John C. Fremont for President, ought to be allowed to breathe the air or to tread the soil of North Carolina."[35]

But no amount of censorship or purging of abolitionists and their ideas could head off a bloody reckoning over slavery. In 1860, Abraham Lincoln was elected as the first Republican president. South Carolina reacted to "the election of a man . . . whose opinions and purposes are hostile to slavery" by seceding from the United States.[36] By February 1861, eleven Southern states had left the union, chosen a new president, and founded the Confederate States of America. The conflict escalated into full-scale civil war in April 1861.

In 1862, at the height of the war, Lincoln issued the Emancipation Proclamation freeing all slaves in Confederate territories captured by Union troops as of January 1, 1863. All slaves were officially freed when the Southern states surrendered to Union forces in 1865, and three constitutional amendments were adopted to secure their legal status as citizens. The Thirteenth Amendment of 1865 formally abolished slavery; the Fourteenth Amendment of 1868 recognized as American citizens "all persons born or naturalized in the United States," including African Americans, and prohibited states from denying "the equal protection of the laws" or restricting the "life, liberty or property" of any person "without due process of law"; and finally, the Fifteenth Amendment of 1870 gave African American men the right to vote.[37]

Black Codes and Red Scares

In spite of their new civil rights, African Americans were still treated as second-class citizens under the growing number of dehumanizing "black codes" and "Jim Crow laws." Racial segregation was legally recognized in the 1896 case *Plessy v. Ferguson*, in which the Supreme Court established the "separate but equal" doctrine, which remained in force into the 1960s.[38] Under this doctrine, the Supreme Court consistently refused to apply the Bill of Rights to state laws, and even approved racial segregation as constitutional. So the First Amendment long remained a dead letter when it came to the numerous state and local laws and practices limiting freedom of speech, association, and assembly. Free speech and the denial thereof played a key role in the nation's long struggle toward equality, particularly during the civil rights movement a century later.

These rights were also assaulted by nonstate actors. The Ku Klux Klan operated with impunity from—or even in tandem with—officials as Reconstruction was demolished and replaced by American apartheid. More than four thousand "racial terror lynchings" were carried out in the twelve Southern states between 1877 and 1950.[39]

In the absence of robust legal protections, the fight for racial equality had to rely on brave and passionate individual activism. Born into slavery in 1862, Ida B. Wells established herself as an important voice for Black rights, not least through her fearless practice of free speech as the editor and co-owner of the Black newspaper the *Memphis Free Speech* and her investigative reporting documenting and exposing lynchings.[40] In 1892, she wrote a now-famous editorial intimating that lynchings were not actually responses to rape, but to white women having consensual sexual affairs with Black men:

> Nobody in this section believes the old thread-bare lie that Negro men assault white women. If Southern white men are not careful they will over-reach themselves and a conclusion will be reached which will be very damaging to the moral reputation of their women.[41]

The editorial caused outrage. One local newspaper protested that "a black scoundrel [was] allowed to live and utter such loathsome and repulsive calumnies."[42] Another white newspaper directed its anger at Wells's male coeditor, declaring that the "black wretch who had written that foul lie should be tied to a stake . . . a pair of tailor's shears used on him, and he should then be burned."[43]

The incitement worked. A mob of whites stormed and destroyed the office of the *Memphis Free Speech*, forcing Wells to permanently leave the South. She eventually settled in Chicago, where she kept fighting for the rights of African Americans and women.[44] In 1910, she cofounded the National Association for the Advancement of Colored People (NAACP), which would play a key role in using the First Amendment as a battering ram against racial segregation.

Racial minorities were not the only targets of systematic intolerance in early twentieth-century America. In 1915, World War I ravaged Europe and threatened to entangle the US. Against this background, President Woodrow Wilson gave an ominous address to Congress accusing naturalized citizens of having "poured the poison of disloyalty into the very arteries of our national life" and having "sought to bring the authority and good name of our Government into contempt." Wilson urged Congress to adopt laws that would "crush" such "creatures of passion, disloyalty, and anarchy."[45]

When America finally entered the fray in 1917, the Espionage Act gave Wilson's warning teeth. Among other things, it banned conveying a long list of false information deemed harmful to US war efforts.[46] In 1918, the Espionage Act was amended with the Sedition Act, which banned a laundry list of speech including incitement to "insubordination" within the military; "disloyal, profane, scurrilous, or abusive language" about the government, the Constitution, the military, or the flag; advocating labor strikes; advocating violations of the act; or supporting countries at war with the United States.[47] It was as if the clock had been set back to 1798.

The Espionage and Sedition Acts had disastrous consequence for free speech, with approximately two thousand prosecutions and more than a thousand convictions resulting in many years of imprisonment.[48] Those targeted included communists, socialists, anarchists, peace activists, and—not least—members of the Industrial Workers of the World union (or "Wobblies"). The anarchist, feminist, and free speech activist Emma Goldman was arrested around forty times and spent considerable time in prison for her activism. Goldman—who was also a Russian-Jewish immigrant—was ultimately deported for opposing the draft.[49] Racism reared its ugly head as well. The editor of a Texas newspaper was sentenced to two years in prison for publishing a letter praising Black soldiers who had been sentenced to death for a deadly race-related mutiny.[50] Women's rights also fell victim to the intolerant atmosphere. In February 1919, at least forty members of the National Woman's Party were arrested after burning an effigy of President Wilson and making "violent speeches" denouncing Wilson as "the leader of an autocratic party" holding "millions of women in political slavery" at a suffragist protest outside the White House.[51]

Following a pattern that would become all too familiar later, private institutions helped create a "cancel culture" in which criticism of the war was seen as bordering on treason. In 1917, the trustees at Columbia University dismissed two professors for their antiwar opinions. The *New York Times* wrote an editorial praising Columbia for cracking down on doctrines "dangerous to the community and to the nation." The editorial declared that "if colleges and universities are not to become breeding grounds of radicalism and socialism, it must be recognized that academic freedom has two sides, that freedom to teach is correlative to the freedom to dispense with poisonous teaching."[52]

The Espionage Act also banned certain publications from being sent by mail. Opposition to the war or the government's policies was sufficient to exclude printed material from circulation by the postmaster general.[53] This affected newspapers pointing out the hypocrisy of urging Blacks to fight in the war abroad when they were denied their equal rights at home.[54] Several issues of the NAACP's

Crisis magazine were excluded from the mail; the Post Office Department found it "exceedingly dangerous" and deemed "exciting race prejudice" to be the publication's principal purpose.[55]

Moreover, when the US entered the war in 1917, a censorship board was established to filter all communication between the US and foreign countries and prevent "false" and "demoralizing" statements. By the end of the war, the board had compiled a list of the names and addresses of more than 250,000 potential suspects.[56]

The First Amendment provided scant protection against this coordinated onslaught. Prior to World War I, press freedom claims—if addressed at all—were uniformly rejected by the Supreme Court on the basis of the "bad tendency" test, or even restrictive Blackstonianism, which limited free speech to protection against prepublication censorship.[57] In a string of cases in 1919, the Supreme Court unanimously upheld convictions of up to ten years in prison for antiwar agitation in pamphlets, political speeches, and newspaper articles.[58] In *Schenck v. United States* (1919), the court affirmed the conviction of Socialist Party leaders Charles Schenck and Elizabeth Baer for violating the Espionage Act when mailing leaflets to US soldiers denouncing their conscriptions as a violation of the Bill of Rights. Still, there were signs that the court's definition of free speech was in flux. In *Schenck*, Justice Oliver Wendell Holmes developed his famous "clear and present danger" test, which sought to narrow the permissible grounds for speech restrictions. According to Holmes, words that are normally "protected by the First Amendment may become subject to prohibition when of such a nature and used in such circumstances as to create a clear and present danger that they will bring about the substantive evils which Congress has a right to prevent." Yet Holmes was not quite ready to provide any real teeth to this particular parchment barrier, and he voted to uphold the conviction of Schenck and Baer, with the now infamous dictum that free speech does "not protect a man in falsely shouting fire in a theatre." This phrase has since become a worn cliché, dragged out whenever someone wants to argue that specific viewpoints should not be protected by free speech.[59]

When a fourth case was decided by the Supreme Court in November 1919, Holmes wrote one of the most influential dissents in First Amendment history. *Abrams v. United States* involved Russian-Jewish communist immigrants who had received sentences of up to twenty years in prison for circulating pamphlets that opposed sending US troops to Russia and denounced the war. For Holmes, this was much too far, since "the ultimate good desired is better reached by free trade in ideas." Holmes acknowledged that free speech was an "experiment," but still counseled that "we should be eternally vigilant against attempts to check the expression of opinions that we loathe . . . unless they so imminently threaten immediate interference with the lawful and pressing purposes of the law that an immediate check is required to save the country."[60]

With the First Amendment being kept on life support by the dissenting opinions of Justice Holmes and his colleague Justice Louis Brandeis, American free speech needed a shot of activism to revive its Madisonian spirit. The end of the war did not end the onslaught on civil rights, as nationwide bombing campaigns by anarchists and leftists mingled with fears raised by the Russian Revolution to fuel the First Red Scare. It culminated with the Palmer Raids and the arrests of thousands of union organizers and socialists, with scant regard for their freedom of speech and assembly.[61] And so, in 1920, the American Civil Liberties Union (ACLU) was founded to strike back. Combating the systematic targeting of trade unionists and socialists was high on the organization's agenda. But the ACLU also fought for African Americans and other minorities hampered by discriminatory acts, such as a Mississippi law from 1920 that made it a misdemeanor to print or distribute "information, arguments or suggestions in favor of social equality or of intermarriage between whites and negroes."[62]

Given the massive "collateral damage" of World War I restrictions and the Red Scare, the ACLU worked from the hypothesis that—in the words of the chronicler of ACLU history Samuel Walker—"the principal strategy for advancing group rights came to be the expansion of constitutionally protected individual rights." This meant rejecting the idea of group libel laws restricting the free speech of bigots and racists, since the ACLU leadership believed that "any proposal to limit individual rights, no matter how narrowly defined, threatened the very basis of their program."[63]

The ACLU's defense of radicals, coupled with the communist sympathies of its key leaders, did not exactly win them universal approval. With the rise of European fascism in the 1930s, the group also came under assault by its own members for defending the rights of American Nazis, whose end goals were the denial of the freedoms that the ACLU was established to protect.

Forced to respond, the ACLU published the 1934 pamphlet *Shall We Defend the Free Speech of Nazis in America?* It made a meticulous case for the ACLU's principled stand by highlighting how free speech restrictions had been used to systematically target progressive movements, how hate speech laws were open to abuse, that punishing Nazis for their speech only made martyrs out of monsters, and that abandoning its principles would seriously undermine the ACLU's position when defending the rights of other unpopular groups.[64]

As the ACLU worked to convince its members that defending the free speech rights of Nazis and unpopular minorities were two sides of the same coin, it was winning landmark legal victories. In the 1930s the organization finally convinced the Supreme Court to strike down state laws violating the First Amendment by way of "incorporation" of the Fourteenth Amendment, subjecting states to the Bill of Rights. Suddenly, state and local governments could no longer consider the First Amendment irrelevant to the battery of laws and practices restricting speech. Madison's attempt to bind the states to the constitutional protection of free speech had originally been killed by Congress. Now, it was being revived by the Supreme Court.

Just how powerful a weapon this new legal avenue could be for proponents of civil liberties was demonstrated in *Herndon v. Lowry* (1937). Angelo Herndon was a Black Communist Party member who was arrested for possessing various communist writings when he went to Atlanta on a recruitment drive in 1932. The state of Georgia pushed for the death penalty, arguing that Herndon was planning to "lead a red army into this country and destroy our civilization," but the jury "only" sentenced him to eighteen to twenty years for incitement to insurrection. The incriminating writings called for unemployment and emergency relief and equal rights for Blacks; there was no evidence that Herndon was advocating a violent overthrow of the government. Herndon appealed his case numerous times. Given his race, politics, and activism, it seemed certain he would not prevail. But after a byzantine legal process, a 5–4 majority of the Supreme Court overturned Herndon's conviction in 1937, finding that "to make membership in the party and solicitation of members for that party a criminal offense . . . is an unwarranted invasion of the right of freedom of speech." Moreover, the opinion held that the Georgia law in question amounted to "a dragnet which may enmesh any one who agitates for a change of government if a jury can be persuaded that he ought to have foreseen his words would have some effect in the future conduct of others."[65]

In *Herndon*, the Supreme Court reined in the "bad tendency" test and replaced it with a version of Oliver Wendell Holmes's "clear and present danger" test that protected a broader swath of speech. It also sent an important signal that African Americans could rely on their constitutional rights to free expression and association, even when advocating doctrines hostile to the prevailing political order and majoritarian sentiments. According to professor of philosophy Timothy Shiell, this was the first time the Supreme Court protected a Black person's free speech and struck down a Southern speech restriction. For Black Americans, liberty and equality seemed to finally converge.[66]

Liberalism and Imperialism
in the British Empire

By the second half of the nineteenth century, America's former colonial masters in the United Kingdom had not only abolished slavery but also widened democratic participation, limited religious discrimination, and ensured a much safer platform for press freedom. In his *Introduction to the Study of the Law of the Constitution* from 1885, the great English jurist A. V. Dicey wrote that despite the lack of any express legal protection of press freedom, "the press, and especially the newspaper press, has practically enjoyed with us a freedom which till recent years was unknown in continental states."[67]

Nor was this supposedly happy state of affairs confined to the British Isles. The *Encyclopedia Britannica* from 1888 declared boldly, "In the British colonies the press is as free as it is in England."[68] Had that been true, the sun would never have set on the free press. But the actual practice of British colonialism was very different from the idealized version described by liberal imperialists in Britain. The British Empire dwarfed all other European colonial powers, ensuring a level of global hegemony through its command and control of land and resources from the Americas to Asia and beyond. And Britain was more than willing to use its global reach to employ bigoted and racially motivated censorship and repression when new ideas were thought to threaten its interests in places like Hong Kong, India, and Africa. So while the enforcement of British speech crimes had discriminated on the basis of class in the early nineteenth century, it discriminated its colonial subjects on the basis of language, ethnicity, and race in the early twentieth century.

India was the crown jewel of the British Empire, and no less an advocate of a free press than John Stuart Mill was an employee of the East India Company, which more or less ran (and exploited) India until the establishment of direct rule by the British, also known as the British Raj, in 1858. To Mill, Indians were on the lower rungs on the "ladder of civilization" and needed "the dominion of foreigners" to carry them up the ladder and "clear away obstacles to improvement."[69] In 1852—seven years before publishing *On Liberty*—Mill showed very little interest in the question of Indian press freedom when queried at a hearing in the House of Lords. Mill thought that "both the dangers and the advantages of the free press in India have been very much overrated." Besides, the comments of the Indian newspaper press were "seldom of any value."[70] A stark contrast to Mill's later categorical advocacy of press freedom in Britain.

The British Raj began relatively liberally in 1858, with Britain confident that it was firmly in control. In the words of historian Robert Darnton, "Britannica ruled and the press remained free, free even to lament the country's lack of independence."[71] But as British anxieties about maintaining power increased, more and more speech restrictions were imposed. The crime of seditious libel was added to the penal code in 1870, defined loosely to ensnare anyone who "excites or attempts to excite feelings of disaffection towards, Her Majesty or the Government." The promotion of "feelings of enmity or hatred between different classes of Her Majesty's subjects" was criminalized in 1898, creating an early form of hate speech law.[72] After all, the Indian was, in the words of the lieutenant-governor of Punjab, "traditionally disposed to believe evil of his government, difficult to arouse, perhaps, but emotional and inflammable when once aroused."[73]

Things really got out of hand after the partition of Bengal in 1905, which separated the largely Muslim eastern areas from the predominantly Hindu western areas of the province. That was when the Indian penal code came in handy; several anticolonial voices, including the prominent nationalist leader and newspaper editor Bal Gangadhar Tilak, were convicted of sedition and promoting enmity between communities.[74] The authorities now saw nationalist publications as an existential threat, which led to a systematic crackdown reminiscent of Pitt's Reign of Terror.[75] But despite—or perhaps because of—the crackdown, Indian independence gained a new, formidable champion.

No one better symbolizes India's anticolonial struggle for independence than Mahatma Gandhi, whose efforts became the gold standard for nonviolent resistance to oppression. Gandhi may have rejected guns, but the principle of free speech was one of the most powerful weapons in his arsenal. He regarded freedom of opinion and association as "the two lungs that are absolutely necessary for a man to breathe the oxygen of liberty."[76] In a 1921 article in his newspaper *Young India*, he even stated that "sedition has become the creed of the [Indian National] Congress"—the nationalist movement he later became the president of.[77] Such dissent landed him in court for sedition in March 1922. At the trial, he gave a famous speech taking aim at the criminalization of sedition, which he denounced as

> designed to suppress the liberty of the citizen. Affection cannot be manufactured or regulated by law. If one has no affection for a person or system, one should be free to give the fullest expression to his disaffection, so long as he does not contemplate, promote or incite to violence.[78]

Gandhi was still sentenced to six years in prison, but his ideas were not so easily silenced. Far from suffocating sedition, what became known as the Great Trial made the crime one of the most prominent of platforms from which to brutally expose the irreconcilable chasm between British liberalism and imperialism for all to see. Gandhi's nonviolent fight for free speech would inspire Martin Luther King and the American civil rights movement as well as Nelson Mandela and the African National Congress in Apartheid South Africa. According to King, "India's Gandhi was the guiding light of our technique of nonviolent social change."[79]

British West Africa came closest to the British ideal of extending press freedom to colonial subjects. A free and vibrant press emerged in what is now the Gambia, Sierra Leone, Ghana, and Nigeria.[80] A 1902 editorial in the newspaper *Gold Coast Leader* told readers, "We are positively thirsting for materials that will be talked about, at the store, office, a social gathering or at home."[81] West African publishers were also keenly aware of the importance of the press, which one editor in 1903 called "the only medium for the people to express their grievances."[82]

But from early on, the British were worried about the power of political ideas. Pan-Africanism, in particular, threatened to unite Black subjects across the empire in the cause of independence. In 1918, the British governor in Guyana warned his colleague in Jamaica about a circular letter intercepted by colonial censors. The letter sought to gather support for an independent African colony among Black Jamaicans. The governor feared the "harmful effects" that its continued circulation might have, addressed as it was to all "Negroes."[83]

The 1930s saw a major reversal in official press tolerance in the colonies, including West Africa. In 1934, the British secretary of state distributed a top secret telegram instructing all colonial governors to ban the importation of the *Negro Anthology*, which contained articles written by a wide range of authors from around the world united by the cause of Pan-Africanism and anticolonialism. The book was edited by Nancy Cunard, a white British heiress who shocked polite society with her procommunist views and interracial relationships. This was a cocktail too explosive for even the relatively permissive environment of West Africa.[84]

Even more unnerving was the return from Europe of African anticolonial activists with connections to international anti-imperialist movements, who set up radical newspapers intent on undermining colonial rule from within. Sedition acts were passed in response, and authors were put under surveillance and exiled for their writings. Foreign publications were steadily added to an index of books prohibited from importation. In the words of the governor of Nigeria, "the time has come to take a less lenient line with the Press generally."[85] It was a huge and humiliating about-face by an empire that for decades had showcased West African press freedom as an example of the blessings of liberal imperialism.

British ideals of press freedom would also create headaches for the government in the crown colony of Hong Kong. There the authorities were worried about anticolonial sentiments which might inflame the local population against British rule. In 1914, Hong Kong's colonial secretary complained of newspapers of a "highly seditious and disloyal character," which, "disseminated amongst ill-educated persons," were "likely to be productive of disturbance and ill feeling in the Colony."[86] Accordingly, the Seditious Publications Ordinance of April 1914 defined sedition as any expression "likely or [which] may have a tendency directly or indirectly . . . to bring into hatred or contempt His Majesty, or the Government . . . or the administration of justice . . . or any class or section of His Majesty's subjects."[87]

While being a hegemonic superpower with colonial possessions straddling the globe had its challenges, it also brought benefits of scale. It allowed the British Empire to establish the world's first global system of mass surveillance and censorship, which was up and running by World War I. In 1914, when Britain controlled nearly 60 percent of the world's undersea cable networks, "cable censors" were dispatched to filter traffic running through vital points along the world's communications infrastructure, including a main cable station in Hong Kong. According to a report from the War Office, British surveillance was supposed to cover "all telegrams that touch British territory at any point." The scope and purpose of the surveillance and censorship system quickly expanded from counter-intelligence to the point where there was hardly "any department of human activity during the war that did not come within the purview of the cable censorship."[88] This included continuing the time-honored British tradition of waging war on "rumors, propaganda and misinformation," but the telegraph was also used to *disseminate* propaganda by both Britain and other participants in the war.[89]

The prepublication censorship in Hong Kong that was introduced with the outbreak of World War I was so useful to the colonial government it was continued after the war, and used to counter all and sundry threats to British interests. In 1922, an Emergency Regulations Ordinance was adopted in response to a series of strikes that fed the government's fear of nationalist and communist movements.[90] It empowered the chief executive in council to institute "censorship, and the control and suppression of publications, writings . . . communications and means of communication" at his sole discretion.[91]

In 1925, the government used another strike as an excuse to expand censorship. Any and all printing, publishing, and distribution of Chinese-language publications had to be submitted to and vetted by the secretary of Chinese affairs prior to publication. The clock in Hong Kong had been turned back to before 1695, when the British Parliament had let the Licensing Act lapse and abolished preventive censorship—but only for the Chinese. The *South China Morning Post* savaged the government's spurious claim that censorship was justified because of the potential state of danger, arguing that it "opens the door to complete denial of the elementary British right of free speech, and must be opposed."

The campaign to abolish preventive censorship picked up pace in 1936, when fifty editors of Chinese newspapers petitioned Lo Man Kam, a Chinese member of the legislative council, to champion the cause of press freedom. Lo stepped up and made an eloquent attack on censorship, demonstrating how the government had "imposed a permanent system of censorship upon the Chinese Press" under the cloak of a temporary emergency law. He also exposed the extreme hypocrisy and double standards of the parallel English and Chinese systems of censorship. Several articles on censorship had been published without restriction in English-language newspapers but were censored when translated by Chinese newspapers. Stressing that the Licensing Act had lapsed in 1695, Lo invoked Blackstone's definition of press freedom and pointed out that *Halsbury's Laws of England*, an encyclopedia of British law, made no colonial exceptions for the liberty of the press. But the Hong Kong government was adamant that "prevention is obviously better than cure."[92] Preventive censorship continued in Hong Kong until the 1950s, when the climate for diversity in opinion became less restrictive, and at the British handover in 1997, Hong Kong was bequeathed a Basic Law ensuring freedom of the press as a parting gift.

Yet, as we will learn in later chapters, the British legacy of censorship and repression still influences the climate for free speech in both India and Hong Kong today, as colonial-era injunctions against sedition, hate speech, and blasphemy remain on the book. Though now used by their former victims against very different targets, such as prodemocracy protestors in Hong Kong and critics of the Modi government's policies on religious (in)tolerance and climate change in India.[93]

———

FROM THE NINETEENTH CENTURY TO THE FIRST DECADES of the twentieth, press freedom advanced significantly in the US, the UK, and beyond. But these advances were unequally distributed. Racial minorities and political radicals in America and the inhabitants of the British colonies were vulnerable to harsh censorship and repression no longer deemed acceptable when deployed against dissent from within majoritarian mainstream opinion in America or Europe. But things were about to get a whole lot worse for European minorities and dissenters.

10

The Totalitarian Temptation

In November 2019, German chancellor Angela Merkel delivered an unusually passionate speech before the German Bundestag. "We have freedom of expression in this country," she declared. "But the freedom of expression has limits. And they begin where there is incitement, where hatred is spread, and where the dignity of other people is violated." She insisted, "we must and will oppose this. Otherwise this society will no longer be what it used to be."[1]

Merkel grew up under a stifling communist dictatorship and came to lead a country where vicious fascist propaganda once helped pave the way for genocide. Few politicians have stronger credentials when it comes to balancing the pros and cons of free speech. And there can be no doubt that the German commitment to "militant democracy" stems from a sincere belief that democracies cannot tolerate intolerance.

It is no accident that the ideas most crucial to the prevailing postwar conception of free speech and its limits were framed by those with firsthand experience of totalitarianism. Karl Loewenstein, an émigré professor from Nazi Germany, coined the term "militant democracy" in 1937. Loewenstein warned that "the lack of militancy of the Weimar Republic against subversive movements, even though clearly recognized as such, stands out in the post-war predicament of democracy both as an illustration and as a warning."[2] In particular, he accused democracies faced by fascist movements of having "gravely sinned by their leniency, or by too legalistic concepts of the freedom of public opinion."[3]

In a similar vein the "paradox of tolerance" was defined in *The Open Society and Its Enemies*, written by Karl Popper in 1945 while in exile from the Nazi regime. Popper held that the very survival of tolerance required defenders of liberal democracy to be willing to fight the intolerant with intolerance.[4]

George Orwell disagreed. Having fought communism with his pen and fascism with guns during the Spanish Civil War, he cautioned against the "widespread tendency to argue that one can only defend democracy by totalitarian methods" in an unpublished preface to his famous novel *Animal Farm* from 1945. He also discussed the dangers of treating as enemies "those who . . . spread mistaken doctrines" and warned that "if you encourage totalitarian methods, the time may come when they will be used against you instead of for you."[5] Even Karl Popper saw restrictions on speech as a last resort in democracies faced by intolerant philosophies "as long as we can counter them by rational argument and keep them in check by public opinion, suppression would certainly be most unwise."[6]

These conflicting approaches to extreme speech are still with us today, shaping debates about the limits of hate speech that are so central to the digital era of instant online discourse and resurgent authoritarianism. On the one hand, freedom of expression is a foundational value ensuring the pluralism and autonomy that is anathema to totalitarianism. On the other, many countries restrict free speech to safeguard against propaganda aimed at undermining democracy and the rights and dignity of minorities. This raises the question: Should open societies be more afraid of totalitarian movements abusing free speech to destroy freedom itself, or of democratic governments abusing the limits on free speech to silence dissent and unwittingly forging the chains with which authoritarians may fetter all speech once in power?

The Red Lines
of the Dictatorship of the Proletariat

The totalitarian chain reaction that devastated so much in the twentieth century started in Russia. Tsar Nicholas I finally freed Russia from the yoke of prepublication censorship in 1905, creating a short-lived burst of newspapers and magazines.[7] But as opposition to tsarism and the popularity of socialism swept through his country, he tried to stem the tide by reimposing ever stricter controls on the press. It was too late: nothing could save the tsarist monarchy now. In early March 1917, amidst the chaos of World War I, Russians took to the streets and the regime came tumbling down. A revolutionary government of opposition politicians, ranging from moderate liberals to revolutionary socialists, took control on March 15. In its very first public announcement, the provisional government established "freedom of speech, press, association, and assembly."[8]

As soon as he heard the news, the revolutionary socialist leader Vladimir Lenin, who had been exiled to Western Europe since 1907, hurried back to Russia and declared "nowhere is there such freedom as exists in Russia today." But Lenin had no intention of preserving this state of affairs. The young Karl Marx may have been a vocal advocate of press freedom in the reactionary atmosphere of the nineteenth century, but Lenin was an entirely different beast. And while he was happy to take advantage of the collapse of tsarist censorship, he held the "Bourgeois conception of freedom of the press" in disdain. To Lenin, press freedom was only a "freedom for the rich systematically, unremittingly, daily, in millions of copies, to deceive, corrupt, and fool the exploited and oppressed mass of the people."[9] He promised to "close down" the bourgeois press "when time [was] ripe."[10]

That time came sooner than expected. Throughout the autumn of 1917, the provisional government was shaken by a new wave of protests, strikes, and a botched counterrevolution. Lenin and the Bolsheviks took this as a cue to launch a new revolution. On November 7, they overthrew the provisional government and established a dictatorship of the proletariat. The first legislative act of the new regime was a Decree on the Press "against the counter-revolutionary press of different shades," which authorized the suppression of publications deemed to be seditious or calling for resistance. According to the decree, "Every one knows that the bourgeois press is one of the most powerful weapons of the bourgeoisie." In fact, the press was "no less dangerous than bombs and machine-guns." And so, "temporary extraordinary measures were taken to stem the torrent of filth and slander."[11]

In Petrograd alone, as many as five newspapers were closed every day between November 16 and the end of the month.[12] The printing presses and property of many shuttered newspapers were requisitioned for Bolshevik and leftist newspapers, with the promise that these measures would end and the press be granted "complete freedom" once things had settled down.[13] Needless to say, the moment of complete freedom never arrived. But those who believed in press freedom did not give up without a fight. Writers, publishers, and printers protested loudly, published bootleg newspapers, and threatened strikes.[14] The liberal editor and politician Vladimir Nabokov—father of the more famous author of *Lolita*—protested the "contemptible and disgusting terror and crazy reprisal established by Lenin" before going into exile.[15]

A week after Lenin's press decree, an intense debate on freedom of speech took place in the Central Executive Committee, the leading organ of Soviet power. It began at the fifth session of the Central Executive Committee on November 17, when the Bolshevik Yuri Larin introduced a motion to revoke the press decree. The pro-Leninist Bolshevik Varlam Avanesov immediately challenged the proposal, arguing, "Having silenced the bourgeois press, [they] would be very naïve if they were to let slip from their hands such a powerful means of influencing the ideals of all workers, soldiers, and peasants." Once the communist society was achieved, "a socialist press [would] ensure freedom of speech for all citizens and for all tendencies of thought."

But the Leninist version of equal free speech was not exactly inspired by the Athenian concepts of *isēgoría* and *parrhēsía*. Avanesov's arguments received the backing of both Lenin and Leon Trotsky, who asked if "newspapers should [be allowed] to exist which depend upon the banks rather than upon the people?" It just so happened that the Bolsheviks represented the voice and will of the people. From this it followed, according to Trotsky, that "all the press media should be handed over to Soviet power."

Boris Malkin, a leading member of the rival Left Socialist-Revolutionaries, condemned the double standards of Lenin and Trotsky: "We Socialist-Revolutionaries were once prisoners of tsarism but we were never its slaves, and we don't want to establish slavery for anyone now." Even so, the motion to revoke the press decree was rejected by thirty-one to twenty-two votes. The new Bolshevik government had formally killed freedom of expression, and it would not be officially revived until the last days and collapse of the Soviet Union in the early 1990s. Another Socialist-Revolutionary, Prosh Proshyan, sadly declared that the resolution "legalizes repression and clearly shows that the Bolshevik members of the [Central Executive Committee] are embarking upon a path of terror."[16]

Proshyan's prediction proved prophetic. When the first free elections in Russian history were held on November 25, 1917, the Socialist-Revolutionaries triumphed while the Bolsheviks received less than a quarter of the votes. Lenin's response was to dissolve the Constituent Assembly. After all, how could the people be properly represented if their genuine representatives were outvoted?

The Bolsheviks were now free to completely muzzle the press, one step at a time. First, they sapped their income with a state monopoly on advertising. Violations were sanctioned with closure and confiscation of assets. Then, on December 20, a secret police force—the *Cheka*—was instituted for the purpose of "watching over the press" and rooting out opposition. A month later, another decree empowered the government to sentence seditious journalists to jail, deportation, and banishment to Siberia—just as the tsar had done.[17] The definition of sedition included "any falsified and distorted news about social events since they provoked infringement of rights and freedoms of the working class."[18] With such a blanket definition, the regime could easily remove any critical voices. The next step was to shut down the remaining independent papers. The entire "bourgeois" (i.e., nonsocialist) press was suppressed in March 1918. Over the following year, papers that were socialist but not strictly Bolshevik were likewise shut down by a special press tribunal. The last nail in the coffin came in March 1919, when the paper of the Moscow Printing Trades Union was forced to close. The flourishing press of the early 1910s had in essence been reduced to a one-party press.[19]

As would also be the case in Fascist Italy and Nazi Germany, censorship went hand in hand with propaganda and tight management of the press, which Lenin viewed as "a collective propagandist . . . agitator [and] organizer."[20] By early 1918, the new regime distributed 884 Bolshevik newspapers and 753 magazines in twenty different languages, and the numbers would only grow. To ensure complete party control, membership of the Communist Party became obligatory for all journalists.[21] In Lenin's eyes, a one-party press and wall-to-wall propaganda was the real definition of press freedom. He even asked rhetorically if there were a country in the world in which the average worker "enjoy[ed] anything approaching such liberty . . . of using the largest printing plants and biggest stocks of paper to express his ideas and to defend his interests . . . as in Soviet Russia?"[22] Of course, the average worker was never allowed to publish any ideas except through the ventriloquism of the party machinery.

To ensure compliance from the intelligentsia, some 160 famous intellectuals and academics were rounded up and deported from the country on account of their "anti-Soviet activities" in the fall of 1922. Deported by steamboats later known as "philosophers' ships," the philosophers, theologians, economists, sociologists, and writers aboard were warned not to return unless they wanted to be shot.[23] The purge was meant, first and foremost, as a warning to ensure strict compliance to the Soviet line of thought. Joseph Stalin—by now appointed general secretary by Lenin—ominously warned any exiles who refused to submit to the omniscience of the party and clung to their outdated ideals to "remember that we carry out our promises. And how we follow up our warnings."[24] A rather ironic injunction given that Stalin was sentenced to no less than seven separate Siberian exiles during tsarist rule.[25]

After winning the bloody civil war following the revolution, Lenin was not about to repeat the mistake of the tsarist regime, which had contributed to its own demise by relaxing censorship and allowing the writings of people like Karl Marx. The perfect Bolshevik state needed full control over the flow of information. So in 1922, a centralized censorship bureau known as *Glavlit* (General Directorate for the Protection of State Secrets in the Press) was established to keep control over all publishing, including fiction and scientific research. Glavlit employed thousands of censors whose job was to weed out "propaganda against the Soviet Union" that "stirred up public opinion through false information" or "aroused nationalistic or religious fanaticism."[26] Glavlit censors confiscated and destroyed thousands of books, movies, and audio records from libraries, bookstores, cinemas, clubs, and theatres.[27] Copying the tried and tested methods of Henry VIII and the Catholic Church, the bureau compiled an annual index of forbidden material. The *Perechen* contained references to forbidden authors and texts as well as long lists of subjects and terms that could not be mentioned in print. The prohibited topics included information about natural disasters, nonauthorized statistics on homelessness and unemployment, information about foreign living standards, and—of course—any mention of Glavlit itself and its activities.[28] To enshrine its constantly changing draft of Russian history, Glavlit worked closely with the secret police, which provided the muscle to arrest and intimidate those who strayed outside the red lines.[29]

As in Old Regime France, the huge amount of published material made it necessary for Glavlit to outsource much of the censorship to editors and publishers, who self-censored for fear of punishment. "Political editors" came to be employed at every publishing house as the first line of defense.[30] As the head of Glavlit remarked in 1936, "the greater the sense of responsibility of each editor, the less work there will be for the employee of the censorship."[31] It was a highly successful strategy. According to an internal Glavlit report from 1928, out of the three hundred thousand manuscripts they inspected from Petrograd and Moscow, the censors rejected merely 0.3 to 1 percent. As the report boasted, "Political and ideological orientation of the Soviet Power is so clear, definite, and firm that harmful material is submitted only by people who either are inveterate foes of socialist construction or are lacking in political literacy."[32] The red lines had been internalized.

In the 1930s, censorship and repression initiated by Lenin reached genocidal proportions under Stalin, to whom "every criticism was a battle of survival," in the words of historian Simon Sebag Montefiore. Stalin—an avid reader of history, philosophy, and world literature—took a direct and personal interest in defining the red lines of the Soviet public sphere. He spent countless hours poring through draft news articles and book manuscripts and screening movies, acting as supreme censor, editor, and critic, whose orders, edits, and "friendly advice" had to be followed scrupulously by publishers, journalists, authors, directors, and playwrights who cared about their careers, freedom, and, ultimately, their lives.[33]

As Stalin's increasing paranoia spread through the entire censorship system, the Glavlit censors became obsessed with removing ambiguity that might be interpreted as remotely suspicious, and were terrified of the consequences if they let anything illegal slip through—and with good reason. In 1937, the head of Glavlit was arrested and later shot in one of Stalin's Great Purges.[34] The censors were instructed to pay close attention to "so-called typographic errors" that could be perceived as a clever way to express dissent. These included such terrible things as hyphens in the words "counter-revolutionary" and "anti-Bolshevik." According to a senior Glavlit official, "Such a hyphenation of words constitutes the gravest political distortion."[35] Images were also scrutinized carefully to ensure that they could not be misinterpreted. This led to absurdities like a 1935 circular from the central Moscow bureau of censorship commenting on a photo of Stalin and Comintern's general secretary Georgi Dimitrov: "The curls on Comrade Dimitrov's forehead interweave in such a way that they create the impression of a drawn swastika. . . . Glavlit categorically forbids further printing of this picture."[36]

By the end of the 1930s, Stalin presided over a highly efficient juggernaut of repression ring-fenced by a Kafkaesque bureaucracy of various offices that controlled not only all publications but also each other. In 1940, Stalin's army of repression consisted of about five thousand censors. From 1938 to 1939 alone, Glavlit ordered the withdrawal of almost eight thousand politically harmful books penned by around nineteen hundred authors. Altogether, more than sixteen thousand titles and more than twenty-four million copies of printed works were removed from libraries and the book trade network.[37] The workings of this machine of literary extermination were entirely unhampered by any semblance of due process or individual freedoms, and the orders could be enforced by the secret police and sanctioned with deportations to concentration camps or a bullet to the back of the head.

One of the most feared instruments of Soviet repression was the infamous Article 58 of the criminal code on "counter-revolutionary crimes." It included a whole laundry list of subarticles criminalizing everything from treason to counterrevolutionary sabotage. Article 58, section 10, on "anti-Soviet agitation," was particularly broad.[38] "Who among us has not experienced its all-encompassing embrace?" asked the dissident author Aleksandr Solzhenitsyn in his 1973 *The Gulag Archipelago*, a clandestinely compiled account of the regime's sprawling system of slave labor camps, where he spent eight years, convicted under Article 58-10 for criticizing Stalin in private letters. "In all truth, there is no step, thought, action, or lack of action under the heavens which could not be punished by the heavy hand of Article 58."[39] Solzhenitsyn was not alone. In addition to "enemies of the people," the gulags were filled with "babblers," convicted under Article 58-10 for criticizing or telling a joke about the party or Stalin. Not infrequently such babblers were denounced by neighbors or colleagues.[40]

Interestingly, Article 123 of the so-called Stalin Constitution from 1936 declared punishable by law "any advocacy of racial or national exclusiveness or hatred and contempt."[41] While this erstwhile commitment to equality did little to stop the demonization and deportation of millions of people from national and ethnic minorities within the Soviet Union, the Soviets later fought hard to include similar hate speech injunctions into international law during the Cold War, with long-term consequences for global free speech that would outlive both Stalin and the Soviet Union as such.

Although the blatant absurdities of the Stalinist regime do have a certain comic quality, they were no laughing matter. Stalin's legacy ranks among history's worst crimes against humanity. About a million people were executed or died from mistreatment in prisons and labor camps during the Great Purge in 1937 to 1938 alone. More than eighteen million prisoners were deported to the gulags from 1934 to 1953, and millions died from famines that were often engineered deliberately to combat "class enemies."[42] Stalin explained the murderous logic behind the terror to his henchman Lavrentiy Beria, head of the dreaded secret police (NKVD), which did most of the terrorizing. "An Enemy of the People," said Stalin, is "one who doubts the rightness of the Party line." And since there were "a lot" of such doubters "we must liquidate them."[43]

The combination of extreme censorship and incessant propaganda facilitated these crimes. Solzhenitsyn noted that the gulags could only metastasize because "there was no public opinion in the Soviet Union."[44] The regime's massive crimes against its own people went unchecked because "no news could leak out. If some muffled rumor did, with no confirmation from newspapers, with informers busily nosing it out, it would not get far enough to matter; there would be no outburst of public indignation."[45]

Soviet propaganda was also internalized outside the USSR, where many members of the communist Left closed their eyes to Stalin's crimes for decades. The *New York Times* correspondent Walter Duranty won the 1932 Pulitzer Prize for his reporting from the Soviet Union, despite his reliance on Stalinist propaganda that obfuscated the fact that millions of Ukrainians were starving to death under the policies of forced collectivization or were murdered in a policy of "liquidating" the "kulaks," whose opposition to Stalin's mass murderous policies made them "class enemies."[46] During World War II, the British Ministry of Information warned a publisher not to publish George Orwell's novella *Animal Farm*, since its thinly veiled criticism of Lenin and Stalin was likely to cause "offence" to the Soviets.[47] The brutal purge or liquidation of millions of "enemies of the people" trailblazed by the Bolsheviks also followed communism's global migration with horrific consequences in places like Maoist China and Cambodia under the Khmer Rouge.

Even today, Russia has not yet exorcized the spirit of Glavlit. In 2017, the Russian Ministry of Culture banned the British film *The Death of Stalin*, which ridiculed the Stalinist system, from distribution in theatres. The ministry assured the public that "we have freedom of speech," but added, "The film desecrates our historical symbols."[48]

Nothing Against the State: Italian Fascism

While Lenin and Stalin were busy with the ideological purification of the Soviet Union, another totalitarian ideology reared its ugly head in Italy. Before gaining office, Mussolini and his squads of black-shirted Fascists silenced their critics and opponents with brute force, terrorizing leftists and burning down newspaper offices. They came into power in the fall of 1922, after thousands of Blackshirts marched on Rome to overthrow the government. The political establishment blinked and appointed Mussolini prime minister in the vain hope that they could make him play by their rules. But the Fascists had nothing but contempt for democracy. Through a mix of repression, intimidation, and violence, Mussolini installed a full dictatorship in 1925—or, as he would later describe it, "an organized, centralized, and authoritative democracy."[49] But the democratic elements of Mussolini's fascist state had little room for pluralism, based as it was on the idea of "Everything in the State, nothing outside the State, nothing against the State."[50]

Under such a system, there was little room for dissent or independence of thought. The Law for the Defense of the State from November 25, 1926, punished a wide range of speech and thought crimes under the guise of national security with harsh sentences ranging from three to fifteen years. The red lines included the propagation of "doctrines, opinions, or methods" of any illegal "association, organization, or party" as well as the communication of "false, exaggerated, or tendentious rumors or information" that might discredit the state abroad.[51] The same decree established a Special Tribunal for "political crimes," resulting in 5,155 convictions and twenty-nine death sentences between 1927 and 1943.[52]

Neither was there any place for a critical press. To Mussolini, a former newspaper editor, the formula was quite simple: "Fascism requires militant journalism," he explained. "Newspapers must strive to find an essential uniformity, to serve the Cause . . . and to ignore the rest, burying it in the darkness of absolute indifference."[53] In 1926, the police were given national security powers to seize any writings "damaging to the prestige of the state or its authorities, or offensive to the national sentiment, to moral sense, and public decency."[54]

Of course, Mussolini insisted that "the press enjoys more freedom in Italy than in any other country in the world."[55] And much like Lenin, he defined press freedom as absolute ideological conformity. In the same speech, he compared journalists to the instruments of an orchestra all using their own voices to play the same tune. That tune consisted of loyally voicing the ideas of *Il Duce*, which embodied those of the Italian people and therefore suffered no dissent. But while Mussolini was a trailblazer for fascist oppression, the full potential of fascism would not be unleashed until Germany's fragile Weimar Republic collapsed and was replaced by the Third Reich. Under Nazi rule, Mussolini's mix of propaganda, repression, and censorship was refined to devastating effect.

The Weimar Fallacy

The short-lived Weimar Republic of 1918 to 1933 represented a remarkable interlude of liberal democracy wedged between a semi-authoritarian empire and a totalitarian Third Reich. But the odds were stacked against the republic from the outset. It was built on the shaky ruins of Germany's catastrophic defeat in the Great War, weighed down by the punitive Versailles Treaty, and destabilized by economic hardship and political violence. From 1918 to 1923, militant groups on the far Left and Right launched at least five unsuccessful coup attempts. By 1922, right-wing extremists had carried out some 354 political assassinations.[56] Victims included prominent politicians as well as the famous socialist Rosa Luxemburg who, unlike Lenin, believed that "freedom is always and exclusively freedom for the one who thinks differently."[57]

Despite the violence, free speech was fundamental to the Weimar Republic. Article 118 of the 1919 Weimar Constitution stated, "Every German has the right within the limits of the general laws, to express his opinion orally, in writing, in print, pictorially, or in any other way. . . . No censorship shall be established." This marked a stark contrast to the early decades of Imperial Germany, when socialist and Catholic publications and journalists were harshly suppressed. But Article 118 still allowed for censorship of cinema, "indecent and obscene literature," public plays, and exhibitions, "for the protection of youth." Most fatal, however, was Article 48, which permitted the president to suspend "fundamental rights," including freedom of speech, "if public safety and order be seriously disturbed or threatened."[58] This instrument would ultimately provide the killer blow to the very democracy it was supposed to protect.

Still, there is no denying that the Weimar Constitution provided the framework for a vibrant and diverse public sphere, as it expanded and guaranteed the freedoms of the 1874 press law. Germany had some 4,700 newspapers by the early 1930s, with a total daily circulation of about twenty million copies.[59] Weimar Germany was also extremely fertile ground for culture, literature, art, and science. Among its long list of famous authors, artists, and intellectuals were Thomas Mann, Bertolt Brecht, Hermann Hesse, Theodor W. Adorno, Hannah Arendt, the filmmaker Fritz Lang, and the photo artist Hannah Höch. Nine Germans won the Nobel Prize during the Weimar Republic. Five of the prize winners were Jewish, including Albert Einstein. The republic also produced the world's second female Nobel laureate in Physics, Maria Goeppert Mayer, exemplifying the giant leap forward in terms of gender equality.

Women won the right to vote in 1918 and equal rights in 1919. The Austrian writer Gina Kaus, an active member of the intellectual circles in Berlin, noted a seismic change. "It has not been such a long time since the woman writer was regarded as a peculiar monster," she remarked in 1929.

> This intellectual mistrust and nearly physical aversion to women writers has persisted almost to the present—however, a radical stop has finally been put to gender prejudices. . . . We meet women authors in all the publishers' catalogues, bookshop windows, newspapers, and magazines.[60]

Not everyone was happy with the fruits of this new and liberal public sphere. On February 24, 1920, two thousand people in Munich listened as a leading member of the German Worker's Party (DAP) read the party's manifesto aloud. His name was Adolf Hitler, and his demands included "legal warfare against conscious political lying and its dissemination in the press." He also insisted that only ethnic Germans should be allowed to edit, write, finance, and influence German-language publications. But that was not all: "It must be forbidden to publish papers which do not promote the national welfare. We demand legal prosecution of all tendencies in art and literature of a kind likely to disintegrate our life as a nation."[61]

Nobody in 1920 would have guessed that these outlandish demands of a political outsider from Austria were to become the law of the land less than fifteen years later. But in hindsight, nobody could say they hadn't been warned. Hitler used his devastating talent for public speaking to whip the crowds of Bavarian beer halls into a frenzy of hatred and to become leader of the National Socialist German Worker's Party, or NSDAP. He leveraged the humiliation

Germans felt after losing World War I to forge a powerful sense of ethnonational pride and destiny. The enemies of the movement were identified as democracy, Marxism, the politicians who had "stabbed the German army in the back" by signing an armistice, and, above all, those he insisted were behind the sinister conspiracy to subjugate the German people: the Jews.[62]

A very direct warning came in 1923 with the ill-fated Beer Hall Putsch. The authorities of Bavaria had already banned several Nazi rallies, during which armed paramilitaries marched around looking for violent clashes with leftists. But the government was too weak to systematically enforce the bans. And on November 8 and 9, Hitler tried to overthrow the government in Bavaria and launch a national revolution in the style of Mussolini's march on Rome. Four police officers lay dead, a Social Democratic newspaper was destroyed, and several Social Democratic city councilors were taken hostage before the disorganized coup fizzled out. Hitler was convicted of high treason but given a ridiculously light sentence of five years after a trial that he was allowed to use as a propaganda platform.[63]

Hitler served just under nine months in prison. While locked away, he wrote his autobiography, *Mein Kampf*, which included further warning signs as to what free speech would look like under National Socialism. Hitler accused the liberal press of "dig[ging] the grave for the German people" while the "lying Marxist Press" was spreading falsehoods to enslave the nation for the benefit of "international finance and its masters, the Jews." The state meekly allowed the media to hide behind "the principle of freedom of the Press and liberty of public opinion," which "allowed poison . . . to enter the national bloodstream and infect public life" with complete impunity. The solution was to wrestle control of the press from the "enemies of the people."[64] A term dear to both Lenin and Hitler.

What might newspapers under state control look like? Once again, Hitler was brutally honest in *Mein Kampf*. To Hitler, the vast majority of the people he claimed to speak for were credulous simpletons who believed everything they read in the press. And since those people also decided democratic elections, state control of the press was of paramount importance, so that it would service "the State and the Nation." Accordingly, they should be fed propaganda aimed exclusively at the masses. He also stated that "all effective propaganda must be confined to a few bare essentials and those must be expressed as far as possible in stereotyped formulas. These slogans should be persistently repeated until the very last individual has come to grasp the idea that has been put forward."

Weimar democrats struggled with how to balance free speech when confronted by sensationalist reporting and fanatical agitation in a country marred by political terror and coordinated street violence. As the mild punishment of Hitler and the NSDAP shows, the courts were often lenient toward right-wing extremism. In his 1922 survey, *Four Years of Political Murder*, the German-Jewish Professor Emil J. Gumbel described how vocal calls for murder in the right-wing press were punished with mere slaps on the wrist: "A fine of a few paper marks, and the one who issued the call can resume stirring up the seeds of hate."[65]

But the government would soon adopt increasingly drastic measures to combat the radical agitation so that ultimately, according to one historian, "in the struggle for the preservation of the Republic the principle of freedom of the press was a major casualty."[66] The first step was the 1922 Law for the Defense of the Republic, which permitted the authorities to suppress newspapers expressing contempt for the existing state structure, the national flag, members of the government, or advocacy of violence.[67] In the 1930s, the combustible mix of violent clashes and sensationalist press reports invoking the language of civil war made even Social Democrats, whose newspapers had been systematically suppressed in Imperial Germany, begin to have doubts about press freedom. Leading Social Democrats lamented that press freedom had degenerated into "freedom for lying and slander" and had become "the most poisonous weapon against democracy." According to historian Bernhard Fulda, "no other Western liberal democracy in this period witnessed [the] joining of democratic forces, from Socialists to Liberals, intended to pass a law curtailing press freedom."[68]

In the final years of the republic, press freedom was eroded by a steady stream of increasingly desperate and draconian laws and emergency decrees. The Law for the Defense of the Republic was expanded in 1930; then the immunities of MPs acting as editors were lifted. A 1931 presidential emergency decree under Article 48 of the constitution expanded the government's power to ban newspapers for up to two months. Initially, even the liberal press was on board with this development. "In order to protect itself effectively against lies and slander, the state has to be allowed to compromise basic rights, like the freedom of the press," wrote one mainstream newspaper.[69] To counter the "assertion of false facts," the emergency press decree also authorized the government to force newspapers to print corrections, announcements, and replies, and ban papers that threatened "public peace and order."[70] Then came yet another emergency decree in June 1932, which further tightened government control of newspapers and expanded the permissible grounds for their suppression. These provisions were not empty threats. During Heinrich Brüning's chancellorship from March 1930 to May 1932, 284 newspapers were temporarily banned in Prussia alone. Ninety-nine were Nazi, seventy-seven were communist, and forty-three belonged to other far-right movements.[71]

All of a sudden, the media realized that the methods of curbing fanaticism and antidemocratic forces they had once supported had become an existential threat to press freedom itself. The liberal *Berliner Tageblatt* compared the estimated one hundred monthly "systematic newspaper bans" in Germany to the press climate in Fascist Italy and Soviet Russia. A few months later, the *Tageblatt* declared "the end of freedom."[72] But it was already too late to protest.

In June 1932, the staunchly conservative Franz von Papen became chancellor, and in the few months before his resignation in November 1932, ninety-five more newspapers were suspended.[73] The plurality were communist, while those sympathetic to the Nazis came in second. In 1932, the communist newspaper *Die Rote Fahne* was banned on more than a third of its publication days. But social-democratic and left-liberal newspapers critical of Nazism were also suppressed. And by that point, publishing an offensive cartoon was enough to be banned. This included caricatures skewering Papen's decision to lift the ban against the Nazi Party's paramilitary wing, the SA, a decision which led to an explosion of street violence, as well as cartoons mocking Papen's rule by emergency decrees.[74] It's difficult not to contrast Weimar Germany's systematic banning of newspapers that *wrote* about political violence with its comparatively lenient attitude toward the various groups and associations that *committed* violence. This contrast paints a more nuanced picture than Loewenstein's lament about the "lack of militancy of the Weimar Republic."

The constant erosion of constitutional principles helped pave the way for Hitler and the Nazis to abolish free speech once and for all. Thus, it is important to examine how Weimar authorities handled the virulent hatred, anti-Semitism, and fanatical antidemocratic agitation of the NSDAP.

As we've already seen, Weimar Germany was not a safe space for Nazi propaganda. The Nazi Party newspaper the *Völkischer Beobachter* was temporarily suspended for anti-Semitic excesses on multiple occasions in the early 1920s.[75] After Hitler's failed coup attempt in 1923, both the NSDAP and its newspaper were banned until 1925.[76] The continued popularity of Adolf Hitler and his fierce propaganda saw most German states prohibit him from speaking publicly between 1925 and 1927 (the injunction persisted until 1928 in Prussia).[77] No doubt, the ban was an impediment to the

NSDAP, which relied on Hitler's mesmerizing speeches for popular support. But the prohibition also provided fodder for fruitful propaganda. Ultimately, Hitler concluded that the ban had been a net benefit, boosting his fame and popularity.[78] Not least because of the efforts of leading Nazis like Joseph Goebbels who organized and spoke at protests against this "illegal" injustice. Posters depicted a muzzled Hitler as a martyr unfairly singled out for repression by The System, with captions like "CROOKS CAN SPEAK ANYWHERE IN GERMANY, BUT HITLER IS BANNED."[79] Goebbels's opportunistic, selective, and deeply hypocritical appeal to free speech only when it serves one's own agenda—still a familiar tactic among right-wing populists today—was also a standard tactic when other Nazi publications were targeted by the authorities.

The two most notorious Nazi newspapers were Goebbels's *Der Angriff* (The Attack) and Julius Streicher's virulently anti-Semitic *Der Stürmer*. The former was founded by Goebbels as a direct response to the NSDAP ban in Berlin. *Der Angriff* specialized in anti-Semitic trolling.[80] Its favorite target was Bernhard Weiss, the Jewish vice president of Berlin's police force, who was demonized with anti-Semitic cartoons and tropes. Weiss consistently pursued *Der Angriff* in court, where he won several libel suits.[81] But the many court cases played into Goebbels's hands; he used them to portray the NSDAP and *Der Angriff* as victims of the very kind of Jewish conspiracy to enslave the German people that the paper was purportedly trying to expose. Goebbels also shamelessly appealed to free speech and legal protections—principles he actually loathed. Between November 1930 and August 1932, *Der Angriff* was administratively banned thirteen times for a combined total of nineteen weeks, allowing Goebbels to proudly proclaim *Der Angriff* to be Germany's "most frequently banned daily." According to historian Russel Lemmons, the legal pursuit of *Der Angriff* was a double-edged sword. On the one hand, press bans hurt the finances of the paper, which came close to folding. But on the other, they generated much-needed attention and crucial propaganda victories that presented the paper as the small victim of severe persecution—which struck a chord with the many Germans who had lost faith in the authorities of Weimar Germany.[82]

Julius Streicher's *Der Stürmer* took anti-Semitism to sickening levels of depravity. After World War II, Streicher—known as "Jew-Baiter Number One"—was sentenced to death by the Nuremberg Tribunal and executed for his "incitement to murder and extermination."[83] But in Weimar times, *Der Stürmer*'s anti-Semitism was less explicitly violent, however stomach-churning. Several Jewish groups and individuals tried to curb *Der Stürmer* through the courts, using libel suits as well as criminal law provisions that prohibited incitement to enmity and violence among classes of citizens and offenses against religion.[84] Streicher was convicted twice of violating the latter for printing blood libels that accused Judaism—and by extension Jews—of the ritual murders of non-Jews. In 1929, Streicher was sentenced to two months in prison, but he left the court cheered by four hundred supporters. Much like *Der Angriff*, *Der Stürmer* used its legal defeats as victories in the realm of propaganda. Apparently, it worked in what may be history's most pernicious example of the Streisand effect. Shortly after Streicher's verdict, the NSDAP tripled its votes in local elections in Thuringia, then more than doubled its votes in Streicher's hometown of Nuremberg in the 1930 federal elections.[85] No doubt, many Germans were horrified by the crude Nazi anti-Semitism and welcomed legal action against it. But to the growing number of Germans who wished to see the end of Weimar democracy, convictions for speech crimes became badges of honor.

More effective against Nazi propaganda was the Weimar radio policy. After the first German radio program was broadcast in October 1923, the number of subscribers surged from one hundred thousand in 1924 to more than four million in 1932.[86] Jittery about the potential dangers of mass communication, the government put the airwaves under ever tighter state control and banned political parties and private companies from owning radio stations. One historian has even characterized Weimar radio policy as an "aesthetic educational dictatorship." Political broadcasts were government-friendly, and both Nazis and Communists were kept from the airwaves.[87] However, the censorship entailed significant politically skewed collateral damage. In 1928, the journalist Kurt Tucholsky complained that "not a word can be spoken on the radio that has not been understood and approved." He also insisted that the Right was given a free pass, but "if a free thinker, a radical worker, or a proponent of abortion attempts to express views . . . they can be certain of being censored."[88]

A number of social scientists have sought to measure how radio affected support for the Nazis during both Weimar Germany and the Third Reich. They found that the progovernment content and ban against Nazi broadcasts helped limit electoral support for the Nazis between 1928 and 1933. The flipside of this approach was that total control of the radio was served wrapped up on a platter to the Nazis once they were in power.[89] Radio helped the Nazis in the tainted election of March 1933, and once it was fully under Nazi control, it played a significant role in convincing anti-Semitic Germans to denounce Jews to the authorities.[90] As Goebbels famously asserted, "Our way of taking power and using it would have been inconceivable without the radio."[91]

The Third Reich

The Wall Street Crash of 1929 hit the vulnerable German economy hard, and the unemployment rate soon skyrocketed to more than 30 percent.[92] An increasing number of Germans longed for a strong man to steer them out of the crisis, and the Nazis' share of the vote surged from a paltry 2.6 percent in the federal election of 1928 to a whopping 37.2 percent in July 1932.[93] Although they never won the majority, the NSDAP was by far the biggest party in the Reichstag.

After much political jockeying and hesitation, President Hindenburg appointed Hitler to chancellor on January 30, 1933.

Hitler had barely been sworn in before he took aim at free speech, enforcing a ban on the communist paper *Die Rote Fahne* and the social democratic paper *Vorwärtz*. Then, on February 4, an emergency decree "For the Protection of the German People" was passed, giving the police authority to ban political meetings and demonstrations and making it illegal for newspapers to publish "incorrect news," as defined by the Nazi minister of interior.[94] Goebbels could hardly contain his glee: "Now we also have a lever against the press, and bans will pop like crazy. . . . All those Jewish organs which caused us so much trouble and grief, will disappear all at once from the streets of Berlin."[95]

At this point, Hitler's attack on the press was merely an escalation of the draconian press policy that Weimar's democratic politicians had set in motion, and that the mainstream press had backed before they came under assault. But like Lenin, Hitler had no intention of relaxing his grip. And on February 27, he was provided with the perfect pretext to remove the remaining constitutional obstacles once and for all when the Reichstag was set on fire by the Communist Marinus van der Lubbe. Though historians still debate the Nazis' involvement, the Nazis certainly took advantage of the situation. "This is a God-given signal!" Hitler raged, practically foaming at the mouth. "If this fire, as I believe, turns out to be the handiwork of Communists, then there is nothing that shall stop us now crushing out this murderous pest with an iron fist."[96] On the very next day, Hitler pushed Hindenburg to issue two emergency decrees. As "a defensive measure against communist acts of violence endangering the state," they immediately suspended seven constitutional rights, including habeas corpus and the freedoms of expression, press, and assembly, "until further notice."[97]

Within days, the regime arrested four thousand Communists, jamming them into makeshift prisons in run-down factories, bars, and basements.[98] According to the Nazis' reinterpretation of the law of *Schutzhaft*, or "protective custody," these political prisoners could be detained indefinitely and without a court order.[99] The next targets were Social Democrats, union officials, and "deviants" like homosexuals.[100] Hitler's brutal crackdown on the Left was widely applauded and contributed to his popularity among many Germans who viewed Marxism as an existential threat to the nation. An editorial in a Bavarian newspaper concluded, "This emergency decree will find no opponent despite the quite draconian measures. . . . The consequences of the most acute struggle against communism have finally been drawn."[101]

On March 20, Heinrich Himmler announced the opening of Germany's first concentration camp in a former gunpowder factory near Dachau for people "who threaten the security of the state."[102] Around one hundred thousand were detained in "protective custody" during 1933. Most were released within two years, but an estimated six hundred—and probably more—died from torture and mistreatment.[103]

Three days later, Hitler's government changed the constitution with the Enabling Act, which allowed "laws passed by the government" to bypass both the Reichstag and the president. With the votes of the Catholic Center Party and the German National People's Party, Hitler had paved the way for the unopposed dictatorship of the Nazi regime.[104] Most of the deputies who would have protested the Enabling Act were already in prison, concentration camps, or exile. But the Social Democrat Otto Wels stood firm: "In this historical hour, we German Social Democrats pledge ourselves to the principles of humanity and justice, of freedom and socialism. No Enabling Act gives you the power to eradicate ideas, which are eternal and indestructible."[105] Yet Hitler had not only the votes but also the rhetorical comeback to checkmate Wels. If Wels was so enthusiastic about equal rights and free speech, why hadn't he defended the Nazis when they were in opposition?

> You should have recognized the beneficial power of criticism when
> we were in the opposition. . . . Back then our press was *verboten*
> and *verboten* and again *verboten*; our assemblies were banned; we
> were not allowed to speak, and I was not allowed to speak—and
> that went on for years! And now you say criticism is beneficial![106]

Hitler never intended to allow political dissent. He had made
that clear as early as 1920. But the many examples of anti-Nazi
repression provided a facade of legitimacy for Hitler's systematic repression and helped deflect criticism, since he could use the potent
weapon of "whataboutery" and accuse the Social Democrats of hypocrisy and double standards. This helped him justify his popular
crackdown so that it appeared in a less authoritarian light.[107]

Social Democrats who weren't deported to concentration camps
were terrorized, humiliated, and beaten into compliance by the paramilitary brownshirts of the SA and blackshirts of the SS. A leading
Social Democrat in Cologne was forced to drink a mixture of oil and
urine, while the Social Democratic minister-president of Mecklenburg
was tortured to death, tied in a sack, and thrown into a river.[108] By the
end of May 1933, the Nazi stormtroopers had forcibly removed some
five hundred municipal administrators and seventy mayors from office.[109] The Communist Party and the Social Democratic Party were
banned by June. After the ban, an estimated three thousand leading
Social Democrats were arrested, beaten, and even killed.[110]

Hitler's enablers on the Right would soon regret their support
when, having muzzled the Left, he turned his attention to the rest
of the political spectrum. One by one, he coerced the remaining
parties into dissolving themselves in a wave of "political suicides."
As the final nail in the coffin, all political parties apart from the
NSDAP were banned by law on July 14.[111] In the span of less than
six months, Hitler had transformed Germany into a one-party
dictatorship, unrestrained by any meaningful protection of constitutional freedoms.

When the worst enemies of the state had been placed in "protective custody," deported to concentration camps, or beaten into silence, the regime formalized its control of the public sphere through legal means that also served to sugarcoat the harsh measures with a veneer of legality and proper procedure. Understandably, we associate the terror of Nazi Germany with the Gestapo and the concentration camps. But according to historian Richard J. Evans, legislation was equally important in consolidating Nazi rule. The regular courts and the already existing state apparatus could be turned into powerful weapons against dissent once unleashed from the restraints of constitutional freedoms. From 1932 to 1937, the number of prisoners in Germany increased from 69,000 to 122,000—around 23,000 of whom were labeled political prisoners. In 1937 alone, the German courts passed a staggering 5,255 convictions for high treason.[112]

This was fueled by a battery of increasingly vague and wide-ranging laws against speech crimes. The Malicious Practices Act of March 1933 banned "malicious gossip," derogatory statements, jokes, and rumors about the regime and its officials. The law effectively banned any criticism of the Nazi party, including subjective opinion, whether expressed in public or private.[113] One Protestant pastor was later indicted for condemning in his sermons as un-Christian the anti-Semitic violence of Kristallnacht, when on November 9, 1938, thousands of Jewish homes, businesses, and synagogues were simultaneously attacked.[114] A treason law passed in April 1933 punished anyone who "planned" to "alter the constitution" with long prison sentences and even execution. In practice, it became an act of high treason to write, print, or distribute leaflets promoting a constitutional alteration like, say, a return to democracy. The slightest association with a perpetrator of such treason could be interpreted as engagement in conspiracy. To protect the authority of Nazi officials, a December 1934 law made hate speech against leading figures in the party or the state punishable with the possibility of a death sentence.[115] At the height of war, in 1942, a hairdresser from Munich got four years behind bars for her "malicious, hateful, agitatory, and base-minded comments" after she had called Hitler "a crazy mass-murderer."[116]

In addition to laws and secret police, informers known as "block wardens" kept an eye on their neighborhoods and workplaces and reported anyone who criticized the regime, cracked a Hitler joke, or forgot to raise the flag on Hitler's birthday. The regime had around two hundred thousand such informants in 1935. By the beginning of the war, two million Germans were keeping a vigilant eye on their neighbors.[117] One of the most sinister forms of surveillance took place in the mandatory youth organization, *Hitlerjugend*, where children were pressed to inform on their own parents. Surveillance and social control were not primarily conducted by sadistic Gestapo officers raiding the homes of ordinary citizens. The bulk of the work was carried out by the ordinary citizens themselves.

The third stage after the power grab was the so-called *Gleichschaltung* of Germany—complete "synchronization" of political, social, and cultural life according to Nazi goals.[118] As Hitler declared in his Reichstag speech on March 23, 1933, "the Reich Government intends to undertake a thorough moral purging of the *Volkskörper* [body of the people]. The entire system of education, the theater, the cinema, literature, the press, and radio—they will be used as a means to this end."[119] He appointed Joseph Goebbels to *Reichsminister* of Popular Enlightenment and Propaganda with the responsibility of overseeing everything from the press to cinema, music, radio, and art.[120]

Nazi control of the press and, by extension, access to define the truth, was a fundamental aspect of the Gleichschaltung.[121] Socialist and openly critical papers had already been dealt with by the Reichstag Fire Decree. Surviving newspapers were now subjected to suffocating laws of ownership or starved of advertising funds by Nazi-controlled advertising agencies. Many were forced to fold or sell themselves cheaply to powerful Nazi media moguls like Franz

Eher, who owned two-thirds of the German newspapers by 1939.[122] The Gleichschaltung of the press effectively killed the vibrant media landscape of the Weimar era. When the Nazis came into power in 1933, Germany had around 4,700 newspapers. By 1944, only 977 papers remained, of which 82 percent were directly controlled by the Nazis.[123]

The surviving papers were micromanaged by the Reich Press Chamber under Goebbels's Ministry of Propaganda. Daily directives were issued on everything from format to the length and content of articles. Anyone who did not comply was punished with a pink slip or even reeducation in a concentration camp.[124] These restrictions were formalized in the Editors Law of October 1933, which prohibited writings "calculated to weaken the strength of the Reich abroad or at home, the resolution of the community, German defence, culture or the economy."[125] In the end, it was easiest for most papers to just copy and paste from the governmental news agency. So effective had Nazi control of journalism become that Goebbels noted: "No decent journalist with any feeling of honour in his bones can stand the way he is handled by the press department of the Reich Government. . . . Any man who still has a residue of honour will be very careful not to become a journalist."[126]

But just as Lenin did not stop at rooting out the "Bourgeois" press, so Hitler was not satisfied with the purge of "Bolshevik" and liberal newspapers. The German press had to be Aryanized. According to the Editors Law, members of the Reich Association of the German Press, the printers guild, had to be "racially pure," leading to a purge of Jewish journalists and editors.

In a now well-rehearsed pattern of authoritarianism, Goebbels's ministry promulgated blacklists of illegal authors and books.[127] On May 10, 1933, Goebbels orchestrated perhaps the most infamous book burning in history. Truckloads of blacklisted books—some twenty-five thousand—were burned in a great bonfire outside the opera in Berlin, and many more were consumed by flames in thirty-four other German towns and cities.[128] In his fiery speech at the book burning in Berlin, Goebbels explained that a Nazi cultural revolutionary had to "be just as good at tearing down what is blameworthy as he is at building up what is praiseworthy." He denounced the "extremist Jewish intellectualism" of writers like Karl Marx, Sigmund Freud, and—ominously—Henrich Heine, the nineteenth-century writer who had warned, "Where they burn books, they will also burn people in the end."[129]

———

THE END GOAL OF THE THIRD REICH WAS TO ENSURE THAT not only people's actions, but also their innermost thoughts conformed to the Nazi ideology. The German-Jewish linguist Victor Klemperer survived the Holocaust and famously observed that the "the most powerful Hitlerian propaganda tool" was not speeches, posters, or flags. It was the gradual erosion of the German language:

> Nazism permeated the flesh and blood of the people through single words, idioms and sentence structures which were imposed on them in a million repetitions and taken on board mechanically and unconsciously. . . . Words can be like tiny doses of arsenic: they are swallowed unnoticed, appear to have no effect, and then after a little time the toxic reaction sets in after all.[130]

Without independent media, opposition parties, civil society, trade unions, or tolerance of dissent, the antidote to the linguistic arsenic of constant Nazi propaganda was seriously diluted.

Still, just how effective the Nazi propaganda was remains disputed.[131] Richard J. Evans argues that the incessant Nazi indoctrination helps explain the shocking brutality of the German war machine once set in motion in 1939, and, by extension, the even more shocking brutality of the Holocaust.[132] Studies have shown that Nazi propaganda was most effective on young Germans—more impressionable, with little experience of living in a free society and subject to institutional indoctrination in schools and Hitler Youth organizations—and in districts where anti-Semitism was already prevalent before the Nazi takeover. On the other hand, the effects of propaganda targeting the population at large in the radio, cinema, and press seem to have been less significant, with the working class and Catholics proving most resistant to Nazi ideology.[133] By the summer of 1940, the Nazi intelligence agency, the *Sicherheitsdienst*, reported widespread criticism of propaganda, diminishing interest in the press, and distrust in the official military reports.[134]

In other words, Nazi propaganda did not succeed in brainwashing all Germans into becoming committed Nazis or anti-Semites, even if the noncommitted were mostly given to passive resignation rather than life-threatening active opposition. As Aldous Huxley, the author of the dystopian novel *Brave New World*, observed in 1936:

> Propaganda gives force and direction to the successive movements of popular feeling and desire; but it does not do much to create these movements. The propagandist is a man who canalizes an already existing stream. In a land where there is no water, he digs in vain.[135]

Hitler's megalomaniac dreams of a racially pure superpower dominating Europe ended in total defeat. But the question of how to prevent the rise of new genocidal regimes is ever present.

It would be dangerously reductionist to explain Germany's democratic collapse and Nazi takeover solely through the lens of free speech and censorship. These were but some (and probably not the most important) among many complex factors that led to the cataclysm of the Third Reich. But the fact that the Weimar Republic unsuccessfully tried to stem the tide of totalitarianism with illiberal laws of increasingly harsh censorship should at the very least give pause to those who demand that democracies today must also sacrifice free speech to counter organized hatred. So should Hitler's use of Weimar Germany's illiberal precedents to destroy the democracy they were supposed to protect.

If one concludes that the genocidal incitement of the Third Reich requires official intolerance of intolerance today, the legacy of communism poses some awkward questions. There are obvious and important ideological differences between communism and Nazism. For one, the latter's genocidal commitment to biological racism was a necessary precondition for the particular evil of the Holocaust. Still, there were also striking similarities between Nazi Germany and the Soviet Union. Like Hitler, Lenin and Stalin built a ruthless one-party state, which combined strict censorship with incessant propaganda demonizing specific groups as "enemies of the people" singled out for punishment, deportation to concentration camps, or even "liquidation." In fact, the global spread, duration, and death toll of communism exceeded that of fascism and Nazism. If most liberal democracies have found that countering communism is possible without resorting to the censorship and repression of previous eras, might robust democracies not also be able to withstand the threat from resurgent Nazism and adjacent far-right extremism without compromising the most essential democratic freedom of all?

11

The Age of Human Rights

Triumph and Tragedy

O n January 6, 1941, US president Franklin Delano Roosevelt used his State of the Union speech to try and convince an isolationist America to support Britain's desperate fight against Nazi Germany.[1] The speech struck a very different tone from the paranoid warnings against fifth column activity of immigrants and communists that President Wilson had given prior to American involvement in World War I. FDR made his case by envisaging a "world founded upon four essential human freedoms. The first is freedom of speech and expression—everywhere in the world."[2]

After the carnage of World War II, the newly established United Nations set out to draw a set of universally recognized human rights, based on Roosevelt's Four Freedoms. Their endeavor bore fruit—not least through the efforts of FDR's widow, Eleanor Roosevelt—in the form of the landmark Universal Declaration of Human Rights (UDHR) from 1948, which set out a series of principles for states to uphold, and the legally binding International Covenant on Civil and Political Rights (ICCPR) from 1966. Both documents contain historic protections of free speech and freedom of opinion. Article

19 of the UDHR stipulates, "Everyone has the right to freedom of opinion and expression; this right includes freedom to hold opinions without interference and to seek, receive and impart information and ideas through any media and regardless of frontiers."[3] The first two paragraphs of Article 19 of the ICCPR were essentially copy-pasted from the UDHR, although paragraph three established criteria for when freedom of expression may be restricted.

But the road leading to these historic achievements was not without ideological friction. Behind the drawing board, the Cold War was slowly taking shape, and the Soviet bloc fought relentlessly to restrict free speech with clauses obliging member states to prohibit hate speech.

Cold War at the Drafting Table

The discussions leading to the UDHR began when the UN set up a Commission on Human Rights in 1946. To make the declaration as universal as possible, the committee consisted of eighteen members of different political, cultural, and religious backgrounds and consulted with philosophers and thinkers from all over the world. It quickly became clear that it was especially difficult to reach an agreement when it came to the limits of free speech.[4] The US proposal was radically absolutist: "There shall be freedom of speech, of the press and of expression by any means whatsoever."[5] But the Soviet Union and its allies not only wanted to *permit* states to prohibit hate speech but *oblige* them to do so. The Soviet Union's own 1936 constitution held out "any advocacy of racial or national exclusiveness or hatred and contempt" for punishment.[6] Moscow now pushed to include a similar injunction—copied almost verbatim—against hate speech in the UDHR.[7]

The burning question that fueled disagreement was the extent to which Nazis and fascists should be allowed to advocate the very ideologies that had covered Europe in totalitarian darkness and culminated in the Holocaust. As the Soviet delegation argued, "the freedom [Article 19] would give to the Nazis would undercut and threaten . . . the very right affirmed in the article; without the limiting clause, the article would be self-destructive."[8] Most tellingly—and perhaps most decisively for the final outcome—the Soviets pushed for a phrase explicitly criminalizing "fascism."

The Canadian delegate Lester Pearson spoke for many members when he warned about such a statement's potential for authoritarian abuse: "The term 'fascism' . . . was now being blurred by the abuse of applying it to any person or idea which was not communist."[9] The Soviet delegate, Alexei Pavlov, did not exactly ease those concerns when his definition of fascism included "the bloody dictatorship of the most reactionary section of capitalism and monopolies" or when he stated that the declaration should guard against the fascists existing in all European countries except the "peoples' democracies" (by which he meant the communist one-party People's Republics in Eastern Europe).[10] In other words, the Soviet position regarded Western capitalism and democracy as a manifestation of fascism and therefore the advocacy of such ideas should be prohibited as incitement to hatred.[11]

Absent from the Soviet proposal was any prohibition against incitement to hatred based on political opinion, class, or social status. This was not surprising given how Lenin and especially Stalin mirrored Hitler's virulent anti-Semitic incitements and labeled anyone supposedly opposing the party as "enemies of the people" while comparing them to "vermin," "filth," and "poisonous weeds" that needed to be uprooted or simply "liquidated," as millions in fact were.[12]

European democracies were presented with an uncomfortable dilemma, since all of them accepted that free speech had its limits. States such as the Netherlands, Denmark, Germany, and Czechoslovakia had adopted various laws against group libel, hate speech, and incitement in order to restrict the advance of fascism in the inter-war period.[13] Accordingly, many, including the British, were initially open to the idea of limiting free speech to protect the broader set of human rights against totalitarian movements. However, they con-sidered it dangerous to include an obligation to prohibit hate speech in an international human rights declaration, fearing that such pro-visions might be abused to justify state control of the public sphere and persecution of opinions that the government did not like. This was not an unreasonable worry given the brutality of Stalinism and the activities of Glavlit, which was still busy scrubbing the Soviet public sphere from any dissent, real or imagined.

These concerns ultimately swayed the British to back the Ameri-can position.[14] The Soviet bloc had overplayed its hand and alienated those Western democracies that were sympathetic to the idea of re-stricting hate speech. Hence the final version of Article 19 included a strong endorsement of free speech with no strings attached.[15]

An overwhelming forty-eight states voted in favor of the UDHR, but while there were no votes against it, eight states abstained. Not surprisingly, this included the six communist states who thought the declaration did not go far enough to restrict the resurgence of Nazism and fascism. But the Soviet bloc was joined by a somewhat unlikely set of allies: Saudi Arabia and the newly established apart-heid regime in South Africa. Saudi Arabia mainly abstained because Article 18 protected the right to change one's religious beliefs, which clashed with the ban against apostasy under Shari'ah law. South Af-rica abstained because the whole apartheid regime was built on the systematic violations of the idea of universal human rights embodied by the UDHR.[16] It would probably be a bad idea to seat a Bolshevik, a Wahhabist, and a Calvinist white supremacist at the same table at a dinner party, but in spite of their mutual animosity, the three regimes had more in common than they cared to admit. All claimed to be in possession of the Truth and all favored punishing religious, ideological, or political heretics under the guise of restricting various forms of hate speech.

Despite the triumphant adoption of the UDHR, the battle over the limits of free speech was far from over. The Soviet delegates eyed a new opportunity to restrict free speech when the UN hunkered down to draft the legally binding ICCPR, a process which began concurrently with the drafting of the UDHR.[17] The US delegate, first chair of the Commission on Human Rights and former First Lady Eleanor Roosevelt, emerged as an eloquent and prophetic champion of principled free speech protections. Under Roosevelt's leadership the commission issued an early draft in 1947 that envisaged prohibiting only "any advocacy of national, racial or religious hostility that constitutes an incitement to violence."[18] But once again, the Soviet bloc pushed for a broader prohibition banning any advocacy of hatred whether inciting to violence or not, still invoking the Nazis. In 1949, Mr. Pavlov insisted that a duty to prohibit hate speech was necessary since "millions had perished because the propaganda of racial and national superiority, hatred and contempt, had not been stopped in time."[19]

Roosevelt vigorously opposed the Soviet agenda. In 1950, she warned that the Soviet proposal

> would be extremely dangerous . . . since any criticism of public or religious authorities might all too easily be described as incitement to hatred and consequently prohibited. . . . It [is] equally difficult to differentiate between the various shades of feeling ranging from hatred to ill-feeling and mere dislike.[20]

She also feared that "it would only encourage Governments to punish all criticisms in the name of protection against religious or national hostility" and warned the commission "not to include . . . any provision likely to be exploited by totalitarian States for the purpose of rendering the other articles null and void."[21]

The US position was supported by several Western democracies at the commission. In 1953, the Swedish delegate argued that free speech prohibitions would not have prevented the "fanatical persecution" of World War II. Instead, she contended that "the effective prophylaxis lay in free discussion, information and education."[22] When challenged by the Soviet Union, the UK representative pointed out that during World War II, Hitler's *Mein Kampf* had not been banned in the UK and said that the UK "would maintain and fight for its conception of liberty as resolutely as it had fought against Hitler."[23] France was more open to free speech restrictions and adopted a middle course "between the two extremes of authoritarianism and unlimited freedom."[24]

Gerhart M. Riegner, author of the Riegner Telegram, which had alerted the world to the unfolding Nazi genocide in 1942, was invited to speak at the UN Commission on Human Rights in 1953 on behalf of the World Jewish Congress. It was less than a decade after the Holocaust had ended, and perhaps understandably, Riegner supported the Soviet argument that hate speech provisions were necessary in the name of human rights. He also emphasized the causal link between verbal propaganda, demonization of certain groups, and genocide.[25]

Ironically, the World Jewish Congress's support for the Soviet hate speech proposal came shortly after an outbreak of anti-Semitism stemming from the very top and fanned by the state media in the Soviet Union. At a party meeting in November 1952, Stalin claimed that "every Jew is a nationalist and an agent of American intelligence."[26] This culminated in the so-called Doctors' Plot, in which a group of doctors—most of whom were Jewish—were accused of planning to cause the death of leading Soviet officials. The Soviet Constitution's injunction against racial hatred did nothing to protect against such government persecution. According to some historians, Soviet Jews were spared a coordinated mass pogrom only by Stalin's death in March 1953—two months before Riegner spoke at the UN.[27]

Though the discussion of the UDHR and ICCPR started around the same time, the latter took much longer to hammer out, and the communist states were determined not to lose out as they felt they had done in 1948. In 1961, a delegate from Poland, part of the Soviet bloc, argued that freedom of expression could be abused and "contribute decisively to the elimination of all freedoms and all rights."[28] Yugoslavia may have been beyond the control of Moscow but agreed that it was "important to suppress manifestations of hatred which, even without leading to violence, constituted a degradation of human dignity and a violation of human rights."[29]

The same year, sixteen countries from Eastern Europe, Latin America, Africa, and the Middle East proposed the text that became the final version of Article 20 (2). It demanded that "any advocacy of national, racial or religious hatred that constitutes incitement to discrimination, hostility or violence shall be prohibited by law."[30]

This time, the US was outnumbered. When put to a vote in the General Assembly, it was adopted with fifty-two votes in favor, nineteen against, and twelve abstentions. It was a reflection of the changes the UN had undergone since the passage of the UDHR. When the Soviet Union had lost that debate in 1948, there were 58 member states of the UN. By 1961 that number had risen to 104. The new members included dozens of states—most of them newly independent African nations—that had experienced systematic, humiliating, and oppressive European racism—including racist censorship—under colonial rule by some of the very nations that were now adopting this deeply principled stand. These experiences made newly independent states sympathetic toward the idea of prohibiting racist hate speech and suspicious of Western sincerity. The nineteen countries that voted against the article included almost all Western liberal democracies, whose delegates feared that the vagueness of the provision might end up legitimizing authoritarian abuse.[31] As a Norwegian diplomat concluded, the article would be "so easy to misconstrue that those whom the provision was supposedly designed to protect might very well find themselves its victims."[32] These concerns would soon be confirmed.

McCarthy, the Civil Rights Movement, and the Fight for Free Speech in Post–World War II America

Even as Eleanor Roosevelt championed free speech maximalism in international human rights law, the First Amendment protections of American citizens were being weakened. The 1930s had brought about landmark achievements as the umbrella of the First Amendment was expanded to protect against speech-restrictive state laws and practices, including those that targeted unpopular racial, religious, or political activists like Angelo Herndon. But just as minorities suffered from the crackdown on socialists, antiwar activists, and anarchists under the Sedition and Espionage Acts of 1917 and 1918, so the gains of the 1930s were halted by the Second Red Scare of the 1940s and 1950s. The Alien Registration Act of 1940 (known as the Smith Act), which on paper prohibited the advocacy of the violent overthrow of the US government, sent more than two hundred people to prison merely for being members of the Socialist and Communist political parties.[33] The Supreme Court rubber-stamped the Smith Act in *Dennis v. United States* in 1951.[34]

This was also the era of McCarthyism, named after the Republican senator Joseph McCarthy, who spearheaded an anticommunist witch hunt. It was kicked off in 1946 when the House Un-American Activities Committee began sniffing out alleged communists in Hollywood who might infiltrate America's most influential form of popular culture. With subversive actors out of the way, McCarthy began his infamous Senate hearings in 1953, as chair of the

Permanent Subcommittee on Investigations charged with identifying secret communists employed in the government. In McCarthy's own words, America was "engaged in a final, all-out battle between communistic atheism and Christianity."[35] Ironically, the House Un-American Activities Committee had been formed in 1938 to investigate Nazi activities. Its metamorphosis into a vehicle for an anticommunist inquisition proved in practice the ACLU's point about the need to defend even Nazis rights.[36]

The fear of being branded a communist put the fight for racial equality through civil liberties on pause, as American tolerance of nonconformists waned.[37] In his classic study on *Communism, Conformity, and Civil Liberties* from 1955, the sociologist Samuel Stouffer found that substantial majorities were unwilling to allow atheists, communists, and socialists to speak publicly, teach at the local college, or work in the local community. Many also wanted communist books removed from the local library.[38] Once the fear of a looming communist takeover subsided by the end of the fifties, Chief Justice Earl Warren took a cue from a shift in public opinion and moved the court in a markedly liberal direction on free expression that chimed with Roosevelt's arguments at the UN. However, much of the impetus behind the expansion of the First Amendment came from those minorities whose voices were being silenced. During the late 1950s, civil rights organizations, and the NAACP in particular, had a hot winning streak of landmark First Amendment cases, as the organization took it upon itself to dismantle segregation one strategic lawsuit at a time.

Southern authorities tried to strangle this new challenge to white supremacy by arresting and imprisoning civil rights activists on seemingly content-neutral charges. Activists were arrested for "distributing literature without a permit" after handing out leaflets to mobilize African Americans to vote in Alabama and Mississippi.[39] In 1963, John Lewis—who would later become a highly influential member of Congress—was arrested for carrying a sign with the slogan "One man, one vote" in Dallas.[40] The great civil rights leader Martin Luther King Jr. was arrested no less than twenty-nine times for offenses including praying outside the city hall and parading without a permit.[41] He penned his famous *Letter from a Birmingham Jail* in 1963 while incarcerated for violating an injunction against "parading, demonstrating, boycotting, trespassing and picketing."[42]

But where the Supreme Court had once been hostile to the free speech claims of minorities, it now welcomed them with open arms.

In 1958, the Supreme Court overturned Alabama's demand that the NAACP disclose a list of its members, stating that the "freedom to engage in association for the advancement of beliefs and ideas is an inseparable aspect of the 'liberty' . . . which embraces freedom of speech."[43] In 1961, the court found that sit-ins conducted by Black activists were "as much a part of the 'free trade in ideas,' . . . as is verbal expression."[44] In 1963, it overturned the convictions of 187 Black students who had protested segregation, holding that a state could not prohibit "the peaceful expression of unpopular views."[45]

Perhaps the most consequential free speech victory was the 1964 case *New York Times Co. v. Sullivan*. In 1960, civil rights leaders had run an ad in the *New York Times* condemning "Southern violators," including the police department of Montgomery, Alabama, for harassing Dr. King and suppressing peaceful protests at Alabama State College. But the article included significant errors and exaggerations: it claimed that Dr. King had been arrested seven times in Alabama (he had only been arrested four times) and alleged that the police had "ringed" the university (they had only been "deployed near" it). Consequently, a lower court awarded Montgomery's police commissioner $500,000 in damages from the *New York Times* for defamation. But in 1964, the Supreme Court reversed the decision, holding that defamation required "actual malice—that is, with knowledge that it was false or with reckless disregard of whether it was false or not." Furthermore, the court held that "debate on public issues should be uninhibited, robust, and wide-open, and that it may well include vehement, caustic, and sometimes unpleasantly sharp attacks on government and public officials."

The *New York Times Co. v. Sullivan* ruling finally managed to decapitate the zombie concept of seditious libel, which so often had been unleashed against critics of state and federal governments. In doing so the court fulfilled—and explicitly cited—James Madison's vision of the First Amendment protecting the "right of freely examining public characters and measures, and of free communication among the people thereon, which has ever been justly deemed, the only effectual guardian of every other right," as he advocated so eloquently when opposing the Sedition Act.[46] This latter-day manifestation took these ideas even further by encompassing the descendants of those slaves whom Madison had excluded. Professor Harry Kalven Jr. noted the sea change in 1965: "We may come to see the Negro as winning back for us the freedoms the Communists seemed to have lost for us."[47]

While these victories were achieved in court rooms, the battles began with resolute activism. The civil rights movement and its allies had to reshape public opinion, making the grim reality of racism and segregation impossible for white Americans to ignore. Free speech was thus crucial to the fight for equality and for more sweeping legislative achievements, such as the Civil Rights Act of 1964 and the Voting Rights Act of 1965. Looking back at the epic struggle in which he had played a pivotal role, John Lewis remarked, "Without freedom of speech and the right to dissent, the Civil Rights movement would have been a bird without wings."[48]

Less than twenty-four hours before Dr. King was assassinated in Memphis on April 4, 1968, he gave a defiant speech rebuking government officials who continued to deny civil rights advocates their First Amendment freedoms. He called upon America to live up to the ideals that set the nation apart from others:

If I lived in China or even Russia, or any totalitarian country, maybe I could understand . . . the denial of certain basic First Amendment privileges. . . . But somewhere I read of the freedom of assembly . . . the freedom of speech . . . the freedom of press. Somewhere I read that the greatness of America is the right to protest for right.[49]

The following year, the Supreme Court demonstrated just how seriously it now took the protections enshrined in the First Amendment. In *Brandenburg v. Ohio*, the court held that speech could only be banned if constituting "incitement to imminent lawless action" likely to result in such action.[50] It was a standard very close to the one suggested by the Commission on Human Rights in the first draft of the ICCPR in 1947, when Roosevelt was at the helm. The Brandenburg standard invalidated an Ohio law used to convict a KKK leader who had denounced and called for government action against "Niggers" and "Jews" in front of armed KKK members and TV cameras. Less than a decade later, the ACLU won a federal lawsuit upholding the right of American Nazis to march through the village of Skokie, Illinois, inhabited by hundreds of Jewish Holocaust survivors.[51]

The Supreme Court's protection of white supremacist speech in *Brandenburg* might seem incompatible with Dr. King's vision of a just and equal society. But the progressive potential of protecting the speech of bigots was clear to one of the justices who joined the unanimous decision. In 1967, Thurgood Marshall became the first African American Supreme Court justice. Central to Marshall's philosophy, as one biographer has explained, was the idea that "liberty and equality, properly understood, complemented each other." Specifically, Marshall's record of protecting free speech claims from the bench underlined his belief that "the First Amendment also promoted equality and social justice because it afforded members of subordinated groups, whose voices are most likely to be suppressed, an opportunity to give voice to their concerns."[52] Indeed, the test articulated in *Brandenburg v. Ohio* would be used to help defeat a new authoritarian assault on free speech at the UN four decades later.

White Fragility and Civil Obedience in Apartheid South Africa

According to Martin Luther King, "the struggle for freedom forms one long front crossing oceans and mountains."[53] To King, the plight of Black South Africans in particular underscored the global nature of the fight against racism. In a 1960 letter to President Dwight D. Eisenhower he wrote, "South Africans cannot hope for help from a government committed to 'apartheid'; nor can we hope for help from local and state governments committed to 'white supremacy.'"[54]

As we've seen, South Africa was among the states that abstained from signing the UDHR back in 1948. Ideas about "the inherent dignity" and "equal and inalienable rights of all members of the human family" were difficult to reconcile with South Africa's constitutional commitment to white supremacy.[55] The regime of apartheid or "apartness" was formerly introduced in May 1948, just a few months before the adoption of the UDHR. South African apartheid institutionalized a strict racial hierarchy with Black Africans at the bottom. And just as Southern states in the US had entrenched first slavery and then segregation through censorship and repression, so South African apartheid rested on the systematic denial of freedom of thought and speech. In the words of the white South African writer and Nobel laureate Nadine Gordimer, "No social system in which a tiny minority must govern without consent over a vast majority can afford to submit any part of control of communication."[56]

The censorship served to guard an ideological trinity of racism, Calvinism, and capitalism.[57] It was illegal to print, publish, display, import, sell, or circulate any "undesirable material," including obscene and blasphemous writings.[58] A Directorate of Publications was responsible for reviewing and identifying undesirable material in order to "uphold a Christian view of life."[59] Banned materials were listed in the Jacobsen's Index of Objectionable Literature—the apartheid version of the Index of Forbidden Books—compiled by the South African publisher Jacobsen. At one point, it included more than twenty thousand titles.[60]

The "undesirable" category also included publications "harmful to the relations between any inhabitants" or that brought "any section of the inhabitants into ridicule or contempt," in effect a form of hate speech ban.[61] On the face of it, these provisions applied to all racial and ethnic groups in South Africa. What they really aimed at, however, was preserving white supremacy. As the chairman of the Publications Appeal Board, an official censorship body, explained:

> The Appeal Board has emphasized that the South African community in no way wants to suppress criticism against whites or the government, but writers should realize that they are on delicate ground and that they have to make sure that what they publish does not assume the character of a hateful attack on the white man.[62]

Not surprisingly, many works were banned for subjecting whites to ridicule or contempt. One novel was banned for portraying the white community as behaving "oppressively" toward the Black community.[63] Nadine Gordimer's *Burger's Daughter* was initially banned because the book contained "various anti-white sentiments." *Roots*, the American miniseries on slavery, was banned out of fear that "viewers would identify with the cause of the oppressed American slaves."[64]

The Suppression of Communism Act gave the government authority to ban publications that might further the aims of "communism," conveniently defined to include the promotion of racial equality.[65] It also allowed the government to ban individuals and organizations. Some banning orders specified that the person could not "be concerned in any way with the preparation, printing, or publication of any newspaper, magazine, pamphlet, book, handbill, or poster."[66] It was even illegal to quote the words of a banned person.[67] Some 1,358 banning orders were issued by the end of 1978.[68]

Legal repression was only one strategy within a larger system of control.[69] The famous (white) South African writer André Brink explained the more subtle tactics:

> It begins, for the writer, with the discovery that all his mail is opened and his phone is tapped. . . . There are other methods, too, all of them extensions of censorship: an "invitation" to visit the Special Branch and "discuss things"; and next they are the visitors, arriving unannounced and with great show of strength, to search one's house and confiscate notes and correspondence and even one's typewriters.[70]

But it could get far uglier than intimidation. Black dissidents were silenced with corporal violence, police brutality, and even murder, as in the case of the famous anti-apartheid activist Steve Biko, who was tortured to death in 1977. The killing of Biko and the crackdown on the anti-apartheid Black Consciousness Movement, which he headed, convinced US President Jimmy Carter to add action to rhetoric and support a UN arms embargo to address "the recent retrogression of South Africa in its dealing with freedom of the press and with freedom of expression of opinion."[71]

Like King and the civil rights movement in America, the African National Congress (ANC) and its Youth League took up Gandhi's strategy of civil disobedience in the early 1950s, spearheaded by the young lawyer Nelson Mandela. He mobilized massive strikes, boycotts, and campaigns like burning the internal passes that Black people were required to carry at all times in white areas.[72] Bridging the racial gap, the ANC helped organize a multiracial Congress of the People in 1955. It adopted a Freedom Charter that insisted that "South Africa belongs to all who live in it, black and white," and that "the law shall guarantee to all their right to speak, to organise, to meet together, to publish, to preach," though it also envisaged banning racial insults.[73] The regime responded with harassment and systematic persecution. Mandela was banned several times from 1952 onward.[74] He likened these restrictions on his speech, writing, and travel to "a kind of walking imprisonment."[75]

As tensions mounted, the regime proved willing to take extreme steps to quell dissent—including mass murder. In March 1960, the police opened fire and killed sixty-seven unarmed anti-apartheid protestors in the Black township of Sharpeville.[76] The Sharpeville massacre became a turning point in the battle over speech. The ANC was banned, and its leaders were arrested or forced underground. Abandoning peaceful civil disobedience, Mandela and the ANC established an armed wing and launched a sabotage campaign.[77] Within a few years, Mandela and several other ANC leaders were tried for sabotage, treason, and violent conspiracy after the authorities raided a safe house that contained weapons to be used for armed insurrection.[78] At the infamous Rivonia Trial in 1964, Mandela delivered an iconic defense of liberty, explaining why the ANC had turned to armed resistance:

> All lawful modes of expressing opposition . . . had been closed by legislation, and we were placed in a position in which we had either to accept a permanent state of inferiority, or to defy the Government. . . . We first broke the law in a way which avoided any recourse to violence; when this form was legislated against, and when the Government resorted to a show of force to crush opposition to its policies, only then did we decide to answer violence with violence.[79]

In other words, Mandela offered a pressure-cooker theory in which peaceful dissent is the antithesis of violence. Only when free speech and peaceful protest is denied can violence be justified. Mandela was sentenced to life in prison, where he spent the next twenty-seven years, becoming perhaps the world's most iconic political prisoner.

The crackdown on the anti-apartheid movement marked a stark contrast to the victories of the American civil rights movement occurring around the same time. In the United States, civil rights activists had been able to appeal to and ultimately rely on constitutional freedoms couched in universalist terms in order to dismantle the Jim Crow system. Anticolonialist movements within the British Empire could also point to the chasm between colonial censorship and Britain's liberal traditions of press freedom. But no such legal or ideological support was available to the opponents of apartheid. The South African constitutions of 1961 and 1983 contained no bills of rights, and they explicitly discriminated on the basis of race.[80] While American constitutional ideals promised freedom and equality—even if long denied in practice—South African constitutional ideals promised only subjugation and inequity. This hampered the people's ability to use dissent as a weapon against apartheid and protracted the excruciatingly long road to freedom.

The Helsinki Effect

The UDHR had ushered in hope and optimism, but lofty principles quickly drowned in Cold War rivalry and colonialism. As historian Samuel Moyn has shown, the real breakthrough for human rights did not come until the 1970s, when they became the common international language of hope and progress—however aspirational.[81] Many factors contributed to this change, including decolonization, the American civil rights movement, the Carter presidency's embrace of human rights, the explosion of human rights NGOs, and communication technology that allowed information to penetrate borders. But the real game changer, at least in Cold War Europe, was the Helsinki Final Act of 1975.

Signed by thirty-five countries under the auspices of the Conference on Security and Cooperation in Europe (CSCE) after two and a half years of negotiation,[82] its primary ambition was to ease Cold War tensions and avoid a nuclear cataclysm. But the two blocs also brought different agendas to the negotiating table. When the participants agreed on a number of basic principles to be negotiated on June 8, 1973, the Soviet bloc stressed the "inviolability of frontiers" and "non-intervention in internal affairs" while the Western bloc emphasized the "respect for human rights and fundamental freedoms, including specifically the freedom of thought, conscience, religion or belief." These principles—not least freedom of expression and information—were fleshed out in more detail as the signatories agreed to "facilitate the freer and wider dissemination of information of all kinds," including newspapers, magazines, books, radio, and TV, as well as to improve working conditions for foreign journalists.[83]

The human rights agenda was initially driven by the Western European democracies of the European Community, while US national security advisor Henry Kissinger counseled presidents Richard Nixon and Gerald Ford to focus on realpolitik rather than useless human rights sloganeering. In 1974, Kissinger was openly dismissive about the drafting of the Final Act: "They can write in Swahili for all I care."[84] But a wide range of factors changed American attitudes and led to the US taking a more proactive role in driving the human rights agenda. One influential factor was a 1975 speech given by Aleksandr Solzhenitsyn. In 1974, he had been deported and stripped of his citizenship after publishing *The Gulag Archipelago*. A year later, Solzhenitsyn warned that the Helsinki principle of noninterference would result in "the funeral of Eastern Europe" unless the US stepped up its game.[85]

The human rights language obviously did not appeal to communist states. They were already fighting an uphill battle to jam the radio signals of Western radio stations like Radio Free Europe, Radio Liberty, and the BBC that broadcast uncensored news and dissident writings into the homes of millions of people behind the Iron Curtain.[86] The Soviet ambassador in Helsinki emphasized that the USSR would under no circumstances tolerate "the dissemination of anti-culture—pornography, racism, fascism, the cult of violence, hostility among peoples and false slanderous propaganda."[87]

But at the end of the day, the Soviet bloc swallowed the human rights concessions and signed the agreement. The prevailing view in Moscow was that the human rights language was little more than empty rhetoric anyway, given the document's commitment to sovereignty and nonintervention. As the Soviet foreign minister Andrei Gromyko confidently proclaimed, "We are masters in our own house."[88]

But through newspaper reports, word of mouth, underground samizdat publishers, and Western radio broadcasts, Central and Eastern Europeans quickly learned about the new rights that their governments had just solemnly promised to respect.[89] Dissident groups throughout the Soviet bloc were emboldened by the Helsinki agreement to act as if their governments had actually committed themselves to basic human rights in good faith, rather than as a calculated gesture to obtain other diplomatic concessions.[90]

In 1975, the Soviet nuclear physicist Andrei Sakharov had been awarded the Nobel Peace Prize for his human rights work. But the government barred him from flying to Oslo to accept it and instead subjected him to a relentless campaign of smears and surveillance when he refused to reject this Western honor.[91] As early as the 1960s, Sakharov had become increasingly critical of the oppressive nature of the Soviet Union, and in 1968 he wrote the essay "Thoughts on Progress, Peaceful Coexistence and Intellectual Freedom":

> Intellectual freedom is essential to human society—freedom to obtain and distribute information, freedom for open-minded and unfearing debate and freedom from pressure by officialdom and prejudices. Such a trinity of freedom of thought is the only guarantee against an infection of people by mass myths, which, in the hands of treacherous hypocrites and demagogues, can be transformed into bloody dictatorship.[92]

Sakharov's eloquent essay was rewarded with the loss of his security clearance.[93]

Given the negative attention surrounding Sakharov, it was a pretty bold move when, in May 1976, a group of Russian dissidents including Natan Sharansky, Yuri Orlov, and Sakharov's wife, Yelena Bonner, held a press conference in Sakharov's apartment. Here they announced the establishment of the Moscow Helsinki Group in order to monitor the implementation of the Helsinki Agreement in the USSR. In the following years, the Moscow Helsinki Group and others like it reported human rights violations to Western journalists or circulated them within the USSR through underground networks and samizdat.[94]

Western NGOs and politicians provided much-needed backing to these groups of dissidents who had no official or public channels of communication. Millicent Fenwick, a Republican congresswoman of New Jersey, came to play an important role after she met dissidents on a trip to the Soviet Union. Against the wishes of President Ford, she convinced Congress to establish the Commission on Security and Cooperation in Europe, consisting of members of both houses of Congress, with a mandate to investigate and report on Soviet and Eastern European compliance with the Final Act. Suddenly, dissidents and human rights activists had powerful friends on

Capitol Hill.[95] Western NGOs also saw an opportunity to punch above their weight with the Final Act. The US Helsinki Watch group—now Human Rights Watch—was established in New York in 1978 to give "moral support for the activities of the beleaguered Helsinki monitors in the Soviet bloc."[96] The reports of Amnesty International from the late 1970s were filled with information about human rights violations obtained from samizdat compiled by dissidents and monitoring groups behind the Iron Curtain and then smuggled across borders. Amnesty and other Western rights groups would then ensure publicity in the media and among Western politicians in order to apply maximum pressure on socialist states to honor the human rights commitments they had ratified.

It is important not to paint too simplistic a picture of US involvement in the "Helsinki effect." The US came around to actively supporting the practice and principle of human rights and free speech against communist regimes in Europe. But the wider fight against communism saw the US government support authoritarian regimes around the globe that had no qualms about using censorship and brutal suppression of dissent that violated core principles of human rights, as the surviving victims of dictators such as Augusto Pinochet in Chile, Park Chung-hee in South Korea, and Joseph Mobutu in Zaire can attest. Moreover, the US support for dissidents behind the Iron Curtain was in stark contrast with the way successive US administrations shunned the ANC and vetoed punitive financial sanctions against the apartheid regime at the UN, until Congress stepped in with the Comprehensive Anti-Apartheid Act of 1986.[97]

For the first couple of years after the Final Act, the Soviet regime met the Helsinki watch groups and the wave of dissident activity with surprising tolerance. From the period between 1968 and 1974 to the period between 1975 and 1978, the average number of dissidents arrested per year dropped by half.[98] It all seemed very promising, but as many dissidents must have sensed, the apparent thaw was too good to last.

The Helsinki Act inspired a wave of human rights activism throughout the Eastern bloc. In Czechoslovakia, the decisive moment was the 1976 arrest of the underground rock band Plastic People of the Universe for "organizing disturbance of the peace" and "corrupting" the youth with its "anti-social" behavior.[99] The band had gained notoriety for its provocative lyrics, which satirized the communist regime and its repression following the Soviet invasion that crushed the so-called Prague Spring of 1968. Now rock 'n' roll itself was put on trial.

The arrests inspired a motley crew of intellectuals, writers, and artists, including the playwright Václav Havel, to take action. They published a charter documenting how the government systematically violated the rights it had promised to respect in the recently ratified ICCPR and Helsinki Final Act. The very first paragraph of the charter protested,

> The right to freedom of expression, for example, guaranteed by Article 19 of the . . . [ICCPR], is in our case purely illusory. Tens of thousands of our citizens are prevented from working in their own fields for the sole reason that they hold views differing from official ones, and are discriminated against and harassed in all kinds of ways by the authorities and public organizations.

The informal group became known as Charter 77—one of the most iconic dissident movements of the Cold War. Crucially, the movement was ideologically neutral and nonpartisan. When the manifesto was published on January 1, 1977, it had 242 signatories who spanned from liberals to socialists and with many more joining in the following weeks. The signatories were united by the Charter's commitment to the "rights accorded to all men by the two mentioned international covenants, by the Final Act of the Helsinki conference and . . . the [UDHR]."[100]

Despite the Czechoslovakian government's censorship, the Charter went viral and was published in influential Western newspapers like *Le Monde*, *The Times*, and the *New York Times*. Charter 77 had caught the government in a catch-22. If it cracked down too hard, it would merely prove the point of the chartists. Yet the memory of 1968 was still fresh, and if it did nothing, liberal sentiments might get out of hand again. So initially the government used propaganda and smear tactics to try to influence public opinion against the signatories. When that failed, Charter signatories were arrested or fired, many losing their careers and being forced to take any job they could get.[101]

At this point, the Czechoslovakian government realized that signing the Helsinki Final Act had been a trap all along. The crackdown on Charter 77 was condemned by the US, Western European states, NGOs, and intellectuals, all of whom protested that the Czech government was violating the human rights provisions in the Final Act.[102] This so-called Helsinki effect put the government on the defensive, while providing an international platform to dissidents who were otherwise powerless in the face of the might of a one-party state and its full apparatus. And as we shall see, prominent members of Charter 77—not least Václav Havel—would fight on to play a key role in Czechoslovakia's Velvet Revolution, which ended communism and brought about democracy.

The Helsinki effect also spread to Poland, where fifty-nine people signed the so-called Letter of 59 in December 1975 to demand the rights and freedoms their leaders had promised when they signed the Helsinki Final Act.[103] In the summer of 1976, the Helsinki Final Act and the blossoming human rights movement in the Soviet Union inspired the formation of the Workers' Defense Committee or KOR. It was established to help workers who were fired or imprisoned for striking, like the young electrical engineer Lech Wałęsa, who joined the organization after he was fired from the Lenin

Shipyard in Gdańsk for engaging in "anti-government activity." But KOR soon united everyone, from the worker to the professor and clergyman, who joined forces and got behind the fight for human rights and free trade unions. Even the Catholic Church became involved with the Polish human rights movement after a Pole was elected John Paul II in October 1978. The new pope, who as a cardinal had spoken against communism's "consequences for human dignity, individual rights, human rights and the rights of nations," became a huge inspiration for Polish dissidents.[104] When he made a triumphant visit to Poland in 1979, he was met by an adorning crowd of around 250,000.[105] The resistance became too big and too broad for the government to crush with brute force. Deputy Prime Minister Mieczysław Jagielski signed an agreement in August 1980 allowing the Poles to organize themselves freely and independently. Later that month, Wałęsa announced the formation of *Solidarność* or "Solidarity," the first independent trade union in the communist world.[106] Before long, it had attracted ten million members, nearly a third of Poland's population.[107]

The Helsinki effect triggered various responses from the communist states. There were periods of tolerance in order not to jeopardize the wider geopolitical gains of the Helsinki Process such as the sanctity of borders. But there were also crackdowns to stop the process from further eroding communist control. Some dissidents were forcibly committed to psychiatric institutions—after all, only the insane would oppose the landmark achievements of socialism.[108] The Moscow Helsinki Group was initially treated leniently. But then, in July 1978, the regime began arresting members of the group. Yuri Orlov and Natan Sharansky were sentenced to seven and thirteen years in prison, respectively, while Sakharov was exiled to Gorky some 250 miles away, where he lived under tight surveillance from 1980. Between 1980 and 1983 more than five hundred Soviet citizens were arrested for Helsinki-related activities.[109] By 1981, the first deputy chairman of the KGB thought that things were under control:

As a result of measures taken by the KGB, implemented in strict accordance with the law and under the leadership of Party organs, the anti-social elements, despite the West's considerable material and moral support, did not succeed in achieving organized cohesion on the platform of anti-Sovietism.[110]

One year later Yelena Bonner officially disbanded the Moscow Helsinki Group, although others would spring up to continue the good fight.

In Czechoslovakia, several members of Charter 77 were arrested throughout 1977. The majority of Czechoslovakian cases taken up by Amnesty International in 1978 concerned members or affiliates of Charter 77 who were imprisoned for writing, distributing, or possessing texts that criticized the government's abuse of human rights. Most were sentenced under three articles from the penal code criminalizing "subversion," "breach of public peace," and "incitement." The latter was the very crime the Soviet bloc—including Czechoslovakia—had fought successfully to include in Article 20 of the ICCPR, and which Eleanor Roosevelt had warned could be abused to render all rights "null and void." True, Article 100 of the Czechoslovakian penal code punished incitement "against the socialist social and state system of the Republic" motivated by "hostility" to these bodies rather than specific groups of people or minorities.[111] But this "mutation" of incitement norms had also been foretold by Roosevelt. A good example of the catchall character of incitement was the case of the Charter 77 affiliate František Pitor, who was sentenced to three years in prison after tape-recording and distributing the Charter 77 manifesto. Others got similar punishments for writing or distributing political leaflets. Václav Havel was initially lucky and only got a suspended sentence of fourteen months for "attempting to harm the interests of the republic abroad."[112]

The crackdown prompted members of Charter 77 to set up a Committee for the Defense of the Unjustly Prosecuted, which documented the repression of their fellow dissidents. This activity cost Havel a sentence of four and a half years in prison in 1979, whereas Jiří Gans was given a stiff sentence of fifteen years for listening to Voice of America broadcasts and founding the Club of Friends of American Music.[113]

Czechoslovakia was not the only communist state to prove Eleanor Roosevelt right on the dangers of hate speech prohibitions; Hungary also prohibited various forms of incitement to hatred, while Yugoslavia criminalized incitement to hatred with punishments of up to ten years in prison. But Yugoslavia's provision was mostly used to curb political criticism as well as the religious and nationalist sentiments of the country's different ethnic groups. In 1981, a number of Muslims, including an imam, were sentenced to four years' imprisonment for provoking national and religious hatred after criticizing the authorities and urging parents to raise their children as Muslims. An Orthodox priest and three other men were given sentences of four to six years for singing nationalist songs at a christening. The liberal Croatian writer and dissident Vladimir "Vlado" Gotovac—sometimes called the Croat Václav Havel—was sentenced to two years of prison and banned from writing and speaking in public for four years for spreading "hostile propaganda" and "inciting national hatred" in interviews with foreign journalists.[114]

The Polish government also felt compelled to reverse its lenient course. Several members of Solidarity were arrested and charged with crimes like "slanderous and offensive allegations about the authorities," "disseminating false information," and "publishing and disseminating material and appeals directed against the allied unity of Poland and the Soviet Union."[115] In December 1981, Poland's new leader Wojciech Jaruzelski declared martial law. Tens of thousands were arrested without charge, and around a hundred were killed.[116] Many of the victims were members, supporters, or officials of Solidarity, including Lech Wałęsa, who was put under house arrest. On January 29, 1982, the government suspended a number of rights from the ICCPR, including the freedoms of expression, assembly, association, and movement.[117] Solidarity was officially banned on October 8, while a new law dissolved existing trade unions and put restrictions on the formation of new ones.[118]

Wałęsa was released in November. Martial law was lifted in July 1983, and many of the suspended rights were reestablished. But Solidarity was still banned, and the criminal code was amended to make it punishable with up to five years in prison to publish, carry, or distribute "anti-state publications." Actions "intended to incite public unrest" could be punished with up to three years in prison, and military courts now assumed the jurisdiction of crimes "against the fundamental political interests of the state."[119] Even so, the crackdown was not enough to shore up the crumbling communist monopoly on power and the public sphere, nor to avert the momentous events that were shortly to wash over the whole of the communist bloc.

―――

IN THE EARLY 1970S, KGB LEADER YURI ANDROPOV HAD warned, "With all the innovations in the domain of information transmission the frontiers of this country will never be watertight again."[120] With the acceptance of the Helsinki Final Act, the Soviet Union had allowed dissidents and the West to further flood its sphere of dominance, and even a brutal crackdown could not stop the dam from bursting. Despite their best efforts, the communist states could not blunt the emancipatory and empowering idea of free expression. The very human rights language they had sought to contain in an awkward embrace ultimately escaped their grasp and ended up eroding the communist stranglehold on power.

When Mikhail Gorbachev assumed the role of general secretary of the Communist Party in 1985, things unraveled fast. Gorbachev's reform of glasnost, or "openness," in the late eighties took inspiration from the Final Act, which he explicitly relied on to push back against protesting hard-liners in the Politburo and KGB. Censorship was relaxed, Sakharov was allowed to return to Moscow, and hundreds of political prisoners were released, including Sharansky and Orlov.[121] The government also moved to stop the jamming of Western radio signals. As a Soviet official stated, "The level of glasnost is now so high in the Soviet Union that we can afford to hear three more voices or 20 more languages."[122]

The spirit of glasnost also spread to Czechoslovakia and Poland. The civic movement around Charter 77 played a major role in the so-called Velvet Revolution that toppled the communist dictatorship in Czechoslovakia in 1989. The same year, Václav Havel won the presidency in a democratic election. That year also saw Jaruzelski and the Polish government cave in after a number of large-scale strikes. Solidarity was allowed to run in the semifree election for parliament in June 1989, and it won by a landslide. The humiliation of the Communist Party and the victory for Solidarity sent shock waves through the communist bloc and became one of the drivers behind the fall of the Berlin Wall later that year.[123] Like Havel in Czechoslovakia, Wałęsa, the former dissident, became the democratically elected president of the newly independent Poland.

Of course, the Helsinki effect was not uniquely responsible for these events; many other crucial economic, military, diplomatic, and geopolitical developments contributed to the fall of communism and the end of the Cold War. But it cannot be denied that human rights became an effective central platform and unifying language for a movement of dissidents backed by Western governments and NGOs. In the words of Moyn, the "Helsinki accords were an essential feature of the crystallization of international human rights consciousness."[124] And among the rights guaranteed by the Helsinki Final Act perhaps none was more important than freedom of expression. In the words of Lech Wałęsa, without freedom of expression "human life becomes meaningless; and once the truth of this hit me, it became part of my whole way of thinking."[125] In a triumphant speech to the US Congress in 1990, Václav Havel—now president of Czechoslovakia—said:

> When they arrested me on Oct. 27, I was living in a country ruled by the most conservative communist government in Europe, and our society slumbered beneath the pall of a totalitarian system. Today, less than four months later, I'm speaking to you as the representative of a country that has set out on the road to democracy, a country where there is complete freedom of speech.[126]

The coming decades would usher in a Golden Age of free speech unsurpassed in human history. But the end of the Cold War was far from the end of history for free speech.

12

The Free Speech Recession

On Thursday, April 30, 1977, fourteen women marched into the Plaza de Mayo in downtown Buenos Aires to protest the "disappearance" of their sons and daughters. Since March 1976, when a violent military coup overthrew the government, thousands of Argentinians had disappeared into torture chambers never to be seen or heard from again. On their heads, the women wore white scarves to symbolize the diapers of their lost children, embroidered with their names and dates of birth.

The mothers returned to the presidential palace on the Plaza de Mayo on the following Thursday. And, in increasing numbers, on every Thursday after that. The Madres de Plaza de Mayo, with their iconic white scarves, became synonymous with Argentina's fight for freedom and democracy. They were still marching in the fall of 1983 when the regime collapsed and the Argentinians elected a democratic president. At this point, up to thirty thousand Argentinians—including some of the marching mothers themselves—had been abducted and killed, many forced onto "death flights" and thrown into the Atlantic Ocean. The Mothers of the Plaza de Mayo would never see their children again. But their tireless protests helped shine a light on the brutality of the dictatorship.[1]

Argentina's neighbors, Brazil, Chile, and Uruguay, also suffered coups and violent military dictatorships in the 1960s and '70s. All of which relied on murder and harassment of activists and journalists, rigorous censorship, and control—directly or indirectly—of the media to maintain their grip on power. Looking at the data in all four countries since the 1960s, there is a clear correlation between the waxing and waning of democracy and freedom of speech and the press.[2] And despite harsh repression, activists like the Mothers of the Plaza de Mayo and alternative media outlets all contributed to toppling these military regimes.[3]

For Black South Africans, the walk to freedom was longer than for the Argentinians, but it too was illuminated by the stubborn persistence of those who refused to be silenced. For much of the Cold War, apartheid South Africa had been able to resist international pressure for change because of its staunch anticommunist credentials. By the 1980s, however, South Africa had become a pariah state, almost universally condemned and heavily sanctioned by the international community, including—belatedly—the US. While imprisonment, intimidation, and even killings prevented Mandela and other activists from speaking out, a rapidly globalized world allowed international media, dissidents, and human rights organizations to speak for those whose voices had been muted. They could take advantage of the speech rights in liberal democracies as well as international human rights norms to expose and denounce the gross injustice. In February 1990, the regime finally wavered. Mandela was released from prison and the ANC was unbanned. The following year, apartheid was abolished, and in April 1994, South Africans elected Mandela as president in the country's first free and multiracial election.

Shortly before winning the 1994 election, Mandela gave a speech to the International Press Institute Congress in which he expressed gratitude to the international media for exposing the evils of white supremacy and giving a voice to the many South Africans who had been silenced by apartheid. Mandela also promised that freedom of expression would constitute a "core value" of the new South African democracy:

> No single person, no body of opinion, no political or religious doctrine, no political party or government can claim to have a monopoly on truth. For that reason truth can be arrived at only through the untrammelled contest between and among competing opinions, in which as many viewpoints as possible are given a fair and equal hearing. It has therefore always been our contention that laws, mores, practices and prejudices that place constraints on freedom of expression are a disservice to society.[4]

Argentina and South Africa represent a trend known as the third wave of democratization taking place between the late 1970s and early 2000s, when democracy and free speech triumphed in the Americas, sub-Saharan Africa, Eastern Europe, and Asia. This ushered in a Golden Age of free speech unsurpassed in human history, aided by new communications technology such as digital broadcast, satellite TV, and—most consequentially—the World Wide Web. According to data from Freedom House, the world's share of free countries surged from 32 percent in 1979 to 46 percent in 2003.[5] In the same period, the percentage of countries with press freedom grew from 25 to 41 percent.[6]

Not all states—nor all people—in the world have been as committed to free speech as the apparent triumph of these values seemed to suggest. In 2003, 41 percent of countries had a free press. By 2016, only 31 percent did, according to Freedom House. In terms of population, the numbers were even starker. Only 13 percent of the world's 7.4 billion people enjoyed free speech in 2016, while 45 percent lived in countries where censorship was the norm.[7] This development had real consequences for media and reporters. According to data from the Committee to Protect Journalists (CPJ),

1,010 journalists were imprisoned from 2011 to 2020. This represents an alarming 78 percent increase from the previous decade of 2001 to 2010.[8]

This free speech recession precipitated a "third wave of autocratization."[9] In 2021, the Economist Intelligence Unit's Democracy Index reported the worst average global score "by far" since its first survey from 2006.[10] No scores have deteriorated as much over the past decade as those "related to freedom of expression and media freedom."[11] Likewise, the V-Dem Institute's *Democracy Report 2020*—the largest global dataset on democracy—found that media censorship intensified in a record-breaking thirty-seven countries in 2019.[12]

The contrasting fates of Cold War–era dissidents like Václav Havel, Lech Wałęsa, and Nelson Mandela on the one hand and Chinese dissident and Nobel Peace Prize winner Liu Xiaobo on the other are a sobering illustration of how the Golden Age of free speech subsided into a free speech recession that continues into the present day. By 1989, twelve years after Havel coauthored Charter 77, Czechoslovakia's communist dictatorship was gone, and Havel—as would Mandela and Wałęsa—had become president of a democracy. In 2017, nine years after Liu Xiaobo sought to emulate Charter 77 and coauthored Charter 08 calling for democracy, human rights, and putting "an end to punishing speech as a crime," he died of cancer after spending almost a decade in prison, and with the Chinese Communist Party firmly in control.[13] Free speech entropy remained a pervasive force.

Roosevelt's Prophesy: The Conflation of Hate Speech and Blasphemy at the UN

On September 30, 2005, the Danish newspaper *Jyllands-Posten* published twelve cartoons of the prophet Muhammad. Coming on the heels of numerous incidents of Islamist violence and intimidation against writers and artists in Europe, commissioning editor Flemming Rose explained the publication as an attempt to show that demanding special protection for religious taboos was "incompatible with secular democracy, in which the individual must be prepared to suffer scorn, mockery, and ridicule."[14] The Danish cartoon affair exploded into a global battle of values with geopolitical implications. However, the controversy was not the result of spontaneous protests but rather of an orchestrated campaign hatched at the highest levels of politics and government.

The main driver behind the protests was the Organization of Islamic Cooperation (OIC)—an intergovernmental umbrella organization for the Muslim world comprising fifty-seven member states.[15] At a high-level summit in December 2005, the OIC's heads of state condemned the cartoons as a "defamation of Islam" and urged states "to criminalize this phenomenon as a form of racism," a goal vigorously pursued by the OIC at the UN.[16] A few months later, much of the Middle East was on fire, stoked by the incitement of governments who normally never allowed their peoples to protest. In Denmark, cartoonists and editors had to go into hiding as unprecedented security measures were implemented by both the government and media organizations, preventing a raft of terrorist attacks, including an attempt to break into *Jyllands-Posten* and decapitate journalists in the newsroom and lob their severed heads onto the square below.[17]

In 1950, Eleanor Roosevelt had warned that if hate speech prohibitions were embedded in human rights law, "any criticism of public or religious authorities might all too easily be described as incitement to hatred and consequently prohibited." Roosevelt's foresight was once again displayed when the OIC sought to exploit the very loopholes that the communist states had introduced with ICCPR Article 20. Instead of protecting an atheistic and materialistic ideology as the communists had done, they insisted that restrictions on free speech under human rights law protected theistic and metaphysical Islamic doctrines from criticism and satire.

During the height of the Rushdie Affair, the OIC had once before tried to advance the idea that free speech exempted—or even prohibited—mocking and insulting religion, but with no success.

At the UN's General Assembly, delegates from Iran and Libya— the latter on behalf of the OIC—took the floor to condemn Rushdie. The Libyan delegate argued:

> Some people had invoked the right to freedom of thought and expression with respect to the publication of the "Satanic Verses" but without taking into account the feelings of millions of Muslims. Freedom of opinion and expression was not an absolute freedom existing in a vacuum. . . . Article 20, paragraph 2 of the [ICCPR] stated that "any advocacy of national, racial or religious hatred that constitutes incitement to discrimination, hostility or violence shall be prohibited by law."[18]

In other words, the Libyan representative justified the OIC's pledge to ban *The Satanic Verses* by referring to hate speech prohibitions in secular international human rights law. The real criminal was Rushdie, not those who sought to kill him.

Founded in 1969, the OIC adopted its own Cairo Declaration on Human Rights in Islam in 1990, based on a theocentric approach subordinating individual rights to Islamic Shari'ah law. Article 22 states, "Everyone shall have the right to express his opinion freely in such manner as would not be contrary to the principles of the Shari'ah."[19] This narrow understanding of free speech had already proved lethal in OIC states. Four years before the Rushdie Affair, Sudanese religious scholar Mahmoud Muhammad Taha was executed for apostasy after advocating a tolerant version of Islam.[20] Egyptian secularist Farag Foda suffered the same fate when assassinated by

Islamist militants in 1992 after being condemned as an apostate by prominent religious authorities.[21] No doubt medieval freethinkers like al-Rāzī and al-Rāwandī would have been in trouble too.

In 1999, the OIC launched a controversial resolution in the Commission on Human Rights—urging all member states to combat "defamation of religions" (the original draft only mentioned defamation of Islam), a euphemism for blasphemy.[22]

UN resolutions against defamation of religions were adopted at the UN every year from 1999 to 2010, often by comfortable majorities that included non-Muslim countries such as Russia, China, and Cuba, who were happy to dilute free speech protections and join ranks against supposedly Western values.[23] In the early years, few attached much weight to these resolutions. Yet, the defamation agenda was strengthened by events such as 9/11 and subsequent Al-Qaeda attacks in London and Madrid and then supercharged by the Danish cartoon affair. These events deeply polarized opinion on Islam and gave voice to genuine anti-Muslim hatred and anti-Islamic political parties in many Western countries, in turn providing a facade of legitimacy to the OIC grievances.

The OIC's diplomats skillfully framed the issue as a matter of protecting and promoting international human rights standards, deliberately conflating blasphemy and hate speech, including Article 20 of the ICCPR.

Western intellectuals and human rights organizations aided the OIC's efforts by blurring the line between blasphemy and hate speech. In 2006, the Nobel Prize–winning German writer Günter Grass compared the Danish cartoons to the virulently anti-Semitic cartoons in Julius Streicher's Nazi magazine *Der Stürmer*, ignoring the fact that the universalist defense of free speech and tolerance that motivated the cartoons was the antithesis of Streicher's genocidal commitment to a racially pure one-party state.[24] Amnesty International—apparently afraid to appear xenophobic or racist—released a statement titled "Freedom of Speech Carries Responsibilities for

All." The statement failed to support *Jyllands-Posten* against calls for censorship and even suggested that the cartoons might violate the ICCPR's Article 20 as constituting "hate speech," a shocking deviation from Amnesty's support for victims of blasphemy laws around the world.[25] Incredibly, even the US State Department under the Bush administration initially sided with the OIC. In February 2006, a spokesperson said, "we all fully recognize and respect freedom of the press and expression but it must be coupled with press responsibility. Inciting religious or ethnic hatreds in this manner is not acceptable."[26] It was a very far cry from Eleanor Roosevelt's position in 1950.

The OIC used another trump card by accusing European democracies of hypocrisy. Several European states retain blasphemy laws—until 2017 this included Denmark. Even more importantly, since the 1990s the European Court of Human Rights has exempted from the protection of free speech satire or criticism of religion that is deemed "gratuitously offensive to others" and that therefore—according to the court—does "not contribute to any form of public debate capable of furthering progress in human affairs." Accordingly, "provocative portrayals of objects of religious veneration" can constitute a "malicious violation of the spirit of tolerance." On this basis, the court has found that freedom of expression does not extend to blasphemous artistic films mocking Christianity, books attributing controversial sexual desires to the prophet Muhammad, or accusing the latter of pedophilia for having married a young girl.[27] Such decisions by a court with jurisdiction over forty-seven states, including all Western European democracies, were a PR gift for the OIC.

The explicit goal of the OIC was to move from nonbinding resolutions in the UN Human Rights Council (which replaced the Commission on Human Rights in 2006) to a new and binding legal instrument. With a raft of successfully passed resolutions, and Western unease about defending free speech in light of rising anti-immigration sentiments and hostility toward Islam, things were looking good for the OIC. The EU group in Geneva was unable to defeat the OIC juggernaut, and in 2006 the outlook became even worse when the Bush administration abandoned the Human Rights Council.

However, the Obama administration decided to reenter the Human Rights Council in 2009, in order to strengthen its multilateralist credentials. This decision proved to be a game changer with profound implications. With a combination of stick and carrot, the State Department—aided by European democracies—launched a multilateral global offensive to undermine OIC's resolutions against "defamation of religions." And it worked. With alarm, the OIC observed their majorities for the annual defamation resolutions shrink as states with no vested interest in the conflict switched sides or voted against instead of merely abstaining.[28] In 2011, their majority was gone and the OIC was forced to abandon its resolution. Instead, the US ensured a majority for the new Resolution 16/18, which provided a rare but important win amidst the larger free speech recession.

According to the new text, human rights law protects people, not religions or ideologies. While the resolution "condemned" advocacy of incitement to hatred, it only called on the criminalization of "incitement to *imminent violence* based on religion or belief," a formulation inspired by the Supreme Court decision in *Brandenburg v. Ohio*.[29] This test not only protects blasphemous speech, it is also more protective of speech than mainstream European hate speech laws, and the hate speech provision in ICCPR Article 20. Eleanor Roosevelt would have been proud.

Yet the defeat of the defamation agenda at the UN has done little to soften blasphemy laws in OIC countries. In 2014, the Saudi Arabian blogger Raif Badawi was sentenced to ten years in prison and a thousand public lashes. His crime: insulting Islam on his blog Free Saudi Liberals. Badawi's offensive words included the al-Rāzīesque warning that "as soon as a thinker starts to reveal his ideas, you will find hundreds of fatwas that accused him of being an infidel just because he had the courage to discuss some sacred topics." He also denounced the "chauvinist arrogance" of Islamists, hailed secularism, and argued that "states which are based on religion confine their people in the circle of faith and fear."[30] In 2019, the Pakistani university lecturer Junaid Hafeez was sentenced to death for allegedly blasphemous statements made on Facebook and during lectures. His conviction followed more than five years in solitary confinement since the beginning of his trial in 2014.[31]

Outside the judicial systems in Pakistan, Afghanistan, and Bangladesh, mobs and vigilante groups have murdered dozens of persons accused of "blasphemy" to enforce extreme interpretations of religious doctrines.[32] These include the young Afghan woman Farkhunda Malikzada, who was falsely accused of burning a Qur'an after she confronted mullahs selling amulets at a shrine in 2015. Based on these false accusations of blasphemy, a frenzied mob beat her to death, then dragged her behind a car before stoning and burning her remains.[33] But the religious repression of dissent and the fanaticism it bred was just one manifestation of the global free speech recession.

Eroding the Bulwark of Liberty

While the bulwark of liberty ultimately held firm against the OIC campaign at the UN, freedom of speech proved much less resilient at the national level. As we have learned, free speech has always been the first target of authoritarians who intend to subvert democracy, from the Council of the Four Hundred in ancient Athens to the Third Reich. Once the immune system of free speech is compromised, more encroachments are sure to follow. This ancient pattern is repeating itself in the twenty-first century, during which free speech has systematically eroded in Hungary, Turkey, Poland, Serbia, Brazil, and India—the six countries that have suffered the worst autocratization in the past decade, according to V-Dem.[34]

After his election in 2010, Prime Minister Viktor Orbán—a former liberal anticommunist activist—systematically began curbing Hungarian press freedom with repressive media laws and strategic changes in media ownership. By 2014, the country's V-Dem scores in freedom and democracy plunged. By 2019, Hungary became the first member of the EU to lose its status as a free democracy.[35] At that point, nearly 80 percent of Hungary's media were owned by allies of Orbán's Fidesz party.[36] Orbán's cronies even began buying up papers and TV stations in neighboring Slovenia and Romania. Like-minded strongmen in the region took notes. Aleksandar Vučić in Serbia and the Law and Justice party in Poland—two other countries where illiberal populism is in ascendancy—copied Orbán's strategy of media capture, turning the fourth estate into government-friendly mouthpieces.[37]

India, the world's largest democracy, also suffered a setback. The 2014 election of Hindu-nationalist strongman Narendra Modi has threatened a collapse of the country's "lungs of liberty," as Gandhi labeled the freedoms of expression and association. Under Modi there were increases in violence against journalists, arrests for online activity, prolonged internet shutdowns, misuse of penal provisions against students, journalists, activists, and academics, as well as systematic attacks against media houses.[38] Tragically, Modi's nationalist government also embraced British colonial-era laws against speech crimes such as sedition, hate speech, and religious offense—once used against Indian champions of independence. In 2016, Human Rights Watch concluded that, though India's hate speech laws are "intended to protect minorities and the powerless, these laws are often used at the behest of powerful individuals or groups, who claim that they have been offended, to silence speech they do not like."[39]

Disha Ravi, a twenty-two-year-old climate activist from Bengaluru, offers a striking example. She was arrested in February 2021 for circulating and contributing to an online "toolkit," which was tweeted by Swedish climate activist Greta Thunberg, in support of Indian farmers protesting a raft of agriculture bills. According to the Delhi police, Ravi was conspiring "to wage economic, social, cultural and regional war against India."[40] She was charged under sections of the Indian penal code that include 153A (promoting enmity between communities) and 124A (sedition)—the same colonial-era laws that British authorities used to silence Bal Gangadhar Tilak and Gandhi a century ago.[41]

When US historian of Mughal India Audrey Truschke published a book on the Mughal emperor Aurangzeb in 2017, she had to remove certain passages on the revered Hindu warrior king Shivaji from the Indian edition. Despite self-censoring, she had to cancel planned talks in India because of protests from Hindu extremists.[42] In her words, "Religious (and nationalist) sentiments are increasingly trumping historical truth in modern India."[43] It seems that modern India can still learn from the rich heritage of Akbar and Ashoka.

Hearkening back to the example of Ottoman sultans who curbed the printing press for centuries, modern Turkey is dominated by a new all-powerful and unusually thin-skinned ruler. President Erdoğan—a former prisoner of conscience—has presided over a dramatic deterioration of free speech since his election in 2014. What was an aspiring democracy less than a decade ago was labeled "Not Free" in 2018.[44] Since his election, sixty-three journalists have been convicted of "insulting the president" under Article 299 of the Turkish penal code.[45] In 2016, Erdoğan even tried to pressure the German authorities into prosecuting the satirist Jan Böhmermann for lèse majesté because of a poem that offended him, though the case was eventually dropped.[46] In a move echoing the suppression of Diderot's *Encyclopédie* in Old Regime France, Wikipedia was ordered offline between April 2017 and

January 2020 for refusing to remove content considered critical of Erdoğan's government.[47] The regime also exploited a failed coup attempt in 2016 to step up its attack on free speech dramatically. At least two hundred journalists and media workers have been imprisoned, many under spurious charges of terrorism, and more than 160 news outlets shut down.[48] Turkey now tops the charts for most journalists in prison, just behind China.[49] Turkish universities have not been spared either. At least 5,800 academics—many liberals and secularists—were fired from public universities for alleged connections with "terrorist organizations."[50]

Russia has had a long and complicated history with speech restrictions, from Catherine's volte-face in the 1790s and the tsarist repression of the nineteenth century to the Soviet war against "enemies of the people" in the twentieth. The future initially looked bright after the collapse of the Soviet Union in the early 1990s, but the country's press freedom score has steadily declined since the election of President Vladimir Putin in 2000. Freedom House has labeled Russia "Not Free" since 2005, adding to a sad statistic of promising democracies suffering autocratization under illiberal strongmen.[51]

The Russian free speech recession has taken a turn for the worse in recent years. Sixteen journalists were imprisoned from 2016 to 2020, compared to three in the period from 2011 to 2015, according to data from the CPJ.[52] At least 122 journalists were arrested, intimidated, or fined for covering protests in support of opposition leader Alexey Navalny, who was poisoned in August 2020 and jailed in February 2021.[53] However, prison is not the worst punishment for journalists shining a critical light on Putin's regime. Since 2000, at least twenty-eight journalists have been murdered in Russia.[54] The victims include the fearless investigative reporter Anna Politkovskaya, who exposed the brutality of Russian military operations in Chechnya. After surviving years of harassment, poisoning, and beatings, Politkovskaya was shot in Moscow in 2006.[55]

As was the case with the Soviet Union, modern Russia has found ways to use laws against hatred and offense to target the expression of ideas not favorable to the government. In January 2003, the exhibition *Caution: Religion!* at the Sakharov Museum in Moscow featured religious symbols and messages, including images of Christ, turned into pop art. After much controversy, several Russian Orthodox thugs vandalized the exhibition. However, after pressure from the Orthodox Church, the museum director, Yuri Samodurov—not the vandals—was charged and convicted for "incitement of ethnic, racial, or religious hatred."[56] Samodurov was convicted again in 2010 on similar charges for another art exhibition.[57] Likewise, three members of Russian female punk band Pussy Riot were sentenced to two years in a prison colony for committing "hooliganism driven by religious hatred" after staging a protest against Putin in an Orthodox cathedral.[58] In 2019, Russia revived the spirit of Article 58 of the Soviet criminal code by criminalizing online insults to the Russian state, including its government and symbols. Within 180 days, more than forty modern-day Russian "babblers" had been indicted for insulting Putin.[59]

Chinese rulers have a long tradition of imposing draconian controls on the free flow of ideas and information, dating back to the first Chinese emperor, Qin Shi Huang, who banned and burned books that might undermine his rule and put obstinate scholars to death for violating the prohibition. In the eighteenth century, the Qianlong Emperor of the Qing dynasty ensured that there would be no Enlightenment in China. The Great Qing Code of 1740 strictly prohibited—on pain of corporal punishment or death—using abusive language against government officials, books aimed at misleading the people, sedition, and of course the publication of "false and malicious report[s]."[60] Mao Zedong's ideological cleansing of China, culminating in the Cultural Revolution of 1966 to 1976, was one of the darkest chapters of repression, when dissidents were tortured, killed, or forced to undergo humiliating "self-criticism."

Much like Robespierre and Stalin, Chairman Mao saw the need for a "reign of terror" and condoned the mass execution of "class enemies."[61] And like Stalin, he was also ultra thin-skinned. Any slight of his person could result in severe consequences. A particularly luckless man was sentenced to several years in prison for the crime of wrapping fresh fish in a newspaper and accidentally smearing a picture of the Great Helmsman in fish oil.[62] Mao even compared his regime to that of the Qin emperor, bragging that the latter "buried only 460 scholars alive; we have buried forty-six thousand scholars alive. . . . We have surpassed Qin Shi Huang a hundred fold."[63] In 1978, the great reformer Deng Xiaoping initiated a brief thaw by encouraging Chinese citizens to air their grievances and contribute to the discussion on how to improve the country's development. This gave voice to democratic aspirations in daring protests and on wall posters throughout major cities. These activities were spearheaded by dissidents such as the young woman Fu Yuehua, and the later Sakharov Prize–winner Wei Jingsheng. However, the new regime quickly got cold feet when the calls for democracy and human rights became a little too vocal and openly challenged the legacy of Mao and the authority of the Communist Party. By 1979, both Fu Yuehua and Wei Jingsheng had been sent to prison.[64] In June 1989, the regime cracked down on student-led demonstrations calling for free speech and democracy in Tiananmen Square, Beijing, with lethal brutality, effectively crushing any hope that prodemocracy activists could inspire anything resembling a Helsinki effect. Today, the Chinese government uses the world's most sophisticated system of censorship and information control to insulate itself from the convulsions of the digital age. It also adopts harshly repressive measures against journalists, dissidents, and minorities deemed insufficiently pliant to the iron rule of the Communist Party. China holds the world record for most imprisoned journalists with at least 121 reporters behind bars—often in life-threatening conditions— as of March 2021.[65]

The Communist Party's handling of the COVID-19 pandemic is a dramatic example of the regime's belief in rigid censorship. On December 30, 2019, the Chinese ophthalmologist Li Wenliang warned a group of doctors about a mysterious SARS-like disease spreading in Wuhan province. On January 3, Dr. Li and seven other doctors were detained by police for "spreading false rumors." He was threatened with prosecution if he "failed to repent and continue illegal activities." Shortly after being released, he began showing signs of what the world soon came to know as COVID-19. Dr. Li died of the illness on February 7, but not before exposing how he had been censored. The Chinese government immediately blocked online content related to the virus, Dr. Li, and the authorities' handling of the outbreak. Next, the regime cracked down on foreign and domestic journalists covering the crisis, expelling at least eighteen foreign correspondents from the country in the first half of 2020.[66]

Chinese president Xi Jinping insisted that China "acted with openness, transparency and responsibility" and informed the world of the outbreak "in a most timely fashion."[67] Yet, the Associated Press has exposed how the Chinese government withheld critical data from the World Health Organization for weeks in the early phases "when the outbreak arguably might have been dramatically slowed."[68] Harvard professor of history Serhii Plokhy compared China's response to that of Soviet Russia to the Chernobyl nuclear disaster of 1986, noting that "lack of freedom of speech helps to turn potential disasters into real ones and national tragedies into international cataclysms."[69]

The Chinese zero-tolerance policy toward dissent is not confined to the mainland. In a highly symbolic and ominous move, China maneuvered to strangle Hong Kong's remaining institutional and civic commitment to democracy, civil liberties, and the rule of law after huge prodemocracy demonstrations in 2019. As the culmination of a wider crackdown, a new National Security Law (NSL) entered into force in June 2020, establishing harsh punishments under its purposefully vague bans on "separatism," "terrorism," and "subversion."[70] The law was particularly devastating to Hong Kong's prodemocracy movement. Forty-seven leading activists, arrested in March 2021, face maximum sentences of life in prison for engaging in "conspiracy to subvert the state power" under the NSL.[71] But the law also applies to nonresidents entering mainland China or Hong Kong. In reality, the NSL claimed universal jurisdiction to prosecute anyone challenging Beijing's rule in Hong Kong. The law's global reach has forced universities in the United States, the UK, Australia, Canada, and New Zealand to adjust class instruction to protect the privacy of students whose participation, especially in history and politics courses, could violate the law.[72]

The situation has also seen the revival of Hong Kong's slumbering colonial-era sedition law. In September, two radio hosts with ties to the antigovernment protests were arrested and charged under the law, which dates back to the nineteenth century and prohibits incitement to "hatred or contempt" for the government.[73] The British sedition ban may thus be more consequential in the long term than the Basic Law ensuring essential freedoms—including freedom of speech—bequeathed to Hong Kong by the British as a parting gift when the Union Jack was lowered for the last time on July 1, 1997.

The long-lasting negative effects of colonial-era speech crimes in India and Hong Kong can be contrasted with recent developments in South Africa that provide grounds for optimism amidst the larger free speech recession. After urging Black South Africans to occupy privately owned land, the controversial politician Julius Malema was charged with incitement to commit an offense under an apartheid-era law.[74] In November 2020, the South African Constitutional Court declared a section of the law unconstitutional in a majority opinion authored by Chief Justice Mogoeng Mogoeng.

In stark contrast to the logic behind sedition acts, Mogoeng noted that "when citizens are very angry or frustrated," freedom of expression "serves as the virtual exhaust pipe through which even the most venomous of toxicities within may be let out to help them calm down, heal, focus and move on." Mogoeng specifically highlighted the "dark past" of the law, and how during apartheid,

> expression was so extensively and severely circumscribed that a person could be arrested, banned, banished or even killed by the apartheid regime for labelling as unjust, what everyone now accepts is unjust. . . . Free expression is thus a right or freedom so dear to us and critical to our democracy and healing the divisions of our past, that it ought not to be interfered with lightly.[75]

The current South African constitution exempts from the protection of free speech "advocacy of hatred that is based on race, ethnicity, gender or religion, and that constitutes incitement to cause harm."[76] Still, in stark contrast to courts in Germany, France, the UK—and indeed the European Court of Human rights—South African courts have been cautious and kept the definition of hate speech narrow.[77]

The Constitutional Court has held that "a court should not be hasty to conclude that because language is angry in tone or conveys hostility, it is therefore to be characterized as hate speech. Even if it has overtones of race and ethnicity." In a similar vein the Supreme Court of Appeal has held that statements that are "hurtful of people's feelings, or wounding, distasteful, politically inflammatory or downright offensive" still constitute protected speech.[78]

These judgments embody Nelson Mandela's words to the effect that "it is only . . . a free press that can temper the appetite of any government to amass power at the expense of the citizen."[79] A pending Prevention and Combating of Hate Speech Bill is a worrying diversion from this trend, but the strong protection of the South African courts may still keep the country from the backsliding that has characterized India and Hong Kong.[80]

The global free speech recession is not only driven by censorious states. From 1992 to 2003, when global press freedom peaked, at least 133 journalists were killed by criminal, political, and religious groups, averaging 11 per year according to CPJ data. From 2004 to 2020, after the free speech recession began, a total of 487 journalists were killed by such nonstate actors, almost tripling the annual average of victims from 11 to 29. Many more journalists worldwide have suffered threats, harassment, violence, torture, and kidnappings. The world's deadliest country for journalists is Mexico, accounting for 9 out of 49 journalists murdered globally in 2020 and a total of 117 since 2000.[81] Jaime Castaño, founder of an online news outlet, was shot by unidentified gunmen in December 2020 after he refused to delete photos of the bodies of two shooting victims from his camera.[82]

Standing up to powerful corporate and state interests that threaten the environment can also be lethal. According to the NGO Global Witness, 212 environmental activists were killed in 2019, many with impunity, with Latin America being the deadliest region.[83]

But even Europe is becoming a more dangerous place for investigative reporters, like Maltese crime journalist Daphne Caruana Galizia, who was killed by a car bomb in 2017.[84] Threats and deadly violence send a clear signal to journalists and activists around the world that even in the twenty-first century, those who pursue truth, justice, and accountability should think twice before shining a light on darkness.

The Decline of the West

In the twenty-first century, the United States remained "the most speech protective of any nation on Earth." According to a 2021 Justitia survey, Americans were also the most supportive of all forms of freedom of expression alongside populations in Scandinavia.[85] Yet, the survey showed somewhat less American tolerance for speech critical of the government and offensive to minorities than a similarly worded Pew survey from 2015.[86] This hinted that the consensus around free speech as a secular article of faith seemed to break down during the presidency of Donald Trump, as hyperpartisan political tribalism became ever more unforgiving and heterodoxy was treated as heresy.

In May 2020, widespread protests erupted across the United States after a video emerged of a white police officer holding down a Black man named George Floyd by placing his knee on Floyd's neck during an arrest. As long minutes ticked by, Floyd pleaded for his life, crying, "I can't breathe!" until going limp and dying. The video shocked Americans as they watched Floyd's final moments in horror.

Millions took to the streets to denounce racial disparities in the criminal justice system under the rallying cry of "Black Lives Matter." Most protests were peaceful, but several cities experienced large-scale violence, looting, and vandalism. As the protests raged on, a disturbing number of incidents of police brutality and excessive force against both peaceful protesters and journalists exercising their First Amendment freedoms were documented.[87] President Trump further fanned the flames when he accused a Black Lives Matter leader of "Treason, Sedition, Insurrection!" and repeatedly labeled protestors as "terrorists."[88]

However, unlike the civil rights movement of the 1950s and '60s, many proponents of racial justice saw free speech as a threat to, rather than a precondition for, justice and equality. Activists called for deplatforming people whose opinions were deemed hostile to, or even insufficiently supportive of, racial justice. Academia was no exception. A letter signed by hundreds of Princeton faculty members, employees, and students demanded a faculty committee be established to "oversee the investigation and discipline of racist behaviors, incidents, research, and publication."[89] Tulane University apologized and canceled a virtual debate of a book about the KKK—and critical of white supremacy—after protests by students and employees, some of whom claimed the book discussion was "not only inappropriate but violent towards the experience of Black people."[90]

"Cancel culture" migrated from campuses to media and cultural institutions; organized attempts to punish—rather than vocally criticize—specific viewpoints, through calling for people to be fired or disciplined, multiplied.[91] A Democratic data analyst was fired after tweeting a study that showed that nonviolent Black-led protests were more effective than violent ones in terms of securing voter support.[92] Staffers at the *New York Times* protested that the newspaper put "Black @NYTimes staff in danger" when it ran a provocative op-ed by Republican senator Tom Cotton that argued for deploying the military to quell riots. The newsroom revolt led to opinion editor James Bennet resigning.[93] The protesting staffers seemed unaware of the fact that they were essentially advocating a "bad tendency" test, judging speech by its potential future harm, rather than any incitement to immediate harm. This test was the first line of defence of Southern states against the dissent of abolitionists and the civil rights movement. The danger of adopting this logic is that, if an incendiary op-ed could be said to threaten journalists' safety, so Donald Trump could use this reasoning to argue that a provocative op-ed, banner, placard, tweet, or slogan constitutes "sedition and insurrection."

So highly charged was the question of race that the mere mentioning or discussion of certain words, regardless of intent, could lead to serious consequences. When prominent Slate journalist Mike Pesca argued that the N-word could—in very specific contexts—be used by white people, he was suspended despite not saying the N-word himself.[94] Nor was it necessarily exculpatory if offensive social media "babbling" occurred many years ago while the offender was a teenager, as the—biracial—Alexi McCammond found out when she was forced to resign shortly after being appointed editor in chief of *Teen Vogue*.[95]

While there was no shortage of loud voices, many Americans chose to hold their tongues. According to a Cato Institute survey from July 22, 2020, 62 percent of Americans self-censor their political views for fear of offending others, with only those who identify as strongly liberal confident of speaking their mind freely.[96]

The fallout from the George Floyd case was the culmination of a development years in the making in which the question of free speech played a polarizing and divisive role, creating an incendiary atmosphere in which Donald Trump acted as a blowtorch. During his one presidential term, Trump repeatedly attacked the "fake news media" as "enemies of the people," mirroring the rhetoric of Robespierre, Lenin, Stalin, Hitler, and Mao.[97] Trump and his campaign also sued several media outlets for defamation—including the *New York Times*, CNN, and the *Washington Post*—and proposed to enact stricter libel laws, as well as stiff punishments for burning the American flag.[98]

All of these initiatives flew in the face of established First Amendment doctrines. Nevertheless, the consistent attacks on the media and free speech seemed to have an impact on conservatives already distrustful of the mainstream media. According to a 2018 poll, 44 percent of Republicans agreed that the president should have the power to close down news outlets for "bad behavior," and 48 percent of Republicans considered the media "enemies of the people."[99] Republican lawmakers supposedly worried about cancel culture's effect on free speech took to fighting fire with fire. In states like Oklahoma and Florida, Republicans have proposed removing critical race theory from classrooms, willfully ignoring that government-mandated restrictions on curricula in and of themselves create the risk of establishing a particular form of ideological orthodoxy.[100]

While Republicans focused their concerns on established media outlets and school curricula, Democrats, liberals, and progressives, on the other hand, were significantly more supportive of banning hate speech and preventing speakers with controversial views on race from speaking at universities.[101] In 2014, the University of California published a list of some fifty microaggressions that might be offensive or hurtful to students and faculty, including statements such as, "There is only one race, the human race."[102] Advocates of "safe spaces" are requesting that ever-growing portions of campus as well as classrooms be designated as such and cleansed of speech that may endanger emotional "safety." In keeping with this movement, speakers who are deemed controversial are being disinvited from campus speaking engagements in reaction to protests from both students and administrators. The Foundation for Individual Rights in Education (FIRE) has recorded over 450 "disinvitation attempts" since 1998, the vast majority of which stem from objections to the speaker's political views (affecting both speakers from the political Left and Right).[103] FIRE also found that more than a fifth of the 478 US colleges and universities surveyed in 2020 had "at least one policy that both clearly and substantially restricts freedom of speech."[104] An alarming 60 percent of surveyed students held back opinions "because of how students, a professor, or the administration would respond." And their fear may be justified, especially on liberal-leaning campuses. Among "extremely liberal" students, 13 percent thought violence to stop a speech or event on campus was "always" or "sometimes" acceptable, while 60 percent thought it was "always" or "sometimes" acceptable to shout down a speaker with opposing views.[105] An ironic development given how radical socialist professors were purged from American elite universities in the early twentieth century.

Yet while many conservatives fulminated about cancel culture establishing a liberal orthodoxy, liberals and progressives were also affected. Professors critical of Israel, Vice President Mike Pence, and Donald Trump have been subject to canceling efforts.[106] And Republican lawmakers have adopted their own ideological red lines in education, not only against critical race theory but also LGBTQ issues. In Tennessee, a proposed bill would prohibit textbooks that "promote, normalize, support, or address . . . LGBT issues or lifestyles."[107] This wording is chillingly similar to Russia's "gay propaganda" law, prohibiting "promotion of nontraditional sexual relations to minors."[108]

All of these developments raised serious questions about the long-term resilience of free speech in the US. As Greg Lukianoff, the president of FIRE, warned, "Free speech culture is more important than the First Amendment. . . . It's what informs the First Amendment today—and it is what will decide if our current free speech protections will survive into the future."[109]

The Quiet Continent 2.0?

Europe was the first laboratory where the practice and principles of free speech were discovered and experimented with in systematic fashion. The outcome of this experiment has varied over time as rulers and governments have adjusted and tinkered with the dosages of freedom and restrictions, respectively. So far in the twenty-first century, more restrictions than freedom have been added to the mix.

According to the Economist Intelligence Unit, Western Europe has experienced a sharp decline in civil liberties since 2008 (the first year when comparable data is available) as "infringements of free speech . . . have increased."[110] Disturbingly, part of this development was driven by a clash between violent religious fundamentalism and the secular values of freedom of thought and tolerance. Once again France was the ground zero of this modern-day reenactment of the conflict between philosophes and Counter-Enlightenment hardliners that characterized the second half of the eighteenth century. Only this time with secular values and institutions dominant and under attack from a small group of extremists willing to use shockingly brutal measures, which were almost universally condemned but nevertheless managed to sow doubt about whether free speech was progressive or oppressive.

Je Suis Charlie

The atmosphere was relaxed in the conference room on the second floor of 10 rue Nicolas-Appert in Paris's hip eleventh arrondissement. The people present shared ideas, jokes, and croissants around the large oval table. What sounded like firecrackers in the lobby only added to the atmosphere. Then, at 11:30 a.m., two armed men stormed in. "You're going to pay for insulting the prophet Muhammad," they shouted, before opening fire at point blank.

By the time the assailants left, eleven people lay dead at the offices of *Charlie Hebdo*, an irreverent French leftist satirical magazine (in)famous for mocking all and sparing none. Since 2006, the prophet Muhammad had become a prominent target of *Charlie Hebdo*'s skewering cartoons and purposely disrespectful prose, resulting in death threats and a fire bombing in 2011.[111]

The jihadist attack on *Charlie Hebdo* on January 7, 2015, sparked a global debate on the limits of free speech. To the millions who adopted the slogan of "Je suis Charlie," the murder of writers and cartoonists armed with pens by religious fanatics armed with AK-47s amounted to an attack on the very Enlightenment values so central to European and, in particular, French national identity.

Then French president François Hollande stated, "Today the entire republic of France was attacked. Its principles of freedom of speech, culture, creation, pluralism and democracy."[112] French academics were shocked that two young Muslims born, raised, and educated in secular France could emulate the bloody intolerance that Enlightenment values were supposed to have inoculated all good *citoyens* against. They rushed to publish a collection of texts on free speech and tolerance by eighteenth-century French thinkers with the apt title *Tolerance: The Beacon of the Enlightenment*.[113] To others, though, the *Charlie Hebdo* affair was more complicated. The magazine, they argued, had abused its supposedly dominant position to "punch down" on an embattled minority already suffering from racism and discrimination. In March 2015, the free speech organization PEN America announced *Charlie Hebdo* as the recipient of its freedom of expression award. However, 242 authors, including Teju Cole and Francine Prose, signed an open letter protesting PEN's decision, which amounted to "valorizing selectively offensive material: material that intensifies the anti-Islamic . . . sentiments already prevalent in the Western world."[114]

The most radical Enlightenment proponents of free speech were accused of abusing this freedom to *erode* the very foundations of legitimate order and authority. Now, the modern critics of *Charlie Hebdo* were accusing the magazine of abusing free speech to *consolidate* oppressive and inequal authority—an argument inverting Spinoza's insistence that freedom of thought and speech are preconditions for diverse and tolerant societies. Rather than uniting the defenders of free speech the *Charlie Hebdo* affair led to fear, self-censorship, and bitter recriminations about the proper relationship between free speech and tolerance in diverse societies. To make matters worse, a continuous wave of bloody jihadist terrorist attacks led France and other Western governments to crack down on civil liberties, including freedom of speech, through increasingly strict national security laws that disproportionately affected minorities, not least Muslims.

After the attack on *Charlie Hebdo* in 2015, the French government declared free speech inviolable. But that very year French police intervened in more than 2,300 cases of "apology for terrorism," which doesn't require that speech reaches the threshold of incitement, but merely that of praise or apology for terrorism. Some 306 people were convicted and 232 sent to prison for this offense in 2016 alone.[115]

In 2016, the Danish parliament enacted a law criminalizing "religious teaching" that "explicitly condones" certain crimes such as murder, violence, and even polygamy, aimed primarily at Islamic "hate preachers."[116] Under the law, an imam or priest who explicitly condones the spanking of children or polygamy as part of his or her religious teaching would face up to three years in prison, whereas a politician or ordinary citizen condoning such practices would be free to do so. The law also bars religious preachers who have expressed "anti-democratic" views from entering the country; almost all of those administratively barred from entry were Muslims. But European antiterrorism laws also affected art. In Spain, more than a dozen leftist antiestablishment rappers have received sentences of up to three and a half years in prison for lyrics "glorifying terrorism" and insulting the monarchy.[117]

More than anything, European speech restrictions are driven by a deep-seated fear of providing oxygen to the modern heirs of the fascist movements that snuffed out democracy and plunged the Continent into total war and genocide. And even today, right-wing extremism can inspire murderous deeds and shocking levels of hatred among Europeans born and raised in peaceful and prosperous democracies.

October 9, 2019, was Yom Kippur—the holiest of Jewish holidays. Members of the Jewish congregation in the German town of Halle were praying inside their synagogue when they heard gunshots. Members watched grainy images on the CCTV in horror as a man tried to shoot his way through the reinforced door. After a short while, Stephan Balliet gave up and turned his murderous attention to other targets, killing two random strangers.[118] Balliet, a twenty-seven-year-old neo-Nazi, livestreamed his attack on Twitch and left a manifesto declaring his intention to "kill as many non-Whites as possible, jews preferred."[119] The Halle attack came only months after another neo-Nazi shot and killed the conservative pro-immigrant politician Walter Lübcke, and on February 19, 2020, yet another neo-Nazi murdered nine immigrants in Hanau. The German government estimates that the country is home to 24,100 far-right extremists, half of whom are inclined toward violence. In a familiar pattern, the German government reacted to the 2019 attacks by proposing further expansions of the country's already strict hate speech laws, which had been given more teeth as late as 2017 with the NetzDG law targeting hate speech on social media (see Chapter 13).[120] Few Germans seemed to question whether the understandable impulse to crack down on Nazi ideology was an efficient weapon against violent extremism. Would Balliet have remained a bigoted and socially awkward loner rather than a hateful killer with less free speech? Such questions are impossible to answer, though as we have seen, the road that led from the Weimar Republic to the Third Reich suggests that censorship is an unreliable weapon in the fight against the enemies of democracy that may backfire and inflict collateral damage on democracy itself.

In fact, European laws against hate speech have at times come uncomfortably close to serving as "sedition acts" threatening punishment for criticism of governments and officials. In 2014, a German named Hans Burkhard Nix published a blog post accusing a public employment agency of racially discriminating against his mixed-race daughter. Nix accompanied the blog post with a quotation from and picture of Nazi leader Heinrich Himmler wearing an SS uniform. Clearly, Nix was neither defending nor advocating Nazism; he was "playing the Nazi card" to underscore his not-so-subtle criticism of a local government agency. Still, a regional court found Nix guilty of violating Germany's ban against displaying symbols of unconstitutional organizations. Nix took his case to the European Court of Human Rights, which found no violation of his freedom of expression.[121] That was hardly surprising, as the court has ruled against the speaker in 62 percent of hate speech cases brought before it.[122]

In June 2020, none other than the German police union filed a criminal complaint for incitement to hatred against the newspaper *Tageszeitung* (or *taz*), which had published a column comparing the police to "trash" that should be "thrown in the landfill," following Black Lives Matter protests in Germany.[123]

In France, too, hate speech laws are used against others beyond merely bona fide Nazis. Several dozen pro-Palestinian activists have been convicted of incitement to discrimination for BDS (Boycott, Divestment, Sanctions) campaigns aimed at boycotting Israeli products in response to Israel's treatment of Palestinians and alleged war crimes in Gaza. The activists distributed leaflets and wore T-shirts with slogans such as "Long live Palestine, Boycott Israel" and "buying Israeli products means legitimizing crimes in Gaza," purportedly aimed at the Israeli government rather than Israelis or Jews. In 2020, the European Court of Human Rights deviated from its usual practice in hate speech cases and ruled that the French prohibition of BDS campaigns violated freedom of expression.[124]

In Scotland, a sweeping new hate crime bill expands the prohibition against "stirring up hatred" to include a raft of new groups and—recalling the Spanish Inquisition—even applies to speech uttered in private homes.[125]

European laws against "hatred" and "offense" have also undergone scope creep as ever more groups have successfully lobbied for the recognition and respect thought to follow from the protected status. However, this development has inadvertently led to situations where some of the marginalized groups supposed to benefit from hate speech laws have been targeted and pitted against each other.

In 2017, two British street preachers were arrested and initially convicted for preaching from the Bible, including statements that were deemed insulting to LGBTQ persons and Muslims.[126] Conversely, a leader of a French LGBTQ rights organization was fined 2,300 euros in 2016 for calling the president of an organization that defends "traditional" family values and opposes same-sex marriage a "homophobe."[127] This development should not come as a surprise. The British Race Relations Act of 1965 prohibited incitement to racial hatred. The first person to be prosecuted for this offense was a Black man.[128] Several other Black Britons were prosecuted for antiwhite hatred, including leading members of Black Power and the Universal Coloured People's Association.[129]

Ominously, European efforts to crack down on illegal hate speech have been centralized. In November 2020, Europol, an EU law enforcement agency, announced that it had coordinated raids in Germany, Italy, France, Greece, Norway, Britain, and the Czech Republic in a clamp down on online hate speech. In Germany alone, police searched more than eighty dwellings, seizing smart phones and laptops, while ninety-six suspects were questioned about hateful posts that included anti-Semitism and "insulting a female politician."[130] Given the scope creep of European hate speech bans, and the sketchy protection under European human rights law, this development seems particularly disturbing for the future of free speech in the EU.

———

PERHAPS THE MOST STRIKING FEATURE OF THE FREE SPEECH recession was that its onset and acceleration coincided with the triumph of the most revolutionary breakthrough in communications technology since the printing press. In theory, the internet should have made free speech invincible, banishing censorship to the ash heap of history. However, as sixteenth-century Europeans living through the combustible cocktail of Gutenberg and Luther found out, radical new communications technologies are as likely to cause major disruptions of the social and political order as to usher in progress and enlightenment.

Just as Gutenberg's printing press was initially praised before its disruption led to regret, censorship, and bans, so the internet was initially hailed as an unstoppable force that would speed up the onward march of global freedom and democracy. Yet unmediated access to free and equal speech soon caused resurgent autocracies to fight back and democracies to think twice about whether the internet should be seen as more of a blessing than a curse.

13

The Internet
and the Future of Free Speech

For years the far-right conspiracy theorist Alex Jones fed his online followers with deranged stories: Barack Obama was born in Kenya; millions of undocumented immigrants voted for Hillary Clinton; the deadly school shooting at Sandy Hook was staged and the grieving family members were "crisis actors."[1] Jones used social media and podcasts to great effect gaining a sizable audience for his media fiefdom called Infowars. Yet in 2018 most major tech companies decided that enough was enough. Within a day in August 2018, Jones was deplatformed by Apple, Facebook, YouTube, and Spotify.[2] Twitter, the only major platform to waver, followed suit in early September.[3] Few mourned the sudden death of Alex Jones from the respectable parts of the internet. Still, the swift and decisive action taken behind closed doors at these huge private tech companies raised very pertinent questions of crucial importance in the digital age: What are the limits of online free speech? And who decides them?

In the most utopian and techno-optimistic days of the internet, the answer to these questions were, respectively, none and yourself.

John Perry Barlow's oft-quoted "A Declaration of the Independence of Cyberspace" from 1996 captured the spirit perfectly: "We are creating a world where anyone, anywhere may express his or her beliefs, no matter how singular, without fear of being coerced into silence or conformity." He also warned governments that "the virus of liberty" could not be warded off "by erecting guard posts at the frontiers of Cyberspace."[4] The architect of the World Wide Web, Tim Berners-Lee, described his vision as "encompassing the decentralized, organic growth of ideas, technology, and society"—a space in which "anything being potentially connected with anything" was unfettered by "hierarchical classification systems." Individual users would filter content according to their own preferences, because "when someone imposes involuntary filters on someone else, that is censorship."[5]

The global nature of the internet meant that the classic tools of censorship could no longer be relied upon by authoritarian states to isolate their citizens from sharing and accessing information. As Professor Lawrence Lessig put it, "Nations wake up to find that their telephone lines are tools of free expression, that e-mail carries news of their repression far beyond their borders, that images are no longer the monopoly of state-run television stations but can be transmitted from a simple modem."[6]

In short, the internet promised to bring about an era of universal free and equal speech, with cyberspace as a global agora. And in 1996, Congress gave this ideal crucial legal protection with the adoption of Section 230 of the Communications Decency Act (CDA 230). It granted online intermediaries broad immunity from user-generated content, as well as from their good-faith efforts to moderate objectionable content.[7] CDA 230 was given further teeth by a string of speech-protective court decisions creating a legal framework of "internet exceptionalism." Online platforms could now give voice to their users without fear of crippling lawsuits from slighted individuals and corporations. In his account of the history of CDA 230,

Jeff Kosseff argues that without it, "the Internet would be little more than an electronic version of a traditional newspaper or TV station, with all the words, pictures, and videos provided by a company and little interaction among users."[8]

The early peer-to-peer versions of social media, such as Usenet, allowed users across the globe to communicate and share news and information in forums, bulletin boards, or newsgroups, hosted and administered by the users themselves.[9] Influential computer scientist Michael Hauben described the difference between Usenet and traditional mass media in 1997:

> Inherent in most mass media is central control of content. Many people are influenced by the decisions of a few. . . . However, Usenet is controlled by its audience. Usenet should be seen as a promising successor to other people's presses, such as broadsides at the time of the American Revolution and the Penny Presses in England at the turn of the 19th Century.[10]

The late 1990s and the early 2000s saw the breakthrough of the blogosphere, which retained an important element of decentralization, or what professor of law David Kaye described as a "horizontal web."[11] Millions of blogs sprouted up touching on every imaginable subject, endlessly linking to and sharing information. The blogosphere soon showed that its distributed knowledge, dispersed among millions of people, could expose the failings and challenge the monopoly on information of traditional top-down, hierarchical elite institutions. In 2004, CBS reporter Dan Rather's story about President George W. Bush's supposed attempts to evade military service fell apart under scrutiny from bloggers who determined that the "smoking gun" document had been forged.[12] In countries like Cuba, Iran, and Egypt, oppressive regimes with an iron grip on information suddenly found their citizens unmuted, instead of mere passive recipients of government propaganda, as blogs and rapidly growing social media platforms like Facebook, YouTube, and Twitter seemed to make John Perry Barlow's utopia a reality.

Nothing so captivated the spirit of techno-optimism as the so-called Arab Spring. On March 3, 2010, the Tunisian street vendor Abdesslem Trimech set himself on fire to protest the regime. Trimech died from his injuries, but the media barely noticed the story and the regime carried on business as usual. Nine months later, another Tunisian street vendor set himself on fire as a protest of last resort against the corrupt and repressive regime. Unlike Trimech's self-immolation, Mohamed Bouazizi's fiery protest was recorded on the cell phones of onlookers, who shared the horrific images on Facebook where they soon went viral, leading to mass protests.[13] The combination of cell phones and social media was not the only difference between the anonymous death of Trimech and the instant fame of Bouazizi. It was a real game changer in the power balance between a decades-old dictatorship and its people that allowed protesters to circumvent government-imposed censorship in order to spread the word and coordinate demonstrations. These new networks proved highly effective in conveying the people's anger with the government and their desire for a more democratic leadership. People from across the world followed the events and cheered on the activists from their screens, while news media amplified the voices of protest by sharing the videos, updates, and angry slogans on cable news that could be viewed throughout the Middle East.[14] Within a month, Tunisia's dictator Zine El Abidine Ben Ali fled to Saudi Arabia. "We're all very happy that Ben Ali has left the country," a civilian in Tunis told the BBC. "We managed to work together to throw him out—and a lot of that was down to the internet and social networking."[15]

Virtually overnight, Tunisia was transformed from an autocracy with strict censorship into an electoral democracy with what Freedom House called a "critical and vibrant" press.[16] By the spring of 2011, similar protests had spread like wildfire throughout North Africa and the Middle East, fueled again by blogs and social media that both energized and organized the hopeful protestors. According to a 2012 study, "social media carried a cascade of messages about freedom and democracy across North Africa and the Middle East, and helped raise expectations for the success of political uprising."[17] The entire region seemed poised to leap toward more democratic rule. For a brief, optimistic moment, the Arab Spring seemed like the biggest victory for free speech since the collapse of Soviet communism.

Yet all too soon the limits of social media revolutions were brutally exposed as a series of repressive counterrevolutions turned the tide against protestors in the MENA region—not unlike the European reaction to the French Revolution and its aftermath. When Saudi activists organized a "Day of Rage" on social media in March 2011, the regime deployed more than ten thousand policemen and security guards to snuff out the protests. King Abdullah issued a royal decree in April, amending the country's press law to criminalize criticism of government officials and religious scholars. The Saudi regime mounted a regional coalition to contain the Arab Spring, sending military assistance to the regime in Bahrain, where dissidents were silenced with mass arrests and torture.[18] The already fatally flawed democracy governed by Islamists in Egypt was crushed by a military coup in July 2013. The number of imprisoned journalists in Egypt exploded from a yearly average of one and a half imprisonments between 2005 and 2012 to a yearly average of twenty-three imprisonments between 2013 and 2020.[19] The country is now one of the world's leading jailers of journalists after Saudi Arabia, Turkey, and China.[20] Syria and Libya both descended into bloody chaos and civil war. With the exception of Tunisia civil and political rights including free speech are now in even worse shape than prior to the popular protests, as regimes have consolidated their grip on power and repressed all dissent.[21]

The Arab uprisings frightened authoritarians around the world into significantly expanding and updating the censorship capabilities that had proved so inadequate when first confronted by tech-savvy bloggers and Silicon Valley's plug and play tool kit for digital revolution. These efforts have largely been successful. By 2020, global internet freedom declined for the tenth consecutive year, with the number of countries where the internet is "free" down to fifteen (out of the sixty-five surveyed) according to Freedom House. As many as 73 percent of the world's internet users were living in countries where political, social, or religious content was liable to result in arrests.[22]

Ironically, this development was greatly aided by a radical change in the World Wide Web, fueled by its own success and subsequent commercialization. When CDA 230 was passed by Congress in 1996, only forty million people worldwide had online access, and the internet they surfed was radically different from the increasingly centralized and commercialized internet of 2021 with its 4.66 billion active users, 4.2 billion of whom also used social media.[23] Simultaneously the horizontal web of the independent blog lost terrain to the vertical and centralized web in the era of "platformization." By 2019, 43 percent of the world's internet traffic ran through the same six tech giants and their subsidiaries: Google (including YouTube), Netflix, Facebook (including Instagram and WhatsApp), Microsoft (including Skype and LinkedIn), Apple, and Amazon, in decreasing order.[24]

These centralized platforms can act as choke points for "undesirable" content, as Alex Jones found out. David Kaye has noted that "a centralizing internet dominated by corporative imperatives . . . is friendlier to censorship . . . than the horizontal web of blogs and websites."[25] Lessig warned of such a development in 2006:

> The first-generation Internet might well have breached walls of control. But there is no reason to believe that architects of the second generation will do so, or not to expect a second generation to rebuild control. There is no reason to think, in other words, that this initial flash of freedom will not be short-lived.[26]

No country has set about policing cyberspace with more ruthless determination than China. In 2000, US president Bill Clinton laughed off China's early attempts at online censorship as akin to "trying to nail Jell-O to the wall."[27] But the so-called Great Firewall of China has turned the techno-optimist utopia of the 1990s and early 2000s into a high-tech dystopia of censorship and surveillance. Using sophisticated technology such as AI, it controls all digital traffic going in and out of the country, blocks access to "problematic" websites like Facebook, Twitter, Google, YouTube, and Wikipedia, and filters keywords related to controversial issues.

On June 3, 2020—one day before the anniversary of the 1989 Tiananmen Square Massacre—the retired Chinese soccer star Hao Haidong made a live appearance on YouTube, criticizing the Communist Party on controversial issues like COVID-19 and the status of Hong Kong and Tibet.[28] In less than twenty-four hours, Hao's account on the social media platform Weibo was gone and his name had become the single most censored term on the website. Hupu, a social media platform for sports fans, warned its users not to discuss Hao's "harmful remarks." Soon the warning disappeared too, and even articles discussing the controversy were wiped from the Chinese-controlled internet.[29]

But Chinese online policing is considerably more sophisticated than traditional forms of censorship. The Chinese government sponsors online users engaged in "strategic distraction" by fabricating hundreds of millions of social media comments a year aimed at drowning out dissent with progovernment cheerleading and hypernationalist trolling.[30] Concurrently, China has adopted mass surveillance on an unprecedented scale, which likely serves as a more efficient tool to foster self-censorship and conformity than blocking, filtering, and draconian punishments.[31]

China has exported the blueprint of its firewall to regimes across the globe as part of President Xi's plans to make China a "cyber superpower." China's digital client states include the Philippines and

Thailand as well as MENA states like Egypt, Saudi Arabia, and the United Arab Emirates, who fear a rerun of the Arab Spring.[32]

Even Western companies have responded to Chinese sticks and carrots. The foundation of the Great Firewall was built by American IT company Cisco.[33] In 2020, the video-meeting platform Zoom admitted to blocking accounts of Chinese dissidents commemorating the anniversary of the Tiananmen Square Massacre and was developing a method to block individual users in China "to comply with requests from local authorities." Apple removed podcast apps from its Chinese online store under pressure from Beijing.[34] Only intense pressure from its employees forced Google to abandon Project Dragonfly—a search engine tailored to the Chinese market that incorporated censorship dictates from the Communist Party, such as blocking out "categories of information related to democracy, human rights, and peaceful protest," as well as disappearing links to sites like Wikipedia and the BBC.[35]

China is not alone in policing the web. The digital rights group Access Now recorded 155 intentional internet shutdowns across twenty-nine countries in 2020.[36] These disruptions often serve authoritarian ends. In April 2019, Egypt held a referendum on a number of sweeping constitutional changes consolidating the powers of its authoritarian president Abdel Fattah al-Sisi. Prior to the referendum, the authorities blocked access to thirty-four thousand websites, including those of the viral opposition campaigns #Batel and #Void. Other countries where the authorities have blocked websites or forced users, social media platforms, or online news outlets to delete information include Bangladesh, Venezuela, and Belarus.[37]

In the most extreme cases, authorities blacked out the internet at large, to manipulate election outcomes or stop protests from migrating from cyberspace into uprisings. In 2019, an election year, India accounted for over 67 percent of global internet shutdowns.[38] Since June 2018, the internet has also been blacked out around election time in Kazakhstan, Malawi, and Pakistan.[39] Such internet shutdowns massively disadvantaged opposition and civil society voices, and gave governments a distinct advantage; as they had better access to—and often control over—traditional media than grass-roots organizations or marginalized opposition groups that lacked the resources to circumvent these restrictions.

Elite Panic (Again)

In principle, liberal democracies should have been as enthusiastic about social media as authoritarian states were hostile. And the relationship did start off as a mutual love affair, with democracies cheering the potential of social media to revitalize democracy at home and tear down the walls of authoritarianism abroad.

In 2006, the junior senator from Illinois released a podcast in which he highlighted the importance of the internet because it allowed him to "say what I want without censorship." On November 5, 2008, now president-elect @BarackObama tweeted, "We just made history. All of this happened because you gave your time, talent and passion. All of this happened because of you. Thanks."[40] There were good reasons why Obama thanked his millions of online friends and followers directly. As an African American junior senator, he was the quintessential political outsider. But through a trailblazing campaign that pioneered the use of the internet and social media, Obama by-passed traditional gatekeepers in the media, corporate donors, and his own party establishment to connect directly with digitally energized voters. Obama's online guerilla tactics upended his political-elite rivals and helped him win the "Facebook generation" by a landslide. In doing so, the new "Communicator-in-Chief" changed the nature of political campaigning and communication for good.[41]

But the dark side of social media became much more visible in the years that followed. Previously, white supremacists and anti-Semites had little reach outside their local environments, since no editor would publish their hateful views in traditional media. The rise of centralized platforms, however, gave them the ability to co-ordinate hateful incitement and target members of minority groups who would have never encountered a neo-Nazi pamphlet or obscure white-supremacist blog otherwise.[42] In some cases, violent right-wing extremists even used social media to livestream acts of mass murder. Roving bands of misogynist trolls found a captive audience of women to harass, abuse, and shame into fear and silence. Jihadists may not support free speech for cartoonists, infidels, and apostates, but terrorist groups like ISIS enthusiastically embraced social media to generate funds and recruits through the "shock and awe" of slick and savvy propaganda, severed heads and all. Disinformation and misleading propaganda thrived in the ecosystem of social media platforms designed to reward user engagement through likes and shares.

It would not have surprised Martin Luther that "false, shocking, negative, exaggerated, and emotionally charged content tends to spread faster and wider on social media platforms" than dry, long-winded, and reasoned arguments.[43] In fact, a 2018 MIT study found that false news stories were 70 percent more likely to be retweeted and diffused significantly farther, faster, deeper, and more broadly than real news.[44] No wonder political hyperpartisans, authoritarian governments, conspiracy theorists, and cynical trolls in it "for the lulz" did their worst to "flood the zone with shit," in the words of Steve Bannon, a former advisor to President Trump.[45] To make matters worse, this happened during a period when political polarization was on the rise and trust in political institutions and traditional media was in decline in several countries, not least the US.[46] In 2021, the annual Global Trust Index measured the highest ever level of "trust inequality" between the "Mass Population"—generally distrustful—and the "Informed Public" (or elite)—generally trustful—when measuring trust in media, government, NGOs, and businesses.[47] Global trust in information sources, whether from traditional or social media, hit record lows.

The decisive game changer in institutional attitudes to social media came in 2016 with the shock of the US presidential election. Donald Trump harnessed online platform power to viciously attack opponents, to spread falsehoods at a dizzying rate, and to win the US presidency. Many established elites in the media, politics, and the commentariat apportioned a large part of the "blame" for Trump on social media, claiming it had facilitated the weaponization of free speech through disinformation and hostile propaganda spread by nefarious actors, not least Putin's Russia and its army of trolls.[48] Given the unprecedented amplification of disinformation and hate speech and the wider potential for harm in terms of election interference, rampant conspiracy theories, targeting of minorities, and what author Jonathan Rauch has called an "epistemic crisis" with truth itself at risk, it was not surprising that many politicians, journalists, and pundits sounded the alarm.[49]

By November 2020, the love affair between Obama and Silicon Valley was over. After losing the 2020 presidential election, President Trump and his team launched a campaign of reckless conspiracy theories and outright lies, turning social media against the very democracy Trump was the head of to cling to power and overturn his defeat. Now Obama viewed the platforms that had helped him rise to power in 2008 as "the single biggest threat to our democracy."[50] Obama's warning was given credence on January 6, 2021, as Trump supporters whipped up by the president's lies, which were regurgitated by several pundits and politicians, stormed the Capitol after an incendiary Trump speech at a "Stop the Steal" rally in Washington, DC. Several of the attackers called for the execution of Vice President Pence, and five people ended up dying, including a police officer.

Social media, it was broadly agreed, had become a clear and present danger to democracy. But for governments and other elite institutions fretting about the corrosive effects of social media, there was a silver lining to the centralized amplification of hate, harm, and hoaxes. If you could persuade or strong-arm Facebook, YouTube, and Twitter into purging illegal and lawful but awful content, its visibility would drop exponentially. Potentially, centralized platforms could even end up serving as the private enforcers of government censorship, entirely inverting the initial promise of egalitarian and unmediated free speech.

After the attack on Congress, Trump was deplatformed and permanently cut off from communicating directly to his more than 120 million fans and followers on Facebook and Twitter. Not everyone thought this was a sign of progress, however. Alexey Navalny criticized Twitter's purge of Trump as "an unacceptable act of censorship" that would be "exploited by the enemies of freedom of speech around the world."[51] The independent Oversight Board established by Facebook to adjudicate user complaints also raised concerns that the indefinite suspension of Trump was arbitrary and disproportionate.[52]

The move to deplatform the most powerful man in the world was the culmination of a long trajectory beginning in the EU. In 2016, the European Commission and a number of Big Tech firms, including Facebook, Twitter, and Google, agreed on a voluntary Code of Conduct to remove illegal hate speech. In 2018, a Code of Practice to tackle disinformation was added.[53] In reality, the EU was making these tech firms an offer they couldn't refuse, as the alternative was legally binding regulations. But these nonbinding instruments were not sufficient to appease all European governments.

As seen in previous chapters, Germany has a long and complicated history of resorting to concerted repression of dissenting opinions that threaten the fundamental values of society and elite control of information. Examples range from the Carlsbad Decrees and Bismarck's crackdown on socialists in the nineteenth century to the Weimar Republic's drastic emergency press laws in the twentieth. In the digital era, Germany's "militant democracy" once again felt vulnerable and bet its continued resilience against resurgent authoritarianism on curbing extremist voices.

Germany's 2017 Network Enforcement Act (NetzDG) obliges larger social media platforms to remove manifestly illegal content within twenty-four hours or risk steep fines. At the time of this writing, the German Bundestag was poised to expand the NetzDG by requiring online platforms to inform the authorities of illegal content, along with the user data (such as IP addresses) of those who post such content.[54] It is not difficult to imagine the potential chilling effect of such government-imposed social control through digital means.

In fact, a more nuanced look at German history might have cautioned the German government against attempts to fight extremism with ever stricter censorship, however well-intentioned. Not only did this strategy fail during the Weimar Republic, the NetzDG can trace its roots back to Bismarck's Imperial Press Law and Criminal Code of the 1870s, which, as we know, was used to crack down on dissent and insults against the Iron Chancellor.[55]

The impact of the NetzDG was not limited to Germany. At least twenty-three countries, ranging from a few European democracies like France and the United Kingdom to a host of authoritarian states like Russia, Belarus, Turkey, Pakistan, and Venezuela, adopted or proposed similar laws—often with explicit reference to the German precedent.[56] Ironically enough, Putin's Russia has transformed a law aimed at *defending* Western democracies into a draconian law used to shore up an authoritarian regime committed to *disrupting* Western democracies. In March 2021, Russia's federal agency for media regulation, Roskomnadzor, accused Twitter—a vital platform for Alexey Navalny—of breaking the law by failing to remove almost three thousand illegal posts since 2017, and threatened the platform with heavy fines.[57] Roskomnadzor also pressured YouTube, TikTok, and Instagram to remove content tied to the protests against Navalny's imprisonment.[58] In a rare instance of institutional pushback, France's Constitutional Council declared parts of the French Avia Law—essentially a NetzDG clone—unconstitutional in June 2020 because it undermined "freedom of expression and communication in a way that is not necessary, adapted nor proportionate."[59]

Time and again, false information is the category of speech most commonly prohibited by rulers and governments fretting about the erosion of their authority. In 2018, even democratic France was so worried about the supposed flood of "fake news" on social media that it adopted a law allowing judges to issue injunctions against disinformation during election periods.[60] And France is not alone. According to Věra Jourová, the EU vice president for Values and Transparency, "the time has come to go beyond self-regulatory measures" on countering digital disinformation.[61]

Interestingly, the European Federation of Journalists—representing over 320,000 journalists across forty-five countries—also pushed for EU regulation and sanctions of online platforms that fail to remove disinformation.[62] Such a scheme would necessarily entail granting some European body the authority to determine what is true and false. Unfortunately, the EU's record in this field is far from promising. In 2015, the EU set up the East StratCom Task Force to expose and combat Russian disinformation via the website EUvsDisinfo.eu. The taskforce soon came under fire for including a number of articles in Dutch news media in its index of disinformation, raising questions about politicization and the reliability of the network of NGOs and journalists doing the *fact checking*.[63]

In the US, the First Amendment prevents the passage of laws like the NetzDG. But both Democrats and Republicans have declared war on CDA 230, though for very different reasons. When he was a senator, President Joe Biden wanted to shred CDA 230, since it allows online platforms to "propagat[e] falsehoods they know to be false."[64] Former president Donald Trump, on the other hand, issued an executive order aimed at stripping online platforms of their CDA 230 immunities because of the perceived anticonservative bias of Facebook and Twitter's content moderation, which Republicans insist is both pervasive and premeditated.[65]

Traditional media outlets have also taken aim at social media and the erosion of institutional gatekeepers ensuring proper editorial standards. "Free Speech Is Killing Us," read the headline of a *New York Times* op-ed by *New Yorker* reporter Andrew Marantz, which captured the zeitgeist among many in legacy media.[66] As an anonymous tech executive told the *Economist*, the pressure from the media is to "remove more, remove more, remove more."[67]

Many of those concerned about the viability of what Jonathan Rauch calls the "Constitution of Knowledge" were motivated by a commitment to the institutions and values of liberal democracy, including safeguarding free speech as a vehicle for approaching truth and discerning falsehood.[68] But the examples above also document a growing loss of faith in this freedom and a willingness to counter the harms at the expense of safeguarding the benefits of free speech. It seems increasingly clear that some elites among politicians and legacy media, who once enjoyed privileged free speech, now view the digital era's direct and egalitarian free speech as a threat to democratic values, as well as to their authority as trusted gatekeepers of the public sphere.

Sociologists Lee Clarke and Caron Chess, who coined the term "elite panic," have almost prophetically described the dynamic which has seen democracies, governments, and institutions demand ever more restrictions on online free speech. Elite panic, they argue, "is an attribution that is almost exclusively applied when looking down at people who do not occupy positions of power or authority." It occurs in a time of crisis "when decision makers are under intense media scrutiny or when considerable financial or reputational resources are at stake." Another driver is "uncertainty or disagreement about distributions of responsibility." Such circumstances generate an unrelenting pressure for elites to act and act now. Consequently, "the need to appear decisive might lead to rash actions," that could potentially be worse than the very real problems they are intended to solve.[69]

In relation to social media, elite panic comes in cascades. Panic in the government and traditional media results in condemnations and regulation, or the threat thereof. This, in turn, causes social media platforms to appease their critics through constant and often contradictory tweaks and changes to their terms of service and content moderation based on the specific controversy of the day—hate speech, disinformation, terrorism, election interference, anti-vaxxers, etc. In the interest of self-preservation, the platforms abandon any principled approach that—through the lens of PR, stakeholder management, or profitability—cannot be defended in the abstract against the specific instance of harmful or offensive content. A striking example of this zigzagging came in 2020, when Mark Zuckerberg announced that Facebook would no longer tolerate Holocaust denial.[70] Just two years before, Zuckerberg had resisted such restrictions, stressing that only "misinformation that is aimed at or going to induce violence . . . [or] result in real harm" should be taken down.[71]

It is also important to note that elite panic relating to social media platforms cascades downward. It is ultimately aimed at restricting the speech and access to information of users, not that of the platforms whose commitment to free expression is quite openly tempered by their commitment to shareholders, advertisers, and other stakeholders. Elite panic is thus focused on social media users, who apparently cannot be trusted to know the difference between truth and lies or remain tolerant and peaceful when given unmediated access to information. As author James B. Meigs notes, "Elite panic frequently brings out another unsavory quirk on the part of some authorities: a tendency to believe the worst about their own citizens."[72]

There are close parallels between the modern democratic elite's mistrust of social media and the nervousness that privileged classes have displayed time and again when the masses gain access to potentially radical ideas. This Roman and elitist conception of free speech calls to mind the justifications, if not the methods, behind Pitt's

Reign of Terror and the Sedition Act of 1798, which stemmed from fears that newspapers and pamphlets would channel dissent and erode respect for governmental authority and institutions.

There is no denying that the backlash against social media has had consequences. Facebook and Twitter originally displayed a strong civil-libertarian impulse inspired by First Amendment ideals.[73] As late as 2012, Twitter only half-jokingly described itself as the "free speech wing of the free speech party."[74] But as the scrutiny grew more intense and the calls for increasing content removal and regulation grew ever louder, the platforms changed their tunes and started emphasizing the values of "safety" and preventing "harm." In a 2017 hearing before a hostile British Parliament, a Twitter VP waved the white flag and announced that the platform was ditching its "John Stuart Mill-style philosophy."[75] And in 2019, Facebook's Mark Zuckerberg called for stronger regulation of the internet, before even agreeing on the need for reform of CDA 230 in Congressional hearings in October 2020, knowing full well that few other platforms will be able to spend as many resources on content moderation as Facebook does.[76]

The terms of service of platforms like Facebook and Twitter have undergone substantial scope creep, banning more and broader categories of speech.[77] Facebook deleted 26.9 million pieces of content for violating its Community Standards on "hate speech" in the last quarter of 2020. That's nearly seventeen times the 1.6 million instances of deleted "hate speech" in the last quarter of 2017. More than 97 percent of the purged hate speech in Q4 of 2020 was proactively identified by AI.[78]

Twitter and YouTube also removed record levels of content in 2019 and 2020, respectively.[79] No government in history has ever been able to exert such extensive control over what is being said, read, and shared by so many people across the world and in real time.

Content moderation by these private platforms does not fall within the First Amendment's scope. Part of the rationale behind

CDA 230 was to encourage responsible moderation by the platforms themselves according to their own rules. Even free speech maximalists would likely ditch platforms that only moderated content violating the First Amendment once deluged by porn, spam, harassment, and abuse. But given the enormous pressure and legal sanctions applied by governments, the idea that the current state of content moderation relies entirely on voluntary principles is more than strained. And as US tech firms adopt increasingly restrictive terms of service to comply with European laws, global social media users are being subjected to moderation without representation. Perhaps more consequential is the potential habituation of social media users to community standards that are significantly less speech protective than what follows under constitutional and human rights law, with the danger that the former will ultimately influence interpretation of the latter rather than the other way around.

Regardless of whether one thinks that social media platforms remove too much or too little content, the lack of transparency about the moderation and algorithmic distribution of content is deeply problematic. As noted by the Centre for Democracy and Technology, automated content moderation is bad at understanding context and nuance, like humor or racist language employed to expose and document racism. Inherently vague and subjective definitions of hate speech and offense also pose a challenge to automated content moderation.[80] These shortcomings may result in extensive collateral damage to permissible speech.

The confidential Implementation Standards developed to guide Facebook's human content moderators is a constantly growing index of prohibited content of around twelve thousand words, which few content moderators truly understand.[81] Whether the millions of posts and comments deleted for hate speech and other prohibited categories each month live up the platform's own standards is an open question, since purged content is not available to the public.

Nor can users expect anything resembling due process normally involved in the adjudication of potential speech transgressions. According to a Justitia survey of hate speech cases in five European countries, domestic legal authorities took 778.47 days, on average, from the date of the alleged offending speech until the conclusion of the trial at first instance.[82] Facebook's content moderators are expected to make such decisions within hours or days. Add to this the fact that content moderation at scale is, in the words of Techdirt editor Mike Masnick, "impossible to do well," given clashing global attitudes on where to draw the line, the vagueness of community standards, and the fallibility of humans and technology.[83] If Facebook made the wrong call in just 0.1 percent of the 6.5 billion deleted fake accounts, 6.5 million genuine ones would have been purged in 2019 alone. This has real consequences. In June 2020, Facebook suddenly deactivated the accounts of up to sixty Tunisian bloggers and political activists, citing "technical error."[84]

According to Facebook's own data from 2020, it makes "mistakes" in about 10 percent of the appealed cases regarding hate speech.[85] But mistakenly deleting posts is not the only cause for concern. The secret algorithms behind the automated content moderation may sometimes be biased against certain groups. A review of Facebook's internal documents by ProPublica suggests that Facebook's hate speech algorithms sometimes "tend to favor elites and governments over grassroots activists and racial minorities." For instance, a post from a Republican congressman inviting people to "hunt" and "kill" radicalized Muslims did not raise any red flags. But a post from a Black Lives Matter activist stating that "all white people are racist" was removed and caused the activist's profile to be suspended.[86] YouTube's hate speech algorithm also appears to have taken on a life of its own, going as far as removing Bob Dylan's song "Neighborhood Bully" for hate speech.[87]

Facebook also maintains a secret list of banned individuals—historical and contemporary—who engage in "organized hate."

Even the mere mention of the British far-right activist Tommy Robinson on Facebook has resulted in deletion of content and the suspension of numerous accounts. This includes content posted by people deeply opposed to Robinson's anti-Muslim bigotry as well as by a journalist from the Danish Broadcasting Corporation who featured Robinson in a televised debate.[88] Meanwhile the more than five thousand members of the Facebook group "In Defense of Stalin," which describes itself as "the world's largest cyber community of Pro-Stalin people," operate smoothly, though Stalin undoubtedly was one of the most dangerous people in history.[89]

Twitter has defined its ban on "hateful conduct" to include "misgendering" and has banned users for statements such as, "only females get cervical cancer." Reddit banned a subgroup of feminists for "hate speech" because of their belief that a person's biological sex is fixed.[90] In October 2020, Twitter blocked all users—including reporters—from sharing or discussing a story from the *New York Post* that exposed incriminating emails allegedly originating from a laptop belonging to presidential candidate Joe Biden's son. Twitter even blocked the account of the *New York Post*, the fifth-largest and oldest continually published newspaper in the US, only to subsequently admit to having made a mistake, thus limiting access to potentially relevant information in the run-up to a presidential election.[91]

These examples demonstrate that governments, journalists, organizations, and activists can endlessly cherry-pick content that "proves" that platforms are biased (for or) against conservatives, liberals, racial minorities, the LGBTQ community, women, Muslims, etc. But the reality may well be that the seemingly chaotic and incoherent approach to content moderation is mostly based on ad hoc damage control following endless media controversies. The end result is poorly conceptualized rules and practices that spawn a host of unintended consequences when applied generally and outside of the specific context of pressure and outrage under which they were adopted.

Take the case of British comedian Sacha Baron Cohen. In 2019, Cohen claimed that hate speech and "fake news" were "facilitated by a handful of internet companies that amount to the greatest propaganda machine in history" and demanded stricter content regulation.[92] But Baron Cohen's own career is a prime example of why imposing more restrictive global rules for online content may be a cure worse than the disease. In 2006, his blockbuster hit movie *Borat*—in which he plays a clueless and offensive journalist from Kazakhstan—was banned from distribution in a number of countries. A Russian official cited the "film's potential to offend religious and ethnic feelings" as a reason to censor the movie.[93] According to a 2021 Justitia global survey, only 61 percent of people in thirty-three surveyed countries think that free speech should protect statements "offensive" to religious beliefs.[94] This begs the question of why more restrictive rules for online content should conform to the subjective standards of liberal Westerners like Baron Cohen, rather than the billions who find his humor beyond the pale. And sure enough, less than two weeks after Baron Cohen had celebrated Facebook's 2020 decision to purge Holocaust denial, Pakistani prime minister Imran Khan wrote a letter to Mark Zuckerberg demanding "a similar ban on islamophobia and against Islam for Facebook."[95] At scale, Milton's Curse sets off a censorship envy race to the bottom, which ultimately affected Baron Cohen himself. In a 2020 article in *Time* magazine, Baron Cohen launched a new attack on Facebook for facilitating a "whirlwind of conspiratorial madness." Ironically, Baron Cohen's article was blocked by Facebook, since it was accompanied by a picture of man wearing a facemask captioned, "COVID-19 IS A HOAX."[96]

Social Media and Democracy

If, as many experts, media personalities, and politicians believe, free speech is as likely to harm as to strengthen democracy in the digital age, then elite panic may be an entirely prudent reaction aimed at reducing the harm while safeguarding the benefits of this fundamental freedom.

In order to try to establish whether this belief is supported by empirical fact, a small army of researchers have explored if and how social media might impact the democratic process. The 2020 edited volume *Social Media and Democracy* provided an overview of recent research, and many of the findings—however preliminary—challenged dominant narratives that guide elite panic. In the words of the editors, Nathaniel Persily and Joshua A. Tucker, "reliance on untested conventional wisdom based on folk theories of technology's impact on democracy is leading to misguided reform proposals that may even worsen the problems they are attempting to solve."[97]

Take French president Emmanuel Macron's 2018 warning about "torrents of hate coming over the Internet."[98] No doubt, the visibility of hate speech was heightened by social media. But hate speech only constitutes a small percentage of the content on social media.[99] A 2021 study analyzed over a billion American tweets from when Trump declared his candidacy in 2015 to six months after his election. Contrary to a popular narrative, the researchers found no systematic increase in hate speech and white nationalist language during Trump's election campaign, with such content hovering between 0.1 and 0.3 percent of tweets at any given time.[100] More limited studies from Ethiopia and Denmark showed a similarly low amount of hate speech on Facebook.[101]

That being said, even if the prevalence of hate speech is exaggerated, hundreds of thousands of hateful comments are uploaded daily across social media platforms, sometimes with very real consequences for those they are directed at. A number of studies suggest that online hate speech may cause harm in terms of fear, psychological trauma, and self-censorship, disproportionately affecting minorities. A few studies of Facebook and Twitter usage and hate crimes have offered "preliminary evidence" that social media can facilitate online hate speech turning into offline violent crime.[102] Scholar Susan Benesch coined the term "dangerous speech"—a more narrow and precisely defined category than "hate speech"—to describe speech that might "increase the risk that its audience will condone or commit violence against members of another group."[103] Dangerous speech can contribute to mass atrocities like the Rwanda genocide of 1994, in which radio played a vital role.[104] Social media can also serve as a vector for dangerous speech, as demonstrated by the ethnic cleansing of Rohingya Muslims in Myanmar carried out by the military, which used Facebook to launch a deceptive campaign of incitement against the Rohingya.[105]

But while online expression may sometimes lead to real-life harm, it does not necessarily follow that placing restrictions on free speech is an effective remedy.[106] On the contrary, studies suggest that, on the whole, freedom of expression is associated with less rather than more violent extremism and social conflict in democracies.[107] The preventive effect of free speech on terrorist attacks seems particularly strong.[108] Conversely, suppression may actually serve to amplify rather than silence hate speech. A 2017 study concluded that violent far-right extremism in Western Europe was partly fueled by "extensive public repression of radical right actors and opinions."[109] Researchers also found an increase in "non-violent hate crimes"—including verbal insults, threats, and bullying—when the Dutch far-right politician Geert Wilders was prosecuted for hate speech, suggesting a "backlash effect" in which "repression of the radical right may be a catalyst [of hate crimes] due to increasing polarization and radicalization."[110] When Trump's Facebook account was locked indefinitely after the attack on Congress in January, it attracted almost 150,000 new likes within a week, proving that the Streisand effect is a force to be reckoned with.[111]

Moreover, far-right extremists and white supremacists often migrate to alternative platforms when purged from Facebook and Twitter for violating hate speech rules. These include encrypted messaging services like Telegram, where extremists may reconnect and network with minimal publicity.[112] After the attack on the Capitol, Twitter and Facebook banned a large swath of Trump's supporters while Google and Apple removed Parler, a social network popular with the far right, from their app stores. Such purges can help limit the visibility of hate speech on larger platforms. However, Telegram then suddenly became the second most downloaded app in the US owing to a sudden influx of Trump supporters and Parler users.[113] The withdrawal of extremists from popular forums not only impedes the efforts of law enforcement agencies to track down future attacks but also hinders targeted counterspeech, which some studies have shown to be effective in reducing hate speech.[114]

The picture is also much more nuanced when it comes to fake news and disinformation, though because of the difficulties and biases involved in defining what constitutes disinformation, such studies should be treated with some caution. A case in point is the so-called lab-leak theory, which pointed to evidence that the SARS-CoV-2 virus may have originated at the Wuhan Institute of Virology in Wuhan, China. So radioactive was this supposed racist right-wing crackpot theory that most traditional media dismissed and generally refused to cover it seriously. Facebook went so far as deleting lab-leak content, which it labeled as misinformation, only to reverse course after a group of independent researchers used social media and blogs to provide information that suddenly made the theory less implausible.[115]

Accordingly, what constitutes disinformation is often debatable, or even unknowable until further facts emerge. Still, multiple studies have found that "fake news" is neither as pervasive nor as detrimental as many assume. An American study from 2019 found that fake news (broadly defined as "fake, deceptive, low-quality, or hyperpartisan news") was "extremely rare," comprising only about 0.15 percent of Americans' daily media diet.[116] Another 2019 study showed much the same picture for Facebook, finding that sharing fake news was a rare activity.[117] A 2018 analysis of data from US desktop and mobile users in the months leading up to and following the 2016 election showed that the ratio of monthly visits to "real" news sites versus "fake" news sites was forty to one.[118] Another study from 2019 found that Russian trolls have no significant influence on US Twitter users.[119] Research has also seriously questioned the effect of mis- and disinformation on democratic elections—not least the 2016 US presidential election which made Donald Trump commander in chief to the chagrin of established elites in both politics and the media. One study suggested that, while fake news favoring Donald Trump vastly outnumbered disinformation favoring Hillary Clinton, the very limited reach of such information would only have changed vote shares in the presidential election "by an amount on the order of hundredths of a percentage point."[120] In France, during the 2017 presidential election, a mere 4,888 out of sixty million tweets (less than 0.01 percent) were deemed to contain "fake news," suggesting that the French fake news law was indeed an instance of elite panic.[121] Finally, a study of the effect of fake news on Twitter during European elections in 2019 found that "disinformation outlets are largely ignored" and "play a peripheral role in online political discussions."[122]

Still, some groups appear to be more susceptible than others. The 2019 study of Russian trolls also found that the US Twitter users who are "most at risk of interacting with trolls" were "those with strong partisan beliefs."[123] This finding is consistent with studies showing how highly partisan users are especially prone to believing online misinformation that conforms to their views.[124] In the United States, partisan conservatives, especially from the older generation, are more likely to share and consume misinformation than liberals and moderates.[125]

A number of studies also challenged the idea that social media users are lost in digital echo chambers and filter bubbles in which their existing prejudices are endlessly confirmed, polarized, and radicalized. Multiple studies showed that "exposure to diverse news is higher [on social media] than through other types of media," and that "ranking algorithms do not have a large impact on the ideological balance of news consumption."[126] As with mis- and disinformation, it seemed that those most vulnerable to stumbling down the rabbit hole of ideological echo chambers and filter bubbles were those already afflicted by political partisanship.[127]

These findings appeared to be in line with the studies on the effect of propaganda and indoctrination in the Third Reich, which showed that Nazi propaganda depended heavily on existing confirmation bias for its effectiveness, and that it was much less effective—or even counterproductive—among Germans who did not already hold anti-Semitic views.

In *Not Born Yesterday*, social scientist Hugo Mercier offers an explanation as to why the supposed torrents of fake news and hate speech thought to tear apart democracies may not be as persuasive as many assume. Mercier argued that human beings have evolved a suite of cognitive tools based on "open vigilance" that help us sort between plausible and implausible information and deduce which arguments to trust.[128] A 2020 study of global media consumption by Reuters Institute may provide a good example of open vigilance in action. Among those surveyed, 38 percent trusted news in traditional media as opposed to a mere 22 percent who trusted news in social media.[129] While trust in mainstream media is worryingly low, many people still seem to appreciate the division of labor in knowledge production and curation, and harbor (more) sound skepticism about news and information that has not undergone the checking and vetting processes developed by professional journalists.

Even if open vigilance shields most humans from falling prey to fake news, the total number of people pulled in by propaganda is still likely to be substantial. This can cause real-life harm, such as anti-vaxxers undermining lifesaving vaccine drives and viral conspiracy theories about voter fraud in the 2020 US presidential election leading to distrust and violence.[130] Open vigilance may thus not be sufficient to counter disinformation and propaganda at scale—particularly when trust breaks down and societies become deeply polarized, which makes the human mind more receptive to otherwise inefficient propaganda. In February 2021, more than two-thirds of Republicans still believed the 2020 presidential election was "invalid."[131] But that does not mean that ever-increasing restrictions on free speech will cure the residual harm. Lost in the incessant focus on the darker sides of free speech—real, perceived, and exaggerated—are the profound benefits of free and open discourse, from the toppling of absolutist rulers to the cross-fertilization of knowledge across cultures and the defeat of institutional racism and discrimination. As thinkers like Spinoza, Cato, Madison, Constant, and Douglass have pointed out, we jeopardize those benefits if we are unwilling to accept any of the harms or costs that inevitably accompany free expression.

After Dr. Li Wenliang was censored, the hashtags "I want freedom of speech" and "We want freedom of speech" were shared by millions of Chinese internet users before being blocked.[132] This is deeply significant because today's hyperfocus on the darker sides of the internet and social media too often obscures the enormous benefits that many—especially in democracies—have come to take for granted.

Around the world, citizen activists have creatively used the digital space to rise against authoritarian regimes and advocate for change in weakened democracies. Following Belarus's tainted presidential election in August 2020, citizens used end-to-end encrypted communication platforms like Telegram to document human rights violations, organize protests, and rally against longtime dictator Alexander Lukashenko.[133] In Russia, Alexey Navalny used YouTube to release a long and detailed video purporting to document Putin's ill-gotten gains through drone footage of an opulent Black Sea residence. The video has been viewed almost 115 million times and inspired Belarussian dissidents to do a similar video on Luka-shenko.[134] Without the internet and social media, Hungarian prime minister Viktor Orbán's media capture would have left his opponents virtually voiceless.

Exiled Turkish journalists publish independent news on overseas platforms like Ahval and #ÖZGÜRÜZ, which many Turks access by using VPNs to bypass government censorship.[135] Social media also played a crucial role in Armenia's peaceful "Velvet Revolution" in 2018, which ended the corrupt presidency of Serzh Sargsyan.[136]

Perhaps nothing better illustrates the internet's potential for speaking truth to power than Bellingcat, a small network of investigative reporters founded by the British citizen journalist Eliot Higgins. Through the innovative use of open-source data and social media, Bellingcat has—among other things—helped document Russian culpability in the downing of a Malaysian Airlines flight over Ukraine, the use of cluster bombs against civilians by Syrian dictator Bashar al-Assad, and the identity and whereabouts of a Russian death squad responsible for poisoning a defected former Russian intelligence officer in Salisbury, England. These exposures of the truth about authoritarian crimes and abuses are likely to be more consequential to the Putins of the world than the uncertain benefits such leaders gain from spreading disinformation and propaganda at scale.[137]

Not even China can avoid digital scrutiny. Unlike the suffering of gulag victims in Stalin's Soviet Union, about which the world was mostly oblivious, the horrific conditions in "China's gulag"—networks of "reeducation camps" in the western Xinjiang province where an estimated one million predominantly Uighur Muslims are being detained and subjected to torture, systematic rape, and forced sterilization—have been exposed by journalists, activists, and victims using smartphones, social media, satellites, and messaging apps.[138] In 2019, citizen activists in Hong Kong protesting China's harsh extradition bill, which threatened to deport Hong Kong citizens to the mainland, used a variety of technologies to mobilize support and weather the heavy crackdown from authorities, from actively engaging on anonymous chatrooms to using GitHub to broadcast livestreams of protests on their smartphones.[139]

As we saw in Chapters 9 and 10, censorship and suppression of speech have been instrumental in sustaining the systemic repression of minorities and other oppressed groups. Many minority and marginalized groups today remain deeply skeptical about the role of the internet and social media, where hatred can be amplified. However, the digital space has in many and important ways strengthened the voice and agency of minorities and vulnerable groups.

When the video of George Floyd's death circulated across social media, it sparked local protests and snowballed into the global Black Lives Matter movement for racial justice, with demonstrations in cities around the world, including the UK, South Africa, Germany, Argentina, the Philippines, and Japan.[140] As the movement grew, social media became instrumental in coordinating protests, livestreaming marches, documenting police excesses, raising bail fund donations, and even organizing town halls.[141] In some cases, authorities were compelled to suspend officers and initiate legal proceedings against those who were captured on camera hurting unarmed protestors.[142]

Social media has helped LGBTQ persons across the globe gain acceptance, form communities, and express their identities in spaces free of prejudice.[143] These liberating online communities are especially helpful for young people in socially conservative countries like Kenya and Uganda where homosexuality is a crime and expressions of LGBTQ identity are censored in the media.[144]

The Iraqi American refugee Faisal Al Mutar and his NGO Ideas Beyond Borders have translated into Arabic and made freely available sixteen prominent books and twenty-one thousand Wikipedia articles on science, tolerance, and humanism, reaching more than forty million people in the Middle East through social media.[145]

Many of the translated works cater to the MENA region's embattled freethinkers and secularists thirsting for more heterodox and daring ideas than those typically available in Arabic.

In India, feminists have used digital tools on multiple occasions to attack prevailing patriarchal and sexist norms. In 2017, the hashtag #LahuKaLagaan (roughly translating to "women's blood") was successfully used to campaign against a 12 percent tax on sanitary napkins and challenge the societal taboo on discussing menstrual hygiene.[146] Globally, technology has also facilitated the #MeToo movement, empowering women to speak out against sexual violence and harassment. The movement was instrumental in bringing a sense of agency to the victims of sexual abuse, enabling them to recount their experiences, publicly expose offenders, and find support through a large online community.[147]

Perhaps the most promising aspect of the digital age is that activists are developing tools to combat the dark side of the internet based on transparency and civic engagement, rather than centralized control and censorship. More importantly, this development also aims to repair the growing sense of popular alienation from and distrust in elite political and media institutions, which has fertilized the ground for misinformation, hate speech, and hostile propaganda in the first place.

In Taiwan, a group of civic hackers mobilized into an online collective called g0v (pronounced Gov Zero).[148] The movement promoted the idea that everybody affected by the government's policies should be able to engage in the decision-making process. G0v quickly became influential in Taiwan, and Audrey Tang, one of its founding members, went on to become Taiwan's digital minister on an agenda of "radical transparency."[149] During Taiwan's 2020 presidential election, Tang's alternative approach played a pivotal role in countering massively coordinated Chinese efforts at misinformation and election interference.[150] Tang stressed that immunizing democracies against disinformation from below requires a nation to trust its citizens and civil society, rather than viewing them as a fickle mob ready to believe whatever outrageous rumors are being spread by the enemies of democracy.

One of g0v's most innovative tools was the collaborative Cofacts initiative, which allowed users of Line—the most popular messaging app in Taiwan—to install a chatbot.[151] Whenever users have doubts about the validity of information, they can submit a link to the chatbot, which forwards it to a group of fact-checkers who can verify or debunk the story. The latest initiative of g0v is the establishment of vTaiwan (virtual Taiwan), which uses the Polis platform to allow citizens to discuss new initiatives while politicians listen to the input. Polis is designed to "successfully decentralise power in organisations of all kind," and unlike Facebook, Twitter, and YouTube, Polis is built to promote consensus and agreement rather than division and outrage. This promising precedent has been used as the basis for a dozen laws and regulations already passed in Taiwan, and has also been used by the government of Singapore and to inform local politics in the UK and the US.[152]

The Future of Free Speech: A Prognosis

When weighing up the pros and cons of the current state of internet freedom, the benefits of social media and the instant access it gives ordinary people to unmediated information do, I believe, outweigh the downsides, even if the harms are real, substantial, and more visible than ever. At the same time, it is increasingly difficult to reconcile the idea of egalitarian free speech with large, centralized, corporate, and increasingly algorithmically driven social media platforms acting as the conduits of global *parrhēsia*. John Stuart Mill feared society's tendency to impose conformity "by other means than civil penalties," such as social and peer pressure, as much as censorship by government. Likewise, George Orwell warned that "unpopular ideas can be silenced, and inconvenient facts kept dark, without the need for any official ban" when the public sphere is dominated by a centralized press owned by a few wealthy men. Since both private and government censorship and surveillance are facilitated by centralization, some free speech advocates argue that decentralizing cyberspace is part of the solution, just as Tocqueville believed that the large number of American newspapers two centuries ago helped to diversify opinion and information.[153] In order to achieve this diversity, scholars like Columbia professor Tim Wu have argued that antitrust laws should be enforced to break up the concentration of power in behemoth platforms like Facebook, without restricting the limits of user content, thus creating a more decentralized social media ecosystem.[154] Mike Masnick has proposed moving toward social media built around open protocols controlled by end users rather than centralized proprietary platforms, which he believes "would allow end users to determine their own tolerances for different types of speech but make it much easier for most people to avoid the most problematic speech, without silencing anyone entirely or having the platforms themselves make the decisions about who is allowed to speak."[155]

A more radical proposal is a peer-to-peer model like Usenet, but updated with blockchain technology, which is being touted as "censorship resistant" by its proponents. Peer-to-peer platforms are not dependent on a company or a government because the individual users host the content and provide the bandwidth, making them much harder to control.[156] In December 2019, Twitter CEO Jack Dorsey announced that his company is funding the development of "an open and decentralized standard of social media."[157]

Critics have raised a number of concerns about this possibility. Blockchain technology is currently too complex and inconvenient for the non-tech-savvy majority, and most people are willing to trade significant parts of their privacy and free speech for the convenience and reach of Facebook and Twitter.[158] And while blockchain technology might promise a new age of complete immunity from government and corporate censorship and surveillance, it would also grant anonymity (and impunity) to nefarious actors like terrorist groups and child abusers.

Still, even the architect of the World Wide Web has acknowledged that the status quo is untenable. In 2019, Tim Berners-Lee announced that he is hard at work to stop the internet's "downward plunge to a dysfunctional future."[159] His solution is to "decentralize the web and take back power from the forces that have profited from centralizing it."[160]

More than two thousand years of history suggest that Berners-Lee is right, and that a more decentralized internet is the best bet for the future of free speech. But we are bound to be disappointed if we expect humanity to ever resolve the ancient but dynamic conflict between the proper spheres of authority and free expression.

Conclusion

If Dirck Coornhert, Baruch Spinoza, John Lilburne, Olympe de Gouges, or Frederick Douglass were alive today they would surely declare the twenty-first century an unprecedented Golden Age for free speech. They would marvel at what can be freely discussed openly in real time between people across the globe with no looming Inquisition, Star Chamber, or Committee of Public Safety. No one in the Netherlands bats an eyelid if the doctrines of the Reformed Church are questioned or rejected. Every "free-born Englishman"—regardless of class or religious belief—has a right to criticize the government with no prior censorship or onerous laws against seditious words. In France, women have the same right to "mount the tribune" as men, and political heretics don't have to fear the guillotine. And in the US, though racism is yet to be defeated, African Americans are no longer "dumb in their chains," nor can they be silenced by repressive "black codes" or violent mobs acting with impunity.

Given the epic struggles, setbacks, false starts, and enormous sacrifices that led to this happy state of affairs, there is indeed much to celebrate about the current condition of free expression. But the

Golden Age of free speech is in decline rather than ascendancy despite the unprecedented ubiquity of speech and information.

In the ninth century CE, Ibn al-Rāwandī could reject prophecy and central doctrines of Islam without serious punishment. But if he were alive today, his life and liberty would be severely threatened in a number of Muslim-majority countries, where blasphemy and apostasy are punishable by death. Even in secular democracies like France and the UK, al-Rāwandī's radical ideas might well be met with the Jihadist's Veto.

Gandhi would surely lament that India still uses colonial-era speech crimes to curtail the freedoms of speech and assembly that Gandhi considered the "two lungs that are absolutely necessary for a man to breathe the oxygen of liberty."

Four decades ago, Western democracies relied on freedom of expression to empower dissidents behind the Iron Curtain, which contributed to the triumph of the Helsinki effect and the end of European communism. Today, the combination of free speech and technology ensuring the free flow of information across borders is increasingly seen as a trojan horse threatening democracy rather than a battering ram knocking down the walls of censorship in closed societies.

At times European democratic leaders have sounded more like a distorted echo of the Soviet apparatchiks who warned against the flood of Western "racism," "fascism," and "false propaganda" than the stewards of democracies built upon the central premise of free and open debate for all. Eleanor Roosevelt's prescient warning that prohibiting incitement to hatred under international human rights law "would encourage governments to punish all criticism under the guise of protecting against religious or national hostility" has been forgotten.

In the US, the robust legal protection afforded by the First Amendment can barely disguise that the underlying assumptions of American "free speech exceptionalism" have lost much of their unifying appeal. As an abstract principle, American faith in free speech remains strong. But the unity collapses along unforgiving tribalist and identarian lines once each side's sacred taboos are violated by the other side.

It was always naïve to assume that the exercise of global free and equal speech at scale would further progress, liberation, truth, and tolerance without harmful and unintended consequences. A free and open network accessible to billions of people across the world will inevitably facilitate organized hatred, lies, malignant propaganda, and divisive rhetoric undermining the civil libertarian ideals of early internet pioneers.

And it was inevitable that those authoritarian regimes whose hold on power was challenged by the internet were going to invest heavily in solutions to reimpose centralized command and control of the means of communication. In the twentieth century, Mussolini, Hitler, and Stalin turned the press and radio into fine-tuned vehicles of totalitarian propaganda combined with ruthless censorship and repression of dissent. Today, authoritarian states—with China's digital juggernaut leading the charge—are reverse engineering the technology that was supposed to make censorship impossible to silence dissent at home and sow division and distrust abroad.

It was also naïve to think that radical developments in communications technology would lead elites and gatekeepers to willingly give up their privilege and admit previously voiceless groups into the public sphere without gnashing of teeth. The ancient conflict between Athens's egalitarian free speech ideals of *isēgoría* and *parrhēsía* on the one hand and Rome's elitist free speech ideal included in *libertas* on the other has morphed along with technological advances. Elite panic is still a phenomenon in modern democracies. Sometimes with good cause, but too often accompanied by questionable methods and counterproductive outcomes, such as Germany's NetzDG law, which has inspired authoritarian regimes across the globe.

These conflicting dynamics are playing out before us with no natural center of legitimate authority, shared values, or clear sets of principles on which to build a global framework for free speech in the digital agora of the twenty-first century. This reflects a much deeper and fundamental disconnect between what the philosopher of technology L. M. Sacasas has called the Digital City of the internet era and the Analog City that characterized life in the industrial era before mass digitization. Modern humans increasingly inhabit the former, while trying to make sense of its unprecedented informational order according to the principles, assumptions, and pace of the latter. The result has been a tendency toward "political and epistemic fragmentation," with plummeting trust in the ecosystem of information and political institutions that is unlikely to have run its course any time soon.[1]

It took seventy years before the printing press helped the Reformation go viral, with all of the dramatic events and fundamental changes it unleashed in the centuries to follow. In comparison, the World Wide Web has only been around for thirty-odd years, while Google, Facebook, and Twitter were founded in 1998, 2004, and 2006, respectively. These may well be the early days of the digital age.

At the time of this writing, a torrent of lies and conspiracy theories have challenged the efforts to contain a deadly pandemic and led millions to reject the legitimacy of a free and fair presidential election in the world's most powerful democracy. If these pathologies are but a harbinger of things to come in the Digital City, no wonder many still cling to the relative certainty and informational structure of the Analog City. As such it might be tempting to simply close off huge swaths of cyberspace as an irreparably contaminated area, like the Ottoman emperors who sought to avoid the political and religious chaos wreaked across Christendom by shunning the printing press. But what might have looked like prudence five centuries ago with hindsight looks like a huge and costly miscalculation, as Europe benefitted from the compound knowledge accumulated by the new ideas spread by the printing press.

Indeed, most thoughtful advocates of free speech, including Baruch Spinoza, Benjamin Constant, James Madison, George Orwell, and Eleanor Roosevelt, have acknowledged that this freedom can be used for malignant ends. Madison warned that "some degree of abuse is inseparable from the proper use of every thing; and in no instance is this more true, than in that of the press." Yet, he insisted that it was "better to leave a few of its noxious branches, to their luxuriant growth, than by pruning them away, to injure the vigor of those yielding the proper fruits."

Today Madison might have noted that online free speech connecting billions of people around the world necessarily provides nourishment to entire networks of noxious branches and their digital offshoots. But he might also have insisted that this is an unavoidable cost of enjoying the unprecedented fruits of having unlimited knowledge at our fingertips and being empowered to speak freely to potentially billions of people globally in real time on any subject. No doubt, Madison would have warned that broad attempts to prune the nasty weeds of the internet might well result in digital Sedition Acts of the sort that would tarnish his vision of the First Amendment as "*that right of freely examining public characters and measures, and of free communication among the people thereon, which has ever been justly deemed the only effectual guardian of every other right.*"[2]

More fundamentally, a political system whose basic values and ruling class are dependent on centralized control of information and opinion for survival can remain neither free nor vibrant. Liberal democracies must come to terms with the fact that in the Digital City one cannot effectively shield citizens and institutions from hostile propaganda, hateful content, or disinformation without compromising the egalitarian and liberal values of democracy as such. Instead democracies and their citizens must rediscover the enormous potential of free and equal speech and harness it to the benefit of liberal democratic values. Already, a whole cottage industry has sprung up to map, analyze, and counter disinformation and propaganda, just as innovative activists and journalists are using online open-source intelligence and data to expose the criminal deeds and human rights violations of authoritarian states for the whole world to see. Developing a more detached attitude to the constant background noise of social media rather than treating each "problematic" tweet or piece of content as a potential threat to democracy or specific groups may also help to develop a healthier information ecosystem.

The larger process is likely to be messy and frustrating. It may well give rise to an outpouring of more division, hostility, and propaganda. Reasserting authority and top-down control of the public sphere through censorship in democracies, however, is as unlikely to install a spirit of trust, understanding, and compromise as it is to succeed in filtering away all undesirable information.

Whatever fundamental reforms are needed to ensure that humans can thrive, trust, and flourish in the Digital City, a robust commitment to free speech should be recognized as a necessary part of the solution rather than an outdated ideal to be discarded on the ash heap of history. As seen throughout this book, free speech still serves as the bulwark of liberty, the foundation of democracy, equality, autonomy, and, yes, even the pursuit of truth. In established democracies these benefits are largely invisible, since we take them for granted, while the harms and pathologies are more visible than ever. But it is surely instructive that embattled prodemocracy activists in Hong Kong, Belarus, Russia, Myanmar, Egypt, and Venezuela depend on the ability to communicate and organize their activities on digital networks outside government control, while the regimes of these countries view the open internet as an existential threat to their survival.

To demonstrate this point, it is instructive to compare the US and Russia. Until recently, both had illiberal presidents willing to subvert the rule of law and democratic norms. In the US, Trump lasted one term after being subjected to relentless and severe criticism and thwarted by courts in his attempts to sue and silence critics and the media. Russia's Putin has been in power since 2000, all the while using state power to kill and imprison journalists, censor independent media and the internet, and turn traditional media into his pliant mouthpieces. When Alexey Navalny challenged Putin's rule, he was poisoned and then imprisoned after a Star Chamber trial in a kangaroo court. To be sure, Trump frequently fantasized about locking up his opponents, but the First Amendment and a culture of free speech underpinned by independent institutions made him powerless to do so. In fact many of Trump's loudest critics became media stars with huge media platforms. If the First Amendment helped Trump win office, it was instrumental in removing him from it again. On the other hand, the absence of free speech in Russia has been a key component in Putin's long and obsessive stranglehold on Russian politics.

Legacy media and experts must remain an essential part of the ecosystem that encourages the disinterested search for truth, knowledge, and accountability. To do so, media outlets and experts must find new and innovative ways to earn the trust of a public that is no longer a passive recipient of hierarchical top-down knowledge production and filtering. Jealously guarding the crumbling pillars of privileged access to the public sphere is unlikely to provide a winning strategy amidst deep mistrust of elites in general and the established media in particular.

As the voices of hatred are leveraged online, purging intolerance at scale is a tempting strategy to ensure the dignity and equality of those minorities who bear the brunt of organized hate speech. Yet, the centrality of censorship and repression in the maintenance of white supremacy and colonialism, and the key role of dissent and persuasion in the dismantling thereof, should remind us of Frederick Douglass's words that "the right of speech is a very precious one, especially to the oppressed." Moreover, while bigoted opinions may be of little social value, *knowing* that someone is a bigot can be of great scientific and practical value. Those who see benefit in silencing "dangerous" opinions coercively have failed to answer the practical question: Are we really *safer* when we know *less* about what motivates our neighbors? A principled defense of free speech in the face of hateful bigots can also be made more persuasive when combined with the recognition of a moral obligation to use one's own freedom to extend solidarity and compassion to those targeted by hatred and exposing and condemning those engaging in it.

More broadly, the idea that free speech perpetuates unequal power relations and that restrictions on this freedom are needed to level the playing field is deeply misguided. In fact, free speech may well be the most powerful engine of equality ever devised by humankind. Free speech is the difference between a political system where a joke or criticism of the political leader, ruling party, or dominant religion results in a one-way ticket to some distant gulag and one where even the most powerful leader cannot punish the most powerless citizen for such irreverence.

Allowing one group to punish the ideas of others doesn't equalize unequal power relations but inverts them, ultimately creating new structures of oppression rather than abolishing them altogether. Christians were once a small and persecuted sect. But once Christianity became the state religion of the Roman Empire, the Church and Christian rulers turned the tables and persecuted both pagans and heretics. Socialists and communists were hounded and censored in much of Europe prior to the Russian Revolution. Yet when the Bolsheviks grabbed political power there was no room for dissent in the dictatorship of the proletariat, whose leaders persecuted not only "enemies of the people" but the entire people in whose name

Lenin and Stalin claimed to govern. Many an advocate of national self-determination was tried and convicted by British colonial-era laws against sedition and enmity. Today British colonialism has been dislodged but colonial-era speech crimes have been left in place and recycled to shield the new rulers from the people whom decolonization was supposed to liberate.

There are of course dilemmas as to when and how democracies should react to movements who threaten to overthrow democracy. A robust commitment to free speech should be accompanied with a zero-tolerance policy toward organized threats, intimidation, and violence by groups seeking to establish parallel systems of authority. Groups of thugs and armed militias policing the streets to challenge democratic institutions and enforce vigilante justice against ideological enemies are a clear and present danger to both democracy and free speech. In an American context, this suggests that the real danger to democracy is not extremists exercising their rights under the First but rather under the Second Amendment.

As Spinoza, Mill, and Orwell warned, societal threats to free speech can be as stifling as government-imposed censorship. Yet, determining whether private action *undermines* or is an *exercise of* the culture of free speech can be difficult. After all, free speech does not grant anyone the right to have an op-ed published in the *New York Times* or a huge following on social media. Still there is a fundamental difference between reacting to ideas one loathes with scorn or criticism and demanding that specific viewpoints be purged and their authors and enablers punished with loss of livelihood or disciplinary sanctions. However committed to liberal and progressive values, influential educational and cultural institutions do not become more diverse, tolerant, and equal by banishing ideas, publications, and speakers that do not conform to the prevailing orthodoxy. It is particularly problematic when media institutions, social media platforms, and universities—who cannot function without free speech—come to internalize the idea that provocative opinions are "dangerous," "unsafe," or even "harmful" to their own staff, students, readers, and users. Such arguments were used to purge Pierre Bayle from the University of Rotterdam for his skepticism in the late seventeenth century, while academics critical of slavery and US participation in World War I were fired at elite American universities in the nineteenth and twentieth centuries after concerted campaigns by fellow academics and the press. There is good reason to believe that today's online inquisitions scouring social media for twenty-first century Cathars and Conversos will be seen as a regressive rather than a progressive force by future generations.

Eternal vigilance against both encroaching state power as well as the opaque, automated, and centralized privatized control of speech will be required for free expression to fulfill its promise as a necessary precondition for democracy, freedom, and equality.

Most important for the future of free speech is that those of us who have benefitted from the unprecedented advances in human affairs that 2,500 years of this counterintuitive, revolutionary, and deeply consequential idea have helped bring about resist the force of free speech entropy. It is up to each of us to defend a culture tolerant of heretical ideas, use our system of "open vigilance" to limit the reach of disinformation, agree to disagree without resorting to harassment or hate, and treat free speech as a principle to be upheld universally rather than a prop to be selectively invoked for narrow tribalist point scoring. Or to quote George Orwell: "If large numbers of people are interested in freedom of speech, there will be freedom of speech, even if the law forbids it; if public opinion is sluggish, inconvenient minorities will be persecuted, even if laws exist to protect them."

Breaking Milton's Curse will require much effort as we strive against the temptation to give in to the intolerant impulses of our biases and ideological blind spots that justify silencing the Others for the common good. Yet, the fact that groups whose religious or ideological differences were once thought to be irreconcilable matters of life and death now flourish side by side in open democracies is a testament to the true power of a vibrant culture of freedom of speech.

Free speech is still an experiment, and no one can guarantee the outcome of providing a free, equal, and instant voice to billions of people. But a careful look at history suggests that the experiment is a noble one. For while free speech may often seem like an abstract and theoretical principle when confronted with concrete and tangible threats and harms, it is a principle based on millennia of practical and often bloody experience with the consequences of its denial and suppression. For all its flaws, a world with less free speech will also be less tolerant, democratic, enlightened, innovative, free, and fun.

Acknowledgments

This book is the culmination of a journey that began some five years ago when I decided to start a podcast series on the history of free speech called *Clear and Present Danger: A History of Free Speech*. There is no way I could have completed this journey without the support of numerous people and institutions for which I am deeply grateful.

First and foremost I want to thank Greg Lukianoff, president of the Foundation of Individual Rights in Education (FIRE). When I pitched my idea to Greg back in 2016, he and FIRE provided me with financial support, an in-house editor (thank you, Araz Shipley!), and the ability to rely on the amazing resource that is FIRE, an organization with free speech encoded in its very DNA. Moreover, throughout my writing I have been able to bounce ideas off Greg, whose refined free speech theories have helped me think more clearly about many of the issues grappled with in this book. Without Greg neither the podcast nor this book would have been possible.

I also owe a huge debt of gratitude to my research assistant, Mathias Meier, who for four years never failed to excel with an attention for detail and the ability to point out weak spots in my argumentation or sources. Watching Mathias grow into a historian in his own right along the way has been a true privilege, and I'm sure he is destined for great things.

A number of historians, scholars, and experts have generously provided invaluable comments, criticism, and perspective on earlier parts of the manuscript. I'm eternally grateful to Peter Adamson, Heidi Tworek, David Nash, Samuel Moyn, Stephen Solomon, Ron Collins, Nadine Strossen, Wiep van Bunge, Raghav Mendiratta, Stephen A. Smith, John Samples, Natalie Alkiviadou, Jonathan Rauch, Flemming Rose, Richard Wingfield, Steven Pinker, Jonas Nordin, Bent Blüdnikov, Christine Caldwell Ames, Randy Robertson, Charles Walton, Frederik Stjernfelt, and above all Paul Cartledge, whose continuous feedback and encouragement over the years have meant so much to me. Needless to say, all errors and shortcomings are my sole responsibility.

I also want to thank David Patrikarakos, without whom I would have never encountered my publisher, Lara Heimert, whose immediate faith in this book project I'll always be grateful for. I'm also deeply grateful for the careful and patient editing of Emma Berry, as well as that of Brandon Proia, Sarah Caro, and Brittany Smail. Finally, I owe a huge debt of gratitude to my wife Sarah and my children Leo and Norma, who have had to put up with an (even more) absent minded husband and father for so long.

Copenhagen, June 2021

Notes

Introduction

1. D. M. Loades, "The Theory and Practice of Censorship in Sixteenth-Century England," *Transactions of the Royal Historical Society* 24 (1974): 147.

2. Dirck Coornhert, *Synod on the Freedom of Conscience* (1582), trans. and ed. Gerrit Voogt (Amsterdam: Amsterdam University Press, 2008), 176.

3. Karl Popper, *The Open Society and Its Enemies* (1945; repr., Princeton: Princeton University Press, 2013).

4. Eric Heinze, *Hate Speech and Democratic Citizenship* (Oxford: Oxford University Press, 2016), 129–137.

5. Erasmus, *Adagia* 2.1.1 (1525), in *The 'Adages' of Erasmus*, trans. Margaret Mann Phillips (Cambridge: Cambridge University Press, 1964), 145–146.

6. Elie Luzac, *Reinier Vryaart openhartige brieven, etc.* [1781–1784], 1:144, trans. Wyger Velema, in *Early French and German Defenses of Freedom of the Press*, ed. Johan Christian Laursen and Johan van der Zande (Leiden: Brill, 2003), 32.

7. "LATEST BY TELEGRAPH," *New York Times*, August 19, 1858, https://timesmachine.nytimes.com/timesmachine/1858/08/19/78859815.pdf?pdf_redirect=true&ip=0.

8. Alexander Meiklejohn, *Political Freedom* (1948; repr., Westport, CT: Greenwood Press, 1979), 86–87.

9. Jeffrey Goldberg, "Why Obama Fears for Our Democracy," *Atlantic*, November 16, 2020, www.theatlantic.com/ideas/archive/2020/11/why-obama-fears-for-our-democracy/617087.

Chapter 1: Ancient Beginnings

1. The Hittite Laws 173a, trans. Harry A. Hoffner, in *Law Collections from Mesopotamia and Asia Minor*, 2nd ed., ed. Martha T. Roth (Atlanta: Scholars Press, 1997), 234.

2. Exodus 22:28; 1 Kings 21:8–14. See also Edwin M. Good, "Capital Punishment and Its Alternatives in Ancient Near Eastern Law," *Stanford Law Review* 19 (1967): 965.

3. The Instruction of Ptah-Hotep, in *The Sacred Books and Early Literature of the East*, ed. Charles F. Horne (New York: Parke, Austin & Lipscomb, 1917), 2:62–78.

4. Confucius, *The Analects* 1.2, trans. Roger T. Ames and Henry Rosemont (New York: Random House, 1998), 71.

5. Sima Qian, *Historical Records*, trans. Raymond Dawson, in *The First Emperor—Selections from the Historical Records*, ed. K. E. Brashier (Oxford: Oxford University Press, 2007), 74–78.

6. Derk Bodde, "The State and Empire of Ch'in," in *The Cambridge History of China*, ed. Denis Twitchett and Michael Loewe, vol. 1, *The Chi'in and Han Empires* (Cambridge: Cambridge University Press, 1986), 72.

7. Code of Ur-Nammu 25, in Roth, *Law Collections*, 20.

8. Middle Assyrian Laws A 2, trans. Daniel D. Luckenbill, Internet Ancient History Sourcebook, ed. Paul Halsall, https://sourcebooks.fordham.edu/ancient/1075assyriancode.asp.

9. Code of Hammurabi 282, 127, in Roth, *Law Collections*, 132, 105.

10. Ezra 1:1–8; Chronicles 36:22–23.

11. See, for example, UN, *Note to Correspondents* no. 3699, October 13, 1971, https://ask.un.org/loader?fid=8500&type=1&key=517c22dc0833d0e1aed9ca958d30fc4c.

12. See, for example, The Behistun Inscription 2.13–14; and Herodotus 3.35.5.

13. The Edicts of King Ashoka 7, 12, trans. Ven. S. Dhammika (Kandy, Sri Lanka: Buddhist Publication Society, 1993).

14. Thorkild Jacobsen, "Primitive Democracy in Ancient Mesopotamia," *Journal of Near Eastern Studies* 2, no. 3 (1943): 159–172; Arnaldo Momigliano, "Freedom of Speech in Antiquity," in *Dictionary of the History of Ideas*, ed. Philip P. Wiener, 252–263, http://xtf.lib.virginia.edu/xtf/view?docId=DicHist/uvaGenText/tei/DicHist2.xml;chunk.id=dv2-31;toc.depth=1;toc.id=dv2-31;brand=default.

15. Aristotle, *The Politics* 2.1273a; Momigliano, "Freedom of Speech in Antiquity," 254.

16. Thucydides 2.37, trans. Rex Warner (Baltimore: Penguin Books, 1972), 117.

17. Herodotus 5.78.

18. Thucydides 2.40.

19. Aeschines, *Against Timarchus* 1.27.

20. Arlene Saxonhouse, *Free Speech and Democracy in Ancient Athens* (Cambridge: Cambridge University Press, 2006), 29.

21. George Grote, *A History of Greece* (New York: Harper & Bros., 1857), 6:149.

22. Momigliano, "Freedom of Speech in Antiquity," 260.

23. Demosthenes, *Against Leptines* 20.

24. Demosthenes, *Funeral Oration* 26, trans. Ian Worthington, in *Demosthenes, Speeches 60 and 61, Prologues, Letters* (Austin: University of Texas Press, 2006), 33.

25. Demosthenes, *For the Liberty of the Rhodians*, trans. J. H. Vince, in *Orations* (Cambridge, MA: Harvard University Press, 1930), 1:413.

26. Mogens Herman Hansen, *The Athenian Democracy in the Age of Demosthenes* (Norman: University of Oklahoma Press, 1999), 205–212.

27. Saxonhouse, *Free Speech and Democracy*, 44.

28. Plato, *Protagoras* 319–320, trans. Stanley Lombardo and Karen Bell (Indianapolis: Hackett, 1992).

29. Aristotle, *The Politics* 7.17, trans. Benjamin Jowett, in *The Politics and the Constitution of Athens*, ed. Stephen Everson (Cambridge: Cambridge University Press, 1996), 193.

30. Alan Sommerstein, "Harassing the Satirist: The Alleged Attempts to Prosecute Aristophanes," in *Free Speech in Classical Antiquity*, ed. Ineke Sluiter and Ralph M. Rosen (Leiden: Brill, 2004), 146.

31. Dawn B. Sova, *Banned Plays: Censorship Histories of 125 Stage Dramas* (New York: Facts on File, 2004), 151.

32. Thucydides 6–7.

33. Thucydides 8.66, trans. Richard Crawley (London, 1874), 587.

34. Aristotle, *The Athenian Constitution* 35.

35. Xenophon, *Hellenica* 2.3.24–25.

36. Diogenes Laertius, *Lives of Eminent Philosophers* 2.40, trans. Robert D. Hicks (Cambridge, MA: Harvard University Press, 1959), 1:171. See also, Mogens Herman Hansen, *The Trial of Sokrates, From the Athenian Point of View* (Copenhagen: The Royal Danish Academy of Sciences and Letters, 1995), 16.

37. Plato, *Gorgias* 521a2–e2, in Marlein van Raalte, "Socratic *Parrhêsia* and Its Afterlife in Plato's *Laws*," in Sluiter and Rosen, *Free Speech in Classical Antiquity*, 293.

38. Paul Cartledge, *Democracy: A Life* (New York: Oxford University Press, 2016), 175.

39. Hansen, *The Trial of Sokrates*.

40. James Madison, "Federalist No. 55," 1788, in *The Federalist*, ed. George W. Carey and James McClellan (Indianapolis: Liberty Fund, 2001), 288.

41. Livy 2.1.

42. Law of the Twelve Tables 8.1, frag. (1a) from Cicero, *On the Republic* 4.12 (Augustine, *The City of God* 2.9), trans. T. L. Mears, in *Freedom of Expression: Foundational Documents and Historical Arguments*, comp. Stephen A. Smith (Oxford: Oxbridge, 2018), 2.

43. Henrik Mouritsen, *Politics in the Roman Republic* (Cambridge: Cambridge University Press, 2017), 16–17, 25–26, 39–41.

44. Arnoldo Momigliano and Tim J. Cornell, "Senate," in *The Oxford Classical Dictionary*, 4th ed., ed. Simon Hornblower et al. (Oxford: Oxford University Press, 2012).

45. Momigliano, "Freedom of Speech in Antiquity," 261.

46. Mouritsen, *Politics in the Roman Republic*, 5, 36, 80.

47. Cicero, *Pro Flacco* 16, trans. Charles D. Yonge (New York: Henry G. Bohn, 1856).

48. Cicero, *Letters to Atticus* 1.16, *Pro Flacco* 18, in *The Fall of the Roman Republic and Related Essays*, comp. Peter A. Brunt (Oxford: Clarendon Press, 1988), 53–54, 315–316.

49. Brunt, *The Fall of the Roman Republic*, 300.

50. Philipp Blom, *A Wicked Company: The Forgotten Radicalism of the European Enlightenment* (New York: Basic Books, 2010), 186, Kindle.

51. Tacitus, *The Annals* 4.35, trans. The Oxford Translation, rev., in *The Works of Tacitus* (New York: Harper & Bros., 1865), 1:177.

52. Frederick H. Cramer, "Bookburning and Censorship in Ancient Rome: A Chapter from the History of Freedom of Speech," *Journal of the History of Ideas* 6, no. 2 (1945): 159.

53. Cassius Dio, *Roman History* 43.10, trans. Earnest Cary (London: William Heinemann, 1916), 4:227.

54. Cassius Dio 45.18–26, 47.39, 47.8, trans. Earnest Cary (Cambridge, MA: Harvard University Press, 1917), 4:227, 5:197.

55. Suetonius, *Augustus* 36, 54–56. See also, Cramer, "Bookburning and Censorship," 163–164.

56. Suetonius, *Augustus* 31.

57. Cramer, "Bookburning and Censorship," 167.

58. Cramer, "Bookburning and Censorship," 168–169.

59. Tacitus, *Annals* 1.72, 4.22, trans. Cramer, "Bookburning and Censorship," 170.

60. Cramer, "Bookburning and Censorship in Ancient Rome."

61. Suetonius, *Caligula* 16.1.

62. Tacitus, *Annals* 1.81; Cramer, "Bookburning and Censorship," 178–179.

63. Tacitus, *Annals* 2.32, 3.50–51.

64. Suetonius, *Tiberius* 58, 61.3, trans. John C. Rolfe (Cambridge, MA: Harvard University Press, 1914), 1:395.

65. Tacitus, *Annals* 4.34.2, trans. Mary R. McHugh, "Historiography and Freedom of Speech: The Case of Cremutius Cordus," in Sluiter and Rosen, *Free Speech in Classical Antiquity*, 393.

66. Tacitus, *Annals* 4.34–35, trans. Cramer, "Bookburning and Censorship," 193, 196.

67. Matthew 26–27.

68. Leonard Levy, *Blasphemy—Verbal Offense Against the Sacred, from Moses to Salman Rushdie* (Chapel Hill: The University of North Carolina Press, 1993), chap. 2.

69. Acts 6–26.

70. Panayotis Coutsoumpos, *Paul of Tarsus: An Introduction to the Man, the Mission and His Message* (Eugene, OR: Wipf & Stock, 2018), 143.

71. Momigliano, "Freedom of Speech in Antiquity," 256, 258, 262.

72. Tacitus, *Annals* 15.44.

73. Eusebius, *Ecclesiastical History* 2.25.

74. William Frend, *Martyrdom and Persecution in the Early Church* (Oxford: Basil Blackwell, 1965), 537.

75. Diarmaid MacCulloch, *Christianity: The First Three Thousand Years* (New York: Viking, 2010), 189–190.

76. Constantine I and Licinius, Edict of Milan, trans. Merrick Whitcomb et al., *Translations and Reprints from the Original Sources of European History* (Philadelphia: University of Pennsylvania, 1897), 4:29–30.

77. Ammianus Marcellinus, *History* 29.1.40–29.2.4. See also, Eric Berkowitz, *Dangerous Ideas: A Brief History of Censorship in the West, From the Ancients to Fake News* (Boston: Beacon Press, 2021), 49–50.

78. Theodosian Code 16.1.12, trans. Clyde Pharr, *The Theodosian Code and Novels and the Sirmondian Constitutions* (Union, NJ: The Lawbook Exchange, 2001), 440.

79. Levy, *Blasphemy*, 44.

80. Daniel P. Sheridan, "The Catholic Case: The Index of Prohibited Books," *Journal of Hindu-Christian Studies* 19 (2006): 22–26; Berkowitz, *Dangerous Ideas*, 72.

81. Demetrios J. Constantelos, "Paganism and the State in the Age of Justinian," *Catholic Historical Review* 50, no. 3 (1964): 372–380.

82. Simon Corcoran, "Anastasius, Justinian, and the Pagans: A Tale of Two Law Codes and a Papyrus," *Journal of Late Antiquity* 2, no. 2 (2009): 198–199.

83. Catherine Brewer, "The Status of the Jews in Roman Legislation: The Reign of Justinian 527–565 CE," *European Judaism: A Journal for the New Europe* 38, no. 2 (2005): 127–139.

84. Justinian Code Novel 77.1, trans. Fred H. Blume, *Annotated Justinian Code*, ed. Timothy Kearley (Laramie, WY: College of Law, George William Hopper Law Library, 2008), www.uwyo.edu/lawlib/blume-justinian/_files /docs/novel61-80/novel61-80.htm.

85. Dirk Rohmann, *Christianity, Book-Burning and Censorship in Late Antiquity* (Berlin: Walter de Gruyter, 2016), 8.

86. Ramsay MacMullen, *Christianizing the Roman Empire, A.D. 100–400* (New Haven: Yale University Press, 1984), 6.

87. Ramsay MacMullen, *Christianity and Paganism in the Fourth to Eighth Centuries* (New Haven: Yale University Press, 1997), 3.

Chapter 2: The Not-So-Dark Ages

1. Anthony C. Grayling, "The Persistence of the Faithful," *Guardian*, January 23, 2007, www.theguardian.com/commentisfree/2007/jan/23/progress andtheromancatholi.

2. See, for example, Charles Homer Haskins, *The Renaissance of the Twelfth Century* (1927; repr., Cambridge, MA: Harvard University Press, 1955), v–vi; and Jacques Le Goff, *Intellectuals in the Middle Ages* (1957; trans. and repr., Oxford: Wiley-Blackwell, 1993).

3. Robert I. Moore, *The Formation of a Persecuting Society: Authority and Deviance in Western Europe 950–1250*, 2nd ed. (Malden, MA: Blackwell, 2007), 10.

4. "37 The Book of Fighting [The Prohibition of Bloodshed]," Sunan an-Nasa'i 4059, vol. 5, bk. 37, Ḥadīth 4064, Sunnah.com, https://sunnah.com /nasai/37/94.

5. Mohammad Hashim Kamali, *Freedom of Expression in Islam* (Cambridge: Cambridge University Press, 1997), 247.

6. Yohanan Friedmann, *Tolerance and Coercion in Islam: Interfaith Relations in the Muslim Tradition* (Cambridge: Cambridge University Press, 2006), 149.

7. Frank Griffel, "Toleration and Exclusion: Al-Shāfiʿī and al-Ghazālī on the Treatment of Apostates," *Bulletin of the School of Oriental and African Studies* 64, no. 3 (2001): 349; Rudolph Peters and Gert J. J. De Vries, "Apostasy in Islam," *Die Welt des Islams* 17, no. 1/4 (1976–1977): 5.

8. Bernard Lewis, "Some Observations on the Significance of Heresy in the History of Islam," *Studia Islamica* 1 (1953): 43–63.

9. Griffel, "Toleration and Exclusion," 349n10.

10. Dimitri Gutas, *Greek Thought, Arabic Culture: The Graeco-Arabic Translation Movement in Baghdad and Early ʿAbbasaid Society* (London: Routledge, 1998), 28–29.

11. Gutas, *Greek Thought*, i.

12. S. Frederick Starr, *Lost Enlightenment: Central Asia's Golden Age from the Arab Conquest to Tamerlane* (Princeton: Princeton University Press, 2013), 75–76.

13. Peter Adamson, "302. On the Eastern Front: Philosophy in Syriac and Armenian," June 3, 2018, in *History of Philosophy Without Any Gaps*, podcast, https://historyofphilosophy.net/syriac-armenian.

14. Gutas, *Greek Thought*.

15. Gutas, *Greek Thought*, 2.

16. Ibn al-Nadim, *The Fihrist* 243.18–20; Gutas, *Greek Thought*, 133; Johannes Pedersen, *The Arabic Book* (1946; trans. and repr., Princeton: Princeton University Press, 1984), 115.

17. Gutas, *Greek Thought*, 152.

18. "Mihna," Oxford Islamic Studies Online, www.oxfordislamicstudies .com/article/opr/t125/e1510.

19. Michael Cooperson, "Two Abbasid Trials: Ahmad Ibn Hanbal and Hunayn b. Ishāq," *Al-Qantara* 22, no. 2 (2001): 383.

20. Lewis, "Some Observations," 79.

21. Cooperson, "Two Abbasid Trials," 375–393.

22. Christine Caldwell Ames, *Medieval Heresies: Christianity, Judaism, and Islam* (Cambridge: Cambridge University Press, 2015), 90.

23. Sarah Stroumsa, *Freethinkers of Medieval Islam: Ibn Al-Rāwandī, Abū Bakr Al-Rāzī and Their Impact on Islamic Thought* (Leiden: Brill, 1999); Sarah Stroumsa, "The Blinding Emerald: Ibn al-Rāwandī's Kitāb al-Zumurrud," *Journal of the American Oriental Society* 114, no. 2 (1994); Starr, *Lost Enlightenment*, 183.

24. Stroumsa "The Blinding Emerald," 177.

25. See, for example, John Leonard Thornton, *Medical Books, Libraries and Collectors* (London: Andre Deutsch / Grafton Books, 1966), 16.

26. Al-Rāzī, quoted in Starr, *Lost Enlightenment*, 181–183.

27. Stroumsa, *Freethinkers of Medieval Islam*, 12, 19.

28. Peter Adamson, "al-Kindi," *Stanford Encyclopedia of Philosophy*, Spring 2020 ed., ed. Edward N. Zalta, https://plato.stanford.edu/entries/al-kindi.

29. Therese-Anne Druart, "al-Farabi," *Stanford Encyclopedia of Philosophy*, Fall 2020 ed., ed. Edward N. Zalta, https://plato.stanford.edu/entries/al -farabi.

30. *Encyclopedia Britannica*, s.v. "Al-Bīrūnī," by George Saliba, last modified April 20, 2011, https://britannica.com/biography/al-Biruni.

31. Robert Audi, ed., *The Cambridge Dictionary of Philosophy*, 2nd ed. (Cambridge: Cambridge University Press, 1999), 63–64.

32. Adamson, *History of Philosophy Without Any Gaps*, episodes 138–142.

33. Eric J. Hanne, *Putting the Caliph in His Place: Power, Authority, and the Late Abbasid Caliphate* (Madison, WI: Fairleigh Dickinson University Press, 2007), 70; Ames, *Medieval Heresies*, 92, 168.

34. Frank Griffel, *Al-Ghazali's Philosophical Theology* (Oxford: Oxford University Press, 2009), 101–103.

35. Alexander Meleagrou-Hitchens, *Incitement: Anwar al-Awklaki's Western Jihad* (Cambridge, MA: Harvard University Press, 2020), 49, Kindle; Bernard Heykel, "On the Nature of Salafi Thought and Action," in *Global Salafism: Islam's New Religious Movement*, ed. Roel Meijer (Oxford: Oxford University Press, 2009), 38.

36. Friedmann, *Tolerance and Coercion in Islam*, 122.

37. Daniel Pipes, *The Rushdie Affair: The Novel, the Ayatollath and the West*, 2nd ed. (Abindgon: Routledge, 2017), 180; Kamali, *Freedom of Expression in Islam*, 299.

38. Emma Wadsworth-Jones, ed., *The Freedom of Thought Report 2020: Key Countries Edition* (Humanists International, 2020), 13.

39. Benjamin Wormald, "Beliefs About Sharia," in *The World's Muslims: Religion, Politics and Society*, Pew Research Center, April 30, 2013, www.pew forum.org/2013/04/30/the-worlds-muslims-religion-politics-society-beliefs-about-sharia.

40. See, for example, Gutas, *Greek Thought*, 176–177, 186.

41. Dirk Rohmann, *Christianity, Book-Burning and Censorship in Late Antiquity* (Berlin: Walter de Gruyter, 2016), 8.

42. Gutas, *Greek Thought*, 175–181.

43. See, for example, G. W. Trompf, "The Concept of the Carolingian Renaissance," *Journal of the History of Ideas* 34 (1973): 3–26; and "Christianity and Pagan Literature," Bede's Library, www.bede.org.uk/literature.htm#loss; Rohmann, *Christianity, Book-Burning and Censorship*, 8.

44. Jacques Le Goff, *Medieval Civilization* (1965; trans. and repr., Oxford: Blackwell, 1988), 326.

45. See, for example, Lynn White, *Medieval Technology and Social Change* (Oxford: Oxford University Press, 1962); and Kim Esmark and Brian Patrick McGuire, *Europa 1000–1300* (Roskilde, DK: Roskilde Universitetsforlag, 1999), 178–180.

46. See, for example, Le Goff, *Intellectuals in the Middle Ages*; and James Hannam, *God's Philosophers: How the Medieval World Laid the Foundations of Modern Science* (London: Icon Books, 2009), 59–60.

47. Jacques Verger, "Patterns," in *Universities in the Middle Ages*, ed. Hilde de Ridder-Symoens (Cambridge: Cambridge University Press, 1992), 55. See also, Alan B. Cobban, *The Medieval Universities: Their Development and Organization* (London: Methuen, 1975), 116.

48. Joseph Henrich, *The WEIRDest People in the World* (New York: Farrar, Straus and Giroux, 2020), 320–321, Kindle.

49. See, for example, Gordon Leff, "The Faculty of Arts," in de Ridder-Symoens, *Universities in the Middle Ages*, 311.

50. See, for example, Hannam, *God's Philosophers*, 380.

51. Edward Grant, *God and Reason in the Middle Ages* (Cambridge: Cambridge University Press, 2001), 356–364.

52. See, for example, Dorothea Weltecke, "The Medieval Period," in *The Oxford Handbook of Atheism*, ed. Stephen Bullivant and Michael Rose (Oxford: Oxford University Press, 2013), 167.

53. Grant, *God and Reason in the Middle Ages*, 9.

54. Weltecke, "The Medieval Period," 166.

55. See, for example, Monika Asztalos, "The Faculty of Theology," in de Ridder-Symoens, *Universities in the Middle Ages*, 420.

56. Hans Thijssen, "Master Amalric and the Amalricians: Inquisitorial Procedure and the Suppression of Heresy at the University of Paris," *Speculum* 71 (1996): 43–65; Hans Thijssen, *Censure and Heresy at the University of Paris 1200–1400* (Philadelphia: University of Pennsylvania Press, 1998), xi, 172.

57. Quoted in Thijssen, "Master Amalric," 45.

58. Robert of Courçon, Rules of the University of Paris, 1215, in *University Records and Life in the Middle Ages*, ed. Lynn Thorndike (New York: Columbia University Press, 1944), 103–104. See also, Asztalos, "The Faculty of Theology," 420–421.

59. Asztalos, "The Faculty of Theology," 421; Leff, "The Faculty of Arts," 320.

60. See, for example, Mia Münster-Swendsen, "Medieval Beginnings: The First Universities," *Fortid* 1 (2011): 29.

61. Edward Grant, ed., *A Source Book in Medieval Science* (Cambridge, MA: Harvard University Press, 1974), 42.

62. Asztalos, "The Faculty of Theology," 422.

63. Gregory IX, *Parens scientiarum*, papal bull, April 13, 1231, in *Chartularium Universitatis Parisiensis*, ed. Heinrich Denifle (Paris, 1889) 1:78–79, trans. Asztalos, "The Faculty of Theology," 422.

64. Leff, "The Faculty of Arts," 320.

65. See, for example, Hans Thijssen, "Condemnation of 1277," *Stanford Encyclopedia of Philosophy*, Winter 2018 ed., ed. Edward N. Zalta, https://plato.stanford.edu/entries/condemnation/; Thijssen, *Censure and Heresy at the University of Paris*, 43–44. See also, Asztalos, "The Faculty of Theology," 424–428.

66. Thijssen, "Condemnation of 1277."

67. Thijssen, *Censure and Heresy at the University of Paris*, 57–72.

68. William J. Courtenay, "Inquiry and Inquisition: Academic Freedom in Medieval Universities," *Church History* 58, no. 2 (1989): 170.

69. Harold J. Berman, *Law and Revolution: The Formation of the Western Legal Tradition* (Cambridge, MA: Harvard University Press, 1983), 23; Diarmaid MacCulloch, *Christianity: The First Three Thousand Years* (New York: Viking, 2010), 377; Jennifer Kolpacoff Deane, *A History of Medieval Heresy and Inquisition* (Plymouth: Rowman & Littlefield, 2011), 16.

70. Deane, *A History*, 4.

71. Moore, *The Formation of a Persecuting Society*.

72. Edward Peters, *Inquisition* (Berkeley: University of California Press, 1989), 44–52.

73. Moore, *The Formation of a Persecuting Society*, 4.

74. Deane, *A History*, 101.

75. Robert I. Moore, *The War on Heresy: Faith and Power in Medieval Europe* (London: Profile Books, 2012), 314.

76. Peters, *Inquisition*, 43; James B. Given, *Inquisition and Medieval Society: Power, Discipline, and Resistance in Languedoc* (Ithaca: Cornell University Press, 1997), 9–10.

77. Lucius III, *Ad abolendam*, papal bull, November 4, 1184, trans. Edward Peters, *Heresy and Authority in Medieval Europe* (Philadelphia: University of Pennsylvania Press, 1980), 171–172. See also, Ames, *Medieval Heresies*, 9, 213; and Deane, *A History*, 89.

78. Innocent III, *Vergentis in senium*, papal bull, March 25, 1199, trans. Peters, *Inquisition*, 48.

79. The Fourth Lateran Council Canon 3, 1215, trans. H. J. Schroeder, *Disciplinary Decrees of the General Councils* (St. Louis: B. Herder, 1937), 236–296, https://history.hanover.edu/courses/excerpts/344lat.html. See also, Peters, *Heresy and Authority*, 173–178; and Deane, *A History*, 90.

80. The Fourth Lateran Council Canons 67–70, 1215, trans. Schroeder, *Disciplinary Decrees*, 236–296, https://history.hanover.edu/courses/excerpts/344latj.html.

81. Ames, *Medieval Heresies*, 144; Moore, *The Formation of a Persecuting Society*, 27–42.

82. Moore, *The Formation of a Persecuting Society*, 10.

83. The Council of Toulouse Canon 14, 1229, trans. Peters, *Heresy and Authority*, 194–195. See also, Deane, *A History*, 95–96.

84. Colin Tatz and Winton Higgins, *The Magnitude of Genocide* (Santa Barbara: Praeger, 2016), 214. See also, Cullen Murphy, *God's Jury: The Inquisition and the Making of the Modern World* (Boston: Houghton Mifflin Harcourt, 2012), 33; and Ames, *Medieval Heresies*, 210–212.

85. Murphy, *God's Jury*, 49.

86. Gregory IX, *Ille humani generis*, papal bull, November 22, 1231, trans. Peters, *Heresy and Authority*, 197.

87. Peters, *Inquisition*, 55–57.

88. Thomas Aquinas, *Summa Theologica*, pt 2, vol. 2 (1271; repr., London: R. & T. Washbourne, 1917), in *Freedom of Religion: Foundational Documents and Historical Arguments*, comp. Stephen A. Smith (Oxford: Oxbridge, 2017), 19–21.

89. Peters, *Inquisition*, 16–17.

90. Moore, *The War on Heresy*, 302.

91. Deane, *A History*, 120.

92. Peters, *Inquisition*, 59.

93. Gregory IX, *Liber extra*, papal bull, 1234, trans. Peters, *Inquisition*, 62.

94. Jessie Sherwood, "The Inquisitor as Archivist, or Surprise, Fear, and Ruthless Efficiency in the Archives," *American Archivist* 75, no. 1 (2012): 56–80.

95. Jean-Louis Biget, "Bernard Gui," in *Oxford Encyclopedia of the Middle Ages*, ed. André Vauchez (Cambridge; James Clarke, 2005). See also, Murphy, *God's Jury*, 44–45.

96. Murphy, *God's Jury*, 45.

97. Given, *Inquisition and Medieval Society*, 79.

98. Given, *Inquisition and Medieval Society*, 65.

99. Bernard Gui, quoted in Given, *Inquisition and Medieval Society*, 54–55.

100. Given, *Inquisition and Medieval Society*, 73.

101. Anne Brenon, "Cathars, Albigensians," in Vauchez, *Oxford Encyclopedia of the Middle Ages*.

102. See, for example, Joanne Maguire Robinson, *Nobility and Annihilation in Marguerite Porete's "Mirror of Simple Souls"* (Albany: State University of New York Press, 2001), 27; and Deane, *A History*, 167–169.

103. Ames, *Medieval Heresies*, 287.

104. Francisco Bethencourt, *The Inquisition: A Global History 1478–1834*, trans. Jean Birrell (Cambridge: Cambridge University Press, 2009); Henry Charles Lea, *The Inquisition in the Spanish Dependencies* (1908; repr., Cambridge: Cambridge University Press, 2010).

105. Ferdinand II and Isabella I, The Alhambra Decree for Expulsion of the Jews, March 31, 1492, in Smith, *Freedom of Religion*, 27–28.

106. Henry Kamen, *The Spanish Inquisition: A Historical Revision*, 4th ed. (New Haven: Yale University Press, 2014), 104, 367–368, Kindle.

107. See, for example, Julián Juderías, *La Layenda Negra* (Madrid, 1914); and Charles Gibson, ed., *The Black Legend: Anti-Spanish Attitudes in the Old World and the New* (New York: Alfred A. Knopf, 1971).

108. Kamen, *The Spanish Inquisition*, 104–107, 330–332.

109. Juan de Mariana, *Historia general de España* (1592; repr., Madrid: Biblioteca de Autores Españoles, 1950), 31:202, trans. Kamen, *The Spanish Inquisition*, 115.

110. Violet Moller, *The Map of Knowledge: How Classical Ideas Were Lost and Found* (London: Picador, 2019), 112, Kindle. See also, Haig Bosmajian, *Burning Books* (Jefferson: McFarland, 2006), 64.

Chapter 3: The Great Disruption

1. See, for example, Elisabeth Eisenstein, *The Printing Press as an Agent of Change*, abridged ed. (New York: Cambridge University Press, 1979).

2. J. M. Lenhart, "Pre-Reformation Printed Books," *Franciscan Studies* 14 (1935): 7. See also, Lucien Febvre and Henri-Jean Martin, *The Coming of the Book: The Impact of Printing 1450–1800*, trans. David Gerard (London: NLB, 1976), 178–179, 184–185.

3. Febvre and Martin, *The Coming of the Book*, 208, 212.

4. Eltjo Buringh and Jan Luiten van Zanden, "Charting the 'Rise of the West': Manuscripts and Printed Books in Europe, A Long-Term Perspective from the Sixth Through Eighteenth Centuries," *Journal of Economic History* 69, no. 2 (2009): 416–417.

5. John Naughton, *From Gutenberg to Zuckerberg: Disruptive Innovation in the Age of the Internet* (London: Quercus, 2012), 25, Kindle.

6. Jerry Brotton, *The Renaissance Bazaar* (Oxford: Oxford University Press, 2002), 79.

7. Buringh and Van Zanden, "Charting the 'Rise of the West,'" 434.

8. See, for example, Eisenstein, *The Printing Press as an Agent of Change*.

9. Jeremiah Dittmar, "Information Technology and Economic Change: The Impact of the Printing Press," *Quarterly Journal of Economics* 126, no. 3 (2011): 1113–1172.

10. See, for example, Elizabeth Eisenstein, *The Printing Revolution in Early Modern Europe*, 2nd ed. (New York: Cambridge University Press, 2005), 141–142.

11. Niccolò Machiavelli, *Discourses on the First Ten Books of Titus Livius* [1516], in *The Historical, Political, and Diplomatic Writings of Niccolo Machiavelli*, ed. and trans. Christian E. Detmold (Boston: J. R. Osgood, 1882).

12. Erasmus, *The Education of a Christian Prince* (1516), trans. Neil M. Cheshire and Michael J. Heath, ed. Lisa Jardine (Cambridge: Cambridge University Press, 1997), 88.

13. See, for example, Johannes Pedersen, *The Arabic Book* (1946; trans. and repr., Princeton: Princeton University Press, 1984), 113–130; Febvre and Martin, *The Coming of the Book*, 212; and Metin Coşgel, Thomas Miceli, and Jared

Rubin, "Guns and Books: Legitimacy, Revolt and Technological Change in the Ottoman Empire," *Economics Working Papers*, Paper 200912 (2009), 2.

14. See, for example, Coşgel et al., "Guns and Books," 15; and Pedersen, *The Arabic Book*, 133.

15. See, for example, Kathryn A. Schwartz, "Did Ottoman Sultans Ban Print?" *Book History* 20 (2017): 1–39.

16. Bernard Lewis, *What Went Wrong? Western Impact and Middle Eastern Response* (Oxford: Oxford University Press, 2002), 142.

17. Coşgel et al., "Guns and Books," 22; Pedersen, *The Arabic Book*, 134.

18. Pedersen, *The Arabic Book*, 133. See also, Buringh and Van Zanden, "Charting the 'Rise of the West,'" 436.

19. See, for example, Jared Rubin, *Rulers, Religion, and Riches: Why the West Got Rich and the Middle East Did Not* (Cambridge: Cambridge University Press, 2017). See also, Lewis, *What Went Wrong?*.

20. Eisenstein, *The Printing Press as an Agent of Change*.

21. See, for example, Irene Bertschek et al., "The Economic Impacts of Broadband Internet: A Survey," *Review of Network Economics* 14, no. 4 (2016): 201–227.

22. See, for example, Eisenstein, *The Printing Press as an Agent of Change*, 437.

23. Erasmus, *Adagia* 2.1.1, 1525, in *The 'Adages' of Erasmus*, trans. Margaret Mann Phillips (Cambridge: Cambridge University Press, 1964), 145–146. See also, Ann M. Blair, *Too Much to Know: Managing Scholarly Information Before the Modern Age* (New Haven: Yale University Press, 2010), 55–56.

24. See, for example, Eisenstein, *The Printing Press as an Agent of Change*, 436–437; and Hans Peter Broedel, *The Malleus Maleficarum and the Construction of Witchcraft* (Manchester: Manchester University Press, 2003).

25. Brian P. Levack, *The Witch-Hunt in Early Modern Europe*, 3rd ed. (Harlow: Pearson Education Limited, 2006), 21–23.

26. Eisenstein, *The Printing Press as an Agent of Change*, 118, 317.

27. Jürgen Wilke, "Censorship and Freedom of the Press," European History Online, May 8, 2013, http://ieg-ego.eu/en/threads/european-media/censorship-and-freedom-of-the-press.

28. Richard A. Glenn, "Indexes," in *Censorship: A World Encyclopedia*, ed. Derek Jones (Abingdon: Routledge, 2001), 1150.

29. Edoardo Tortarolo, *The Invention of Free Press: Writers and Censorship in Eighteenth Century Europe* (Dordrecht: Springer, 2016), 7.

30. See, for example, Andrew Pettegree, *Brand Luther* (New York: Penguin Books, 2015), 70–71.

31. Peter J. Riga, "Marsiglio of Padova: Father and Creator of the Modern Legal System," *Hastings Law Journal* 29, no. 6 (1978): 1421–1445.

32. Niall Ferguson, "When Gutenberg Met Luther," in *The Square and the Tower* (New York: Penguin, 2017), 108, Kindle.

33. Martin Luther to Archbishop Albrecht of Mainz, October 31, 1517, trans. Gottfried Krodel, in *Documents from the History of Lutheranism, 1517–1750*, ed. Eric Lund (Minneapolis: Fortress Press, 2002), 17.

34. Martin Luther to Leo X, May 30, 1518, trans. Hans J. Hillerbrand, *The Reformation: A Narrative History Related by Contemporary Observers and Participants* (New York: Harper & Row, 1964), 54.

35. Pettegree, *Brand Luther*, 81. See also, Robert W. Scribner, *For the Sake of Simple Folk: Popular Propaganda for the German Reformation* (Oxford: Clarendon Press, 1994).

36. See, for example, Ferguson, "When Gutenberg Met Luther," 108.

37. Arthur G. Dickens, *Reformation and Society in Sixteenth Century Europe* (New York: Harcourt, Brace and World, 1968), 51.

38. Pettegree, *Brand Luther*, 145.

39. Martin Luther, quoted in M. H. Black, "The Printed Bible," in *Cambridge History of the Bible*, ed., S. L. Greenslade, vol. 3, *The West from the Reformation to the Present Day* (Cambridge: Cambridge University Press, 1963), 432. See also, Eisenstein, *The Printing Press as an Agent of Change*, 304.

40. Ferguson, "When Gutenberg Met Luther," 109.

41. Leo X, *Exsurge domine*, papal bull, June 15, 1520, Papal Encyclicals Online, www.papalencyclicals.net/Leo10/l10exdom.htm.

42. Scott W. Hahn and Benjamin Wiker, *Politicizing the Bible: The Roots of Historical Criticism and the Secularization of Scripture 1300–1700* (New York: Herder & Herder, 2017), loc. 5253, Kindle.

43. Martin Luther, *The Babylonian Captivity of the Church* 3.30 (1520), in *Works of Martin Luther with Introductions and Notes*, comp. J. J. Schindel and C. M. Jacobs (Philadelphia: A. Holman Company, 1915), 2:179–187; Diarmaid MacCulloch, *Christianity: The First Three Thousand Years* (New York: Viking, 2010), 610.

44. "How Luther Went Viral," *Economist*, December 17, 2011, www.economist.com/christmas-specials/2011/12/17/how-luther-went-viral.

45. Hahn and Wiker, *Politicizing the Bible*, loc. 5253–5265.

46. Charles V, The Edict of Worms, May 25, 1521, trans. James Harvey Robinson, *Readings in European History* (Boston: Ginn, 1905), 2:83–88.

47. Jonathan Israel, *The Dutch Republic: Its Rise, Greatness, and Fall 1477–1806* (Oxford: Oxford University Press, 1995), 79–80.

48. Allyson F. Creasman, *Censorship and Civic Order in Reformation Germany, 1517–1648: 'Printed Poison & Evil Talk'* (London: Routledge, 2012), 51.

49. Patrick Collinson, *The Reformation* (London: Weidenfeld & Nicolson, 2003), chap. 4.

50. Brotton, *The Renaissance Bazaar*, 79.

51. Joseph Henrich, *The WEIRDest People in the World* (New York: Farrar, Straus and Giroux, 2020), 9–16, Kindle.

52. James 5:1–6, *The New Oxford Annotated Bible*, ed. Michael D. Coogan et al. (Oxford: Oxford University Press, 2018), 1772.

53. Peter Marshall, *The Reformation: A Very Short Introduction* (Oxford: Oxford University Press, 2009), 20–21.

54. Martin Luther, *Against the Robbing and Murdering Hordes of Peasants* (1525), trans. Ernest G. Rupp and Benjamin Drewery, *Martin Luther, Documents of Modern History* (London: Edward Arnold, 1970), 121–126. See also, Pettegree, *Brand Luther*, 242–243.

55. Hans J. Hillerbrand, *The World of the Reformation* (New York: Scribner's, 1973), 83. See also, *Encyclopedia Britannica*, s.v. "Peasants' War," last modified August 20, 2020, www.britannica.com/event/Peasants-War.

56. See, for example, Quentin Skinner, *The Foundation of Modern Political Thought* (Cambridge: Cambridge University Press, 1978), 77–80; and Roland H. Bainton, *Here I Stand: A Life of Martin Luther* (New York: Abingdon-Cokesbury Press, 1950), 267, 375.

57. Skinner, *The Foundation of Modern Political Thought*, 80.

58. Martin Luther, 1527, quoted in Bainton, *Here I Stand*, 375–376.

59. See, for example, Norman Cohn, *The Pursuit of the Millennium: Revolutionary Millenarians and Mystical Anarchists of the Middle Ages* (Oxford: Oxford University Press, 1970), 267; and Marshall, *The Reformation*, 114.

60. Philipp Melanchthon and Martin Luther, memorandum, 1536, quoted in Bainton, *Here I Stand*, 376–377. See also, Marshall, *The Reformation*, 113–114.

61. Romans 13:1–2, Coogan et al., *The New Oxford Annotated Bible*, 1632. See also, Skinner, *The Foundation of Modern Political Thought*, 15–16.

62. Paul F. Grendler, "Printing and Censorship," in *The Cambridge History of Renaissance Philosophy*, ed. C. B. Schmitt et al. (Cambridge: Cambridge University Press, 1988), 44; Creasman, *Censorship and Civic Order*, 10–11.

63. Bainton, *Here I Stand*, 376.

64. MacCulloch, *Christianity*, 210.

65. Martin Luther, *An exposition of the eighty-second Psalm*, 1530, trans. Henry E. Jacobs and Adolph Spaeth, *Works of Martin Luther, with Introductions and Notes* (Philadelphia: A.J. Holman Company, 1932), vol. 4. See also Bainton, *Here I Stand*, 376.

66. Martin Luther, *The Jews and their Lies*, 1543, trans. Franklin Sherman and Helmut T. Lehmann, *Luther's Works* (Philadelphia: Fortress Press, 1971), 47:268–293.

67. Diarmaid MacCulloch, *Reformation: Europe's House Divided* (London: Penguin, 2003), 274–275.

68. Creasman, *Censorship and Civic Order*, 118–119.

69. World Values Survey, www.worldvaluessurvey.org/wvs.jsp; Christine Tamir, Aidan Connaughton, and Ariana Monique Salazar, *The Global God Divide*, Pew Research Center, July 20, 2020, www.pewresearch.org /global/2020/07/20/the-global-god-divide; Joey Marshall, "The World's Most Committed Christians Live in Africa, Latin America—and the U.S.," Pew Research Center, August 22, 2018, www.pewresearch.org/fact-tank/2018/08/22 /the-worlds-most-committed-christians-live-in-africa-latin-america-and-the-u-s.

70. *Encyclopedia Britannica*, s.v. "Defender of the faith," last modified November 29, 2011, www.britannica.com/topic/defender-of-the-faith.

71. Hahn and Wiker, *Politicizing the Bible*, loc. 6272–6283; MacCulloch, *Reformation*, 203.

72. Cyndia Susan Clegg, "Tudor Literary Censorship," Oxford Handbooks Online, Oxford University Press, October 2014, www.oxfordhand books.com/view/10.1093/oxfordhb/9780199935338.001.0001/oxfordhb-9780 199935338-e-9; Wilke, "Censorship."

73. Thomas More, quoted in *Tudor Royal Proclamations*, ed. Paul L. Hughes and James F. Larkin (New Haven: Yale University Press, 1964), 1:194. See also, Alison Hudson, "The Book Banner Who Inspired Banned Books," *British Library*, September 28, 2016, https://blogs.bl.uk/digitisedmanuscripts/2016 /09/utopias-and-banned-books.html.

74. Hahn and Wiker, *Politicizing the Bible*, loc. 6881–6888; Collinson, *The Reformation*, 37; MacCulloch, *Reformation*, 203.

75. Hahn and Wiker, *Politicizing the Bible*, loc. 6899.

76. MacCulloch, *Reformation*, 203.

77. D. M. Loades, "The Theory and Practice of Censorship in Sixteenth-Century England," *Transactions of the Royal Historical Society* 24 (1974): 144, 147.

78. Edward I, Scandalum Magnatum, 1275, in *Freedom of Expression: Foundational Documents and Historical Arguments*, comp. Stephen A. Smith (Oxford: Oxbridge, 2018), 17.

79. Clegg, "Tudor Literary Censorship."

80. Collinson, *The Reformation*, 114.

81. Loades, "The Theory and Practice of Censorship," 144, 152; D. M. Loades, "The Press Under the Early Tudors: A Study in Censorship and Sedition," *Transactions of the Cambridge Bibliographical Society* 4, no. 1 (1964): 43, 45. See also, Wilke, "Censorship."

82. Loades, "The Theory and Practice of Censorship," 144; Debora Shuger, *Censorship and Cultural Sensibility: The Regulation of Language in Tudor-Stuart England* (Philadelphia: University of Pennsylvania Press, 2006), 73.

83. Quoted in Thomas Dunbar Ingram, *England and Rome: A History of the Relations Between the Papacy and English State and Church* (London, 1892), 248–249.

84. Loades, "The Theory and Practice of Censorship," 153–154.

85. Wilke, "Censorship"; Leonard Levy, *Blasphemy—Verbal Offense Against the Sacred, from Moses to Salman Rushdie* (Chapel Hill: The University of North Carolina Press, 1993), 89–90.

86. Peter Wentworth, "Speech in the House of Commons," February 1576, in *The Journals of All the Parliaments During the Reign of Queen Elizabeth* (Shannon, Ire.: Irish University Press, 1682), 236–251.

87. Smith, *Freedom of Expression*, 26, 35; "Elizabethan government," BBC, https://www.bbc.co.uk/bitesize/guides/zppbtv4/revision/5.

88. Shuger, *Censorship and Cultural Sensibility*.

89. Shuger, *Censorship and Cultural Sensibility*, 9.

90. Cyndia Susan Clegg, "Censorship and the Courts of Star Chamber and High Commission in England to 1640," *Journal of Modern European* 3, no. 1 (2005): 50–80.

91. Norman Davies, *Europe: A History* (London: Pimlico, 1997), 490–492.

92. Davies, *Europe*, 493.

93. Marshall, *The Reformation*, 110–111.

94. *Encyclopedia Britannica*, s.v. "Michael Servetus," last modified October 23, 2020, https://www.britannica.com/biography/Michael-Servetus#ref161410.

95. Davies, *Europe*, 493; Collinson, *The Reformation*, 80–81; Stefan Zweig, *Erasmus: The Right to Heresy*, trans. Eden and Cedar Paul (London: Souvenir Press, 1979), 291.

96. Zweig, *Erasmus*, 297.

97. Teresa M. Bejan, *Mere Civility: Disagreement and the Limits of Toleration* (Cambridge, MA: Harvard University Press, 2017), 31, Kindle.

98. Zweig, *Erasmus*, 239.

99. Sebastian Castellio, *Concerning Heretics*, 1554, trans. Roland H. Bainton (New York: Columbia University Press, 1935), 122–123, 145.

100. Philip Benedict, "*Un roi, une loi, deux fois*: Parameters for the History of Catholic-Reformed Co-existence in France, 1555–1685," in *Tolerance and Intolerance in the European Reformation*, ed. Ole Peter Grell and Robert W. Scribner (Cambridge, 1996); MacCulloch, *Reformation*, 306–308.

101. Henry IV of France, Edict of Nantes, April 13, 1598, *Translations and Reprints from the Original Sources of European History*, ed. Merrick Whitcomb et al. (Philadelphia: University of Pennsylvania, 1897), 3:30–32. See also, Benedict, "*Un roi*," 75; Michael Clodfelter, *Warfare and Armed Conflicts: A Statistical Encyclopedia of Casualty and Other Figures*, 4th ed. (Jefferson, NC: McFarland, 2017), 14.

102. The Council of Trent, Fourth Session, April 8, 1546, *The Canons and Decrees of the Sacred and Œcumenical Council of Trent*, ed. and trans. J. Waterworth (Chicago, 1848).

103. Grendler, "Printing and Censorship," 45.

104. Grendler, "Printing and Censorship," 45.

105. See, for example, Cullen Murphy, *God's Jury: The Inquisition and the Making of the Modern World* (Boston and New York: Houghton Mifflin Harcourt, 2012), 118–119.

106. Jesús Martinez de Bujanda and Marcella Richter, *Index des Livres Interdits*, vol. 11: *Index Librorum Prohibitorum* (Québec, 2002), 34.

107. Robert E. McNally, SJ, "The Council of Trent and Vernacular Bibles," *Theological Studies* 27, no. 2 (1966): 226.

108. Patrizia Delpiano, *Church and Censorship in Eighteenth-Century Italy*, (Routledge, 2017), 9, Kindle.

109. Grendler, "Printing and Censorship," 52.

110. Murphy, *God's Jury*, 120, 122.

111. MacCulloch, *Reformation*, 299–300; Creasman, *Censorship and Civic Order*, 9–10.

112. Charles V to Juana of Austria, May 25, 1558, in Henry Kamen, *The Spanish Inquisition: A Historical Revision*, 4th ed. (New Haven: Yale University Press, 2014), 155, Kindle.

113. Kamen, *The Inquisition*, 152–155 (numbers on 157–160).

114. Murphy, *God's Jury*, 131.

115. 1 Chron 16:30, Psalm 96:10, Coogan et al., *The New Oxford Annotated Bible*, 608, 862.

116. See, for example, Alberto A. Martínez, *Burned Alive: Bruno, Galileo and the Inquisition* (London: Reaktion Books, 2018).

117. Galileo, *Istoria e dimostrazioni intorno alle macchie solari e loro accidenti* (Rome, 1613), trans. Stillman Drake, quoted in Martínez, *Burned Alive*, 137.

118. Robert S. Westman, *The Copernican Question: Prognostication, Skepticism, and Celestial Order* (Oakland: University Of California Press, 2011), 491; Murphy, *God's Jury*, 131.

119. Murphy, *God's Jury*, 130; MacCulloch, *Christianity*, 684.

120. Marshall, *The Reformation*, 111.

121. Clodfelter, *Warfare*, 40.

122. MacCulloch, *Reformation*, 262.

123. Katalin Péter, "Tolerance and Intolerance in Sixteenth-Century Hungary," in Grell and Scribner, *Toleration and Intolerance in the European Reformation*, 256.

124. Peter Schimert, "Zápolya, János Zsigmond," in *The Oxford Encyclopedia of the Reformation*, ed. Hans J. Hillerbrand (New York: Oxford University Press, 2005).

125. John Sigismund Zapolya II, The Edict of Torda, January 6, 1568, trans. Alexander St. Ivanyi, in *The Epic of Unitarianism*, comp. David B. Parke (Boston: Starr King Press, 1957), 19–20. See also, MacCulloch, *Reformation*, 262.

126. Stanisław Hozjusz, quoted in "The Confederation of Warsaw of 28th of January 1573: Religious Tolerance Guaranteed," UNESCO, www.unesco. org/new/en/communication-and-information/memory-of-the-world/register /full-list-of-registered-heritage/registered-heritage-page-8/the-confederation -of-warsaw-of-28th-of-january-1573-religious-tolerance-guaranteed.

127. MacCulloch, *Reformation*, 340–344. See also, Michael G. Müller, "Protestant Confessionalisation in the Towns of Royal Prussia and the Practice of Religious Toleration in Poland-Lithuania," in Grell and Scribner, *Tolerance and Intolerance in the European Reformation*, 262–281.

128. Warsaw Confederation, 1573, quoted in MacCulloch, *Reformation*, 343.

129. Müller, "Protestant Confessionalisation," 269.

130. Warsaw Confederation, 1573, quoted in MacCulloch, *Reformation*, 344.

131. Levy, *Blasphemy*, 73–74.

132. Abu'l-Fazl, *A'in-i-Akbari* 5.12.46, "The Happy Sayings of His Majesty," trans. Henry Sullivan Jarrett (1894), 3:422–452, www.columbia.edu/itc/mealac /pritchett/oolitlinks/abulfazl/ain_3_5_12.html. See also, Andre Wink, *Akbar (Makers of the Muslim World)* (Oxford: Oneworld Publications, 2009), 95.

133. John F. Richards, *The Mughal Empire* (Cambridge: Cambridge University Press, 1996), 38–39.

134. Tadd Graham Fernée, *Enlightenment and Violence: Modernity and Nation-Making* (New Delhi: SAGE, 2014), 1–3, 51.

135. Savitri Chandra, "Akbar's Concept of Sulh-Kul, Tulsi's Concept of Maryada and Dadu's Concept of Nipakh: A Comparative Study," *Social Scientist* 20, no. 9/10 (1992): 31.

136. Chandra, "Akbar's Concept of Sulh-Kul," 34.

137. Ebba Koch, "The Intellectual and Artistic Climate at Akbar's Court," in *The Adventures of Hamza: Painting and Storytelling in Mughal India*, ed. John Seyller (Washington, DC: Freer Gallery of Art 2002), 23–24.

138. Abu'l-Fażl, quoted in Wink, *Akbar*, 99.

139. Fernée, *Enlightenment and Violence*, 16.

140. Koch, "The Intellectual and Artistic Climate at Akbar's Court," 23.

141. *Encyclopedia Britannica*, s.v. "Dīn-i Ilāhī," last modified October 7, 2020, www.britannica.com/topic/Din-i-Ilahi.

142. Wink, *Akbar*, 93–95.

143. Rahul Sapra, "A Peaceable Kingdom in the East: Favourable Early Seventeenth-Century Representations of the Moghul Empire," *Renaissance and Reformation* 27, no. 3 (2003): 21.

144. Sapra, "A Peaceable Kingdom in the East," 21–22.

145. See, for example, Joelle Fiss and Jocelyn Getgen Kestenbaum, *Respecting Rights? Measuring the World's Blasphemy Laws* (US Commission on International Religious Freedom, July 2017), 5, 25.

146. Richards, *The Mughal Empire*, 122, 176.

147. Wink, *Akbar*, 108.

148. Sapra, "A Peaceable Kingdom in the East," 21.

149. Neil Postman, *Technopoly: The Surrender of Culture to Technology* (New York: Vintage Books, 1992), 18.

Chapter 4: The Seeds of Enlightenment

1. Jonathan Israel, *The Dutch Republic: Its Rise, Greatness, and Fall 1477–1806* (Oxford: Oxford University Press, 1995), 79–80. See also, Henry Kamen, *The Spanish Inquisition: A Historical Revision*, 4th ed. (New Haven: Yale University Press, 2014), 159–160, Kindle.

2. The Union of Utrecht, 1579, in Jean Dumont, *Corps universel diplomatique du droit des gens* (Amsterdam, 1728), 5.1:328, in *Freedom of Religion: Foundational Documents and Historical Arguments*, comp. Stephen A. Smith (Oxford: Oxbridge, 2017), 53.

3. Eltjo Buringh and Jan Luiten van Zanden, "Charting the 'Rise of the West': Manuscripts and Printed Books in Europe, A Long-Term Perspective from the Sixth Through Eighteenth Centuries," *Journal of Economic History* 69, no. 2 (2009): 421–423, 439.

4. Maarten Prak, *The Dutch Republic in the Seventeenth Century* (Cambridge: Cambridge University Press, 1998), 226, 232–233.

5. Michiel van Groesen, "Reading Newspapers in the Dutch Golden Age," *Media History* 22, no. 3–4 (2016): 336.

6. Willem Frijhoff and Marijke Spies, *1650: Bevochten eendracht* (The Hague: Sdu Uitgevers, 1999), 218; Prak, *The Dutch Republic*, 2–3.

7. Van Groesen, "Reading Newspapers," 341.

8. Prak, *The Dutch Republic*, 3–5, 219–220, 225–228, 232–233.

9. Joris van Eijnatten, *Liberty and Concord in the United Provinces* (Leiden: Brill, 2003), 3–4.

10. Prak, *The Dutch Republic*, 211–220. See also, Andrew Pettegree, "The Politics of Toleration in the Free Netherlands, 1572–1620," in *Tolerance and Intolerance in the European Reformation*, ed. Ole Peter Grell and Robert W. Scribner (Cambridge: Cambridge University Press, 1996), 183; and Wiep van Bunge, *The Early Enlightenment in the Dutch Republic, 1650–1750* (Leiden: Brill, 2003), 248.

11. Eijnatten, *Liberty and Concord*, 3–4; Judith Pollmann, *Religious Choice in the Dutch Republic: The Reformation of Arnoldus Buchelius* (Manchester: Manchester University Press, 1999), 7; Ernestine van der Wall, "Toleration and Enlightenment in the Dutch Republic," in Grell and Porter, *Toleration in Enlightenment Europe*, 114–132.

12. Israel, *The Dutch Republic*, 375–378.

13. Gerrit Voogt, introduction to *Synod on the Freedom of Conscience*, by Dirck Coornhert, trans. and ed. Gerrit Voogt (Amsterdam: Amsterdam University Press, 2008), 8–9.

14. Coornhert, *Synod on the Freedom of Conscience*, 167, 176.

15. Wiep van Bunge, "Censorship of Philosophy in the Seventeenth-Century Dutch Republic," in *The Use of Censorship in the Enlightenment*, ed. Mogens Lærke (Leiden: Brill, 2009), 105.

16. Van Bunge, "Censorship of Philosophy," 95.

17. Van Bunge, "Censorship of Philosophy," 98; Israel, *The Dutch Republic*, 91.

18. Philipp Blom, *A Wicked Company: The Forgotten Radicalism of the European Enlightenment* (New York: Basic Books, 2010), 101, Kindle.

19. Van Bunge, "Censorship of Philosophy," 96–97.

20. Steven Nadler, "Judging Spinoza," *New York Times*, May 25, 2018, https://opinionator.blogs.nytimes.com/2014/05/25/judging-spinoza.

21. Baruch Spinoza, Letter IV/36/8 (1662), in *The Collected Works of Spinoza*, ed. and trans. Edwin Curley, one-volume digital edition (Princeton: Princeton University Press, 1985), 188. See also, Israel, *The Dutch Republic*, 914.

22. Israel, *The Dutch Republic*, 918–919.

23. Van Bunge, "Censorship of Philosophy," 107–109.

24. Israel, *The Dutch Republic*, 918.

25. Baruch Spinoza, *Tractatus Theologico-Politicus* (1670), trans. Robert Willis (London: Trübner, 1862), 246–247, 342, 344–345, 351.

26. "Tractatus Theologico-Politicus," Beacon for Freedom of Expression, http://search.beaconforfreedom.org/search/censored_publications/publication.html?id=9703297.

27. Quoted in Roger Scruton, *Spinoza: A Very Short Introduction* (Oxford: Oxford University Press, 1986), 11; Steven Nadler, *A Book Forged in Hell: Spinoza's Scandalous Treatise and the Birth of the Secular Age* (Princeton: Princeton University Press, 2011), xi.

28. Jonathan Israel, *Radical Enlightenment: Philosophy and the Making of Modernity 1650–1750* (Oxford: Oxford University Press, 2001), 276.

29. Quoted in Israel, *Radical Enlightenment*, 292.

30. Van Bunge, "Censorship of Philosophy," 107; Israel, *Radical Enlightenment*, 292–293.

31. Perez Zagorin, *How the Idea of Religious Toleration Came to the West* (Princeton: Princeton University Press, 2003), 358; Israel, *Radical Enlightenment*, 99.

32. Israel, *Radical Enlightenment*, 334.

33. Zagorin, *How the Idea*, 363.

34. Israel, *The Dutch Republic*, 1046.

35. Pierre Bayle, *Nouvelles de la Republique des Lettres* 1 (Amsterdam: Henry Desbordes, 1684), pref. 3. See also, Hubert Bost, "Pierre Bayle and Censorship," in Lærke, *The Use of Censorship in the Enlightenment*, 41.

36. Bost, "Pierre Bayle and Censorship."

37. Pierre Bayle, *Philosophical Commentary* [1686–1688], ed. John Kilcullen and Chandran Kukathas (Indianapolis: Liberty Fund, 2005). See also, Zagorin, *How the Idea*, 273.

38. Louis XIV, Edict of Fontainebleau, October 22, 1685, in *Recueil général des anciennes lois françaises*, ed. Isambert (Paris, 1829), 19:530, in *Readings in European History*, comp. J. H. Robinson (Boston: Ginn, 1906), 2:180–183.

39. Marisa Linton, "Citizenship and Religious Toleration in France," in *Toleration in Enlightenment Europe*, ed. Ole Peter Grell and Roy Porter (Cambridge: Cambridge University Press, 2000), 160.

40. Israel, *Radical Enlightenment*, 335–336; Zagorin, *How the Idea*, 280.

41. Israel, *Radical Enlightenment*, 337–338.

42. Pierre Bayle, "Catius," in *Dictionnaire historique et critique*, 3rd ed. (Rotterdam, 1720), 821, a, b, quoted in *The Rules of Art*, by Pierre Bourdieu, trans. Susan Emanuel (Stanford: Meridian Books, 1995), 204.

43. Israel, *Radical Enlightenment*, 99.

44. Thomas Helwys, *A Short Declaration of the Mystery of Inquity* [1611–1612], ed. Richard Groves (Macon, GA: Mercer University Press, 1998), 53. See also, Leonard Levy, *Blasphemy—Verbal Offense Against the Sacred, from Moses to Salman Rushdie* (Chapel Hill: The University of North Carolina Press, 1993), 105.

45. Levy, *Blasphemy*, 104.

46. Thomas R. McKibbens, *The Forgotten Heritage: A Lineage of Great Baptist Preaching* (Macon, GA: Mercer University Press, 1986), 6.

47. Levy, *Blasphemy*, 105–106.

48. Joe Early Jr., *The Life and Writings of Thomas Helwys* (Macon, GA: Mercer University Press, 2009), 45.

49. Edward Coke, *Commons Protestation to James I*, 1621, in *The Parliamentary or Constitutional History of England* (London: T. Osborne and W. Sandby, 1753), 5:512–513. See also, Stephen A. Smith, *Freedom of Expression: Foundational Documents and Historical Arguments* (Oxford: Oxbridge, 2018), 35–36.

50. Randy Robertson, *Censorship and Conflict in Seventeenth-Century England: The Subtle Art of Division* (University Park: Pennsylvania State University Press, 2009), 3, 31.

51. See, for example, Levy, *Blasphemy*, 109.

52. Robertson, *Censorship and Conflict*, 49–59.

53. Cyndia Susan Clegg, *Press Censorship in Caroline England* (Cambridge: Cambridge University Press, 2008), 179–180.

54. Robertson, *Censorship and Conflict*, 66.

55. David Cressy, *Travesties and Transgressions in Tudor and Stuart England: Tales of Discord and Dissension* (Oxford: Oxford University Press, 1999), 224; Clegg, *Press Censorship in Caroline England*, 181.

56. John Rushworth, "The Star Chamber on Printing, 1637," in *Historical Collections of Private Passages of State* (London: D. Browne, 1721), 3:306–316, British History Online, www.british-history.ac.uk/rushworth-papers/vol3/pp306-316; Clegg, *Press Censorship in Caroline England*, 202.

57. Clegg, *Press Censorship in Caroline England*, 207.

58. Michael Kent Curtis, "In Pursuit of Liberty: The Levellers and the American Bill of Rights," *Constitutional Commentary*, Wake Forest University Legal Studies Paper 956931 (1991), 362.

59. *Encyclopedia Britannica*, s.v. "Long Parliament," last modified June 23, 2019, www.britannica.com/topic/Long-Parliament.

60. Maija Jansson, ed., *Proceedings in the Opening Session of the Long Parliament: House of Commons* (Rochester, NY: University of Rochester Press, 2000), 1:572; Clegg, *Press Censorship in Caroline England*, 220.

61. Clegg, *Press Censorship in Caroline England*, 208.

62. An Ordinance for the Regulating of Printing (June 1643), in *Acts and Ordinances of the Interregnum, 1642–1660*, ed. C. H. Firth and R. S. Rait (London, 1911), 184–186, British History Online, www.british-history.ac.uk/no-series/acts-ordinances-interregnum/pp184-186.

63. An Ordinance for the Regulating of Printing. See also, Clegg, *Press Censorship in Caroline England*, 226–227.

64. See, for example, Kevin R. Davis, "John Milton," *First Amendment Encyclopedia*, Free Speech Center, Middle Tennessee State University, 2009, https://www.mtsu.edu/first-amendment/article/1259/john-milton.

65. John Milton, *Areopagitica* (1644), ed. Ricard C. Jebb (Cambridge: Cambridge University Press, 1918), 1, 6, 57, 60, 64; Euripides, *Suppliant Women*, 430–440.

66. Levy, *Blasphemy*, 156.

67. Robertson, *Censorship and Conflict*, 126–127.

68. See, for example, Tony Harcup, "Areopagitica," in *A Dictionary of Journalism* (Oxford: Oxford University Press, 2014); and George Frank Sensebaugh, *Milton in Early America* (Princeton: Princeton University Press, 1994), 122, 240.

69. John Nalson, *An Impartial Collection of the Great Affairs of States* (London, 1682), 2:809.

70. Thomas Hobbes, *Leviathan* (London, 1651; repr. Oxford: Clarendon Press, 1909), 137.

71. Thomas Hobbes, *Appendix* iii.2.1202, quoted in Teresa M. Bejan, *Mere Civility: Disagreement and the Limits of Toleration* (Cambridge, MA: Harvard University Press, 2017), 110, Kindle.

72. See, for example, Jon Parkin, "The Reception of Hobbes's *Leviathan*," in *The Cambridge Companion to Hobbes's "Leviathan,"* ed. Patricia Springborg (Cambridge: Cambridge University Press, 2007), 452; and Glen Newey, *The Routledge Guidebook to Hobbes' "Leviathan"* (London: Routledge, 2008), 320.

73. Joad Raymond, *Pamphlets and Pamphleteering in Early Modern Britain* (Cambridge: Cambridge University Press, 2006), 228.

74. William Walwyn, *The Compassionate Samaritane* (London, 1644), 46, in *Tracts on Liberty by the Levellers and Their Critics (1638–1659)*, ed. David M. Hart and Ross Kenyon (Indianapolis: Liberty Fund, 2014), 2:177, https://quod.lib.umich.edu/e/eebo2/A97096.0001.001?rgn=main;view=fulltext.

75. William Walwyn, *Good Counsel to All* (London, 1644), in Hart and Kenyon, *Tracts on Liberty by the Levellers*, 2:190.

76. Randy Robertson, "Debating Censorship: Liberty and Press Control in the 1640s," in *Texts and Readers in the Age of Marvell*, ed. Christopher D'Addario and Matthew C. Augustine (Manchester: Manchester University Press, 2018), 138–139.

77. William Walwyn, *England's Lamentable Slaverie* (London, 1645), in Hart and Kenyon, *Tracts on Liberty by the Levellers*, 2:370–381.

78. Richard Overton, *A Remonstrance of Many Thousand Citizens* (Yeer, 1646; repr. Ann Arbor: Text Creation Partnership, 2011), 19, https://quod.lib .umich.edu/e/eebo2/A90246.0001.001?rgn=main;view=fulltext. See also, Andrew Sharp, *The English Levellers* (Cambridge: Cambridge University Press, 1998), 51; and Leonard Levy, *Emergence of a Free Press* (Oxford: Oxford University Press, 1985), 91.

79. *The Putney Debates of the General Council of the Army* (1647), in *Sources and Debates in English History 1485–1714*, ed. Newton Key and Robert Bucholz, 2nd ed. (Hoboken, NJ: Wiley-Blackwell, 2009), 189.

80. *Humble Petition for Revoking the Press Licensing Ordinances* (1649), in Smith, *Freedom of Expression*, 53–54; Levy, *Emergence of a Free Press*, 91.

81. Don Marion Wolfe, *Leveller Manifestoes of the Puritan Revolution* (New York: Humanities Press, 1967), 328–329, quoted in Curtis, "In Pursuit of Liberty," 377–378.

82. *Walwyn's Just Defense* (1649), in *The Leveller Tracts: 1647–1653*, ed. William Haller and Godfrey Davis (New York: Columbia University Press, 1944), 350, 368, quoted in Curtis, "In Pursuit of Liberty," 387.

83. John Lilburne, William Walwyn, Thomas Prince, and Richard Overton, *An Agreement of the Free People of England* (London: Gyles Calvert, May 1, 1649), in Hart and Kenyon, *Tracts on Liberty by the Levellers*, 6:243–255, https://oll .libertyfund.org/titles/hart-tracts-on-liberty-by-the-levellers-and-their-critics -vol-6-1649-forthcoming. See also, Curtis, "In Pursuit of Liberty," 373.

84. John Lilburne, *The Dissembling Scot . . . Or a Vindication of Lieu. Col. John Lilburne and Others* (1652), quoted in Levy, *Emergence of a Free Press*, 92.

85. An Ordinance for the punishing of Blasphemies and Heresies, with the several penalties therein expressed (May, 1648), in Firth and Rait, *Acts and Ordinances*, 1133–1136, British History Online, www.british-history.ac.uk /no-series/acts-ordinances-interregnum/pp1133-1136; Robertson, *Censorship and Conflict*, 125–126.

86. Curtis, "In Pursuit of Liberty," 377, 380.

87. Patrick Chinnery, "John Lilburne," *First Amendment Encyclopedia*, Free Speech Center, Middle Tennessee State University, 2009, www.mtsu.edu/first -amendment/article/1256/john-lilburne.

88. Charles II, The Declaration of Breda, April 1660, in *Journal of the House of Lords* (London: His Majesty's Stationery Office, 1767–1830), 11:6–9.

89. Levy, *Blasphemy*, 207.

90. Richard C. Allen, "Restoration Quakerism, 1660–1691," in *The Oxford Handbook of Quaker Studies*, ed. Stephen W. Angell and Pink Dandelion (Oxford: Oxford University Press, 2013), 29–32.

91. Charles II, "An Act for preventing the frequent Abuses in printing seditious treasonable and unlicensed Bookes [. . .]," 1662, in *Statutes of the Realm*, ed. John Raithby, (S.L.: Great Britain Record Commission, 1819), 5:428–435.

92. Robertson, *Censorship and Conflict*, 10.

93. Robert Tombs, *The English and Their History* (Penguin, 2014), 254, Kindle.

94. John Locke, *A Letter Concerning Toleration*, 1689, ed. Mark Goldie (Indianapolis: Liberty Fund, 2010), 51–53, 58–59, https://oll.libertyfund.org /titles/locke-a-letter-concerning-toleration-and-other-writings. See also, Bejan, *Mere Civility*, 114.

95. Scott Sowersby, *Making Toleration: The Repealers and the Glorious Revolution* (Cambridge, MA: Harvard University Press, 2013), 12.

96. Tombs, *The English and Their History*, 257–259.

97. William III and Mary II, Toleration Act (1689), in *English Historical Documents, 1600–1714*, ed. Andrew Browning (London: Eyre & Spottiswoode, 1953).

98. Ole Peter Grell, Jonathan Israel, and Nicholas Tyacke, eds., *From Persecution to Toleration: The Glorious Revolution and Religion in England* (Oxford: Oxford University Press, 1991), 10.

99. Levy, *Blasphemy*, 225–226.

100. Israel, *Radical Enlightenment*, 152–153; Grell et al., *From Persecution to Toleration*, 11.

101. Israel, *Radical Enlightenment*, 154.

102. An Act Declaring the Rights and Liberties of the Subjects and Settling the Succession of the Crown (Bill of Rights) (1689), Constitution Society, www.law.gmu.edu/assets/files/academics/founders/English_Billof Rights.pdf.

103. John Locke, *John Locke to Edward Clarke*, December 1794, in *The Life of John Locke*, ed. Lord Peter King (London: Henry Colburn, 1829), 202, 206. See also, Geoff Kemp, "The 'End of Censorship' and the Policies of Toleration, from Locke to Sacheverell," *Parliamentary History* 31, no. 1 (2012): 51–52.

104. Robertson, *Censorship and Conflict*, 203.

105. Quoted in Robertson, *Censorship and Conflict*, 201. See also, Raymond Astbury, "The Renewal of the Licensing Act in 1693 and Its Lapse in 1695," *Library* 5, no. 4 (1978): 317.

106. William III, An Act for the more effectual suppressing of Blasphemy and Profaneness (1697–1698), in *Statutes of the Realm*, ed. John Raithby (S.L.: Great Britain Record Commission, 1820), 7:409; Grell, *From Persecution to Toleration*, 9; Levy, *Blasphemy*, 228–229.

107. Charles II, Act against the cryme of blasphemie (May 16, 1661), Records of the Parliaments of Scotland to 1707, National Records of Scotland, www.rps.ac.uk/search.php?action=fetch_jump&filename=charlesii_trans& jump=charlesii_m1661_1_263_d4_ms&type=trans&fragment=t1661_1_264 _d7_trans.

108. Levy, *Blasphemy*, 232–234.

Chapter 5: Enlightenment Now

1. See, for example, Jonathan Israel, *Radical Enlightenment: Philosophy and the Making of Modernity 1650–1750* (Oxford: Oxford University Press, 2001), 4.

2. Margaret Jacob, *The Enlightenment: A Brief History with Documents*, (Boston and New York: Bedford/St. Martin's, 2000), loc. 1311, Kindle.

3. Anthony Collins, preface to *A Discourse of Freethinking* (London, 1713), quoted in Israel, *Radical Enlightenment*, 4–5.

4. Israel, *Radical Enlightenment*, 114–115.

5. Israel, *Radical Enlightenment*, 104.

6. Eltjo Buringh and Jan Luiten van Zanden, "Charting the 'Rise of the West': Manuscripts and Printed Books in Europe, A Long-Term Perspective from the Sixth Through Eighteenth Centuries," *Journal of Economic History* 69, no. 2 (2009): 417.

7. Buringh and Van Zanden, "Charting the 'Rise of the West,'" 417, 421, 434.

8. See, for example, James Van Horn Melton, *The Rise of the Public in Enlightenment Europe* (Cambridge: Cambridge University Press, 2001).

9. Tom Standage, *Writing on the Wall: Social Media—The First 2,000 Years* (New York: Bloomsbury, 2013), 106.

10. Melton, *The Rise of the Public*, 240.

11. Israel, *Radical Enlightenment*, 92; Melton, *The Rise of the Public*, 197–225. See also, Dena Goodman, *The Republic of Letters: A Cultural History of the*

French Enlightenment (Ithaca: Cornell University Press, 1994); and Antoine Lilti, *The World of the Salons: Sociability and Worldliness in Eighteenth-Century Paris* (Oxford: Oxford University Press, 2015).

12. Jacob, *The Enlightenment*, loc. 836.

13. Diarmaid MacCulloch, *Reformation: Europe's House Divided* (London: Penguin, 2003), 672.

14. *Traité des trois Imposteurs* (1777 ed.), chap. 4, section 1, in *The Treatise of the Three Impostors and the Problem of Enlightenment*, trans. Abraham Anderson (Lanham, MD: Rowman & Littlefield, 1997), 33.

15. Wiep van Bunge, *From Bayle to the Batavian Republic: Essays on Philosophy in the Eighteenth-Century Dutch Republic* (Boston: Brill, 2018), 260.

16. See, for example, Philipp Blom, *A Wicked Company: The Forgotten Radicalism of the European Enlightenment* (New York: Basic Books, 2010), 53–56, Kindle.

17. Johan Christian Laursen and Johan van der Zande, eds., *Early French and German Defenses of Freedom of the Press* (Leiden: Brill, 2003), 15.

18. Elie Luzac, *Essay on Freedom of Expression* (1749), trans. John Paul McDonald, in Laursen and Van der Zande, *Early French and German Defenses of Freedom of the Press*, 25, 49.

19. Court of Holland, *Plan, om door middel van de aanstelling van Censores Librorum*, 1769, quoted in Joris van Eijnatten, "Between Practice and Principle: Dutch Ideas on Censorship and Press Freedom, 1759–1795," *Redescriptions: Yearbook for Political Thought and Conceptual History* (2004): 12.

20. Elie Luzac, "Memorie van consideratien [. . .]," in *Nieuwe Nederlandsche jaerboeken* 5, no. 2 (1770): 788–896; Eijnatten, "Between Practice and Principle," 13–14.

21. Quoted in Robert W. T. Martin, *The Free and Open Press: The Founding of American Democratic Press Liberty* (New York: New York University Press, 2001), Kindle; *Arguments Relating to a Restraint Upon the Press* (London: R. and J. Bonwicke, 1712), 45.

22. John Holt at the trial of John Tutchin, 1704, quoted in Lee Sonsteng Horsley, "The Trial of John Tutchin, Author of the 'Observator,'" *Yearbook of English Studies* 3 (1973): 135.

23. Stephen D. Solomon, *Revolutionary Dissent: How the Founding Generation Created the Freedom of Speech* (New York: St. Martin's Press, 2016), loc. 710–716, Kindle.

24. William Blackstone, *Commentaries on the Laws of England* (1769; repr., Chicago: University of Chicago Press, 1979), 4:150–153.

25. Matthew Tindal, *A letter to a member of Parliament* (London: J. Darby, 1698; repr. Ann Arbor: Text Creation Partnership, 2011), 8, https://quod.lib.umich.edu/e/eebo/A48197.0001.001?rgn=main;view=fulltext.

26. Matthew Tindal and John Toland, *Reasons Against Restraining the Press* (London, 1704), in *Freedom of Expression: Foundational Documents and Historical Arguments*, comp. Stephen A. Smith (Oxford: Oxbridge, 2018), 80–82.

27. See, for example, Stephen Lalor, *Matthew Tindal, Freethinker: An Eighteenth-Century Assault on Religion* (London: Continuum, 2006), 16.

28. Bernard Bailyn, *The Ideological Origins of the American Revolution*, enlarged ed. (Cambridge, MA: The Belknap Press of Harvard University Press, 1992), 35–36.

29. Thomas Gordon, *Cato's Letter, No. 15: Of Freedom of Speech*, February 4, 1721, in John Trenchard and Thomas Gordon, *Cato's Letters, or Essays on Liberty, Civil, and Religious, and Other Important Subjects*, vol. 1, ed. Ronald Hamowy (Indianapolis: Liberty Fund, 1995), https://oll.libertyfund.org/title/gordon-cato-s-letters-vol-1-november-5-1720-to-june-17-1721-lf-ed.

30. Thomas Gordon, *Cato's Letter No. 32: Reflections upon Libelling*, June 10, 1721, in Trenchard and Gordon, *Cato's Letters*, vol. 1.

31. John Trenchard, *Cato's Letter No. 101: Second Discourse upon Libels*, November 3, 1722, in Trenchard and Gordon, *Cato's Letters*, vol. 3.

32. Quoted in Bailyn, *The Ideological Origins of the American Revolution*, 36.

33. See, for example, Martin, *The Free and Open Press.*

34. John Wilkes, *The North Briton* 40, March 5, 1763, in *The North Briton, From No I. to No XLVI* (London: W. Bingley, 1769), 132. See also, Arthur H. Cash, *John Wilkes: The Scandalous Father of Civil Liberty* (New Haven: Yale University Press, 2006), 80.

35. Horace Walpole, *Letters of Horace Walpole*, ed. Paget Toynbee (Oxford, 1903–1905), 5:315.

36. John Wilkes, *The North Briton* 45, April 23, 1763. See also, Cash, *John Wilkes*, 99–100.

37. *Encyclopedia Britannica*, s.v. "John Wilkes," by Ian R. Christie, last modified September 27, 2018, www.britannica.com/biography/John-Wilkes/The-Middlesex-elections.

38. Edoardo Tortarolo, *The Invention of Free Press: Writers and Censorship in Eighteenth Century Europe* (Dordrecht: Springer, 2016), 45.

39. Pauline Maier, "John Wilkes and American Disillusionment with Britain," *William and Mary Quarterly* 20, no. 3 (1963): 373–393.

40. Israel, *Radical Enlightenment*, 103–104.

41. Charles Walton, *Policing Public Opinion in the French Revolution: The Culture of Calumny and the Problem of Free Speech* (Oxford: Oxford University Press, 2009), 25.

42. See, for example, Robert Darnton and Daniel Roche, *Revolution in Print: The Press in France, 1775–1800* (Oakland: University of California Press, 1989); and Robert Darnton, "Bourbon France: Privilege and Repression,"

in *Censors at Work: How States Shaped Literature* (New York: W. W. Norton, 2014), 22–86, Kindle.

43. Quoted in Tortarolo, *The Invention of Free Press*, 63. On the culture of honor in Old Regime France, see Walton, *Policing Public Opinion*, 39–50.

44. See, for example, Robert Darnton, "Reading, Writing, and Publishing in Eighteenth-Century France: A Case Study in the Sociology of Literature," *Daedalus* 100, no. 1 (1971): 229.

45. Thierry Rigogne, "Printers into Booksellers: The Structural Transformation of the French Print Trades in the Age of Enlightenment," *Papers of the Bibliographical Society of America* 101, no. 4 (2007): 551.

46. Darnton, *Censors at Work*, 60. See also, Robert Darnton, *The Literary Underground of the Old Regime* (Cambridge, MA: Harvard University Press, 1985).

47. See, for example, Darnton, *Censors at Work*, 47, 60–61.

48. Darnton and Roche, *Revolution in Print*, 23–24.

49. See, for example, Jeremy Popkin, *News and Politics in the Age of Revolution: Jean Luzac's "Gazette de Leyde"* (Ithaca and London: Cornell University Press, 1989), 36–37. See also, Standage, *Writing on the Wall*, 162–164.

50. See, for example, Robert Darnton, *The Forbidden Best-Sellers of Pre-Revolutionary France* (London: Harper Collins, 1996), 78–80. See also, Standage, *Writing on the Wall*, 166–174.

51. Chief of Police J.-C.-P. Lenoir, quoted in Darnton, *The Literary Underground of the Old Regime*, 201–202. See also, Standage, *Writing on the Wall*, 166.

52. Darnton, *Censors at Work*, 32–33, 58. See also, Israel, *Radical Enlightenment*, 103–104.

53. C. G. de Lamoignon de Malesherbes, *Mémoires sur la librairie et sur la liberté de la presse* (1788; repr. Geneva, 1969), 300, quoted in Darnton, *Censors at Work*, 32.

54. Buringh and Van Zanden, "Charting the 'Rise of the West,'" 417.

55. See, for example, Blom, *A Wicked Company*, 58.

56. Denis Diderot, *Oeuvres* (Paris: Laffont, 1997), 5:537, trans. Blom, in *A Wicked Company*, 169.

57. See, for example, Charles T. Wolfe and J. B. Shank, "Denis Diderot," *Stanford Encyclopedia of Philosophy*, Spring 2021 ed., ed. Edward N. Zalta, https://plato.stanford.edu/entries/diderot. See also, Blom, *A Wicked Company*, 72–74.

58. Andrew Curran, "How Diderot's Encyclopedia Challenged the King," *Longreads*, January 2019, https://longreads.com/2019/01/30/how-diderots-encyclopedia-challenged-the-king.

59. "ANTHROPOPHAGES," in *Encyclopédie, ou Dictionnaire Raisonné des sciences, des arts et des métiers*, vol. 1, ed. Denis Diderot and Jean le Rond

d'Alembert (Paris, 1751), 498. For a critical assessment of this example, see Jeff Loveland, *The European Encyclopedia: From 1650 to the Twenty-First Century* (Cambridge: Cambridge University Press, 2019), 193–194.

60. "Autorité Politique," in Diderot and d'Alembert, *Encyclopédie*, vol. 1, 898, in *Encyclopedic Liberty: Political Articles in the Dictionary of Diderot and D'Alembert*, trans. and ed. Henry C. Clark and Christine Dunn Henderson (Indianapolis: Liberty Fund, 2016), 13.

61. Darnton, *Censors at Work*, 58.

62. Darrin M. McMahon, *Enemies of the Enlightenment: The French Counter-Enlightenment and the Making of Modernity* (Oxford: Oxford University Press, 2002), 21.

63. Abbé Jean Pey, *La Tolérance chrétienne oppose au tolérantisme philosophique* (Fribourg, 1794), iii, quoted in McMahon, *Enemies of the Enlightenment*, 42.

64. Darnton, *Censors at Work*, 56; Tortarolo, *The Invention of Free Press*, 71–76.

65. Claude-Adrien Helvétius, *De l'esprit; or, Essays on the mind* (1758), trans. William Mudford (London: 1807). See also, David Wootton, "Helvétius: From Radical Enlightenment to Revolution," *Political Theory* 28, no. 3 (June 2000), 307–336.

66. "Censure de la Faculté de théologie," in *Correspondance générale d'Helvétius*, ed. A. Dainard et al. (Toronto: University of Toronto Press, 1984), 2:420, trans. Wootton, "Helvétius," 316.

67. Darnton, *Censors at Work*, 57–58; Jonathan Israel, *Democratic Enlightenment: Philosophy, Revolution, and Human Rights 1750–1790* (Oxford: Oxford University Press, 2011), 79; Blom, *A Wicked Company*.

68. Paraphrased in Israel, *Democratic Enlightenment*, 80.

69. Raymond Birn, "*Encyclopédie*," in *Censorship: A World Encyclopedia*, ed. Derek Jones (Oxfordshire: Routledge, 2001), 735.

70. Darnton, *Censors at Work*, 59.

71. Blom, *A Wicked Company*, 68.

72. Blom, *A Wicked Company*, 287.

73. Joseph Henrich, *The WEIRDest People in the World* (New York: Farrar, Straus and Giroux, 2020), 457, Kindle.

74. Walton, *Policing Public Opinion*, 52.

75. Montesquieu, *The Spirit of Laws* (1748), trans. Thomas Nugent (Dublin: G. and A. Ewing and G. Faulkner, 1751), 237, 363. See also, Tortarolo, *The Invention of Free Press*, 66.

76. The apocryphal quotation first appeared in Evelyn Beatrice Hall (S. G. Tallentyre), *The Friends of Voltaire* (New York: G.P. Putnam's sons, 1907), 199.

77. Voltaire, *Treatise on Tolerance* (1763), in *Toleration and Other Essays by Voltaire*, ed. and trans. Joseph McCabe (New York: G. P. Putnam's Sons, 1912), 30–31.

78. See, for example, Simon Harvey, introduction to *Voltaire: "Treatise on Tolerance" and Other Writings* (Cambridge: Cambridge University Press, 2000), xii–xiv.

79. Voltaire, "Liberty of the Press," in *Philosophical Dictionary*, vol. 7 (1764), trans. William F. Fleming (Paris: E. R. DuMont, 1901).

80. Parlement de Paris, *Arrêt de parlement qui condamne deux libelles ayant pour titres [. . .]* (Lyon: P. Valfray, 1765), https://gallica.bnf.fr/ark:/12148/btv1b86179374.

81. See, for example, Blom, *A Wicked Company*, 300–301. See also, Guilhem Gil, "Blasphemy in French Law: From the Chevalier de la Barre to *Charlie Hebdo*," in *Blasphemy and Freedom of Expression: Comparative, Theoretical and Historical Reflections After the "Charlie Hebdo" Massacre*, ed. Jaroen Temperman (Cambridge: Cambridge University Press, 2018), 29.

82. Voltaire, "Liberty of the Press," and "Liberty of Opinion," in *Philosophical Dictionary*, vol. 7 (1764).

83. Walton, *Policing Public Opinion*, 49.

84. Voltaire, *Jusqu'à quel point on doit tromper le peuple* (1771), trans. Jonathan Israel, "*Libertas Philosophandi* in the Eighteenth Century: Radical Enlightenment Versus Moderate Enlightenment (1750–1776)," in *Freedom of Speech: The History of an Idea*, ed. Elizabeth Powers (Lewisburg, PA: Bucknell University Press, 2011), 8.

85. John Dugdale, "Voltaire's *Treatise on Tolerance* Becomes Bestseller Following Paris Attacks," *Guardian*, January 16, 2015, www.theguardian.com/books/2015/jan/16/voltaire-treatise-tolerance-besteller-paris-attack.

86. Tortarolo, *The Invention of Free Press*, 78.

87. Walton, *Policing Public Opinion*, 56.

88. Louis de Jaucourt, "Press," in Diderot and d'Alembert, *Encyclopédie*, in *Encyclopedic Liberty: Political Articles in the Dictionary of Diderot and D'Alembert*, trans. and ed. Henry C. Clark and Christine Dunn Henderson (Indianapolis: Liberty Fund, 2016), 532.

89. Blom, *A Wicked Company*, 372.

90. Jean-Jacques Rousseau, *Discourse on the Arts and Sciences* (1750), in *The Social Contract and the First and Second Discourses*, ed. Susan Dunn (New Haven/London: Yale University Press, 2002), 65, quoted in Tortarolo, *The Invention of Free Press*, 90.

91. Tortarolo, *The Invention of Free Press*, 90.

92. Jean-Jacques Rousseau, *The Social Contract* (1762), trans. and ed. Jonathan Bennett (Early Modern Texts, 2017), 9, 67, 72, www.earlymoderntexts.com/assets/pdfs/rousseau1762.pdf. See also, Blom, *A Wicked Company*, 251.

93. Marie-Jean-Antoine-Nicolas de Cariat, Marquis de Condorcet, *Fragments Concerning Freedom of the Press* (1776), in *Oeuvres de Condorcet* (Paris:

Firmin Didot, 1847–1849), 11:277, 304, quoted in Tortarolo, *The Invention of Free Press*, 97.

94. Declaration of the Rights of Man and Citizen art. 11, August 26, 1789, in *La Constitution française, Présentée au Roi par l'Assemblée Nationale, le 3 Septembre 1791* (Paris: De l'Imprimerie de Baudoin, 1791), in *The French Revolution and Human Rights*, ed. and trans. Lynn Hunt (Boston and New York: Bedford/St. Martin's, 1996), 79.

95. See, for example, Jonathan Israel, *Enlightenment Contested: Philosophy and the Making of Modernity 1650–1750* (Oxford: Oxford University Press, 2006), 295.

96. K. A. Papmehl, *Freedom of Expression in Eighteenth Century Russia* (The Hague: Martinus Njihoff, 1971), 42–43.

97. Papmehl, *Freedom of Expression in Eighteenth Century Russia*, 54.

98. Catherine I, Grand Instruction art. 482, 1767, trans. Papmehl, *Freedom of Expression in Eighteenth Century Russia*, 55.

99. Catherine I, Decree on Serfs, 1767, in *A Source Book for Russian History*, ed. George Vernadsky (New Haven: Yale University Press, 1972), 2:453–454.

100. Catherine I, quoted in Robert K. Massie, *Catherine the Great: Portrait of a Woman* (New York: Random House, 2011), 253.

101. See, for example, Johan van der Zande, "Prussia and the Enlightenment," in Philip G. Dwyer, *The Rise of Prussia 1700–1830* (London: Routledge, 2000), 101.

102. John Moore, *A View of Society and Manners in France, Switzerland and Germany* (1779), in *The Works of John Moore*, ed. Robert Anderson (Edinburg, 1820), 1:257.

103. Frederick II, quoted in Thomas Campbell, *Frederick the Great, and His Court and Times* (London: Henry Colburn, 1843), 4:166, 171.

104. Pamela Selwyn, *Everyday Life in the German Book Trade: Friedrich Nicolai as Bookseller and Publisher in the Age of Enlightenment* (University Park: Pennsylvania State University Press, 2000), 191; Tortarolo, *The Invention of Free Press*, 90.

105. See, for example, Christopher Clark, *Iron Kingdom: The Rise and Downfall of Prussia 1600–1947* (London: Penguin, 2006), 249–250.

106. See, for example, Eckhart Hellmuth, "Enlightenment and Freedom of the Press: The Debate in the Berlin Mittwochsgesellschaft, 1783–1784," *History* 83, no. 271 (July 1998): 420–444. See also, Clark, *Iron Kingdom*, 251–252.

107. Clark, *Iron Kingdom*, 251.

108. Johann Heinrich Wlömer, comment in *Berlin Mittwochsgesellshaft*, December 23, 1783, trans. Hellmuth, "Enlightenment and Freedom of the Press," 431.

109. Moses Mendelssohn, comment in *Berlin Mittwochsgesellschaft*, December 26, 1783, trans. Hellmuth, "Enlightenment and Freedom of the Press," 429.

110. Immanuel Kant, "An Answer to the Question: What Is Enlighten-ment?" in *Berlinische Monatsschrift* 4 (1784): 481–494, in *Eighteenth-Century Answers and Twentieth-Century Questions*, ed. James Schmidt (Oakland: University of California Press, 1996), 58–64.

111. "The History of the Riksdag," Sveriges Riksdag, May 7, 2019, www.riksdagen.se/en/how-the-riksdag-works/democracy/the-history-of-the-riksdag.

112. Jonas Nordin, "The Swedish Freedom of Print Act of 1776—Background and Significance," *Journal of International Media & Entertainment* 7, no. 2 (2018): 137–144.

113. Kristina Örtenhed and Bertil Wennberg, eds., *Press Freedom 250 Years: Freedom of the Press and Public Access to Official Documents in Sweden and Finland—A Living Heritage from 1766* (Sveriges Riksdag, 2018), www.riksdagen.se/globalassets/15.-bestall-och-ladda-ned/andra-sprak/tf-250-ar-eng-2018.pdf.

114. Peter Forsskål, *Tankar om borgerliga friheten* [Thoughts on Civil Liberty] (Stockholm, 1759), trans. David Goldberg et al., www.peterforsskal.com/thetext.html.

115. Anders Chydenius, *Additional Report [. . .] on the Freedom of Printing*, April 21, 1766, in *Anders Chydenius Selected Works*, https://chydenius.kootut teokset.fi/en/kirjoitukset/betankande-om-tryckfriheten-1766.

116. Adolph Friedrik, His Majesty's Gracious Ordinance Regarding the Freedom of Writing and of the Press (1766), trans. Ian Giles and Peter Graves, in *Freedom of Expression: Foundational Documents and Historical Arguments*, comp. Stephen A. Smith (Oxford: Oxbridge, 2018), 126.

117. Marie-Christine Skuncke, "Press Freedom in the Riksdag 1760–62 and 1765–66," in Örtenhed and Wennberg, *Press Freedom 250 Years*, 132.

118. Nordin, "The Swedish Freedom of Print Act of 1776."

119. Skuncke, "Press Freedom in the Riksdag," 134.

120. Buringh and Van Zanden, "Charting the 'Rise of the West,'" 421. See also, Jonas Nordin, "En revolution i tryck: Tryckfrihet och tryckproduktion i Sverige 1766–1722 och däromkring," *Vetenskapssocieteten i Lund. Årsbok 2020*, 87–112.

121. Christian VII of Denmark, rescript, September 14, 1770, in Bolle Willum Luxdorph and Rasmus Nyerup, *Luxdorphiana, eller Bidrag til den danske Literairhistorie* (Copenhagen, 1791), 1–2, trans. John Christian Laursen, "David Hume and the Danish Debate About Freedom of the Press in the 1770s," *Journal of the History of Ideas* 59, no. 1 (1998): 168.

122. See, for example, Frederik Stjernfelt and Jacob Mchangama, *MEN: Ytringsfrihedens Historie i Danmark* (Copenhagen: Gyldendal, 2016), 152.

123. Voltaire, *Épître au roi de Danemark*, January 1771, in *Œuvres complètes de Voltaire* (Garnier, 1877), 10:421–427.

124. See, for example, Henrik Horstbøll, Ulrik Langen, and Frederik Stjernfelt, *Grov Konfækt: Tre Vilde År med Trykkefrihed, 1770–73* (Copenhagen: Gyldendal, 2020).

125. John Christian Laursen, "Censorship in the Nordic Countries, ca. 1750–1890: Transformations in Law, Theory, and Practice," *Journal of Modern European History* 3, no. 1 (2005): 100–121.

126. See, for example, Asser Amdisen, *Struensee: til nytte og fornøjelse* (Copenhagen: Lindhardt and Ringhof, 2012), 207–212; and Israel, *Democratic Enlightenment*, 825.

127. Stjernfelt and Mchangama, *MEN*, 174.

Chapter 6: Constructing the Bulwark of Liberty

1. William Berkeley quoted in William Waller Hening, *The Statutes at Large Being a Collection of All the Laws of Virginia (1619–1776)* (Richmond, 1905–1915), 2:517. See also, Leonard Levy, *Emergence of a Free Press* (Oxford: Oxford University Press, 1985), 18.

2. Lee C. Bollinger and Geoffrey R. Stone, *The Free Speech Century* (Oxford: Oxford University Press, 2019), 1.

3. West Virginia State Bd. Of Educ. v. Barnette, 319 U.S. (1943) at 642.

4. Alan Taylor, *American Colonies: The Settling of North America* (London: Penguin Books, 2001), 181.

5. Larry Eldridge, *A Distant Heritage: The Growth of Free Speech in Early America*, (New York: New York University Press, 1994), 23, Kindle.

6. Eldridge, *A Distant Heritage*, 3.

7. Not including county and local records. Susan Juster, "Heretics, Blasphemers, and Sabbath Breakers: The Prosecution of Religious Crime in Early America," in *The First Prejudice: Religious Tolerance and Intolerance in Early America*, ed. Chris Beneke and Christopher S. Grenda (Philadelphia and Oxford: University of Pennsylvania Press, 2011), 131.

8. Taylor, *American Colonies*, 181.

9. "Way More Than the Scarlett Letter: Puritan Punishments," New England Historical Society, last modified 2020, www.newenglandhistorical society.com/way-more-than-the-scarlet-letter-puritan-punishments.

10. Quoted in Juliet Haines Mufford, *The Devil Made Me Do It!: Crime and Punishment in Early New England* (Guilford: Global Pequot Press, 2012), 67.

11. Carla Gardina Pestana, "The Quaker Executions as Myth and History," *Journal of America History* 80, no. 2 (1993): 441.

12. Nathaniel B. Shurtleff, ed., *Records of the Governor and Company of the Massachusetts Bay in New England (1628–86)* (Boston, 1853–1854), 1:160, quoted in Levy, *Emergence of a Free Press*, 26. See also, Taylor, *American Colonies*, 182.

13. Roger Williams, *The Bloody Tenent, of Persecution for Cause of Conscience* (1644), in *Church and State in the United States*, ed. Anton Phelps Stokes (New York: Harper & Bros., 1950), 1:196–199.

14. Charles II, Rhode Island Royal Charter, 1663, Rhode Island State Archives, https://catalog.sos.ri.gov/repositories/2/resources/410.

15. Maryland Toleration Act, April 21, 1649, in *Colonial Origins of the American Constitution: A Documentary History*, ed. Donald S. Lutz (Indianapolis: Liberty Fund, 1998), 309–314, https://oll.libertyfund.org/title/lutz-colonial-origins -of-the-american-constitution-a-documentary-history#lf0013_head_310.

16. Pennsylvania, An Act for Freedom of Conscience, December 7, 1682, in Lutz, *Colonial Origins*, 287–290.

17. Maryland Toleration Act, in Lutz, *Colonial Origins*, 311.

18. Pennsylvania, An Act for Freedom of Conscience, in Lutz, *Colonial Origins*, 288.

19. Teresa M. Bejan, *Mere Civility: Disagreement and the Limits of Toleration* (Cambridge, MA: Harvard University Press, 2017), 47, Kindle.

20. Eldridge, *A Distant Heritage*, 25–26, 28.

21. Frame of Government of Pennsylvania, Laws Agreed Upon in England, &c. art. 30, May 5, 1682, in Lutz, *Colonial Origins*, 285. See also, Levy, *Emergence of a Free Press*, 22–23; and John Smolenski, "William Bradford," in *Censorship: A World Encyclopedia*, ed. Derek Jones (New York: Routledge, 2001), 280.

22. Quoted in Eldridge, *A Distant Heritage*, 93.

23. Publick Occurrences No. 1 (September 25, 1690), National Humanities Center, 2006, http://nationalhumanitiescenter.org/pds/amerbegin/power /text5/PublickOccurrences.pdf. See also, Tom Standage, *Writing on the Wall: Social Media—The First 2,000 Years* (New York: Bloomsbury, 2013), 135–136.

24. Public order (September 29, 1690), National Humanities Center, 2006, http://nationalhumanitiescenter.org/pds/amerbegin/power/text5/Publick Occurrences.pdf.

25. Benjamin Franklin (Silence Dogood), Essay 8, "Sir, I prefer," July 2–9, 1722, *New-England Courant* No. 49, *Massachusetts Historical Society*, www .masshist.org/online/silence_dogood/img-viewer.php?item_id=646&img _step=1&tpc=&pid=6&mode=transcript&tpc=&pid=6#page1.

26. Standage, *Writing on the Wall*, 142–143; "Silence Dogood Essay 8," Massachusetts Historical Society, www.masshist.org/database/viewer.php ?ft=Silence%20Dogood&item_id=646&pid=6.

27. Benjamin Franklin, *On Freedom of Speech and the Press* (1737), quoted in Robert Shibley, "For the Fourth: Ben Franklin on Freedom of Speech—50 Years Before the Constitution," FIRE, July 4, 2016, www.thefire.org/for-the -fourth-ben-franklin-on-freedom-of-speech-50-years-before-the-constitution.

28. *New York Gazette*, January 7, 1734, quoted in Stephen D. Solomon, *Revolutionary Dissent: How the Founding Generation Created the Freedom of Speech* (New York: St. Martin's Press, 2016), loc. 626, Kindle.

29. See, for example, Solomon, *Revolutionary Dissent*, loc. 752.

30. *New-York Weekly Journal*, December 10, 1733, quoted in Solomon, *Revolutionary Dissent*, loc. 784.

31. Thomas Gordon, *Cato's Letter No. 15*.

32. William Cosby, Governor Cosby to the Lords of Trade, June 19, 1734, in *Documents Relative to the Colonial History of the State of New-York*, ed. John Romeyn Brodhead (Albany, NY: Weed, Parsons, 1856), 6:4–7, quoted in Solomon, *Revolutionary Dissent*, loc. 840.

33. Robert W. T. Martin, *The Free and Open Press: The Founding of American Democratic Press Liberty* (New York: New York University Press, 2001), loc. 1055–1056, Kindle.

34. Solomon, *Revolutionary Dissent*, loc. 858.

35. Martin, *The Free and Open Press*, loc. 858

36. Levy, *Emergence of a Free Press*, 44.

37. Solomon, *Revolutionary Dissent*, loc. 899; Martin, *The Free and Open Press*, loc. 1049.

38. Solomon, *Revolutionary Dissent*, loc. 488.

39. John Peter Zenger and James Alexander, *A Brief Narrative of the Case and Tryal of John Peter Zenger* (Boston, 1738), 15, 18, 20, 27, 43–44, 46. See also, Levy, *Emergence of a Free Press*, 43–44; and Solomon, *Revolutionary Dissent*, loc. 488.

40. Standage, *Writing on the Wall*, 132.

41. Levy, *Emergence of a Free Press*, 46–47.

42. Levy, *Emergence of a Free Press*, 51–58.

43. Quoted in Levy, *Emergence of a Free Press*, 53.

44. Benjamin Franklin, *Documents on the Hearing of William Smith's Petition*, April 27, 1758, in *The Papers of Benjamin Franklin*, vol. 8, ed. Leonard W. Labaree (New Haven, CT: Yale University Press, 1965), 28, https://franklinpapers.org/yale?vol=8&page=028a. See also, Levy, *Emergence of a Free Press*, 57.

45. Ralph L. Ketcham, "Benjamin Franklin and William Smith: New Light on an Old Philadelphia Quarrel," *Pennsylvania Magazine of History and Biography* 88, no. 2 (1964): 156n44.

46. Martin, *The Free and Open Press*, loc. 1341.

47. John Adams to Thomas Jefferson, 1815, quoted in Bailyn, *The Ideological Origins of the American Revolution*, 1.

48. Bernard Bailyn, *The Ideological Origins of the American Revolution*, enlarged ed. (Cambridge, MA: The Belknap Press of Harvard University Press, 1992), 43.

49. Joseph M. Adelman, *Revolutionary Networks: The Business and Politics of Printing the News, 1763–1789* (Baltimore: John Hopkins University Press, 2019), 143.

50. Richard Henderson to Cunningham Corbett, July 30, 1774, in *American Archives: Fourth Series*, ed. Peter Force (Washington, DC, 1837–1846), 3:54, quoted in *A History of the Book in America*, vol. 1: *The Colonial Book in the Atlantic World*, ed. Hugh Armory and David D. Hall (Chapel Hill: University of North Carolina Press, 2007), 483.

51. See, for example, Bailyn, *The Ideological Origins of the American Revolution*, 4–5, 17.

52. *Rivington's New York Gazetteer*, March 9, 1775, quoted in Solomon, *Revolutionary Dissent*, loc. 1195.

53. See, for example, Paul Revere to Jeremy Belknap, 1798, in *Paul Revere's Three Accounts of His Famous Ride*, ed. Edmund Morgan (Boston: Massachusetts Historical Society, 1968).

54. See, for example, Arthur M. Schlesinger, "The Colonial Newspapers and the Stamp Act," *New England Quarterly* 8, no. 1 (1935): 65.

55. Solomon, *Revolutionary Dissent*, loc. 1092–1095.

56. *Constitutional Courant*, September 21, 1765, repr., in Albert Matthews, "The Snake Devices, 1754–1776, and the Constitutional Courant, 1765," *Publications of The Colonial Society of Massachusetts* 11 (1906–1907), 417, 421–436. See also, Schlesinger, "The Colonial Newspapers and the Stamp Act," 69.

57. Cadwallader Colden to H.S. Conway, secretary of state for the colonies, in *Documents Relative to the Colonial History of the State of New-York*, ed. E. B. O'Callaghan and B. Fernow (Albany, 1856–1887), 7:759, quoted in Schlesinger, "The Colonial Newspapers and the Stamp Act," 68.

58. Solomon, *Revolutionary Dissent*, loc. 1060.

59. *Boston Gazette*, July 8, 1765, quoted in Solomon, *Revolutionary Dissent*, loc. 1465.

60. John Adams, "A Dissertation on the Canon and the Feudal Law," No. 4., *Boston Gazette*, October 21, 1765, in *The Adams Papers*, ed. Robert J. Taylor (Cambridge, MA: Harvard University Press, 1977), 1:123–128, Founders Online, National Archives, https://founders.archives.gov/documents/Adams/06-01-02-0052-0007.

61. Solomon, *Revolutionary Dissent*, loc. 1443.

62. The Virginia Resolves, May 30, 1765, Teaching American History, https://teachingamericanhistory.org/library/document/the-virginia-resolves-of-1765. See also, Solomon, *Revolutionary Dissent*, loc. 1419–1434.

63. Solomon, *Revolutionary Dissent*, 1095–1896.

64. See, for example, Schlesinger, "The Colonial Newspapers and the Stamp Act," 74.

65. The Declaratory Act (March 18, 1766), in *The Statutes at large . . . from 1225 to 1867*, ed. Danby Pickering (Cambridge: Benthem, for C. Bathhurst: London, 1762–1869), Lillian Goldman Law Library, https://avalon.law.yale.edu/18th_century/declaratory_act_1766.asp.

66. Bailyn, *The Ideological Origins of the American Revolution*, 4.

67. John Dickinson, *Letters from a Farmer in Pennsylvania* 3, 1767, in *Empire and Nation: Letters from a Farmer in Pennsylvania (John Dickinson). Letters from the Federal Farmer (Richard Henry Lee)*, ed. Forrest McDonald (Indianapolis: Liberty Fund, 1999), https://oll.libertyfund.org/titles /dickinson-empire-and-nation-letters-from-a-farmer.

68. Solomon, *Revolutionary Dissent*, loc. 33.

69. In the House of Representatives, March 3, 1768, in *Reports of Cases Argued and Adjudged*, ed. Josiah Quincy (Boston: Little, Brown, 1865), 274–275. See also, Solomon, *Revolutionary Dissent*, loc. 34–42.

70. Samuel Adams (Populus) in *Boston Gazette*, March 14, 1768, quoted in Solomon, *Revolutionary Dissent*, loc. 1637. See also, Levy, *Emergence of a Free Press*, 67.

71. Actions of the Citizens of Philadelphia, in Opposition to the Importation of Tea, January 3, 1774, in *Principles and Acts of the Revolution in America [. . .]*, ed. Hezekiah Niles (Baltimore: William Ogden Niles, 1822), 201, quoted in "On This Day, the Boston Tea Party Lights a Fuse," *Constitution Daily*, December 16, 2019, https://constitutioncenter.org/blog/on-this -day-the-boston-tea-party-lights-a-fuse.

72. John Adams, quoted in Bailyn, *The Ideological Origins of the American Revolution*, 118.

73. Bailyn, *The Ideological Origins of the American Revolution*, 17.

74. Martin, *The Free and Open Press*, loc. 1831–1849.

75. James Madison to William Bradford, March 1775, in *The Papers of James Madison*, vol. 1, ed. William T. Hutchinson and William M. E. Rachal (Chicago: The University of Chicago Press, 1962), 141–142, Founders Online, National Archives, https://founders.archives.gov/documents/Madison/01-01 -02-0041. See also, Martin, *The Free and Open Press*, loc. 1852–1876.

76. John Adams, quoted in Standage, *Writing on the Wall*, 139.

77. Thomas Paine, *Common Sense*, January 10, 1776, in *Common Sense, Rights of Man, and Other Political Writings*, ed. Mark Philip (Oxford: Oxford University Press, 1995).

78. Josiah Barlett to John Langdon, January 13, 1776, in *Letters of Delegates to Congress, 1774–1789*, vol. 3, ed. Paul H. Smith (Washington, DC: Library of Congress, 1976–2000), American Memory: Remaining Collections, Library of Congress, Washington, DC, http://memory.loc.gov/cgi-bin/query/r?am mem/hlaw:@field(DOCID+@lit(dg00371)).

79. Trish Loughran, *The Republic in Print: Print Culture in the Age of U.S. Nation Building, 1770–1870* (New York: Columbia University Press, 2007), 56; Ray Raphael, "Thomas Paine's Inflated Numbers," *Journal of the American Revolution*, March 20, 2013, https://allthingsliberty.com/2013/03 /thomas-paines-inflated-numbers.

80. George Washington to Lieutenant Colonel Joseph Reed, April 1, 1776, in *The Papers of George Washington*, vol. 4, ed. Philander D. Chase (Charlottesville: University Press of Virginia, 1991), 9–13, Founders Online, National Archives, https://founders.archives.gov/documents/Washington/03-04-02-0009.

81. John Adams to Thomas Jefferson, 1819, quoted in Standage, *Writing on the Wall*, 160.

82. Virginia Declaration of Rights, arts. 12 (June 12, 1776), in James McClellan, *Liberty, Order, and Justice: An Introduction to the Constitutional Principles of American Government*, 3rd ed. (Indianapolis: Liberty Fund, 2000), 188–190.

83. Constitution of Pennsylvania, art. XII (September 28, 1776), in *The Federal and State Constitutions Colonial Charters*, ed. Francis Newton Thorpe (Washington, DC: Government Printing Office, 1909), 3083.

84. Articles of Confederation, art. V, § 5 (March 1, 1781). See also, Akhil Reed Amar, "How America's Constitution Affirmed Freedom of Speech Even Before the First Amendment," *Capital University Law Review* 38, no. 3 (2010): 507.

85. John Adams to William Stephens Smith, December 26, 1787, Founders Online, National Archives, https://founders.archives.gov/documents/Adams/99-02-02-0298.

86. Amar, "How America's Constitution Affirmed Freedom of Speech," 509.

87. U.S. Const. art. I, § 6.

88. "Sentiments of Many," *Virginia Independent Chronicle*, June 18, 1788, in *The Complete Anti-Federalist*, ed. H. J. Storing (Chicago: The University of Chicago Press, 1981), 275.

89. Alexander Hamilton, Federalist No. 84, May 28, 1788, in *The Papers of Alexander Hamilton*, vol. 4, ed. Harold C. Syrett (New York: Columbia University Press, 1962), 702–714.

90. James Madison to Thomas Jefferson, October 17, 1788, in *The Papers of James Madison*, vol. 11, ed. Robert A. Rutland and Charles F. Hobson (Charlottesville: University Press of Virginia, 1977), 295–300.

91. Martin, *The Free and Open Press*, loc. 2398–2405.

92. Philadelphiensis I, *Independent Gazetteer*, November 7, 1787, in *The Documentary History of the Ratification of the Constitution*, ed. John P. Kaminski et al. (Madison: Wisconsin Historical Society Press, 1981), 13:578.

93. Martin, *The Free and Open Press*, loc. 2107–2113.

94. James Madison, "Speech in Congress," June 8, 1789, *Cong. Register* 1:418–419, in *The Papers of James Madison*, vol. 12, ed. Charles F. Hobson and Robert A. Rutland (Charlottesville: University Press of Virginia, 1979), 196–210, Founders Online, National Archives, https://founders.archives.gov/documents/Madison/01-12-02-0126.

95. Madison, "Speech in Congress," June 8, 1789.

96. U.S. Bill of Rights, amend. I.

97. James Madison, "Speech in Congress," June 8, 1789.

98. James Madison, "Speech in Congress," August 17, 1789, *Cong. Register* 2:227, in *The Papers of James Madison*, 12:344, Founders Online, National Archives, https://founders.archives.gov/documents/Madison/01-12-02-0227.

99. James Madison, "Speech in Congress," August 15, 1789, *Cong. Register* 2:195, in *The Papers of James Madison*, 12:339–342, Founders Online, National Archives, https://founders.archives.gov/documents/Madison/01-12-02-0224.

Chapter 7: Revolution and Reaction

1. Jonathan Israel, *The Expanding Blaze: How the American Revolution Ignited the World, 1775–1848* (Oxford: Princeton University Press, 2017), 3.

2. Israel, *The Expanding Blaze*, 231–232.

3. Joris van Eijnatten, "Between Practice and Principle: Dutch Ideas on Censorship and Press Freedom, 1759–1795," *Redescriptions: Yearbook for Political Thought and Conceptual History* (2004): 16–17.

4. Joan Derk van der Capellen tot den Pol, *An Address to the People of the Netherlands* (London, 1782), 136–137.

5. Van Eijnatten, "Between Practice and Principle," 16.

6. *De Post van den Neder-Rhyn*, VIII, nr. 400, 774, in Wyger Velema, *Republicans: Essays on Eighteenth-Century Dutch Political Thought* (Leiden and Boston: Brill, 2007), 148.

7. Simon Schama, *Patriots and Liberators: Revolution in the Netherlands, 1780–1813* (London: Collins, 1977), 80.

8. Elie Luzac, *Reinier Vryaart openhartige brieven, etc.* [1781–1784], 2:4:144, trans. Wyger Velema, in Laursen and Van der Zande, *Early French and German Defenses of Freedom of the Press*, 32.

9. See, for example, Jonathan Israel, *The Dutch Republic: Its Rise, Greatness, and Fall 1477–1806* (Oxford: Oxford University Press, 1995), 1100–1115; and Wiep van Bunge, *From Bayle to the Batavian Republic: Essays on Philosophy in the Eighteenth-Century Dutch Republic* (Boston: Brill, 2018), 266.

10. See, for example, William Doyle, *The Oxford History of the French Revolution*, 2nd ed. (Oxford: Oxford University Press, 2002), 27, 68–69; or, for a brief introduction, William Doyle, *The French Revolution: A Very Short Introduction* (Oxford: Oxford University Press, 2001), 19–37.

11. Charles Walton, *Policing Public Opinion in the French Revolution: The Culture of Calumny and the Problem of Free Speech* (Oxford: Oxford University Press, 2009), 51, 74.

12. The Declaration of the Rights of Man and Citizen, art. 1, in *The French Revolution and Human Rights*, ed. and trans. Lynn Hunt (Boston and New York: Bedford/St. Martin's, 1996), 78.

13. Hunt, *The French Revolution and Human Rights*, 10.

14. Hunt, *The French Revolution and Human Rights*, 19, 23–26.

15. See, for example, Jonathan Israel, *The Enlightenment That Failed: Ideas, Revolution, and Democratic Defeat, 1748–1830* (Oxford: Oxford University Press, 2019), 737.

16. Olympe de Gouges, Les Droits de la femme, arts. 1, 10 (Paris, 1791), trans. Hunt, *The French Revolution and Human Rights*, 125.

17. Marie-Jean-Antoine-Nicolas de Cariat, Marquis de Condorcet, "On giving Women the Right of Citizenship" (1790), in *Condorcet: Foundations of Social Choice and Political Theory*, trans. and ed. Iain McLean and Fiona Hewitt (Cheltenham: Edward Elgar, 1994), 297.

18. Jean Baptiste Amar, speech in the National Convention, October 30, 1793, in *Archives parlementaires* 78 (Paris, 1911), 20–22, 33–35, 48–51, trans. Hunt, *The French Revolution and Human Rights*, 135–138.

19. The Declaration of the Rights of Man and of the Citizen, art. 11, trans. Hunt, *The French Revolution and Human Rights*, 79.

20. Georg Jallinek, *The Declaration of the Rights of Man and of Citizens: A Contribution to Modern Constitutional History*, trans. Max Farrand (New York: Henry Holt, 1901), https://oll.libertyfund.org/titles/jellinek-the-declaration-of-the-rights-of-man-and-of-citizens/simple#lf0162_label_046.

21. Walton, *Policing Public Opinion*, 86–91.

22. Walton, *Policing Public Opinion*, 102, 106.

23. Jean-Paul Marat, *L'Ami du peuple* no. 181, August 4, 1790, trans. Walton, *Policing Public Opinion*, 106–107.

24. Jean-Paul Marat, placard, July 26, 1790, in *Encyclopedia Britannica*, s.v. "Jean-Paul Marat," by Jean Vidalenc, last modified July 9, 2020, www.britannica.com/biography/Jean-Paul-Marat.

25. See, for example, Doyle, *The Oxford History of the French Revolution*, 191; and Doyle, *The French Revolution*, 51.

26. Walton, *Policing Public Opinion*, 109–110.

27. François Xavier Lanthenas, *De la liberté indéfinie de la presse* (Paris, 1791), 26, trans. Walton, *Policing Public Opinion*, 110.

28. Walton, *Policing Public Opinion*, 109, 124.

29. Walton, *Policing Public Opinion*, 129.

30. Walton, *Policing Public Opinion*, 129–130.

31. Doyle, *The French Revolution*, 52–54.

32. Walton, *Policing Public Opinion*, 133.

33. Thomas Paine to George Danton, May 6, 1793, French National Archives, Thomas Paine National Historical Association, https://thomaspaine.org/letters/other/to-george-jacques-danton-may-6-1793.html. See also, Walton, *Policing Public Opinion*, 133.

34. Declaration des droits naturels, civils et politiques des hommes, arts. 4 and 5, Constitution Girondine 1793, Archivio de Diritto e Storia Constituzionali, Università de Torino, www.dircost.unito.it/altriDocumenti/docs/17930215__progettoDiCostitiuzioneGirondina.pdf.

35. Declaration of the Rights of Man and Citizen, Constitution of Year I, 1793, in *The Constitutions and Other Select Documents Illustrative of the History of France 1789–1901*, ed. Frank Maloy Anderson (Minneapolis: H. W. Wilson, 1904), 170–174.

36. The Law of Suspects (September 17, 1793), in *Liberty, Equality, Fraternity: Exploring the French Revolution*, ed. Jack R. Censer and Lynn Hunt (American Social History Productions, 2001), Columbia University, www.columbia.edu/~iw6/docs/suspects.html.

37. Olympe de Gouges, *The Three Urns, or the Welfare of the Motherland*, July 19, 1793, trans. Clarissa Palmer, Olympe de Gouges, www.olympedegouges.eu/three_urns.php.

38. The Trial of Olympe de Gouges, November 2, 1794, in *Women in Revolutionary Paris, 1789–1795*, ed. Darline Gay Levy, trans. Harriet B. Applewhite and Mary D. Johnson (Champaign: University of Illinois Press), 254–259, Liberté, Égalité, Fraternité: Exploring the French Revolution, https://revolution.chnm.org/d/488.

39. Doyle, *The Oxford History of the French Revolution*, 144–145.

40. Hunt, *The French Revolution and Human Rights*, 23.

41. Doyle, *The Oxford History of the French Revolution*, 260–262, 397.

42. Law of 14 Frimaire (December 4, 1793), trans. Walton, *Policing Public Opinion*, 129.

43. Maximilien Robespierre, "Citizens, Representatives of the People," speech to the National Convention, February 5, 1794, in *Report Upon the Principles of Political Morality Which Are to Form the Basis of the Administration of the Interior Concerns of the Republic* (Philadelphia, 1794).

44. Law of 22 Prairial (June 10, 1794), trans. Walton, *Policing Public Opinion*, 135.

45. Maris Linton, "Robespierre and the Terror," *History Today* 56, no. 8 (2006): 23, www.historytoday.com/archive/robespierre-and-terror.

46. Donald Greer, *The Incidence of the Terror During the French Revolution: A Statistical Interpretation* (Cambridge, MA: Harvard University Press, 1935), 85. See also, Walton, *Policing Public Opinion*, 186.

47. Greer, *The Incidence of the Terror During the French Revolution*, 85, quoted in Walton, *Policing Public Opinion*, 186.

48. Peter McPhee, *Robespierre: A Revolutionary Life* (New Haven: Yale University Press, 2012), 214–220; Doyle, *The French Revolution*, 58.

49. Declaration of Rights and Duties of Man and Citizen, Const. of the Year III, art. 9, October 26, 1795, in Anderson, *The Constitutions*, 170–174.

50. Walton, *Policing Public Opinion*, 231.

51. Catherine I, quoted in Norman Davies, *Europe: A History* (London: Pimlico, 1997), 717.

52. Douglas Smith, "Alexander Radishchev's *Journey from St. Petersburg to Moscow* and the Limits of Freedom of Speech in the Reign of Catherine the Great," in *Freedom of Speech: The History of an Idea*, ed. Elizabeth Powers (Lewisburg, PA: Bucknell University Press, 2011), 61–80. See also, Allen McConnell, *A Russian* Philosophe, *Alexander Radishchev 1749–1802* (The Hague: Martinus Nijhoff, 2012).

53. D. S. Babkin, *Protsess A. N. Radishcheva* (Moscow-Leningrad: Izd-vo Akademii Nauk, 1952), 33–35, 151, 156–164, quoted in Smith, "Alexander Radishchev's *Journey from St. Petersburg to Moscow*," 75.

54. Smith, "Alexander Radishchev's *Journey from St. Petersburg to Moscow*," 77.

55. Quoted in Smith, "Alexander Radishchev's *Journey from St. Petersburg to Moscow*," 61.

56. Aleksandr Radishchev, *A Journey from St. Petersburg to Moscow*, trans. Leo Wiener (Cambridge, MA: Harvard University Press, 1958), 164–165, 168–169, 171–172, quoted in Smith, "Alexander Radishchev's *Journey from St. Petersburg to Moscow*," 65, 67.

57. Radishchev, *A Journey from St. Petersburg to Moscow*, in K. A. Papmehl, *Freedom of Expression in Eighteenth Century Russia* (The Hague: Martinus Nijhoff, 1971), 125.

58. *Journal of the Kantselariya of the Imperial Academy of Sciences*, no. 602, 1791, quoted in Semennikov, *A Contribution to the History of Censorship in the Age of Catherine* (Russkiy Bibliofil, 1913), no.1:52, quoted in Papmehl, *Freedom of Expression in Eighteenth Century Russia*, 116.

59. Papmehl, *Freedom of Expression in Eighteenth Century Russia*, 118, 122; Smith, "Alexander Radishchev's *Journey from St. Petersburg to Moscow*," 77.

60. Christopher Clark, *Iron Kingdom: The Rise and Downfall of Prussia 1600–1947* (London: Penguin, 2006), 269.

61. Johan Christian Laursen and Johan van der Zande, eds., *Early French and German Defenses of Freedom of the Press* (Leiden: Brill, 2003), 103.

62. Edoardo Tortarolo, *The Invention of Free Press: Writers and Censorship in Eighteenth Century Europe* (Dordrecht: Springer, 2016), 153.

63. Pamela E. Selwyn, *Everyday Life in the German Book Trade: Friedrich Nicolai as Bookseller and Publishers in the Age of Enlightenment 1750–1810* (University Park: Pennsylvania State University Press, 2000), 210.

64. Clark, *Iron Kingdom*, 269.

65. James J. DiCenso, *Kant: Religion Within the Boundaries of Mere Reason: A Commentary* (Cambridge: Cambridge University Press, 2012).

66. Johann Christoph von Wöllner, royal proclamation (October 1, 1794), in Immanuel Kant, *The conflict of the faculties* 7:6 (Königsberg: Friedrich Nicolovius, 1798), in *Immanuel Kant: Religion and Rational Theology*, trans. Allen W. Wood and George di Giovvani (Cambridge: Cambridge University Press, 2001), 240.

67. Immanuel Kant to J. C. von Wöllner, October 1794, in *The conflict of the faculties* 7:10, in Wood and Giovanni, *Immanuel Kant*, 242.

68. Richard Price, *A Discourse on the Love of Our Country*, November 4, 1789, in *Richard Price: Political Writings*, ed. D. O. Thomas (Cambridge: Cambridge University Press, 1991), 195–196.

69. George H. Smith, "Thomas Paine Versus Edmund Burke, Part 6," Libertarianism.org, Cato Institute, May 30, 2014, www.libertarianism.org /columns/thomas-paine-versus-edmund-burke-part-6.

70. Edmund Burke, *Substance of the speech of the Right Honourable Edmund Burke, in thr [sic] debate on the army estimates, in the House of Commons*, February 9, 1790 (London: J. Debrett, 1790), Eighteenth Century Collections Online, https://quod.lib.umich.edu/e/ecco/004902170.0001.000 ?rgn=main;view=fulltext.

71. Edmund Burke, *Reflections on the Revolution in France*, 1790, in *Revolutionary Writings*, ed. Iain Hampsher-Monk (Cambridge: Cambridge University Press, 2014), 39, 81, 89, 224.

72. Mark Philip, *The French Revolution and British Popular Politics* (Cambridge: Cambridge University Press, 1991), 5.

73. Mary Wollstonecraft, *A Vindication of the Rights of Men*, 2nd ed. (London: J. Johnson, 1790), 25, 88.

74. Joseph Priestley, "Letter XIII: Of the Prospect of the general Enlargement of Liberty, civil and religious, opened by the Revolution in France," in *Letters to the Right Honourable Edmund Burke* (Birmingham: Thomas Pearson, 1791), 140.

75. See, for example, Martin Fitzpatrick, "Priestley, Joseph," in *An Oxford Companion to the Romantic Age*, ed. Iain McCalman et al. (Oxford: Oxford University Press, 2009).

76. Joseph Priestley, "Letter XII: Of the Danger of the Church, and of the Test Laws," in *Letters to the Right Honourable Edmund Burke*, 131.

77. See, for example, Fitzpatrick, "Priestley, Joseph"; and John G. McEnvoy, "Priestley, Joseph," in *Encyclopedia of the Enlightenment*, ed. Alan C. Kors (Oxford: Oxford University Press, 2005).

78. Thomas Paine, *Rights of Man*, 1791, in *"Rights of Man," "Common Sense" and Other Political Writings*, ed. Mark Philip (Oxford: Oxford University Press, 1995), 134–135, 137, 141.

79. Edmund Burke, *An Appeal from the New to the Old Whigs*, August 3, 1791, in *The Writings and Speeches of Edmund Burke*, ed. P. J. Marshall and Donald Bryant (Oxford: Oxford University Press, 2015), 4:439.

80. Thomas Paine, *Rights of Man, Part the Second*, 1792, in *"Rights of Man," "Common Sense" and Other Political Writings*, 210, 225, 233.

81. Thomas Paine, quoted in John Keane, *Tom Paine: A Political Life* (London: Bloomsbury, 1995), 341.

82. Philip, *The French Revolution and British Popular Politics*, 5.

83. Keane, *Tom Paine*, 426.

84. Philip, *The French Revolution and British Popular Politics*, 5.

85. George III, A Proclamation, May 21, 1792, in *Journal of the House of Lords*, vol. 39, 1790–1793 (London: His Majesty's Stationery Office, 1767–1830), 431–458, British History Online, www.british-history.ac.uk/lords-jrnl/vol39/pp431-458. See also, Philip, *The French Revolution and British Popular Politics*, 7; and Jennifer Mori, *Britain in the Age of the French Revolution 1785–1820* (London: Routledge, 2000), 94–96.

86. Keane, *Tom Paine*, 335–336.

87. Frank O'Gorman, "The Paine Burnings of 1792–1793," *Past & Present* 193 (2006): 111.

88. Keane, *Tom Paine*, 431.

89. *The Trial of Thomas Paine: for a libel contained The second part of rights of man[. . .]*, 1792, 5–9, 20, Eighteenth Century Collections Online, https://quod.lib.umich.edu/e/ecco/004809446.0001.000/1:2?rgn=div1;view=fulltext.

90. Thomas Paine, *The Age of Reason, Part II* (London, 1795), in *The Writings of Thomas Paine*, ed. Moncure Daniel Conway (New York: G. P. Putnam's Sons, 1894), 4:186.

91. Leonard Levy, *Blasphemy—Verbal Offense Against the Sacred, from Moses to Salman Rushdie* (Chapel Hill: University of North Carolina Press, 1993), 333.

92. Mori, *Britain in the Age of the French Revolution*, 96. See also, Mark Philip, "Britain and the French Revolution," BBC, last modified February 17, 2011, www.bbc.co.uk/history/british/empire_seapower/british_french_rev_01.shtml.

93. Philip, *The French Revolution and British Popular Politics*, 7–8.

94. Mori, *Britain in the Age of the French Revolution*, 100. See also, Marjorie Bloy, "The Age of George III," A Web of English History, last modified April 23, 2017, www.historyhome.co.uk/c-eight/france/pitfrwar.htm.

95. William Pitt, "Speech to the House of Commons," April 30, 1792, in *The Speeches of the Right Honourable William Pitt, in the House of Commons,*

ed. W. S. Hathaway (London: J. Hatchard; printed for Longman, Hurst, Rees & Orme, 1806), 92.

96. *The Annual Register, or a View of the History, Politics, and Literature For the Year 1794* (London: G. Auld, Greville-Street, 1799), 268–271, 275.

97. George III, Treasonable and Seditious Practices Act, 1795, University of Victoria, https://web2.uvcs.uvic.ca/courses/lawdemo/DOCS/TREASON.htm. See also, Mori, *Britain in the Age of the French Revolution*, 99; and Bloy, "The Age of George III."

98. Bloy, "The Age of George III."

99. Philip, "Britain and the French Revolution."

100. Michael Duffy, "War, Revolution and the Crisis of the British Empire," in Philip, *The French Revolution and British Popular Politics*, 118–145.

101. George III, Act Against Unlawful Combinations and Confederacies, 1799, University of Victoria, https://web2.uvcs.uvic.ca/courses/lawdemo/DOCS/COMBCONF.htm.

102. Mori, *Britain in the Age of the French Revolution*, 93–94.

103. Charles Slack, *Liberty's First Crisis: Adams, Jefferson, and the Misfits Who Saved Free Speech* (New York: Grove Atlantic, 2015), 56–86, Kindle.

104. Solomon, *Revolutionary Dissent*, loc. 5126–5157.

105. James Madison to Thomas Jefferson, May 13, 1798, in *The Papers of James Madison*, vol. 17, ed. David B. Mattern et al. (Charlottesville: University Press of Virginia), 130–131, Founders Online, National Archives, https://founders.archives.gov/documents/Madison/01-17-02-0088.

106. Slack, *Liberty's First Crisis*, loc. 1041.

107. The Alien and Sedition Act, sec. 2 (July 6, 1798).

108. Wendell Bird, *Criminal Dissent: Prosecutions Under the Alien and Sedition Acts of 1798* (Cambridge: Harvard University Press, 2020), 2.

109. Charles O. Lerche Jr., "Jefferson and the Election of 1800: A Case Study in the Political Smear," *William and Mary Quarterly* 5, no. 4 (1948): 467–491.

110. Bird, *Criminal Dissent*.

111. Alexander Hamilton to Oliver Wolcott Jr., June 29, 1798, in *The Papers of Alexander Hamilton*, vol. 21, ed. Harold C. Syrett (New York: Columbia University Press, 1974), 522–523, Founders Online, National Archives, https://founders.archives.gov/documents/Hamilton/01-21-02-0296.

112. Alexander Hamilton to Jonathan Dayton, October–November 1799, in *The Papers of Alexander Hamilton*, 2:599–604, Founders Online, National Archives, https://founders.archives.gov/documents/Hamilton/01-23-02-0526.

113. George Hay, *An Essay on the Liberty of the Press* (Philadelphia: Aurora, 1799), 35, 40, 43, 47, 49, 50, Evans Early American Imprint Collection, https://quod.lib.umich.edu/e/evans/N26756.0001.001?rgn=main;view=full text. See also, Slack, *Liberty's First Crisis*, 151–152.

114. James Madison and Thomas Jefferson, *The Resolutions of Virginia and Kentucky* (1798; repr. Richmond: Shepherd and Pollard, 1826), 38. See also, Bird, *Criminal Dissent*, 154–156.

115. Thomas Jefferson, quoted in Bird, *Criminal Dissent*, 4.

116. James Madison, *The Report of 1800*, January 7, 1800, in *The Papers of James Madison*, vol. 17, ed. David B. Mattern et al. (Charlottesville: University Press of Virginia, 1991), 303–351, Founders Online, National Archives, https://founders.archives.gov/documents/Madison/01-17-02-0202.

117. Matthew Lyon, letter in *Spooner's Vermont Journal*, July 31, 1798, quoted in Francis Wharton, *State Trials of the United States During the Administrations of Washington and Adams* (Philadelphia, 1849), 333.

118. Bird, *Criminal Dissent*, 91–95.

119. Bird, *Criminal Dissent*, 133–138.

120. Slack, *Liberty's First Crisis*, 84.

121. Slack, *Liberty's First Crisis*, 78.

122. George Washington to Timothy Pickering, August 4, 1799, in *The Papers of George Washington*, ed. W. W. Abbott (Charlottesville: University Press of Virginia, 1799), 4:221–223, Founders Online, National Archives, https://founders.archives.gov/documents/Washington/06-04-02-0184.

123. Solomon, *Revolutionary Dissent*, loc. 5347–5348.

124. Benjamin Franklin Bache, *Aurora General Advertiser*, August 28, 1798, in *American Aurora: A Democratic-Republican Returns*, ed. Richard N. Rosenfeld (New York: St. Martin's Press, 1998), 222.

125. Bird, *Criminal Dissent*, 9, 369.

126. Thomas Jefferson, "First Inaugural Address," March 4, 1801, in *The Papers of Thomas Jefferson*, ed. Barbara B. Oberg (Princeton: Princeton University Press, 2006), 33:148–152.

127. Thomas Jefferson to Thomas McKean, February 19, 1803, in *The Papers of Thomas Jefferson*, ed. Barbara B. Oberg (Princeton: Princeton University Press, 2012), 39:552–555.

128. Bird, *Criminal Dissent*, loc. 8643.

129. Judge Learned Hand, "The Spirit of Liberty," May 21, 1944, FIRE, www.thefire.org/first-amendment-library/special-collections/the-spirit-of-liberty-speech-by-judge-learned-hand-1944.

Chapter 8: The Quiet Continent

1. Louis de Jaucourt, "Press," in *Encyclopédie, ou Dictionnaire Raisonné des sciences, des arts et des métiers*, ed. Denis Diderot and Jean le Rond d'Alembert, in *Encyclopedic Liberty: Political Articles in the Dictionary of Diderot and D'Alembert*, trans. and ed. Henry C. Clark and Christine Dunn Henderson (Indianapolis: Liberty Fund, 2016), 532.

2. See, for example, *Encyclopedia Britannica*, s.v. "Concert of Europe," last modified February 22, 2016, www.britannica.com/event/Concert-of-Europe.

3. Jonathan Israel, *The Enlightenment That Failed: Ideas, Revolution, and Democratic Defeat, 1748–1830* (Oxford: Oxford University Press, 2019), 771–773.

4. James Curran and Jean Seaton, *Power Without Responsibility: Press, Broadcasting and the Internet in Britain*, 7th ed. (London: Routledge, 2010), 7.

5. Philip Harling, "The Law of Libel and the Limits of Repression, 1790–1832," *Historical Journal* 44, no. 1 (2001): 109–110.

6. Michael Lobban, "From Seditious Libel to Unlawful Assembly: Peterloo and the Changing Face of Political Crime," *Oxford Journal of Legal Studies* 10, no. 3 (1990): 325.

7. Charles Tilly, *Popular Contention in Great Britain, 1758–1834* (London: Routledge, 2005), 251.

8. Donald Read, *Peterloo: The Massacre and Its Background* (Manchester: Manchester University Press, 1958), 2.

9. Read, *Peterloo*, 55–56, 115.

10. Tilly, *Popular Contention*, 260.

11. Read, *Peterloo*, 129–131.

12. Read, *Peterloo*, 134–140.

13. Lobban, "From Seditious Libel," 349.

14. Percy B. Shelley, *The Masque of Anarchy. A Poem* (1918; repr., London: Edward Moxon, 1832), 47. See also, John Sutherland, quoted in "Londoner's Diary: Jeremy Corbyn's Romantic Notions Traced Back to Percy Shelley," *Evening Standard*, May 17, 2017, www.standard.co.uk/news/londoners-diary/londoner-s-diary-jeremy-corbyn-s-romantic-notions-traced-back-to-percy-shelley-a3541276.html.

15. Great Britain, Parliament, *Notes and Observations, Critical and Explanatory* (London, 1820), 68.

16. Lord Sidmouth, quoted in Harling, "The Law of Libel," 126.

17. Harling, "The Law of Libel," 131.

18. Read, *Peterloo*, 73.

19. Rex v. Taylor (1676). See Elliott Visconsi, "The Invention of Criminal Blasphemy: Rex v. Taylor (1676)," *Representations* 103, no. 1 (2008): 30–52. See also, Leonard Levy, *Blasphemy—Verbal Offense Against the Sacred, from Moses to Salman Rushdie* (Chapel Hill: University of North Carolina Press, 1993), 345.

20. Lobban, "From Seditious Libel," 327; E. P. Thompson, *The Making of the English Working Class* (New York: Pantheon Books, 1963), 700.

21. Levy, *Blasphemy*, 352.

22. Richard Carlile, *The Republican*, August 27, 1819. See also, "The Republican," Spartacus Educational, https://spartacus-educational.com/PRrepublican.htm.

23. Quoted in Richard Carlile, *The Report of the Proceedings of the Court of King's Bench [. . .] Being the Mock Trial of Richard Carlile* (London, 1822), 7, 13. See also, Levy, *Blasphemy*, 357–358.

24. Levy, *Blasphemy*, 364.

25. David S. Nash, *Blasphemy in Modern Britain: 1789 to the Present* (Brookfield: Ashgate, 1999), 86–88.

26. Christina Parolin, "The 'She-Champion of Impiety': Female Radicalism and Political Crime in Early Nineteenth-Century England," in *Radical Spaces: Venues of Popular Politics in London, 1790–c. 1845* (Canberra: ANU E Press, 2010), 83–104; Tansy Barton, "World Press Freedom Day: The Pregnant Woman Jailed for Publishing 'Blasphemous' Books," *University of London Senate House Library*, May 3, 2018, https://london.ac.uk/senate-house-library/blog/world-press-freedom-day-pregnant-woman-jailed-publishing-%E2%80%98blasphemous%E2%80%99-books.

27. James Mill, "Liberty of the Press," in *Supplement to the Encyclopedia Britannica* (London: J. Innes, 1825), https://oll.libertyfund.org/title/mill-liberty-of-the-press-1825.

28. Christopher Macleod, "John Stuart Mill," *Stanford Encyclopedia of Philosophy*, Summer 2020 ed., ed. Edward N. Zalta, https://plato.stanford.edu/entries/mill.

29. Levy, *Blasphemy*, 376–378.

30. Curran and Seaton, *Power Without Responsibility*, 7.

31. Curran and Seaton, *Power Without Responsibility*, 17–19, 21.

32. Curran and Seaton, *Power Without Responsibility*, 8.

33. Ellis Archer Wasson, "The Whigs and the Press, 1800–50," *Parliamentary History* 25, no. 1 (2006): 78.

34. Wasson, "The Whigs and the Press," 85. For the 2009 repeal, see "UK Government Abolishes Seditious Libel and Criminal Defamation," *Human Rights House Foundation*, July 13, 2009, https://humanrightshouse.org/articles/uk-government-abolishes-seditious-libel-and-criminal-defamation.

35. Curran and Seaton, *Power Without Responsibility*, 8.

36. Spring Rice, *Parliamentary Debates* 34 (1836), cols. 627–634, 37 (1837), col. 1165, quoted in Curran and Seaton, *Power Without Responsibility*, 8.

37. Curran and Seaton, *Power Without Responsibility*, 8.

38. Robert Justin Goldstein, *The War for the Public Mind: Political Censorship in Nineteenth-Century Europe* (Westport and London: Praeger, 2000), 29.

39. Wasson, "The Whigs and the Press," 84.

40. Curran and Seaton, *Power Without Responsibility*, 21

41. Goldstein, *The War for the Public Mind*, 29.

42. John Stuart Mill, *Principles of Political Economy with some of their Applications to Social Philosophy* (1848), in *The Collected Works of John Stuart Mill*, ed. John M. Robson (Toronto: University of Toronto Press, 1965), 3:762, Liberty

Fund, https://oll.libertyfund.org/title/mill-the-collected-works-of-john-stuart-mill-volume-iii-principles-of-political-economy-part-ii.

43. Wasson, "The Whigs and the Press," 85.

44. Mogens Herman Hansen, *The Tradition of Ancient Greek Democracy and Its Importance for Modern Democracy* (Copenhagen: The Royal Danish Academy of Sciences and Letters, 2005), 19.

45. George Grote, *A History of Greece* (New York: Harper & Bros., 1857), 6:150.

46. John Stuart Mill, *On Liberty* (1859), in *On Liberty and The Subjection of Women* (New York: Henry Holt and Co., 1879), 15, 33, 35–36, Liberty Fund, https://oll.libertyfund.org/title/mill-on-liberty-and-the-subjection-of-women-1879-ed.

47. Curran and Seaton, *Power Without Responsibility*, 6–7, 21, 36.

48. Quoted in Robert Justin Goldstein, *Political Censorship of the Arts and the Press in Nineteenth-Century Europe* (Basingstoke: Palgrave Macmillan, 1989), 30.

49. Klemens von Metternich, quoted in E. Ziegler, *Literarische Zensur in Deutschland 1819–1848* (Munich: C. Hanser, 1983), 119, trans. Robin Lenman, "Germany," in Goldstein, *The War for the Public Mind*, 40.

50. Lenman, "Germany," 41–42.

51. Goldstein, *The War for the Public Mind*, 127.

52. See, for example, John Roach, "Education and Public Opinion," in *The New Cambridge Modern History*, vol. 9, *War and Peace in an Age of Upheaval, 1793–1830*, ed. C. W. Crawley (Cambridge: Cambridge University Press, 1965), 188.

53. Mads Andenæs and Ingeborg Wilberg, eds., *The Constitution of Norway: A Commentary* (Oslo: Universitetsforlaget, 1987), 157.

54. John Christian Laursen, "Censorship in the Nordic Countries, ca. 1750–1890," *Journal of Modern European History* 3, no. 1 (2005): 114–115.

55. Israel, *The Enlightenment That Failed*, 785–788.

56. Israel, *The Enlightenment That Failed*, 777–778.

57. Lenman, "Germany," 40–42.

58. Benjamin Constant, *Principles of Politics Applicable to All Governments* (1815), trans. Dennis O'Keeffe, ed. Etienne Hofmann (Indianapolis: Liberty Fund, 2003), 133, 137, https://oll.libertyfund.org/titles/861#Constant_0452_482.

59. Jonathan Sperber, *Revolutionary Europe, 1780–1850* (London: Routledge, 2000), 279.

60. John M. Merriman, *The Margins of City Life: Explorations on the French Urban Frontier, 1815–1851* (Oxford: Oxford University Press, 1991), 76.

61. Standage, *Writing on the Wall*, 171; Goldstein, *The War for the Public Mind*, 134.

62. Pamela M. Pilbeam, *The 1830 Revolution in France* (Basingstoke, UK: MacMillan, 1991), 30.

63. Pilbeam, *The 1830 Revolution in France*, 60–61.

64. Goldstein, *The War for the Public Mind*, 139.

65. Fr. Const. of 1830, August 14, 1830, in *The Constitutions and other select documents illustrative of the history of France 1789–1901*, ed. Frank Maloy Anderson (Minneapolis: H. W. Wilson, 1904), 507–513. See also, Pilbeam, *The 1830 Revolution in France*.

66. Helena Rosenblatt, *The Lost History of Liberalism: From Ancient Rome to the Twenty-First Century* (Princeton: Princeton University Press, 2018), 88–89.

67. Heinrich Heine, *Almansor* (1821), in *Werke in fünfzehn Teilen*, ed. Erwin Kalischer and Raimund Pissin (Berlin: Bong; Project Gutenberg, 2014), 20, www.gutenberg.org/files/45600/45600-h/45600-h.htm. My translation.

68. Heinrich Heine, *Reisebilder. Das Buch Le Grand* (Hamburg: Hoffman und Campe, 1826), 236–237.

69. Lenman, "Germany," 42.

70. Quoted in Goldstein, *The War for the Public Mind*, 19.

71. Sperber, *Revolutionary Europe*, 258.

72. The German Confederation, The Six Articles, art. 5 (June 28, 1832), trans. Jeremiah Riemer, in *Deutsche Verfassungsdokumente 1803–1850*, vol. 1, *Dokumente zur deutschen Verfassungsgeschichte*, 3rd ed., rev. and enl., ed. Ernst Rudolf Huber (Stuttgart: W. Kohlhammer, 1978), 132–133. See also, Lenman, "Germany," 42.

73. Lenman, "Germany," 42.

74. Lenman, "Germany," 43.

75. Rosenblatt, *The Lost History of Liberalism*, 91.

76. Goldstein, *The War for the Public Mind*, 131.

77. Pilbeam, *The 1830 Revolution in France*, 93–94.

78. Maxime du Camp, quoted in Goldstein, *The War for the Public Mind*, 142.

79. Goldstein, *Political Censorship*, 41.

80. Goldstein, *The War for the Public Mind*, 15.

81. Goldstein, *The War for the Public Mind*, 10.

82. Lenman, "Germany," 47.

83. Karl Marx, "Censorship," in *Rheinische Zeitung* no. 135, May 15, 1842, Marx/Engels Internet Archive, www.marxists.org/archive/marx/works/download/Marx_On_freedom_of_the_Press.pdf. See also, Padmaja Shaw, "Marx as Journalist: Revisiting the Free Speech Debate," *TripleC* 10, no. 2 (2012): 218–220.

84. David McLellan, *Karl Marx: A Biography* (Basingstoke, UK: Macmillan, 1995), 39–49.

85. McLellan, *Karl Marx*, 116–126.

86. Christian Karl Josias, baron von Bunsen, *Aus seinen Briefen und nach eigener Erinnerung geschildert von seiner Witwe* (1847; repr. Leipzig: F.A. Brockhaus, 1869), 392, trans. Goldstein, *The War for the Public Mind*, 13.

87. Quoted in T. C. Jones, "French Republicanism After 1848," in *The 1848 Revolutions and European Political Thought*, ed. Douglas Moggach and Gareth Stedman Jones (Cambridge: Cambridge University Press, 2018), 73. See also, Goldstein, *The War for the Public Mind*, 147–148.

88. Quoted in Frederik Ohles, *Germany's Rude Awakening: Censorship in the Land of the Brothers Grimm* (Kent, OH: Kent State University Press, 1992), 164.

89. See, for example, Lenman, "Germany," 49.

90. Goldstein, *The War for the Public Mind*, 20–21.

91. Jonathan Sperber, *The European Revolutions, 1848–1851*, 2nd ed. (Cambridge: Cambridge University Press, 2005), 160.

92. Sperber, *The European Revolutions*, 160–162; Sperber, *Revolutionary Europe*, 247.

93. Quoted in Goldstein, *The War for the Public Mind*, 147–148.

94. Goldstein, *The War for the Public Mind*, 149.

95. Lothar Höbelt, "The Austrian Empire," in Goldstein, *The War for the Public Mind*, 224.

96. Lenman, "Germany," 50–51.

97. Goldstein, *The War for the Public Mind*, 131–132.

98. Quoted in Goldstein, *The War for the Public Mind*, 150.

99. Goldstein, *The War for the Public Mind*, 132.

100. Alice Catherine Carls, "France," in *World Press Encyclopedia: A Survey of Press Systems Worldwide*, ed. Amanda C. Quick (Farmington Hills, MI: Gale, 2002), 316.

101. Goldstein, *The War for the Public Mind*, 156–157.

102. Lenman, "Germany," 51–53.

103. Gary D. Stark, "Trials and Tribulations: Authors' Responses to Censorship in Imperial Germany, 1885–1914," *German Studies Review* 12, no. 3 (1989): 448–449.

104. Quoted in Gary D. Stark, *Banned in Berlin: Literary Censorship in Imperial Germany, 1871–1918* (New York: Berghahn Books, 2012), 2.

105. Lenman, "Germany," 56.

106. Stark, *Banned in Berlin*, 155.

107. Lenman, "Germany," 57–58.

108. Heidi J. S. Tworek, *News from Germany: The Competition to Control World Communications, 1900–1945* (Cambridge, MA: Harvard University Press), 31.

109. Lenman, "Germany," 60.

110. Quoted in Goldstein, *The War for the Public Mind*, 9.

111. Lenman, "Germany," 58.

112. John B. Bury, *A History of Freedom of Thought* (1918; repr. Oxford: Oxford University Press, 1951), 2.

Chapter 9: White Man's Burden

1. Alexis de Tocqueville, *Democracy in America* [1835–1840], trans. Henry Reeve, ed. John C. Spencer (New York: Edward Walker, 1850), 181–185, 264.

2. *Population of the United States in 1860; Compiled from the Original Returns of the Eighth Census* (Washington, DC: Government Printing Office, 1864), vii, www2.census.gov/library/publications/decennial/1860/population/1860a-02.pdf.

3. Michael Kent Curtis, *Free Speech, "The People's Darling Privilege": Struggles for Freedom of Expression in American History* (Durham, NC: Duke University Press, 2000), 121.

4. Curtis, *Free Speech*, 128–129, 293–294.

5. Curtis, *Free Speech*, 137; An Act to Suppress the Circulation of Incendiary Publications (March 23, 1836), in *Acts of the General Assembly of Virginia, Passed at the Session of 1835–36* (Richmond, VA: Thomas Ritchie, 1836), 44–45.

6. The State of Alabama, Copy of Indictment, 1835, in *Documents of the Assembly of the State of New York*, 59th Ses. (Albany, 1836), 2.

7. Michael Kent Curtis, "The Curious History of Attempts to Suppress Antislavery Speech, Press, and Petition in 1835–37," *Northwestern University Law Review* 89, no. 3 (1995): 786.

8. Curtis, *Free Speech*, 155

9. Curtis, *Free Speech*, 176.

10. Curtis, *Free Speech*, 163.

11. Cong. Globe, 24th Cong., 1st Sess., 3rd vol. (1836): 77.

12. Quoted in Curtis, *Free Speech*, 135.

13. "Protest of the American Anti-Slavery Society," *Evening Post* (NY), January 28, 1836, 2, quoted in Curtis, *Free Speech*, 159.

14. Thomas Jefferson to Thomas Cooper, September 10, 1814, in *The Papers of Thomas Jefferson*, vol. 7, ed. J. Jefferson Looney (Princeton: Princeton University Press, 2010), 649–655, Founders Online, National Archives, https://founders.archives.gov/documents/Jefferson/03-07-02-0471.

15. Curtis, *Free Speech*, 140–141.

16. Curtis, "The Curious History," 789.

17. Cincinnatus, *Freedom's Defence, or, A Candid Examination of Mr. Calhoun's Report on Freedom of the Press* (Worcester, MA: Dorr, Howland, 1836), 14, quoted in Curtis, *Free Speech*, 168.

18. Curtis, *Free Speech*, 20, 22, 169.

19. "Proposed Bill on Incendiary Publications Fails to Pass in the Senate," The History Engine, The University of Richmond, https://historyengine.rich mond.edu/episodes/view/513.

20. Martin Gruberg, "Gag Rule in Congress," *First Amendment Encyclopedia*, Free Speech Center, Middle Tennessee State University, 2009, https:// mtsu.edu/first-amendment/article/1210/gag-rule-in-congress.

21. Angelina Grimké, "Speech at the State House in Boston," February 21, 1838, quoted in "Angelina Grimke Addresses Legislature," Mass Moments, Mass Humanities, www.massmoments.org/moment-details/angelina-grimke -addresses-legislature.html.

22. "*Uncle Tom's Cabin*: A 19th-Century Bestseller," Publishers' Bindings Online, 1815–1930: The Art of Books, University of Alabama, https://bindings .lib.ua.edu/gallery/uncletom.html.

23. Claire Parfait, *The Publishing History of "Uncle Tom's Cabin," 1852–2002* (Farnham, UK: Ashgate, 2007), 95–96.

24. Curtis, *Free Speech*, 129.

25. See, for example, "Lovejoy, Elijah Parish," in *The Oxford Companion to American Literature*, 6th ed., ed. James D. Hart and Philip W. Leininger (Oxford: Oxford University Press, 1995).

26. Curtis, *Free Speech*, 228–230.

27. "Pennsylvania Hall Historical Marker," Explore PA History, https:// explorepahistory.com/hmarker.php?markerId=1-A-104.

28. Angelina Grimké, "Speech at Pennsylvania Hall," May 16, 1838, in *History of Pennsylvania Hall Which Was Destroyed by a Mob on the 17th of May, 1838* (New York: Negro Universities Press, A Division of Greenwood Publishing, 1969).

29. "Pennsylvania Hall Historical Marker," Explore PA History, https:// explorepahistory.com/hmarker.php?markerId=1-A-104.

30. Frederick Douglass, "The Kansas-Nebraska Bill," speech, October 30, 1854, Frederick Douglass Project, River Campus Libraries, University of Rochester, https://rbscp.lib.rochester.edu/4400.

31. Frederick Douglass, "A Plea for Free Speech in Boston," December 10, 1860, Jack Miller Center, https://jackmillercenter.org/cd-resources/free -speech-slavery.

32. See, for example, Curtis, *Free Speech*, 205.

33. Quoted in Curtis, *Free Speech*, 281.

34. The affair is described in detail and with copies of relevant correspondence in Joseph Grégoire de Roulhac Hamilton, ed., *Benjamin Sherwood Hedrick* (Chapel Hill: University of North Carolina, 1910), Documenting the American South, University Library, The University of North Carolina at Chapel Hill, 2005, https://docsouth.unc.edu/true/hamilton/hamilton.html.

35. Benjamin Sherwood Hedrick, *Mr. Hedrick Once More*, November 5, 1856, in Hamilton, *Benjamin Sherwood Hedrick*.

36. The State of South Carolina, Declaration of the Immediate Causes Which Induce and Justify the Secession of South Carolina from the Federal Union (Charleston, 1860), 9.

37. U.S. Const. amend. XIII, XIV (1), XV.

38. Plessy v. Ferguson, 163 U.S. 537 (1896).

39. Equal Justice Initiative, *Lynching in America: Confronting the Legacy of Racial Terror*, 3rd ed. (2017), https://lynchinginamerica.eji.org/report.

40. See, for example, Robin Hardin and Marcie Hinton, "The Squelching of Free Speech in Memphis: The Life of a Black Post-Reconstruction Newspaper," *Race, Gender & Class Journal* 8, no. 4 (2001): 78–95.

41. Ida B. Wells, editorial in *Memphis Free Speech* (1892), quoted in *Crusade for Justice: The Autobiography of Ida B. Wells*, 2nd ed., ed. Alfreda M. Duster (Chicago: University of Chicago Press, 2020), 57.

42. *Daily Commercial* (May 1892), quoted in Hardin and Hinton, "The Squelching of Free Speech in Memphis," 87.

43. Quoted in The Gale Group, "Ida B. Wells-Barnett (1862–1931)," *CBN*, www.cbn.com/special/blackhistory/bio_idabwells.aspx.

44. Hardin and Hinton, "The Squelching of Free Speech in Memphis," 90.

45. Woodrow Wilson, "Third Annual Message," 1915, Miller Center, https://millercenter.org/the-presidency/presidential-speeches/december-7-1915-third-annual-message.

46. Espionage Act, 40 Stat. 217 (1917). See also, David Asp, "Espionage Act of 1917," *First Amendment Encyclopedia*, Free Speech Center, Middle Tennessee State University, last modified May 2019, www.mtsu.edu/first-amendment/article/1045/espionage-act-of-1917.

47. Sedition Act, 40 Stat. 553 (1918). See also, Christina L. Boyd, "Sedition Act of 1918," *First Amendment Encyclopedia*, Free Speech Center, Middle Tennessee State University, 2009, www.mtsu.edu/first-amendment/article/1239/sedition-act-of-1918.

48. Boyd, "Sedition Act of 1918."

49. Timothy C. Shiell, *African Americans and the First Amendment: The Case of Liberty and Equality* (Albany: State University of New York Press, 2019), 29, Kindle.

50. William G. Jordan, *Black Newspapers and America's War for Democracy, 1914–1920* (Chapel Hill: University of North Carolina Press, 2001), 92–96.

51. "SUFFRAGISTS BURN WILSON IN EFFIGY; MANY LOCKED UP," *New York Times*, February 10, 1919, www.nytimes.com/1919/02/10/archives/suffragists-burn-wilson-in-effigy-many-locked-up-police-stop.html?smid=url-share.

52. "Columbia's Deliverance," *New York Times*, October 10, 1917, www .nytimes.com/1917/10/10/archives/columbias-deliverance.html.

53. Michael J. Klarman, "Rethinking the Civil Rights and Civil Liberties Revolutions," *Virginia Law Review* 82, no. 1 (1996): 1–67.

54. Shiell, *African Americans and the First Amendment*.

55. Theodore Kornweibel Jr., *"Investigate Everything": Federal Efforts to Ensure Black Loyalty During World War I* (Bloomington: Indiana University Press, 2002), 136–138.

56. Robert A. Hill, ed., *The Marcus Garvey and Universal Negro Improvement Association Papers*, vol. 11 (Durham, NC: Duke University Press, 2011), 110.

57. David M. Rabbant, "The First Amendment in Its Forgotten Years," *Yale Law Journal* 90 (1981): 514.

58. Schenck v. United States, 249 U.S. 47 (1919); Debs v. United States, 249 U.S. 211 (1919); Frohwerk v. United States, 249 U.S. 204 (1919). See also, Thomas Healy, *The Great Dissent: How Oliver Wendell Holmes Changed His Mind—and Changed the History of Free Speech in America* (New York: Metropolitan Books, 2013), Kindle.

59. Schenck v. United States, 249 U.S. 48, 52 (1919). See also, David Asp, *"Schenck v. United States (1919)," First Amendment Encyclopedia*, Free Speech Center, Middle Tennessee State University, www.mtsu.edu/first-amendment /article/193/schenck-v-united-states.

60. Abrams v. United States, 250 U.S. 630 (1919). See also, Healy, *The Great Dissent*, loc. 1915.

61. Shiell, *African Americans and the First Amendment*, 28.

62. *Laws of the State of Mississippi*, ch. 214 (1920), quoted in "Separate Is Not Equal," *Smithsonian National Museum of America*, www.americanhistory. si.edu/brown/history/1-segregated/detail/jim-crow-laws.html.

63. Samuel Walker, *Hate Speech: The History of an American Controversy* (Lincoln and London: University of Nebraska Press, 1994), 15–16.

64. Samuel Walker, *In Defense of American Liberties: A History of the ACLU*, 2nd ed. (Carbondale: Southern Illinois University Press, 1999), 116.

65. Herndon v. Lowry, 301 U.S. 261–64 (1937). See also, John R. Vile, *"Herndon v. Lowry (1937)," First Amendment Encyclopedia*, Free Speech Center, Middle Tennessee State University, 2009, www.mtsu.edu/ first-amendment/article/268/herndon-v-lowry; David L. Hudson Jr., "Black History Month: Remembering Angelo Herndon," *Freedom Forum Institute*, February 23, 2011, www.freedomforuminstitute.org/2011/02/23/black -history-month-remembering-angelo-herndon.

66. Shiell, *African Americans and the First Amendment*, xi–xii, 91.

67. Albert Venn Dicey, *Introduction to the Study of the Law of the Constitution* (1885), ed. Roger E. Michener (Indianapolis: Liberty Fund, 1982), 152, https://

oll.libertyfund.org/title/michener-introduction-to-the-study-of-the-law-of-the
-constitution-lf-ed.

68. *Encyclopedia Britannica*, 9th ed. (1888), s.v. "Press Laws in the British Colonies and India."

69. John Stuart Mill, quoted in Thomas R. Metcalf, *Ideologies of the Raj* (Cambridge: Cambridge University Press, 1995), 31–33.

70. John Stuart Mill, "Speech to the House of Lords," June 21–22, 1852, in *Writings on India*, ed. John M. Robson et al. (Toronto: University of Toronto Press, 1990), 70.

71. Robert Darnton, *Censors at Work: How States Shaped Literature* (New York: W. W. Norton, 2014), 120.

72. The Indian Penal Code of 1860, sec. 124A (added by Act 27 of 1870, sec. 5) and sec. 153A (added by the Indian Penal Code Amendment Act 4 of 1898, sec. 5), in Government of India, *The Unrepealed General Acts of the Governor General in Council: 1834–67*, 3rd ed. (Calcutta: Office of the Super-intendents of Government Printing, India, 1893), 1:273, 279. See also, Robert Darnton, "British India: Liberalism," in *Censors at Work*, 126, 142, 274; Bhairav Acharya, "Free Speech in India: Still Plagued by Pre-modern Laws," *Media Asia* 42, no. 3–4 (2015): 157–160; and Bhairav Acharya, "The Second Coming of Sedition," *The Wire*, February 18, 2016. https://thewire.in/law/the-second-coming-of-sedition.

73. Denzil Ibbetson, April 30, 1907, P/7590, pro. no. 183, quoted in Darnton, *Censors at Work*, 124, 273n90.

74. Emperor v. Bal Gangadhar Tilak, 10 BOMLR 848 (1908).

75. See, for example, Acharya, "The Second Coming of Sedition"; and Darnton, *Censors at Work*, 125–127.

76. Mahatma Gandhi, "Speech at the Indian National Congress," December 29, 1921, in *The Pilgrim's March: Their Messages* (Madras: Ganesh, 1921), 136.

77. Mahatma Gandhi, "Tampering with Loyalty," *Young India*, September 29, 1921, 309–310, *Bombay Sarvodaya Mandal / Gandhi Book Centre*, www.mkgandhi.org/law_lawyers/appendix1.htm.

78. Mahatma Gandhi, statement in the Great Trial, March 18, 1922, in *Selected Writings*, ed. Ronald Duncan (Mineola, NY: Dover Publications, Inc., 2005), 144–145.

79. Martin Luther King Jr., *The Autobiography of Martin Luther King, Jr.*, chap. 13, *Stanford University Libraries*, https://swap.stanford.edu/20141218230026/http://mlk-kpp01.stanford.edu/kingweb/publications/autobiography/chp_13.htm.

80. Stephanie Newell, "Paradoxes of Press Freedom in Colonial West Africa," *Media History* 22, no. 1 (2016): 101–122.

81. *Gold Coast Leader* (August 9, 1902), 4, quoted in Newell, "Paradoxes of Press Freedom in Colonial West Africa," 104.

82. *Lagos Weekly Record* (February 14, 1903), 6, quoted in Newell, "Paradoxes of Press Freedom in Colonial West Africa," 105.

83. Wilfred Collet, *To Leslie Probyn, Governor, Jamaica*, August 1918, in Hill, *The Marcus Garvey and Universal Negro Improvement Association Papers*, 11:107.

84. Newell, "Paradoxes of Press Freedom in Colonial West Africa," 107.

85. Newell, "Paradoxes of Press Freedom in Colonial West Africa," 109.

86. Michael Ng, "When Silence Speaks: Press Censorship and Rule of Law in British Hong Kong, 1850s–1940s," *Law & Literature* 29, no. 3 (2017): 432.

87. Seditious Publications Ordinance (April 24, 1914), Historical Laws of Hong Kong Online, https://oelawhk.lib.hku.hk/items/show/1282.

88. British War Office, *Report on Cable Censorship During the Great War* (1920), quoted in Andreas Marklund, "Global Connectivity and Weaponized Information: Information and Communications Technologies from World War I to the Present Day," *Bloomsbury Cultural History of Technology*, vol. 6 (forthcoming).

89. Marklund, "Global Connectivity."

90. Ng, "When Silence Speaks."

91. The Emergency Regulations Ordinance (February 28, 1922), Hong Kong e-Legislation, www.elegislation.gov.hk/hk/cap241?pmc=1&m=1&pm=0.

92. Ng, "When Silence Speaks," 438, 441–442, 446.

93. Acharya, "Free Speech in India."

Chapter 10: The Totalitarian Temptation

1. Angela Merkel, "Speech at the General Budget Debate in the German Bundestag," November 27, 2019, *Die Bundesregierung*, www.bundesregierung.de/breg-en/news/kanzlerin-bei-generaldebatte-1699808.

2. Karl Loewenstein, "Militant Democracy and Fundamental Rights, I," *American Political Science Review* 31, no. 3 (1937): 426.

3. Karl Loewenstein, "Militant Democracy and Fundamental Rights, II," *American Political Science Review* 31, no. 4 (1937): 653.

4. Karl Popper, *The Open Society and Its Enemies* (1945; repr., Princeton: Princeton University Press, 2013), 581.

5. George Orwell, proposed preface to *Animal Farm*, first published in the *Times Literary Supplement*, September 15, 1972, Orwell Foundation, www.orwellfoundation.com/the-orwell-foundation/orwell/essays-and-other-works/the-freedom-of-the-press.

6. Popper, *The Open Society and Its Enemies*, 581.

7. See, for example, Charles A. Ruud, "Russia," in Robert Justin Goldstein, *The War for the Public Mind: Political Censorship in Nineteenth-Century Europe* (Westport and London: Praeger, 2000), 247; and Dmitry Strovsky and

Greg Simons, "The Bolsheviks' Policy Towards the Press in Russia: 1917–1920," (working paper no. 109, Department of Eurasian Studies, Uppsala University, Sweden, 2007), 10.

8. Quoted in Albert Resis, "Lenin on Freedom of the Press," *Russian Review* 36, no. 3 (1977): 275–276.

9. Vladimir Lenin, quoted in Resis, "Lenin on Freedom of the Press," 276, 282.

10. Vladimir Lenin, quoted in Strovsky and Simons, "The Bolsheviks' Policy Towards the Press in Russia," 5.

11. Decree on the Press, November 9, 1917, trans. Yuri Akhapkin, in Martin McCauley, *The Russian Revolution and the Soviet State 1917–1921* (London: Palgave, 1980), 190.

12. Resis, "Lenin on Freedom of the Press," 285.

13. Council of People's Commissars, Decree on the Press, November 9, 2017, in *Decrees of the Soviet Government* (Moscow: Institute of Marxism-Leninism, 1957), 1:24–25.

14. Resis, "Lenin on Freedom of the Press," 288.

15. Strovsky and Simons, "The Bolsheviks' Policy Towards the Press in Russia," 6.

16. Fifth Session of the Central Executive Committee, November 17, 1917, trans. John L. H. Keep, *The Debate on Soviet Power* (Oxford: Oxford University Press, 1979), 68–89.

17. Resis, "Lenin on Freedom of the Press," 292–293.

18. Strovsky and Simons, "The Bolsheviks' Policy Towards the Press in Russia," 8.

19. Resis, "Lenin on Freedom of the Press," 293–294.

20. Vladimir Lenin, quoted in Peter Kenez, *Lenin and the Freedom of the Press* (Kennan Institute for Advanced Russian Studies, 1981), 2.

21. Strovsky and Simons, "The Bolsheviks' Policy Towards the Press in Russia," 11–13, 15.

22. Resis, "Lenin on Freedom of the Press," 295.

23. Stuart Finkel, "Purging the Public Intellectual: The 1922 Expulsions from Soviet Russia." *Russian Review* 62, no. 4 (2003): 589; Alexander V. Razin and Tatiana J. Sidorina, "The Philosophers' Ship," *Philosophy Now*, 2001, https://philosophynow.org/issues/31/The_Philosophers_Ship.

24. Joseph Stalin, quoted in "Stalin preduprezhdaet o novoi polose krasnogo terrora," *Segodnia* (Riga), September 16, 1922, trans. Finkel, "Purging the Public Intellectual," 607.

25. Simon Sebag Montefiore, *Stalin: The Court of the Red Tsar* (New York: Vintage, 2018), 28.

26. Herman Ermolaev, *Censorship in Soviet Literature, 1917–1991* (Lanham, MD: Rowman & Littlefield, 1997), 3.

27. Jan Plamper, "Abolishing Ambiguity: Soviet Censorship Practices in the 1930s," *Russian Review* 60, no. 4 (2001): 528.

28. Martin Dewhirst and Robert Farrell, *The Soviet Censorship* (Metuchen: The Scarecrow Press, 1974), 55–58; Ermolaev, *Censorship in Soviet Literature*, 6.

29. Ermolaev, *Censorship in Soviet Literature*, 3.

30. Samantha Sherry, *Discourses of Regulation and Resistance* (Edinburgh: Edinburgh University Press, 2015), 52.

31. Sherry, *Discourses of Regulation and Resistance*, 55.

32. Ermolaev, *Censorship in Soviet Literature*, 10.

33. Montefiore, *Stalin*, 55, 99, 162.

34. Sherry, *Discourses of Regulation and Resistance*, 47.

35. Karlit chairman Sviridov, November 27, 1938, trans. Plamper, "Abolishing Ambiguity," 535–536.

36. Glavlit Moscow, circular, December 27, 1935, trans. Plamper, "Abolishing Ambiguity," 537.

37. Martin Dewhirst, "Soviet Socialist Realism and the Soviet Censorship System," in *In the Party Spirit*, ed. Hilary Chung (Amsterdam: Editions Rodopi, 1996), 29.

38. Anne Applebaum, *Gulag: A History* (New York: Anchor Books, 2003) 46, 294.

39. Aleksandr Solzhenitsyn, *The Gulag Archipelago, 1918–1956: An Experiment in Literary Investigation*, trans. Thomas P. Whitney (New York, Evanston, San Francisco, and London: Harper Perennial, 2007), 1:60. See also, "Alexandr Solzhenitsyn: Biographical," The Nobel Prize, May 1, 2021, www .nobelprize.org/prizes/literature/1970/solzhenitsyn/biographical.

40. Applebaum, *Gulag*, 294.

41. USSR Const. art. 123 (adopted December 1936), Bucknell University, 1996, www.departments.bucknell.edu/russian/const/36cons04.html#chap10.

42. Michael Ellman, "Soviet Repression Statistics: Some Comments," *Europe-Asia Studies* 54, no. 7 (2002): 1151–1172; Stephen Wheatcroft, "The Turn Away from Economic Explanations for Soviet Famines," *Contemporary European History* 27, no. 3 (2018): 465–469.

43. Montefiore, *Stalin*, 243.

44. Solzhenitsyn, *The Gulag Archipelago*, 1:473.

45. Solzhenitsyn, *The Gulag Archipelago*, 3:94.

46. "New York Times Statement About 1932 Pulitzer Prize Awarded to Walter Duranty," The New York Times Company, www.nytco.com/company /prizes-awards/new-york-times-statement-about-1932-pulitzer-prize-awarded -to-walter-duranty.

47. Orwell, proposed preface to *Animal Farm*.

48. Quoted in Matthew Luxmoore, "In Russia, 'The Death of Stalin' Is No Laughing Matter," *New York Times*, January 24, 2018, www.nytimes .com/2018/01/24/movies/death-of-stalin-banned-russia.html?smid=url-share.

49. Benito Mussolini, "The Doctrine of Fascism," in *Enciclopedia Italiana*, vol. 14 (1932), trans. Jane Soames, *Political Quarterly*, in *The Living Age* (November 1933), 240.

50. Benito Mussolini, speech, October 28, 1925, in *Opera Omnia di Benito Mussolini*, ed. Edoardo and Duilio Susmel (Florence: La Fenice, 1951–1963), 21:425, in *Mediterranean Fascism 1919–1945*, ed. Charles F. Delzell (New York: Macmillan, 1970), xvii.

51. The Exceptional Decrees: Law for the Defense of the State, arts. 4, 5, (November 25, 1926), trans. Delzell, *Mediterranean Fascism*, 67–68.

52. Delzell, *Mediterranean Fascism*, 67.

53. Benito Mussolini, *Il popolo d'Italia*, November 2, 1933, in Doug Thompson, *State Control in Fascist Italy: Culture and Conformity, 1925–43* (Manchester and New York: Manchester University Press, 1991), 131.

54. Single Text on Public Security, November 1926, in Guido Bonsaver, *Censorship and Literature in Fascist Italy* (Toronto, Buffalo, and London: University of Toronto Press, 2007), 20.

55. Benito Mussolini, *Della missione del giornalisme nel regime*, October 10, 1928, in Susmel and Susmel, *Opera Omnia di Benito Mussolini*, 23:231–232, in Bonsaver, *Censorship and Literature in Fascist Italy*, 9.

56. Emil J. Gumbel, *Vier Jahre politischer Mord* [Four Years of Political Murder] (Berlin: Verlag der Gesellschaft, 1922), 145–149, in *The Weimar Republic Sourcebook*, trans. and ed. Anton Kaes, Martin Jay, and Edward Dimendberg (Berkeley: University of California Press, 1994), 101. See also, Ian Kershaw, *Hitler: A Biography* (London: Penguin, 2010), 130.

57. Rosa Luxemburg, *The Russian Revolution* (1918), Marxist Internet Archive, www.marxists.org/archive/luxemburg/1918/russian-revolution/ch06 .htm. See also, Kershaw, *Hitler*, 132.

58. Weimar Constitution, arts. 48 and 118 (August 11, 1919), in Howard Lee McBain and Lindsay Rogers, *The New Constitutions of Europe* (New York: Doubleday, 1922).

59. Bernhard Fulda, *Press and Politics in the Weimar Republic* (Oxford: Oxford University Press, 2009), 13–14. See also, David Welch, *The Third Reich: Politics and Propaganda*, 2nd ed. (New York: Routledge, 2002), 47.

60. Gina Kaus, "Die Frau in der modernen Literatur," *Die literarische Welt* 5 no. 11 (March 15, 1929): 1, in Kaes, Jay, and Dimendberg, *The Weimar Republic Sourcebook*, 515–517.

61. German Workers' Party (DAP), The Twenty-five Points, art. 23 (February 24, 1920), in *Das Programm der NSDAP und seine weltanschaulichen*

Grundgedanken (Munich: Franz Eher Nachfolger, 1932), 15–19, in Kaes, Jay, and Dimendberg, *The Weimar Republic Sourcebook*, 124–126.

62. Kershaw, *Hitler*, 106–112, 143.

63. Kershaw, *Hitler*, 143–147, 158–160.

64. Adolf Hitler, *Mein Kampf,* trans. James Murphy (London: Hurst and Blackett, 1939), vol. 1, chap. 10.

65. Gumbel, *Vier Jahre politischer Mord*, 145–149, in Kaes, Jay, and Dimendberg, *The Weimar Republic Sourcebook*, 102.

66. Oron James Hale, *The Captive Press in the Third Reich* (Princeton, Princeton University Press, 1964), 11.

67. Jürgen Wilke, "Censorship and Freedom of the Press," European History Online, May 8, 2013, http://ieg-ego.eu/en/threads/european-media/censorship-and-freedom-of-the-press.

68. Fulda, *Press and Politics in the Weimar Republic*, 219–220.

69. Fulda, *Press and Politics in the Weimar Republic*, 220.

70. Fulda, *Press and Politics in the Weimar Republic*, 176.

71. Hale, *The Captive Press in the Third Reich*, 11–12.

72. Fulda, *Press and Politics in the Weimar Republic*, 220.

73. Hale, *The Captive Press in the Third Reich*, 11–12.

74. Fulda, *Press and Politics in the Weimar Republic*, 220–221.

75. Hale, *The Captive Press in the Third Reich*, 29.

76. Russel Lemmons, *Goebbels and "Der Angriff"* (Lexington: University Press of Kentucky, 1994), 6.

77. Kershaw, *Hitler*, 194, 213–214.

78. Ian Kershaw, *Hitler, the Germans, and the Final Solution* (New Haven: Yale University Press, 2008), 51.

79. NSDAP poster [1925/1926], in German Propaganda Archive, ed. Robert D. Brooks and Randall Bytwerk, poster no. 10, www.bytwerk.com/gpa/posters1.htm; Detlef Mühlberger, *Hitler's Voice: The Völkischer Beobachter, 1920–1933*, vol. 1, *Organisation and Development of the Nazi Party* (Bern: Peter Lang, 2004), 110.

80. Welch, *The Third Reich*, 13.

81. Lemmons, *Goebbels and "Der Angriff,"* 112.

82. Lemmons, *Goebbels and "Der Angriff,"* 120–125.

83. United States v. Goering, "Judgment, Streicher" (September 30, 1946) (International Military Tribunal: Nuremberg, Germany, 1947), 302–304, at Library of Congress, www.loc.gov/rr/frd/Military_Law/pdf/NT_Vol-I.pdf.

84. Dennis E. Showalter, "Jews, Nazis, and the Law: The Case of Julius Streicher," *Museum of Tolerance*, www.museumoftolerance.com/education/archives-and-reference-library/online-resources/simon-wiesenthal-center-annual-volume-6/annual-6-chapter-6.html.

85. Showalter, "Jews, Nazis, and the Law."

86. Kaes, Jay, and Dimendberg, *The Weimar Republic Sourcebook*, 594.

87. Kaes, Jay, and Dimendberg, *The Weimar Republic Sourcebook*, 594. See also, Heidi J. S. Tworek, *News from Germany: The Competition to Control World Communications 1900–1945* (Cambridge, MA: Harvard University Press), 117; and Heidi J. S. Tworek, "A Lesson from 1930s Germany: Beware State Control of Social Media," *Atlantic*, May 26, 2019, www.theatlantic.com/international /archive/2019/05/germany-war-radio-social-media/590149.

88. Kurt Tucholsky (Ignaz Wrobel), "Rundfunkzensur," *Die Weltbühne* 24, no. 16 (April 17, 1928), 590–593, in Kaes, Jay, and Dimendberg, *The Weimar Republic Sourcebook*, 603.

89. Maja Adena, Ruben Enikolopov, Maria Petrova, Veronica Santarosa, and Ekaterina Zhuravskay, "Radio and the Rise of the Nazis in Prewar Germany," June 3, 2015, https://papers.ssrn.com/sol3/papers.cfm?abstract_id=2242446; Tworek, "A Lesson from 1930s Germany."

90. Adena et al., "Radio and the Rise of the Nazis in Prewar Germany."

91. Quoted in Tworek, "A Lesson from 1930s Germany."

92. Eric Weitz, *Weimar Germany: Promise and Tragedy* (Princeton: Princeton University Press, 2007), 161.

93. "Reichstagswahl 1928," Gonschior.de, www.gonschior.de/weimar/Deutsch land/RT4.html; "Reichstagswahl Juli 1932," Gonschior.de, www.gonschior.de /weimar/Deutschland/RT6.html.

94. Fulda, *Press and Politics in the Weimar Republic*, 221.

95. Joseph Goebbels, diary entry, February 15, 1933, in *Joseph Goebbels Tage-bücher*, ed. Ralf Georg Reuth (Munich: Piper, 1992), 2:764, in Fulda, *Press and Politics in the Weimar Republic*, 221.

96. Adolf Hitler, quoted in Denis Sefton Delmer, *Daily Express*, February 23, 1933, Spartacus Educational, https://spartacus-educational.com/Jdelmer .htm.

97. The Decree of the Reich President for the Protection of the People and the State (Reichstag Fire Decree) (February 28, 1933), Reichsgesetzblatt I (1933), 83, in "Reichstag Fire Decree," *Holocaust Encyclopedia*, United States Holocaust Memorial Museum, https://encyclopedia.ushmm.org/content/en /article/reichstag-fire-decree. See also, Richard J. Evans, "Coercion and Consent in Nazi Germany," *Proceedings of the British Academy* 151 (2007): 67.

98. Richard J. Evans, *The Third Reich in Power 1933–1939* (New York: Allen Lane / Penguin Books, 2005), 11.

99. "Law and Justice in the Third Reich," *Holocaust Encyclopedia*, United States Holocaust Memorial Museum, https://encyclopedia.ushmm.org /content/en/article/law-and-justice-in-the-third-reich; Evans, "Coercion and Consent in Nazi Germany," 67.

100. Evans, "Coercion and Consent in Nazi Germany," 58–61.

101. Kershaw, *Hitler, the Germans, and the Final Solution*, 131–132.

102. Heinrich Himmler, quoted in Facing History and Ourselves, "Outlawing the Opposition," in *Holocaust and Human Behavior* (2017), www.facing history.org/holocaust-and-human-behavior/chapter-5/outlawing-opposition.

103. Evans, "Coercion and Consent in Nazi Germany," 66.

104. Evans, "Coercion and Consent in Nazi Germany," 62–63, 67.

105. Otto Wels, Speech Against the Passage of the "Enabling Act," March 23, 1933, German History in Documents and Images, German Historical Institute, Washington, DC, http://germanhistorydocs.ghi-dc.org/sub_document .cfm?document_id=1497; "Otto Wels," *Holocaust Encyclopedia*, United States Holocaust Memorial Museum, https://encyclopedia.ushmm.org/content/en /article/otto-wels.

106. Adolf Hitler, "Official Speech on the Enabling Act to the Reichstag," March 23, 1933, World Future Fund, www.worldfuturefund.org/Reports2013 /hitlerenablingact.htm.

107. Kershaw, *Hitler, the Germans, and the Final Solution*, 51.

108. Evans, "Coercion and Consent in Nazi Germany," 59–60.

109. "Nazi political violence in 1933," *Holocaust Encyclopedia*, United States Holocaust Memorial Museum, https://encyclopedia.ushmm.org/content/en /article/nazi-political-violence-in-1933.

110. Evans, "Coercion and Consent in Nazi Germany," 59.

111. United States Holocaust Memorial Museum, "Nazi Political Violence in 1933."

112. Evans, "Coercion and Consent in Nazi Germany," 67.

113. Evans, "Coercion and Consent in Nazi Germany," 66. See also, Facing History and Ourselves, "Outlawing the Opposition."

114. Kershaw, *Hitler, the Germans, and the Final Solution*, 170.

115. Evans, "Coercion and Consent in Nazi Germany," 66.

116. Kershaw, *Hitler, the Germans, and the Final Solution*, 204.

117. Evans, "Coercion and Consent in Nazi Germany," 78.

118. See, for example, "Gleichschaltung: Coordinating the Nazi State," *Holocaust Encyclopedia*, United States Holocaust Memorial Museum, https:// encyclopedia.ushmm.org/content/en/article/gleichschaltung-coordinating -the-nazi-state.

119. Adolf Hitler, "Reichstag Speech," March 23, 1933, in Thomas Childers, *The Third Reich: A History of Nazi Germany* (New York: Simon & Schuster, 2017), 291.

120. See, for example, "Nazi Propaganda and Censorship," *Holocaust Encyclopedia*, United States Holocaust Memorial Museum, https://encyclopedia

.ushmm.org/content/en/article/nazi-propaganda-and-censorship; and "Culture in the Third Reich," *Holocaust Encyclopedia*, United States Holocaust Memorial Museum, https://encyclopedia.ushmm.org/content/en/article/culture-in-the-third-reich-overview?parent=en%2F81.

121. Welch, *The Third Reich*, 44. See also, "The Press in the Third Reich," *Holocaust Encyclopedia*, United States Holocaust Memorial Museum, https://encyclopedia.ushmm.org/content/en/article/the-press-in-the-third-reich.

122. Welch, *The Third Reich*, 45.

123. Welch, *The Third Reich*, 47.

124. United States Holocaust Memorial Museum, "The Press in the Third Reich."

125. The Editors' Law (October 4, 1933), quoted in Welch, *The Third Reich*, 46.

126. Joseph Goebbels, quoted in Welch, *The Third Reich*, 48.

127. See, for example, Anson Rabinbach and Sander L. Gilman, eds., *The Third Reich Sourcebook* (Berkeley and Los Angeles: University of California Press, 2013), 447, 451.

128. Rabinbach and Gilman, *The Third Reich Sourcebook*. See also, "Book Burning," *Holocaust Encyclopedia*, United States Holocaust Memorial Museum, https://encyclopedia.ushmm.org/content/en/article/book-burning?parent=en%2F11510.

129. Joseph Goebbels, quoted in *Deutsche Allgemeine Zeitung*, May 12, 1933, 179–181, in Rabinbach and Gilman, *The Third Reich Sourcebook*, 453–454; Heinrich Heine, *Almansor*, in *Werke in fünfzehn Teilen*, ed. Erwin Kalischer and Raimund Pissin (Berlin: Bong; Project Gutenberg, 2014), 20, www.gutenberg.org/files/45600/45600-h/45600-h.htm. My translation.

130. Victor Klemperer, *The Language of the Third Reich*, trans. Martin Brady (London: Bloomsbury, 2013), 16–17.

131. See, for example, David Welch, ed., *Nazi Propaganda: The Power and the Limitations* (Kent: Croom Helm, 1983); Christopher R. Browning, *Ordinary Men* (London: Penguin Books, 1992); Daniel J. Goldhagen, *Hitler's Willing Executioners* (New York: Alfred A. Knopf, 1996).

132. Evans, "Coercion and Consent in Nazi Germany," 79.

133. Ian Kershaw, "How Effective Was Nazi Propaganda?" in Welch, *Nazi Propaganda*, 183–188, 190; Nico Voigtländer and Hans-Joachim Voth, "Nazi Indoctrination and Anti-Semitic Beliefs in Germany," *Proceedings of the National Academy of Sciences of the United States of America* 112, no. 26 (2015): 7931–7936.

134. Kershaw, "How Effective Was Nazi Propaganda," 196.

135. Aldous Huxley, "Notes on Propaganda," *Harper's Magazine*, December 1936.

Chapter 11: The Age of Human Rights

1. See, for example, "FDR and the Four Freedoms Speech," FDR Presidential Library and Museum, www.fdrlibrary.org/four-freedoms.

2. Franklin D. Roosevelt, "The Four Freedoms," January 6, 1941, American Rhetoric: Top 100 Speeches, www.americanrhetoric.com/speeches/fdrthefourfreedoms.htm.

3. Universal Declaration of Human Rights (UDHR), art. 19 (adopted December 10, 1948), G.A. Res. 217A (III), U.N. GAOR, 3d Sess., (Resolutions, pt. 1), U.N. Doc. A/810 at 71 (1948).

4. Johannes Morsink, *The Universal Declaration of Human Rights: Origins, Drafting, and Intent* (Philadelphia: University of Pennsylvania Press, 1999); Stephanie Farrior, "Molding the Matrix: The Theoretical and Historical Foundations of International Law and Practice Concerning Hate Speech," *Berkeley Journal of International Law* 14, no. 1 (1996): 1–98; Jacob Mchangama, "The Sordid Origin of Hate-Speech Laws," *Policy Review* 170 (2011): 45–58.

5. U.N. ESCOR, Comm'n on Hum. Rts., 1st Sess., U.N. Doc. E/CN.4/21/ANNEX C at 44 (1947).

6. USSR Const. art. 123 (adopted December 1936), Bucknell University, 1996, www.departments.bucknell.edu/russian/const/36cons04.html#chap10.

7. U.N. ESCOR, Comm'n on Hum. Rts., Sub-Commission on Prevention of Discrimination and Protection of Minorities, U.N. Doc. E/CN.4/Sub.2/21 (1947). See also, Morsink, *The Universal Declaration of Human Rights*, 70; and Lee C. Bollinger and Geoffrey R. Stone, *The Free Speech Century* (Oxford: Oxford University Press, 2019), 218–219.

8. Morsink, *The Universal Declaration of Human Rights*, 66.

9. Morsink, *The Universal Declaration of Human Rights*, 69.

10. Alexei Pavlov, quoted in Morsink, *The Universal Declaration of Human Rights*, 66.

11. Mchangama, "The Sordid Origin of Hate-Speech Laws."

12. Anne Applebaum, *Gulag: A History* (London: Penguin, 2012), loc. 2408, Kindle.

13. Karl Loewenstein, "Legislative Control of Political Extremism in European Democracies," *Columbia Law Review* 38, no. 4 (1938): 741–745.

14. Morsink, *The Universal Declaration of Human Rights*, 66–67.

15. Article 7 of the UDHR obliges states to protect everyone equally against incitement to discrimination, but without specifically obliging them to prohibit speech.

16. Morsink, *The Universal Declaration of Human Rights*, 21. See also, Peter Danchin, "Drafting History," Columbia Center for Teaching and Learning, https://ccnmtl.columbia.edu/projects/mmt/udhr/udhr_general/drafting_history_10.html.

17. Farrior, "Molding the Matrix," 21. See also, Evelyn M. Aswad, "To Ban or Not to Ban Blasphemous Videos," *Georgetown Journal of International Law* 44, no. 4 (2013): 1320.

18. U.N. ESCOR, Comm'n on Hum. Rts., 2d Sess., U.N. Doc. E/CN.4/77 /ANNEX B at 12 (1947).

19. U.N. ESCOR, Comm'n on Hum. Rts., 5th Sess., U.N. Doc. E/CN.4 /SR.123 at 4 (1949). See also, Farrior, "Molding the Matrix," 22.

20. U.N. ESCOR, Comm'n on Hum. Rts., 6th Sess., 174th mtg., ¶ 25, U.N. Doc. E/CN.4/SR.174 at 6 (1950).

21. U.N. Doc. E/CN.4/SR.174, ¶ 27–29, at 6–7.

22. U.N. ESCOR, Comm'n on Hum. Rts., 9th Sess., 378th mtg., U.N. Doc. E/CN.4/SR.378 at 10 (1953); See also, Farrior, "Molding the Matrix," 29.

23. U.N. ESCOR, Comm'n on Hum. Rts., 9th Sess., 379th mtg., U.N. Doc. E/CN.4/SR.379 at 12–13 (1953).

24. U.N. ESCOR, Comm'n on Hum. Rts., 6th Sess., 174th mtg., ¶ 25, U.N. Doc. E/CN.4/SR.174 at 10 (1950).

25. U.N. ESCOR, Comm'n on Hum. Rts., 9th Sess., 378th mtg., U.N. Doc. E/CN.4/SR.378 at 4–5 (1953). See also, Farrior, "Molding the Matrix," 28–29.

26. Joseph Stalin, quoted in Applebaum, *Gulag*, loc. 9184.

27. Applebaum, *Gulag*, loc. 475.

28. U.N. GAOR, 16th Sess., 3d Comm., 1073d mtg., ¶ 28, U.N. Doc. A/C.3/SR.1073 at 67 (1961).

29. U.N. GAOR, 16th Sess., 3d Comm., 1079th mtg., ¶ 9, U.N. Doc. A/C.3 /SR.1079 at 97 (1961). See also, Farrior, "Molding the Matrix," 28.

30. ICCPR art. 20(2); U.N. Doc. A/C.3/L.933. The sixteen cosponsors of the amendment were Brazil, Cambodia, Congo, Ghana, Guinea, Indonesia, Iraq, Lebanon, Mali, Morocco, Philippines, Poland, Saudi Arabia, Thailand, United Arab Republic, and Yugoslavia. See Aswad, "To Ban or Not to Ban Blasphemous Videos," 1321.

31. Mchangama, "The Sordid Origin of Hate-Speech Laws."

32. U.N. GAOR, 16th Sess., 3d Comm., 1084th mtg., ¶ 5, U.N. Doc. A/C.3 /SR.1084 at 121 (1961). See also, Farrior, "Molding the Matrix," 41.

33. Smith Act (Alien Registration Act), 54 Stat. 670, ch. 439 (1940). See also, Timothy C. Shiell, *African Americans and the First Amendment: The Case of Liberty and Equality* (Albany: State University of New York Press, 2019), 75, Kindle.

34. Dennis v. United States, 341 U.S. 494 (1951). See also, Shiell, *African Americans and the First Amendment*, 75.

35. Joseph McCarthy, "Enemies from Within," speech, February 9, 1950, Digital History Project, University of Houston, https://liberalarts.utexas.edu /coretexts/_files/resources/texts/1950%20McCarthy%20Enemies.pdf.

36. David Schultz, "House Un-American Activities Committee," *First Amendment Encyclopedia*, Free Speech Center, Middle Tennessee State University, 2009, www.mtsu.edu/first-amendment/article/815/house-un-american-activities-committee.

37. Shiell, *African Americans and the First Amendment*.

38. Samuel Stouffer, *Communism, Conformity, and Civil Liberties* (1955; repr., Brunswick: Transaction Publishers, 1992), 30.

39. Stanley, "Civil Rights Movement Is a Reminder That Free Speech Is There to Protect the Weak," *American Civil Liberties Union*, May 26, 2017, www.aclu.org/blog/free-speech/civil-rights-movement-reminder-free-speech-there-protect-weak.

40. Vanessa Murphree, *The Selling of Civil Rights: The Student Nonviolent Coordinating Committee* (New York: Routledge, 2009), 53.

41. Christopher Klein, "10 Things You May Not Know About Martin Luther King Jr.," *History*, last modified January 20, 2021, www.history.com/news/10-things-you-may-not-know-about-martin-luther-king-jr. See also, "Albany Movement," *Martin Luther King, Jr. Encylopedia*, Martin Luther King, Jr. Research and Education Institute, Stanford University, https://kinginstitute.stanford.edu/encyclopedia/albany-movement; Stanley, "Civil Rights Movement Is a Reminder"; and Taylor Branch, *Parting the Waters: America in the King Years 1954–63*, (New York: Simon & Schuster, 2007), Kindle.

42. "Birmingham Campaign," *Martin Luther King, Jr. Encylopedia*, Martin Luther King, Jr. Research and Education Institute, Stanford University, https://kinginstitute.stanford.edu/encyclopedia/birmingham-campaign. See also, Stanley, "Civil Rights Movement Is a Reminder"; and Branch, *Parting the Waters*.

43. NAACP v. Patterson, 357 U.S. at 460 (1958). See also, David L. Hudson Jr., "Civil Rights Movement," *First Amendment Encyclopedia*, Free Speech Center, Middle Tennessee State University, 2009, www.mtsu.edu/first-amendment/article/1463/civil-rights-movement.

44. Garner v. Louisiana, 368 U.S. at 201 (1961); David L. Hudson, Jr., "Civil Rights Movement" and "First Amendment Freedoms Crucial to Success of Civil Rights Movement," *Freedom Forum Institute*, January 15, 1999, www.freedomforuminstitute.org/1999/01/15/first-amendment-freedoms-crucial-to-success-of-civil-rights-movement.

45. Edwards v. South Carolina, 372 U.S. at 237 (1963); Hudson, "Civil Rights Movement" and "First Amendment Freedoms."

46. New York Times Co. v. Sullivan, 376 US 254, 270–71, 289 (1964); James Madison, *The Report of 1800*, January 7, 1800, in *The Papers of James Madison*, vol. 17, ed. David B. Mattern et al. (Charlottesville: University Press of Virginia, 1991), 303–351, Founders Online, National Archives, https://founders.archives.gov/documents/Madison/01-17-02-0202.

47. Harry Kalven Jr., *The Negro and the First Amendment* (Columbus: Ohio State University Press, 1965), 6. See also, Hudson, "Civil Rights Movement."

48. John Lewis, quoted in Nadine Strossen, *HATE: Why We Should Resist It with Free Speech, Not Censorship* (Oxford: Oxford University Press, 2018), 41. See also, Russel L. Weaver et al., *Constitutional Law: Cases, Materials, and Problems*, 4th ed., 2019 Case Supplement (New York: Wolters Kluwer, 2019), 200.

49. Martin Luther King Jr., "I've Been to the Mountaintop," April 3, 1968, Martin Luther King, Jr. Research and Education Institute, Stanford University, www.kinginstitute.stanford.edu/king-papers/documents/ive-been-mountaintop-address-delivered-bishop-charles-mason-temple.

50. Brandenburg v. Ohio, 395 U.S. 444 (1969).

51. Village of Skokie v. Nat'l Socialist Party of America, 69 Ill. 2d 605, 373 N.E. 2d 21 (1978). See also, David Goldberger, "The Skokie Case; How I Came to Represent the Free Speech Rights of Nazis," *American Civil Liberties Union*, March 2, 2020, www.aclu.org/issues/free-speech/rights-protesters/skokie-case-how-i-came-represent-free-speech-rights-nazis; and Chris Demaske, "Village of Skokie v. National Socialist Party of America (Ill) (1978)," *First Amendment Encyclopedia*, Free Speech Center, Middle Tennessee State University, 2009, www.mtsu.edu/first-amendment/article/728/village-of-skokie-v-national-socialist-party-of-america-ill.

52. Lynn Adelman, "The Glorious Jurisprudence of Thurgood Marshall," *Harvard Law and Policy Review* 7, no. 1 (2013): 129.

53. Martin Luther King Jr., "Address to the South Africa Benefit of the American Committee on Africa," December 10, 1965, African Activist Archive, Michigan State University, https://projects.kora.matrix.msu.edu/files/210-808-282/GMHACOA68MLK.pdf.

54. Martin Luther King Jr. to Dwight D. Eisenhower, March 26, 1960, WCFG, KAbE, White House Central Files (General File), Dwight D. Eisenhower Library, Abilene, Kansas, The Martin Luther King, Jr. Research and Education Institute, Stanford University, https://kinginstitute.stanford.edu/king-papers/documents/dwight-d-eisenhower-3.

55. UDHR preamble.

56. Nadine Gordimer, "Apartheid and 'The Primary Homeland,'" *Index of Censorship* 1, no. 3–4 (1972): 26.

57. Michael Drewet, "Exploring Transitions in Popular Music: Censorship from Apartheid to Post-Apartheid South Africa," in *The Oxford Handbook of Music Censorship*, ed. Patricia Hall (Oxford, Oxford University Press, 2017), 584.

58. Publications and Entertainment Act, sec. 26 (2) (1963); Publications Act, sec. 47 (2), in *Republic of South Africa Government Gazette* 4426 (1974): 62–63. See also, Margreet de Lange, *The Muzzled Muse: Literature and Censorship in South Africa* (Amsterdam: John Benjamins Publishing Company, 1997), 8.

59. Quoted in Christopher Merrett, "Political Censorship in South Africa: Aims and Consequences." *Reality* 14, no. 2, (March 1982): 3–6.

60. André Brink, "A Long Way from Mandela's Kitchen," *New York Times*, September 11, 2010, www.nytimes.com/2010/09/12/opinion/12brink.html.

61. Publications and Entertainment Act, sec. 26 (2) (c); Publications Act, sec. 47 (2) (c). See also, de Lange, *The Muzzled Muse*, 8.

62. Jacobus C. W. van Rooyen, *Publikasie Beheer in Suid-Afrika* (Beperk: Juta, 1978), 117, in de Lange, *The Muzzled Muse*, 23.

63. Jacobus C. W. van Rooyen, paraphrased in de Lange, *The Muzzled Muse*, 25.

64. Quoted in J. M. Coetzee, "Censorship in South Africa," *English in Africa* 17, no. 1 (1990): 12.

65. "South Africa's Censorship Laws," *Index on Censorship* 4, no. 2 (1975): 38. See also, Anthony Sampson, *Mandela: The Authorized Biography* (New York: Vintage, 2012), 12, Kindle.

66. Internal Security Act (1976), quoted in Sean Moroney and Linda Ensor, *The Silenced: Banning in South Africa* (Johannesburg: South African Institute of Race Relations, 1979), 3–4.

67. de Lange, *The Muzzled Muse*, 10.

68. Merrett, "Political Censorship in South Africa," 3.

69. Drewett, "Exploring Transitions in Popular Music," 594.

70. André Brink, *Mapmakers: Writings in a State of Siege* (London: Faber & Faber, 1983), 246–247, quoted in de Lang, *The Muzzled Muse*, 11.

71. Thomson, *U.S. Foreign Policy Towards Apartheid South Africa*, 173–174.

72. *Encyclopedia Britannica*, s.v. "Nelson Mandela," last modified July 27, 2020, www.britannica.com/biography/Nelson-Mandela.

73. The Freedom Charter (June 26, 1955), African National Congress, https://web.archive.org/web/20110629074215/http:/www.anc.org.za/show.php?id=72.

74. *Encyclopedia Britannica*, "Nelson Mandela."

75. Nelson Mandela, *Long Walk to Freedom* (Boston, New York, and London: Little, Brown, 1995), 153.

76. "Sharpeville Massacre," *A Dictionary of World History*, 3rd ed. (Oxford: Oxford University Press: 2015).

77. *Encyclopedia Britannica*, "Nelson Mandela."

78. "Nelson Mandela Writes from Prison," *History*, last modified June 9, 2020, www.history.com/this-day-in-history/mandela-writes-from-prison.

79. Nelson Mandela, "I Am Prepared to Die," April 20, 1964, Nelson Mandela Foundation, http://db.nelsonmandela.org/speeches/pub_viewasp?pg=item&ItemID=NMS010&txtstr=prepared%20to%20die.

80. Republic of South Africa Constitution Act, secs. 34 (d), 46 (c) (April 25, 1961); and Republic of South Africa Constitution Act, sec. 52 (September

28, 1983). See also, "South Africa," ConstitutionNet, International Institute for Democracy and Electoral Assistance, http://constitutionnet.org/country /south-africa; and "South African Constitution: The Bill of Rights," South African History Online, last modified August 27, 2019, www.sahistory.org.za /article/south-african-constitution-bill-rights.

81. Samuel Moyn, *The Last Utopia: Human Rights in History* (Cambridge, MA: Harvard University Press, 2012), Kindle. See also, Michael Cotey Morgan, "The Seventies and the Rebirth of Human Rights," in *The Shock of the Global: The 1970s in Perspective*, ed. Niall Ferguson, Charles S. Maier, Erez Manela, and Daniel J. Sargent (Harvard University Press, 2011), 238.

82. Daniel C. Thomas, *The Helsinki Effect: International Norms, Human Rights, and the Demise of Communism* (Princeton: Princeton University Press, 2001), 56; Moyn, *The Last Utopia*, loc. 1737.

83. Conference on Security and Cooperation in Europe: Final Act (Helsinki Accord) (August 1, 1975), reprinted in 14 I.L.M. 1292 (1975). See also, Thomas, *The Helsinki Effect*, 42–43, 61–62.

84. Henry Kissinger in *The Kissinger Transcripts: The Top Secret Talks with Beijing and Moscow*, ed. William Burr (New York: New Press, 1999), 326, quoted in Jussi M. Hanhimäki, "'They Can Write It in Swahili': Kissinger, the Soviets, and the Helsinki Accords, 1973–75," *Journal of Transatlantic Studies* 1, no. 1 (2003): 37.

85. Aleksandr Solzhenitsyn, *Détente* (New Brunswick, N.J.: Transaction Books, 1980), 19–50, quoted in Thomas, *The Helsinki Effect*, 124.

86. Michael Cotey Morgan, *The Final Act: The Helsinki Accords and the Transformation of the Cold War* (Princeton: Princeton University Press, 2018), 171–172, Kindle.

87. Quoted in Morgan, *The Final Act*, 179.

88. Quoted in Thomas, *The Helsinki Effect*, 93; and Morgan, *The Final Act*, 201.

89. Daniel C. Thomas, "The Helsinki Accords and Political Change in Eastern Europe," in *The Power of Human Rights: International Norms and Domestic Change*, ed. Thomas Risse, Stephen C. Ropp, and Kathryn Sikkink (Cambridge: Cambridge University Press, 1999), 209; "Chipping Away at Czechoslovak Communism: The Helsinki Final Act and Charter 77," Association for Diplomatic Studies and Training, December 7, 2016, https://adst.org/2016/12/chipping-away-czechoslovak-communism -helsinki-final-act-charter-77.

90. Eric Posner, *The Twilight of Human Rights* (Oxford: Oxford University Press, 2014), 18.

91. David K. Shipler, "Sakharov Denied Visa to Get Prize," *New York Times*, November 13, 1975, www.nytimes.com/1975/11/13/archives/sakharov-denied -visa-to-get-prize.html.

92. Andrei Sakharov, "Thoughts on Progress, Peaceful Coexistence and Intellectual Freedom," *New York Times*, July 22, 1968, https://timesmachine.nytimes.com/timesmachine/1968/07/22/76953998.html.

93. Shipler, "Sakharov Denied Visa to Get Prize."

94. Thomas, *The Helsinki Effect*, 160–161.

95. Thomas, *The Helsinki Effect*, 125.

96. US Helsinki Watch Committee, *The First Fifteen Months, A Summary of the Activities of the U.S. Helsinki Watch Committee from Its Founding in February 1979 Through April 1980* (unpublished report), 3–4, quoted in Thomas, *The Helsinki Effect*, 151.

97. Comprehensive Anti-Apartheid Act, 100 Stat. 1086 (1986). See also, Alex Thomson, *U.S. Foreign Policy Towards Apartheid South Africa, 1948–1994* (New York: Palgave Macmillan, 2008), 1–3, 14–15, 99, 169–174.

98. Thomas, *The Helsinki Effect*, 165.

99. Mihaela Teodor, "Plastic People of the Universe: Rock and Roll, Human Rights and the Velvet Revolution," *Valahian Journal of Historical Studies* 12 (2009): 29–39.

100. Charter 77, January 1, 1977, trans. H. Gordon Skilling, *Charter 77 and Human Rights in Czechoslovakia* (London: Allen & Unwin, 1981), 209–212; Thomas, *The Helsinki Effect*, 177–179.

101. Thomas, *The Helsinki Effect*, 180.

102. Thomas, *The Helsinki Effect*, 180–181.

103. Jan Eckel and Samuel Moyn, *The Breakthrough: Human Rights in the 1970s* (Philadelphia: University of Pennsylvania Press, 2015), 175–176, Kindle.

104. Karol Józef Wojtyła, quoted in "Notable and Quotable," *Wall Street Journal*, November 9, 1978. See also, Thomas, *The Helsinki Effect*, 105.

105. Thomas, *The Helsinki Effect*, 201–203.

106. John Lewis Gaddis, *The Cold War* (London: Allen Lane, 2005), 196–197.

107. Thomas, *The Helsinki Effect*, 204.

108. Morgan, *The Final Act*, 177.

109. Thomas, *The Helsinki Effect*, 177, 209–211, 217.

110. S. Tsvigun, KGB First Deputy Chairman (1981), quoted in Thomas, *The Helsinki Effect*, 195.

111. Amnesty International, *Czechoslovakia: Amnesty International Briefing* (London: Amnesty International Publications, 1981), 6, www.amnesty.org/download/Documents/200000/eur160091981en.pdf.

112. Amnesty International, *Amnesty International Report 1978* (London: Amnesty International Publications, 1979), 206–210, quotation at 207, www.amnesty.org/download/Documents/POL10001I978ENGLISH.PDF.

113. Commission on Security and Cooperation in Europe, *Implementation of the Final Act of the Conference on Security and Cooperation in Europe* (Washington, DC: US Government Printing Office, 1980), 62.

114. Charles E. M. Kolb, "The Criminal Trial of Yugoslav Poet Vlado Gotovac: An Eyewitness Account," *Human Rights Quarterly* 4, no. 2 (1982): 184–211; Amnesty International, *Yugoslavia: Prisoners of Conscience* (1981), 16–18, www.amnesty.org/download/Documents/200000/eur480311981en.pdf.

115. Amnesty International, *Amnesty International Report 1982* (London: Amnesty International Publications, 1982), 280–285, quotations at 281–282, www.amnesty.org/download/Documents/POL1000041982ENGLISH.PDF.

116. "Poland Marks Communist Crackdown," *BBC*, December 13, 2006, http://news.bbc.co.uk/2/hi/europe/6175517.stm.

117. Amnesty International, *Amnesty International Report 1983* (London: Amnesty International Publications, 1983), 266, www.amnesty.org/download/Documents/POL1000011983ENGLISH.PDF.

118. *Amnesty International Report 1983*, 269.

119. Quoted in *Amnesty International Report 1983*, 269.

120. Quoted in Morgan, *The Final Act*, 205.

121. Morgan, *The Final Act*, 241–244.

122. Quoted in Morgan, *The Final Act*, 244.

123. Thomas, *The Helsinki Effect*, 247.

124. Moyn, *The Last Utopia*, loc. 1732–1733.

125. Lech Wałęsa, *A Way of Hope* (New York: Henry Holt, 1987), 97. See also, Thomas, *The Helsinki Effect*, 200.

126. Václav Havel, "Speech to Congress," February 21, 1990, in "Text of Havel's Speech to Congress," *Washington Post*, www.washingtonpost.com/archive/politics/1990/02/22/text-of-havels-speech-to-congress/df98e177-778e-4c26-bd96-980089c4fcb2.

Chapter 12: The Free Speech Recession

1. "Argentina Declassification Project—The 'Dirty War' (1976–83)," CIA, www.cia.gov/readingroom/collection/argentina-declassification-project-dirty-war-1976-83; Uki Goñi, "40 Years Later, the Mothers of Argentina's 'Disappeared' Refuse to Be Silent," *Guardian*, April 28, 2017, www.theguardian.com/world/2017/apr/28/mothers-plaza-de-mayo-argentina-anniversary; "Argentina 'Death Flight' Pilots Sentenced for Deaths Including Pope's Friend," *Guardian*, November 29, 2017, www.theguardian.com/world/2017/nov/29/argentina-death-flight-pilots-sentenced-for-deaths-including-popes-friend.

2. See, for example, "Country Graph," V-Dem Institute, University of Gothenburg, www.v-dem.net/en/analysis/CountryGraph.

3. Colin Sparks, "Media and Transition in Latin America," *Westminster Papers in Communication and Culture* 8, no. 2 (2011): 10; Carlos M. Vilas, "Participation, Inequality and the Whereabout of Democracy," in *The New Politics of Inequality in Latin America*, ed. Douglas A. Chalmers et al. (Oxford: Oxford University Press, 1997), 8.

4. Nelson Mandela, "Address to the International Press Institute Congress," February 14, 1994, Nelson Mandela Foundation, www.mandela.gov.za /mandela_speeches/1994/940214_press.htm.

5. Freedom House, Country and Territory Ratings and Statuses, 1973–2021, data set, https://freedomhouse.org/sites/default/files/2020-02/2020_Country _and_Territory_Ratings_and_Statuses_FIW1973-2020.xlsx.

6. Freedom House, Freedom of the Press, data set, https://freedomhouse. org/sites/default/files/2020-02/FOTP1980-FOTP2017_Public-Data.xlsx; Freedom House, *Freedom of the Press 2003: A Global Survey of Media Independence*, 8, https://freedomhouse.org/sites/default/files/FOTP%202003%20Full %20Report.pdf.

7. Freedom House, *Freedom of the Press 2017*, 25, https://freedomhouse.org /sites/default/files/2020-02/FOTP_2017_booklet_FINAL_April28_1.pdf.

8. Committee to Protect Journalists (CPJ), Database of Attacks on the Press, https://cpj.org/data.

9. Anna Lührmann and Staffan I. Lindberg, "A Third Wave of Autocratization Is Here: What Is New About It?" *Democratization* 26, no. 7 (2019): 1095–1113; Anna Lührmann and Staffan I. Lindberg, eds., *V-Dem Democracy Report 2020: Autocratization Surges—Resistance Grows* (V-Dem Institute, 2020), www.v-dem.net/media/filer_public/de/39/de39af54-0bc5-4421-89ae -fb20dcc53dba/democracy_report.pdf.

10. Economist Intelligence Unit, *Democracy Index 2020: In Sickness and in Health?* (2021), 4, www.eiu.com/n/campaigns/democracy-index-2020/#mkto Form_anchor.

11. Economist Intelligence Unit, *Democracy Index 2019: A Year of Democratic Setbacks and Popular Protest* (2020), 6–7, www.eiu.com/public/topical_report .aspx?campaignid=democracyindex2019&zid.

12. Lührmann and Lindberg, *V-Dem Democracy Report 2020*, 6, 19–20. This trend has been confirmed by other reports such as ARTICLE 19, *The Global Expression Report 2019/2020* (London, 2020), www.article19.org/wp-content /uploads/2020/10/GxR2019-20report.pdf; and Adrian Shahbaz and Allie Funk, *Freedom on the Net 2020: The Pandemic's Digital Shadow* (Freedom House, 2020), https://freedomhouse.org/sites/default/files/2020-10/10122020_FOTN2020 _Complete_Report_FINAL.pdf.

13. Liu Xiaobo et al., *Charter 08*, December 9, 2008, Human Rights in China, www.hrichina.org/en/content/238. See also, "Liu Xiaobo," Human Rights Watch, www.hrw.org/tag/liu-xiaobo.

14. Flemming Rose, *The Tyranny of Silence*, trans. Martin Aitken (Washington, DC: Cato Institute, 2014), 43–44.

15. Jytte Klausen, *The Cartoons That Shook the World* (New Haven: Yale University Press, 2009), 74.

16. 3rd Extraordinary Islamic Summit, Final Communiqué, sec. 2 (December 7–8, 2005). See also, Lorenz Langer, *Religious Offence and Human Rights: The Implications of Defamation of Religion* (Cambridge, Cambridge University Press, 2014), 178.

17. See, for example, Morten Skjoldager, "Terrorists Lack Imagination When Choosing Targets in Denmark," in *Understanding Terrorism Innovation and Learning: Al-Qaeda and Beyond*, ed. Magnus Ranstorp and Magnus Normark (London: Routledge, 2015), 247.

18. U.N. ESCOR, Comm'n on Hum. Rts., 45th Sess., 41st mtg., ¶ 17–19, U.N. Doc. E/CN.4/1989/SR.41 at 5–6 (1989).

19. Cairo Declaration on Human Rights in Islam, art. 22 (a) (August 5, 1990), trans. reprinted in U.N. GAOR, World Conf. on Hum. Rts., 4th Sess., U.N. Doc. A/CONF.157/PC/62/Add.18 at 10 (1993).

20. George Packer, "The Moderate Martyr," *New Yorker*, September 3, 2006, www.newyorker.com/magazine/2006/09/11/the-moderate-martyr.

21. Amnesty International, *Egypt: Human Rights Abuses by Armed Groups*, September 1998, 11–12, www.amnesty.org/download/Documents/156000/mde120221998en.pdf.

22. Marie Juul Petersen and Heini í Skorini, "Freedom of Expression vs. Defamation of Religions: Protecting Individuals or Protecting Religions?" *London School of Economics and Political Science*, March 1, 2017, https://blogs.lse.ac.uk/religionglobalsociety/2017/03/freedom-of-expression-vs-defamation-of-religions-protecting-individuals-or-protecting-religions.

23. Peter S. Henne, "The Domestic Politics of International Religious Defamation," *Politics and Religion* 6, no. 3 (2013): 3.

24. Günter Grass, interview by *Visão*, February 16, 2006. See also, Lawrence Van Gelder, "Arts, Briefly," *New York Times*, February 17, 2006, www.nytimes.com/2006/02/17/books/arts-briefly.html.

25. Amnesty International, "Freedom of Speech Carries Responsibilities for All," February 6, 2006, www.amnesty.org/download/Documents/80000/pol300072006en.pdf.

26. Quoted in Edward Michael Lenert, "Are Free Expression and Fundamentalism Two Colliding Principles?" in *Fundamentalism and the Media,* ed. Stewart M. Hoover and Nadia Kaneva (London: Continuum, 2009), 46.

27. Otto-Preminger-Institut v. Austria, 295 Eur. Ct. H.R. (ser. A) (1994); Wingrove v. UK, 1996-V Eur. Ct. H.R. (1996); İ.A. v. Turkey, 2005-VIII Eur. Ct. H.R. 235 (2005); E.S. v. Austria, Eur. Ct. H.R., no. 38450/12 (2018).

28. Heini í Skorini, *Free Speech, Religion and the United Nations: The Political Struggle to Define International Free Speech Norms* (Abingdon, UK: Routledge, 2020), 177–200.

29. Hum. Rts. Council Res. 16/18, U.N. GAOR, Hum. Rts. Council, 16th Sess., art. 5 (f), U.N. Doc. A/HRC/RES/16/18 at 3 (2011). My emphasis.

30. Ian Black, "A Look at the Writings of Saudi Blogger Raif Badawi—Sentenced to 1,000 Lashes," *Guardian*, January 14, 2015, www.theguardian.com/world/2015/jan/14/-sp-saudi-blogger-extracts-raif-badawi.

31. "Pakistan Blasphemy Death Sentence 'Travesty of Justice,' Say UN Experts," *UN News*, December 27, 2019, https://news.un.org/en/story/2019/12/1054361.

32. Nafees Takar and Paul Alexander, "Pakistan University Mob Kills Fellow Student over Blasphemy Allegations," *VOA News*, April 13, 2017, www.voanews.com/east-asia-pacific/pakistan-university-mob-kills-fellow-student-over-blasphemy-allegations; Matt Vasilogambros, "Bloody Fight over Bangladesh's Secularism," *Atlantic*, April 26, 2016, www.theatlantic.com/international/archive/2016/04/bangladesh-secularism/479820.

33. Joseph Goldstein and Ahmad Shakib, "A Day After a Killing, Afghans React in Horror, but Some Show Approval," *New York Times*, March 20, 2015, https://nyti.ms/1DGQ84m; "Afghan Woman Farkhunda Lynched in Kabul 'For Speaking Out,'" March 23, 2015, *BBC*, www.bbc.com/news/world-asia-32014077.

34. V-Dem, *Autocratization Surges*, 16–17.

35. V-Dem, *Autocratization Surges*, 4, 6, 13, 16.

36. Sarah Repucci, *Freedom and the Media 2019: A Downward Spiral* (Freedom House, 2019), 2, https://freedomhouse.org/sites/default/files/2020-02/FINAL07162019_Freedom_And_The_Media_2019_Report.pdf.

37. Ole Nyeng, "Kaprede medier," *Weekendavisen*, April 1, 2021, www.weekendavisen.dk/2021-13/kultur/kaprede-medier.

38. Sarah Repucci and Amy Slipowitz, *Freedom in the World 2021: Democracy Under Siege* (Freedom House, 2021), 2, 7–8. See also, Vindu Goel and Jeffrey Gettleman, "Under Modi, India's Press Is Not So Free Anymore," *New York Times*, April 2, 2020, www.nytimes.com/2020/04/02/world/asia/modi-india-press-media.html.

39. Human Rights Watch, *Stifling Dissent: The Criminalization of Peaceful Expression in India*, www.hrw.org/report/2016/05/24/stifling-dissent/criminalization-peaceful-expression-india.

40. Hannah Ellis-Petersen, "India: Activist Arrested over Protest 'Toolkit' Shared by Greta Thunberg," *Guardian*, February 15, 2021, www.theguardian

.com/world/2021/feb/15/india-activist-arrested-over-protest-toolkit-shared
-by-greta-thunberg.

41. "Delhi Police Arrest Climate Activist for Drafting Farm Protest Note Tweeted by Greta Thunberg," Scroll.in, February 14, 2021, https://scroll.in /latest/986851/greta-thunberg-toolkit-case-delhi-police-arrest-21-year-old -activist-from-bengaluru-say-reports.

42. Audrey Truschke, "Censoring Indian History: Laws Against Religious Offence in India Have Altered the Writing and Understanding of the Nation's Past," *History Today* 67, no. 8 (August 2017); Audrey Truschke, Facebook update, August 7, 2018, www.facebook.com/AudreyTruschke/photo s/a.163965790930054/227348797925086/?type=3.

43. Audrey Truschke, "Censoring Indian History."

44. Freedom House, Country and Territory Ratings and Statuses 1973–2020.

45. "Turkey—Press Freedom in Figures," Reporters Without Borders, January 29, 2021, https://rsf.org/en/news/turkey-press-freedom-figures.

46. "Germany Drops Turkey President Erdogan Insult Case," *BBC*, October 4, 2016, www.bbc.com/news/world-europe-37554167.

47. "Turkey's Wikipedia Ban Ends After Almost Three Years," *BBC*, January 16, 2020, www.bbc.com/news/technology-51133804.

48. Reporters Without Borders, "Turkey—Press Freedom in Figures."

49. CPJ, Database of Attacks on the Press. See also, Didem Tali, Freedom House, and RIWI, *Perceptions Towards Freedom of Expression in Turkey* (RIWI and Freedom House, 2020), www.freedomhouse.org/sites/default /files/2020-07/Perceptions%20towards%20Freedom%20of%20Expression %20in%20Turkey%202020%20%281%29.pdf.

50. "Turkey: Government Targeting Academics," Human Rights Watch, May 14, 2018, www.hrw.org/news/2018/05/14/turkey-government-targeting -academics.

51. Freedom House, Country and Territory Ratings and Statuses 1973–2020.

52. CPJ, Database of Attacks on the Press.

53. "Russian Police Detain or Harass More Than 100 Journalists amid January 31 Pro-Navalny Protests," CPJ, February 3, 2021, https://cpj.org/2021/02 /russian-police-detain-or-harass-more-than-100-journalists-amid-january-31 -pro-navalny-protests.

54. CPJ, Database of Attacks on the Press.

55. "Anna Politkovskaya," CPJ, https://cpj.org/data/people/anna-politkov skaya.

56. Cathy Young, "Religion in Art? Nyet!" *Reason*, March 23, 2005, https:// reason.com/2005/03/23/religion-in-art-nyet.

57. Sophia Kishkovsky "Organizers of Art Show Convicted in Moscow," *New York Times*, July 12, 2012, www.nytimes.com/2010/07/13/arts/design /13curators.html.

58. Miriam Elder, "Pussy Riot Sentenced to Two Years in Prison Colony for Hooliganism," *Guardian*, August 17, 2012, www.theguardian.com /music/2012/aug/17/pussy-riot-sentenced-two-years.

59. "How Russia's Law Against Insulting the Government Online Has Been Enforced in Its First Half Year," Meduza, September 30, 2019, https://meduza .io/en/short/2019/09/30/how-russia-s-law-against-insulting-the-government -online-has-been-enforced-in-its-first-half-year.

60. Qianlong Emperor, Qing Legal Code (1740), in *Tsa Tsing Leu Lee*, trans. and ed. George Thomas Staunton (London: 1810), 3–5, 354–357, 418, 547–549, in Stephen A. Smith, *Freedom of Expression: Foundational Documents and Historical Arguments* (Oxford: Oxbridge, 2018), 101–103.

61. Richard Baum, "The Fall and Rise of China," lecture 28, Teaching Company, 2010, CD, 20:56.

62. Baum, "The Fall and Rise of China," lecture 29, 26:34.

63. Mao Zedong, "Speech at the Second Session of the Eight Party Congress," May 1958, in *Long Live Mao Zedong Thought* (Red Guard Publication, 1968), in June Grasso et al., *Modernization and Revolution in China* (Armonk, NY: M. E. Sharpe, 1997), 219.

64. Baum, "The Fall and Rise of China," lecture 32, 9:27.

65. "China: Harassment of Foreign Correspondents Intensified During Covid-19," Reporters Without Borders, updated March 25, 2021, https:// rsf.org/en/news/china-harassment-foreign-correspondents-intensified -during-covid-19-0. See also, CPJ, Database of Attacks on the Press.

66. "Li Wenliang: Coronavirus Kills Chinese Whistleblower Doctor," *BBC*, February 7, 2020, www.bbc.com/news/world-asia-china-51403795; Raymond Zhong et al., "No 'Negative' News: How China Censored the Coronavirus," *New York Times*, December 20, 2020, www.nytimes.com/2020/12/19/technology /china-coronavirus-censorship.html; Reporters Without Borders, "China: Harassment of Foreign Correspondents Intensified During Covid-19."

67. Xi Jinping, "Statement at Virtual Event of the Opening of the 73rd World Health Assembly," May 18, 2020, *China Daily*, May 18, 2020, www .chinadaily.com.cn/a/202005/18/WS5ec273d1a310a8b2411568f1.html.

68. "China Delayed Releasing Coronavirus Info, Frustrating WHO," Associated Press, June 6, 2020, https://apnews.com/3c061794970661042b18d5 aeaaed9fae.

69. Serhii Plokhy, "The World Stopped Another Chernobyl by Working Together. Coronavirus Demands the Same," *Guardian*, May 5, 2020, www.theguardian.com/commentisfree/2020/may/05/prevent-coronavirus -chernobyl-international-disaster.

70. Javier C. Hernández, "Harsh Penalties, Vaguely Defined Crimes: Hong Kong's Security Law Explained," *New York Times*, June 30, 2020, https://nyti .ms/2ZonpzT.

71. Oiwan Lam, "With 47 More Charged, Every Prominent Hong Kong Activist Is Now Either in Jail or in Exile," Global Voices, March 1, 2021, https:// globalvoices.org/2021/03/01/with-47-charged-every-prominent-hong-kong -activist-is-now-either-in-jail-or-in-exile/?utm_source=twitter.com&utm _medium=social&utm_campaign=targetings-Testglobalvoicestest&utm _content=Oiwan-Lam&utm_term=730123#0_8_9097_8078_2307_226510071.

72. "Tracker: University Responses to Chinese Censorship," FIRE, www .thefire.org/resources/home-abroad-resources/universities-respond-to-chinas -censorship-efforts.

73. AFP, "Second Hong Kong Radio Host Arrested Under Colonial Era Sedition Law," *Hong Kong Free Press*, February 7, 2021, https://hongkongfp .com/2021/02/07/second-hong-kong-radio-host-arrested-under-colonial -era-sedition-law.

74. Riotous Assemblies Act 18 (2)(b), *Union Gazette Extraordinary* 17 (1956): 3–45, www.gov.za/sites/default/files/gcis_document/201505/act-17-1956_2.pdf.

75. Economic Freedom Fighter and Another v. Minister of Justice and Correctional Services and Another, ZACC 25 (2020), at 1, 16, www.saflii.org/za /cases/ZACC/2020/25.pdf.

76. South Africa Const. 16 (c) (adopted May 8, 1996).

77. S v. Mamabolo (E TV and others intervening), ZACC 17 (2001).

78. Hotz v. UCT, (730/2016 /2016) 2016 ZASCA 159 (2016), www.saflii .org/za/cases/ZASCA/2016/159.pdf.

79. Mandela, "Address to the International Press Institute Congress."

80. Republic of South Africa, Prevention and Combating of Hate Crimes and Hate Speech Bill, *Government Gazette* 41543 (2018), https://globalfreedom ofexpression.columbia.edu/wp-content/uploads/2019/01/Prevention-and -Combating-of-Hate-Crimes-and-Hate-Speech-Bill.pdf.

81. CPJ, Database of Attacks on the Press.

82. "Jaime Castaño Zacarías," CPJ, https://cpj.org/data/people/jaime -castano-zacarias.

83. Global Witness, *Defending Tomorrow* (July 2020), 6, 10, www.global witness.org/documents/19938/Defending_Tomorrow_EN_high_res_-_July _2020.pdf.

84. "Daphne Caruana Galizia," CPJ, https://cpj.org/data/people/daphne -caruana-galizia; "Daphne Caruana Galizia," *Guardian*, www.theguardian .com/world/daphne-caruana-galizia.

85. Svend-Erik Skaaning and Suthan Krishnarajan, *Who Cares About Free Speech? Findings from a Global Survey of Support for Free Speech* (Copenhagen: Justitia, 2021), https://futurefreespeech.com/wp-content/uploads/2021/06 /Report_Who-cares-about-free-speech_21052021.pdf. For survey data, see https://futurefreespeech.com/wp-content/uploads/2021/06/Justitia-data-and -questionnaire.zip.

86. Richard Wike and Katie Simmons, "Global Support for Principle of Free Expression, but Opposition to Some Forms of Speech," *Pew Research Center*, November 18, 2015, www.pewresearch.org/global/2015/11/18/global-support-for-principle-of-free-expression-but-opposition-to-some-forms-of-speech.

87. See, for example, US Press Freedom Tracker database since May 26, 2020, https://pressfreedomtracker.us/all-incidents/?categories=10&date_lower=2020-05-26&search=protest&endpage=3. See also, Jameel Jaffer, "Protest, the Press and the First Amendment Imperiled," *Columbia News*, June 5, 2020, https://news.columbia.edu/news/george-floyd-protests-free-speech.

88. Donald Trump (@realDonaldTrump), (tweet deleted),Twitter, June 25, 2020; See also, Colby Itkowitz, "Trump Lashes Out at Black Lives Matter, Accuses One Member of 'Treason'," *Washington Post*, June 25, 2020, www.washingtonpost.com/politics/trump-lashes-out-at-black-lives-matter-accuses-one-member-of-treason/2020/06/25/45667ec8-b70f-11ea-a510-55bf26485c93_story.html; Angela Dewan, "Trump Is Calling Protesters Who Disagree with Him Terrorists. That Puts Him in the Company of the World's Autocrats," *CNN*, July 27, 2020, https://edition.cnn.com/2020/07/25/politics/us-protests-trump-terrorists-intl/index.html.

89. Tracy K. Smith et al., Faculty Letter, July 4, 2020, https://docs.google.com/forms/d/e/1FAIpQLSfPmfeDKBi25_7rUTKkhZ3cyMICQicpo5ReVaeBpEdYUCkyIA/viewform.

90. Robby Soave, "Tulane Canceled a Talk by the Author of an Acclaimed Anti-Racism Book After Students Said the Event Was 'Violent,'" *Reason*, August 6 2020, https://reason.com/2020/08/06/tulane-cancels-life-of-a-klansman-edward-ball-students-racist.

91. Greg Lukianoff (@glukianoff), "THREAD: As you may have noticed, 'cancel culture' has intensified in recent weeks [. . .]," Twitter, June 26, 2020, 6:22 a.m., https://twitter.com/glukianoff/status/1276506207352750081.

92. Jonathan Chait, "The Still-Vital Case for Liberalism in a Radical Age," *New York Magazine*, June 11, 2020, https://nymag.com/intelligencer/2020/06/case-for-liberalism-tom-cotton-new-york-times-james-bennet.html.

93. Marc Tracy, "Senator's 'Send In the Troops' Op-Ed in The Times Draws Online Ire," *New York Times*, June 3, 2020, www.nytimes.com/2020/06/03 business/tom-cotton-op-ed.html?smid=url-share.

94. Kelsey McKinney, "Slate Podcast Host Mike Pesca Suspended Following Internal Discussion About Use of Racial Slur," Defector, February 22, 2021, https://defector.com/mike-pesca-slate-suspended.

95. Katie Robertson, "Teen Vogue Editor Resigns After Fury over Racist Tweets," *New York Times*, March 18, 2021, www.nytimes.com/2021/03/18/business/media/teen-vogue-editor-alexi-mccammond.html.

96. Emily Ekins, "Poll: 62% of Americans Say They Have Political Views They're Afraid to Share," Cato Institute, July 22, 2020, www.cato .org/survey-reports/poll-62-americans-say-they-have-political-views-theyre -afraid-share.

97. Brett Samuels, "Trump Ramps Up Rhetoric on Media, Calls Press 'the Enemy of the People,'" *The Hill*, April 5, 2019, https://thehill.com/homenews /administration/437610-trump-calls-press-the-enemy-of-the-people.

98. Michael M. Grynbaum and Maggie Haberman, "Trump Demands CNN Retract a Poll, as OANN Teases a Rosier View," *New York Times*, June 10, 2020, https://nyti.ms/2AXjvW6.

99. "Americans' Views on the Media," Ipsos, August 7, 2018, www.ipsos .com/en-us/news-polls/americans-views-media-2018-08-07.

100. Senate Bill 803, State of Oklahoma, 1st sess. of the 58th Legislature (2021), http://webserver1.lsb.state.ok.us/cf_pdf/2021-22%20INT/SB/SB803 %20INT.PDF; Chris Pandolfo, "Oklahoma Republican's Bill Would Ban Critical Race Theory from Being Taught in School," Blaze Media, February 24, 2021, www.theblaze.com/news/oklahoma-republican-ban-critical-race -theory-from-schools#toggle-gdpr; Brooke Singman, "DeSantis Condemns Critical Race Theory, Says It Won't Be Taught in Florida Classrooms," *Fox News*, March 18, 2021, www.foxnews.com/politics/desantis-critical -race-theory-florida-classrooms.

101. Emily Ekins, "The State of Free Speech and Tolerance in America," Cato Institute, October 31, 2017, www.cato.org/survey-reports/state-free -speech-tolerance-america.

102. "Tool: Recognizing Microaggressions and the Messages They Send," University of California Santa Cruz, https://academicaffairs.ucsc.edu/events /documents/Microaggressions_Examples_Arial_2014_11_12.pdf.

103. FIRE, Disinvitation Database, www.thefire.org/research/disinvitation -database.

104. FIRE, *Spotlight on Speech Codes 2021*, www.thefire.org/resources /spotlight/reports/spotlight-on-speech-codes-2021.

105. FIRE, *2020 College Free Speech Rankings*, report, https://reports .collegepulse.com/college-free-speech-rankings.

106. Scott Jaschik, "Temple Board Won't Try to Punish Professor for Speech," Inside Higher Ed, December 12, 2018, www.insidehighered.com /news/2018/12/12/temple-board-announces-it-respects-professors-controversial -speech-protected; "Collin College: Faculty Member Issued Warnings over Tweets About Vice President Pence, Deceased Professor," FIRE, www.thefire .org/cases/collin-college-email-alludes-to-discipline-under-personnel-policies -after-tweets-criticizing-vice-president-pence; Madison Hahamy and Beatriz Horta, "Former Professor Says Yale Fired Her over Tweet on Trump, Dershowitz,"

Yale News, March 23, 2021, https://yaledailynews.com/blog/2021/03/23/former
-professor-says-yale-fired-her-over-tweet-on-trump-dershowitz.

107. House Bill 800 (March 21, 2021). See also, Riley Gillis, "Tennessee
Republican Wants to Ban LGBTQ Books in Schools," *Metro Weekly*, March
30, 2021, www.metroweekly.com/2021/03/tennessee-republican-wants-to-ban
-lgbtq-books-in-schools.

108. "No Support: Russia's 'Gay Propaganda' Law Imperils LGBT Youth,"
Human Rights Watch, 2018, www.hrw.org/report/2018/12/11/no-support/russias
-gay-propaganda-law-imperils-lgbt-youth.

109. Ken White and Greg Lukianoff, "What's the Best Way to Protect Free
Speech?" *Reason*, August 4, 2020, https://reason.com/2020/08/04/whats-the
-best-way-to-protect-free-speech-ken-white-and-greg-lukianoff-debate-cancel
-culture.

110. Economist Intelligence Unit, *Democracy Index 2019*, 6–7.

111. Par Soren Seelow, "Attentat à « Charlie Hebdo »: « Vous allez payer car
vous avez insulté le Prophète »," *Le Monde*, January 8, 2015, www.lemonde
.fr/societe/article/2015/01/08/vous-allez-payer-car-vous-avez-insulte-le-prophete
_4551820_3224.html; Harriet Alexander, "Inside Charlie Hebdo Attack:
'We All Thought It Was a Joke,'" *Telegraph*, January 9, 2015, www.telegraph
.co.uk/news/worldnews/europe/france/11334812/Inside-Charlie-Hebdo-attack
-We-all-thought-it-was-a-joke.html.

112. Claire Williams, "Charlie Hebdo Attack," *France 24*, https://webdoc
.france24.com/france-paris-charlie-kosher-terrorism.

113. Société Française d'Étude du Dix-Huitième Siècle, *Tolérance: le combat des Lumières* (Paris, 2015), www.openbookpublishers.com/shopimages
/resources/Tolerance-Original-French.pdf.

114. "Pen Receives Letters from Members About Charlie Hebdo Award,"
PEN America, May 5, 2015, https://pen.org/pen-receives-letter-from-members
-about-charlie-hebdo-award.

115. Nadim Houry, "France's Creeping Terrorism Laws Restricting Free
Speech," Human Rights Watch, May 30, 2018, www.hrw.org/news/2018/05/30
/frances-creeping-terrorism-laws-restricting-free-speech.

116. Udlændinge- og Integrationsministeriet, LOV nr 1743, December 12,
2016, www.retsinformation.dk/eli/lta/2016/1743.

117. Guy Hedgecoe, "The Spanish Rappers Getting 'Terror' Sentences for
Songs," *BBC*, March 17, 2018, www.bbc.com/news/world-europe-43407694.

118. Jenny Hill, "Halle Shooting: Trial Begins for Germany Synagogue Attack
Suspect," *BBC*, July 21, 2020, www.bbc.com/news/world-europe-53471496.

119. Stephan Balliet, "A Short Pre-action Report," quoted in Andreas
Önnerfors, "The Germany Synagogue Terrorist's Manifesto Highlights Threat

of Neo-Nazism," Centre of Analysis of the Radical Right, October 24, 2019, www.radicalrightanalysis.com/2019/10/24/the-germany-synagogue-terrorists -manifesto-highlights-threat-of-neo-nazism.

120. Melissa Eddy, "Germany Moves to Tighten Gun and Hate Speech Laws After Far-Right Attacks," *New York Times*, October 30, 2019, www .nytimes.com/2019/10/30/world/europe/germany-gun-hate-speech-laws.html.

121. Hans Burkhard Nix v. Germany, Eur. Ct. H.R., no. 35285/16 (2018).

122. Jacob Mchangama and Natalie Alkiviadou, "Hate Speech and the European Court of Human Rights: Whatever Happened to the Right to Offend, Shock or Disturb?," *International Human Rights Law Review* (forthcoming).

123. Elliot Douglas, "German Interior Minister to File Criminal Complaint Against 'Police Are Trash' Journalist," *DW*, June 21, 2020, www .dw.com/en/german-interior-minister-to-file-criminal-complaint-against -police-are-trash-journalist/a-53893014.

124. JTA, "French High Court: BDS Activists Guilty of Discrimination," *Times of Israel*, October 23, 2015, www.timesofisrael.com/french-high-court-bds -activists-guilty-of-discrimination/; "France: Landmark ECtHR Judgement Finds Boycott Campaign Against Israel Cannot Be Criminalized," Amnesty International, June 11, 2020, www.amnesty.org/en/latest/news/2020/06/france -landmark-ecthr-judgment-finds-boycott-campaign-against-israel-cannot -be-criminalized.

125. "MSPs Approve Scotland's Controversial Hate Crime Law," *BBC*, March 11, 2021, www.bbc.com/news/uk-scotland-scotland-politics-56364821.

126. Laura Churchill, "Christian Street Preachers Who Read from Bible Found Guilty of Abusing Bristol Shoppers and Causing Angry Scenes," *Bristol Live*, February 28, 2017, www.bristolpost.co.uk/news/bristol-news /christian-street-preachers-who-read-4603.

127. Nico Lang, "French Hate Crime Ruling Sets a Dangerous Precedent for LGBT People: It's Now Illegal to Call Someone a 'Homophobe' in France," *Salon*, November 8, 2016, www.salon.com/2016/11/07/french-hate -crime-ruling-sets-a-dangerous-precedent-for-lgbt-people-it-is-now-illegal -to-call-someone-a-homophobe-in-france.

128. Sandra Fredman et al., *Comparative Hate Speech Law: Annexure*, University of Oxford, March 2012, 5n14, 19.

129. Anne Twomey, "Laws Against Incitement to Racial Hatred in the United Kingdom," *Australian Journal of Human Rights* 15, no. 1 (1995).

130. "European Police in Coordinated Raids Against Online Hate Speech," Reuters, November 3, 2020, www.reuters.com/article/us-europe-crime-internet -idUSKBN27J1C3.

Chapter 13:
The Internet and the Future of Free Speech

1. Eric Killelea, "Alex Jones' Mis-Infowars: 7 Bat-Sh*t Conspiracy Theories," *Rolling Stone*, February 21, 2017, www.rollingstone.com/culture /culture-lists/alex-jones-mis-infowars-7-bat-sht-conspiracy-theories-195468; Brian Stelter and Tom Kludt, "While Other Outlets Fact-Check Trump, Infowars Provides Alternative Facts," *CNN*, January 26, 2017, https:// money.cnn.com/2017/01/26/media/infowars-alex-jones-donald-trump/index .html; Amanda Sakuma, "Alex Jones Blames 'Psychosis' for His Sandy Hook Conspiracies," *Vox*, March 31, 2019, www.vox.com/2019/3/31/18289271/alex -jones-psychosis-conspiracies-sandy-hook-hoax.

2. Alex Hern, "Facebook, Apple, YouTube and Spotify Ban Infowars' Alex Jones," *Guardian*, August 6, 2018, www.theguardian.com/technology/2018 aug/06/apple-removes-podcasts-infowars-alex-jones.

3. "Twitter Bans Alex Jones and Infowars for Abusive Behaviour," *BBC*, September 6, 2018, www.bbc.com/news/world-us-canada-45442417.

4. John Perry Barlow, A Declaration of the Independence of Cyberspace (February 8, 1996), Electronic Frontier Foundation, www.eff.org/cyberspace -independence.

5. Tim Berners-Lee, *Weaving the Web: The Original Design and Ultimate Destiny of the World Wide Web* (New York: HarperCollins, 2000), 1, 134.

6. Lawrence Lessig, *Code: Version 2.0* (New York: Basic Books, 2006), 236.

7. See, for example, Casey Newton, "Everything You Need to Know About Section 230: The Most Important Law for Online Speech," *The Verge*, May 28, 2020, www.theverge.com/21273768/section-230-explained-internet-speech-law -definition-guide-free-moderation.

8. Jeff Kosseff, *The Twenty-Six Words That Created the Internet* (Ithaca: Cornell University Press, 2019), 4, 78, 96, 102.

9. See, for example, Michael Hauben and Ronda Hauben, *Netizens: On the History and Impact of Usenet and the Internet* (Hoboken, NJ: Wiley, 1997); and Vince Tabora, "The Evolution of the Internet, From Decentral- ized to Centralized," Hacker Noon, March 25, 2018, https://hackernoon.com/ the-evolution-of-the-internet-from-decentralized-to-centralized-3e2fa65898f5.

10. Hauben and Hauben, *Netizens*, 48.

11. David Kaye, *Speech Police: The Global Struggle to Govern the Internet* (New York: Columbia Global Reports, 2019), 6–7, Kindle.

12. Martin Gurri, *The Revolt of the Public and the Crisis of Authority in the New Millennium* (San Francisco: Stripe Press, 2018), 10, Kindle.

13. Gurri, *The Revolt of the Public*, 48.

14. Colin Delany, "How Social Media Accelerated Tunisia's Revolution: An Inside View," *Huffington Post*, February 13, 2011, www.huffpost.com/entry /how-social-media-accelera_b_821497.

15. Quoted in "Tunisians React as President Steps Down," January 14, 2011, *BBC*, www.bbc.com/news/world-africa-12196242.

16. Arch Puddington et al., *Freedom in the World 2012* (Freedom House, 2013), 8, 691–692.

17. Philip Howard, quoted in Catherine O'Donnell, "New Study Quantifies Use of Social Media in Arab Spring," *University of Washington News*, September 12, 2011, www.washington.edu/news/2011/09/12/new-study-quantifies-use-of-social-media-in-arab-spring.

18. Puddington et al., *Freedom in the World 2012*, 8, 61–62, 582–583.

19. Committee to Protect Journalists (CPJ), Database of Attacks on the Press, https://cpj.org/data.

20. Reporters Without Borders, "Journalists' Deaths After Release—Alarm Signal for Egypt and Saudi Arabia," Reporters Without Borders, July 29, 2020, https://rsf.org/en/news/journalists-deaths-after-release-alarm-signal-egypt-and-saudi-arabia.

21. Freedom House, Country and Territory Ratings and Statuses 1973–2020.

22. Shahbaz and Funk, *Freedom on the Net 2020*, 1, 4, 24–25.

23. Joseph Johnson, "Worldwide Digital Population as of October 2020," Statista, January 27, 2021, www.statista.com/statistics/617136/digital-population-worldwide.

24. Cam Cullen, "Over 43% of the Internet Is Consumed by Netflix, Google, Amazon, Facebook, Microsoft, and Apple: Global Internet Phenomena Spotlight," Sandvine, August 30, 2019, www.sandvine.com/blog/netflix-vs.-google-vs.-amazon-vs.-facebook-vs.-microsoft-vs.-apple-traffic-share-of-internet-brands-global-internet-phenomena-spotlight.

25. Kaye, *Speech Police*, 6.

26. Lessig, *Code*, 237.

27. Bill Clinton, "Speech at the Paul H. Nitze School of Advanced International Studies," March 8, 2000, *New York Times*, https://archive.nytimes.com/www.nytimes.com/library/world/asia/030900clinton-china-text.html.

28. #郭文贵 #GTV #六四, "🔔郭文贵gtv直播💧 6/3/2020 郝海東宣讀 🔒紀念六四🔒 新中國聯邦建國," streamed live on June 3, 2020, YouTube video, www.youtube.com/watch?v=e4aN5hoRqD8&feature=youtu.be&t=4496.

29. Gerry Shih, "Chinese Soccer Superstar Calls for Ouster of Communist Party, Stunning Nation," *Washington Post*, June 5, 2020, www.washingtonpost.com/world/asia_pacific/chinese-soccer-superstar-hao-haidong-calls-for-ouster-of-communist-party-stunning-nation/2020/06/05/9ae91df2-a6ec-11ea-898e-b21b9a83f792_story.html.

30. Gary King et al., "How the Chinese Government Fabricates Social Media Posts for Strategic Distraction, Not Engaged Argument," *American Political Science Review* 111, no. 3 (2017): 484–501.

31. Jacob Mchangama, "Episode 26—Oslo Freedom Forum Special with Megha Rajagopalan and Yuan Yang," *Clear and Present Danger: A History of Free Speech*, June 4, 2019, podcast, www.freespeechhistory.com/2019/06/04/episode-26-oslo-freedom-forum-special-with-megha-rajagopalan-and-yuan-yang.

32. Adrian Shahbaz, *Freedom on the Net 2018: The Rise of Digital Authoritarianism* (Freedom House, 2018), 7–8.

33. Jack Goldsmith and Tim Wu, *Who Controls the Internet? Illusions of a Borderless World* (Oxford: Oxford University Press, 2006), 93.

34. Yuan Yang, "Zoom Plan Will Enable China to Censor Individual Users," *Financial Times*, June 12, 2020, www.ft.com/content/a18e3bd5-b1a2-4426-9056-369ad83d8f30.

35. Ryan Gallagher, "Google's Secret China Project 'Effectively Ended' After Internal Confrontation," The Intercept, December 17, 2018, https://theintercept.com/2018/12/17/google-china-censored-search-engine-2.

36. Access Now and #KeeptItOn, *Shattered Dreams and Lost Opportunities* (March 2021), www.accessnow.org/cms/assets/uploads/2021/03/KeepItOn-report-on-the-2020-data_Mar-2021_3.pdf.

37. Shahbaz and Funk, *Freedom on the Net 2020*, 9–10.

38. Reuters, "India Leads the World with 67% of Total Internet Shutdowns," *Business Today*, December 21, 2019, www.businesstoday.in/top-story/india-leads-the-world-with-67-of-total-internet-shutdowns/story/392411.html.

39. Adrian Shahbaz and Allie Funk, *Freedom on the Net 2019: The Crisis of Social Media* (Freedom House, 2019), 9.

40. Barack Obama, "Network Neutrality," June 8, 2006, podcast, http://obamaspeeches.com/076-Network-Neutrality-Obama-Podcast.htm; Barack Obama (@BarackObama), "We just made history [. . .]," Twitter, November 5, 2008, 11:34 a.m., https://twitter.com/barackobama/status/992176676?lang=en.

41. Soumitra Dutta and Matthew Fraser, "Barack Obama and the Facebook Election," *U.S. News*, November 19, 2008, www.usnews.com/opinion/articles/2008/11/19/barack-obama-and-the-facebook-election; John Allen Hendricks and Robert E. Denton Jr., eds., *Communicator-in-Chief: How Barack Obama Used New Technology to Win the White House* (Lanham, MD: Lexington Books, 2010). See also, David Carr, "How Obama Tapped into Social Networks' Power," *New York Times*, November 9, 2008, www.nytimes.com/2008/11/10/business/media/10carr.html.

42. Daryl Johnson, *Hateland: A Long, Hard Look at America's Extremist Heart* (Amherst, NY: Prometheus, 2019).

43. Shahbaz and Funk, *Freedom on the Net 2019*, 7.

44. Soroush Vosoughi, Deb Roy, and Sinan Aral, "The Spread of True and False News Online," *Science* 359 (2018): 1146–1151.

45. David Remnick, "Trump vs. the Times: Inside an Off-the-Record Meeting," *New Yorker*, July 30, 2018, www.newyorker.com/news/news-desk/trump-vs-the-times-inside-an-off-the-record-meeting.

46. According to the OECD, the share of Americans who have trust in their government fell from 46.8 percent in 2006 to 33.3 percent in 2018. See OECD, Trust in Government (data set), https://data.oecd.org/gga/trust-in-government.htm.

47. Edelman, *2021 Edelman Trust Barometer* (2021), 12, www.edelman.com/sites/g/files/aatuss191/files/2021-03/2021%20Edelman%20Trust%20Barometer.pdf.

48. Nathaniel Persily and Joshua A. Tucker, eds., *Social Media and Democracy: The State of the Field, Prospects for Reform* (Cambridge: Cambridge University Press, 2020), 1.

49. Jonathan Rauch, *The Constitution of Knowledge: A Defense of Truth* (Washington, DC: Brookings Institution, 2021).

50. Barack Obama, quoted in Peter Kafka, "Obama: The Internet Is 'the Single Biggest Threat to Our Democracy,'" *Vox*, November 16, 2020, www.vox.com/recode/2020/11/16/21570072/obama-internet-threat-democracy-facebook-fox-atlantic.

51. Alexey Navalny (@navalny), "1. I think that the ban of Donald Trump on Twitter is an unacceptable act of censorship (THREAD)," Twitter, January 9, 2021, 10:13 a.m., https://twitter.com/navalny/status/1347969772177264644.

52. Oversight Board, Case decision 2021-001-FB-FBR, May 5, 2021, www.oversightboard.com/decision/FB-691QAMHJ.

53. "Code of Practice on Disinformation," European Union, September 26, 2021, https://ec.europa.eu/digital-single-market/en/news/code-practice-disinformation.

54. Natasha Lomas, "Germany Tightens Online Hate Speech Rules to Make Platforms Send Reports Straight to the Feds," *Tech Crunch*, June 19, 2020, https://techcrunch.com/2020/06/19/germany-tightens-online-hate-speech-rules-to-make-platforms-send-reports-straight-to-the-feds/?guccounter=1.

55. Heidi Tworek, "Fighting Hate with Speech Law: Media and German Visions of Democracy," *Journal of Holocaust Research* 35, no. 2 (2021): 114.

56. Jacob Mchangama and Natalie Alkiviadou, *The Digital Berlin Wall: How Germany (Accidentally) Created a Prototype for Global Online Censorship—Act Two* (Copenhagen: Justitia, 2020). For an infogram of NetzDG's global spread, see https://infogram.com/netzdg-1h17495pggyl2zj.

57. "Russia Accuses Twitter of Breaking Law by Failing to Delete Content," Reuters, March 1, 2021, www.reuters.com/article/us-russia-twitter-idUSKCN2AT1R7?taid=603cb4227bab020001310123&utm_campaign=trueAnthem:+Trending+Content&utm_medium=trueAnthem&utm_source=twitter.

58. Kat Lonsdorf, "Social Media Fueled Russian Protests Despite Government Attempts to Censor," NPR, January 24, 2021, www.npr.org/2021/01/24/960113653/social-media-fueled-russian-protests-despite-government-attempts-to-censor?t=1614767493916.

59. Constitutional Council, Décision n° 2020-801 DC, June 18, 2020, www.conseil-constitutionnel.fr/decision/2020/2020801DC.htm, trans. Laura Kayali, "French Constitutional Court Strikes Down Most of Hate Speech Law," *Politico*, June 18, 2020, www.politico.eu/article/french-constitutional-court-strikes-down-most-of-hate-speech-law.

60. "Against Information Manipulation," Government of France, November 20, 2018, www.gouvernement.fr/en/against-information-manipulation.

61. "Disinformation: EU Accesses the Code of Practice and Publishes Platform Reports on Coronavirus Related Disinformation," European Commission, September 10, 2020, https://ec.europa.eu/commission/presscorner/detail/en/ip_20_1568.

62. "The EFJ Calls for Stronger Measures to Tackle Online Platforms' Disinformation," *European Federation of Journalists*, June 15, 2020, https://europeanjournalists.org/blog/2020/06/15/the-efj-calls-for-stronger-measures-to-tackle-disinformation-on-online-platforms.

63. Michael Peel, Mehreen Khan, and Max Seddon, "EU Attack on Pro-Kremlin 'Fake News' Takes a Hit," *Financial Times*, April 2, 2018, www.ft.com/content/5ec2a204-3406-11e8-ae84-494103e73f7f.

64. "Joe Biden: Former Vice President of the United States," *New York Times*, January 17, 2020, www.nytimes.com/interactive/2020/01/17/opinion/joe-biden-nytimes-interview.html?smid=nytcore-ios-share.

65. Executive Order 13925, Preventing Online Censorship, 85 Fed. Reg. 34069 (May 28, 2020), https://trumpwhitehouse.archives.gov/presidential-actions/executive-order-preventing-online-censorship.

66. Andrew Marantz, "Free Speech Is Killing Us," *New York Times*, October 4, 2019, www.nytimes.com/2019/10/04/opinion/sunday/free-speech-social-media-violence.html.

67. "Social Media's Struggle with Self-Censorship," *Economist*, October 22, 2020, www.economist.com/briefing/2020/10/22/social-medias-struggle-with-self-censorship.

68. Rauch, *The Constitution of Knowledge*.

69. Lee Clarke and Caron Chess, "Elites and Panic: More to Fear than Fear Itself," *Social Forces* 87, no. 2 (2008): 1006–1008.

70. Nathan Bomey, "Facebook Vows to Remove Content Denying the Holocaust in Reversal for Mark Zuckerberg," *USA Today*, October 12, 2020, https://eu.usatoday.com/story/tech/2020/10/12/facebook-bans-holocaust-denial-content-mark-zuckerberg/5966973002.

71. Sam Levin, "Zuckerberg Defends Facebook Users' Right to Be Wrong—Even Holocaust Deniers," *Guardian*, July 18, 2018, www.theguardian.com /technology/2018/jul/18/zuckerberg-facebook-holocaust-deniers-censorship.

72. James B. Meigs, "Elite Panic vs. the Resilient Populace," *Commentary*, May 2020, www.commentarymagazine.com/articles/james-meigs/elite-panic -vs-the-resilient-populace.

73. Kate Klonick, "The Facebook Oversight Board: Creating an Independent Institution to Adjudicate Online Free Expression," *Yale Law Journal* 129 (2020): 2436.

74. Tony Wang, quoted in Josh Halliday, "Twitter's Tony Wang: 'We Are the Free Speech Wing of the Free Speech Party,'" *Guardian*, March 22, 2012, www.theguardian.com/media/2012/mar/22/twitter-tony-wang-free-speech.

75. Shona Ghosh, "Twitter Was Once a Bastion of Free Speech but Now Says It's 'No Longer Possible to Stand Up for All Speech,'" *Business Insider*, December 19, 2017, https://nordic.businessinsider.com/twitter -no-longer-possible-to-stand-up-for-all-speech-2017-12?r=US&IR=T.

76. Press Association, "Mark Zuckerberg Calls for Stronger Regulation of Internet," *Guardian*, March 30, 2019, www.theguardian.com/technology /2019/mar/30/mark-zuckerberg-calls-for-stronger-regulation-of-internet; Jessica Guynn, "Facebook's Mark Zuckerberg Calls for Section 230 Reform, 'Congress Should Update the Law,'" *USA Today*, https://eu.usatoday.com/story /tech/2020/10/27/facebook-ceo-mark-zuckerberg-calls-congress-reform-section -230/3754266001.

77. Justitia, forthcoming 2022.

78. Facebook, *Community Standards Enforcement Report* (February 2021), https://transparency.facebook.com/community-standards-enforcement.

79. Mchangama and Alkiviadou, *The Digital Berlin Wall*.

80. Natasha Duarte, Emma Llansó, and Anna Loup, *Mixed Messages? The Limits of Automated Social Media Content Analysis* (Center for Democracy and Technology, 2017), www.cdt.org/wp-content/uploads/2017/11/Mixed-Messages -Paper.pdf.

81. Andrew Marantz, "Why Facebook Can't Fix Itself," *New Yorker*, October 12, 2020, www.newyorker.com/magazine/2020/10/19/why-facebook-cant -fix-itself.

82. Jacob Mchangama, Natalie Alkiviadou, and Raghav Mendiratta, *Rushing to Judgment: Are Short Mandatory Takedown Limits for Online Hate Speech Compatible with the Freedom of Expression?* (Justitia, 2021), 30.

83. Mike Masnick, "Masnick's Impossibility Theorem: Content Moderation at Scale Is Impossible to Do Well," Techdirt, November 20, 2019, www .techdirt.com/articles/20191111/23032743367/masnicks-impossibility-theorem -content-moderation-scale-is-impossible-to-do-well.shtml.

84. Simon S. Cordall, "Facebook Deactivates Accounts of Tunisian Political Bloggers and Activists," *Guardian*, June 4, 2020, www.theguardian.com/global-development/2020/jun/04/facebook-deactivates-accounts-of-tunisian-political-bloggers-and-activists.

85. Jack Goldsmith and Andrew Keane Woods, "Internet Speech Will Never Go Back to Normal," *Atlantic*, April 25, 2020, www.theatlantic.com/ideas/archive/2020/04/what-covid-revealed-about-internet/610549.

86. Julia Angwin, "Facebook's Secret Censorship Rules Protect White Men from Hate Speech but Not Black Children," ProPublica, June 28, 2017, www.propublica.org/article/facebook-hate-speech-censorship-internal-documents-algorithms; Captain Clay Higgins, Facebook update, June 4, 2017, via Archive.ph, https://archive.ph/95FO1; June 4, 2017, via Archive.ph, https://archive.ph/95FO1; The Dido Delgado, Facebook update, May 3, 2017, www.facebook.com/THEDiDiDelgado/photos/a.271621723285520.1073741828.268977940216565/278984872549205/?type=1&theater.

87. Jacob Siegel, "Bob Dylan's 'Neighborhood Bully' Gets Memory-Holed," *Tablet*, December 22, 2020, www.tabletmag.com/sections/arts-letters/articles/neighborhood-bully-memory-holed.

88. Anton Lind, "Facebook sletter danske opslag for at nævne navnet på radikal britisk hørefløjsaktivist," *Danmarks Radio* [Danish Broadcasting Corporation], September 20, 2019, www.dr.dk/nyheder/indland/facebook-sletter-danske-opslag-naevne-navnet-paa-radikal-britisk; Frederik V. Kock, "Tommy Robinson er ikke alene: Står på hemmelig liste over bandlyste brugere hos Facebook," *Berlingske*, www.berlingske.dk/samfund/tommy-robinson-er-ikke-alene-staar-paa-hemmelig-liste-over-bandlyste.

89. In Defense of Stalin, Facebook group, www.facebook.com/groups/InDefenseOfStalin.

90. Hateful Conduct Policy, Twitter, https://help.twitter.com/en/rules-and-policies/hateful-conduct-policy; Alessandra Aster (@AlessandraAster), (suspended tweet), Twitter, October 20, 2020, https://twitter.com/Alessandra Aster/status/1318449503767244801; M. K. Fain, "My Whole Conversation with Kaitlyn Tiffany for the Atlantic," 4W, December 8, 2020, https://4w.pub/my-whole-conversation-with-kaitlyn-tiffany-for-the-atlantic.

91. Kate Conger and Mike Isaac, "In Reversal, Twitter Is No Longer Blocking New York Post Article," *New York Times*, October 16, 2020, https://nyti.ms/3dKsuJP.

92. Sacha Baron Cohen, "Read Sacha Baron Cohen's Scathing Attack on Facebook in Full: 'Greatest Propaganda Machine in History,'" *Guardian*, November 22, 2019, www.theguardian.com/technology/2019/nov/22/sacha-baron-cohen-facebook-propaganda.

93. Steven Lee Myers, "'Borat' Is Not Approved for Distribution in Russia," *New York Times*, November 10, 2006, www.nytimes.com/2006/11/10/movies/10bora.html.

94. Svend-Erik Skaaning and Suthan Krishnarajan, *Who Cares About Free Speech? Findings from a Global Survey of Support for Free Speech* (Copenhagen: Justitia, 2021), https://futurefreespeech.com/wp-content/uploads/2021/06/Report_Who-cares-about-free-speech_21052021.pdf.

95. "Pakistan's PM Asks Facebook to Ban Islamophobic Content," *BBC*, October 26, 2020, www.bbc.com/news/world-asia-54689283.

96. Sacha Baron Cohen (@SachaBaronCohen), "@Facebook—I criticized you for not blocking false info about Covid. Now your AI is blocking my article [. . .]," Twitter, October 13, 2020, 11:17 a.m., https://twitter.com/SachaBaronCohen/status/1316080610956455938.

97. Persily and Tucker, *Social Media and Democracy*, 2.

98. Emmanuel Macron, "Speech at Internet Governance Forum 2018," November 12, 2018, Internet Governance Forum, www.intgovforum.org/multilingual/content/igf-2018-speech-by-french-president-emmanuel-macron.

99. Alexandra Siegel, "Online Hate Speech," in Persily and Tucker, *Social Media and Democracy*, 66–71.

100. Alexandra Siegel et al., "Trumping Hate on Twitter? Online Hate Speech in the 2016 U.S. Election Campaign and Its Aftermath," *Quarterly Journal of Political Science* 16, no. 1 (2021): 71–104.

101. Jacob Mchangama, Eske Vinther-Jensen, and Ronne Brandt Taarnborg, *Digital Ytringsfrihed og Sociale Medier* (Copenhagen: Justitia, 2020); Iginio Gagliardone et al., *Mechachal: Online Debates and Elections in Ethiopia: From Hate Speech to Engagement in Social Media* (2016), 6, working paper, https://eprints.soas.ac.uk/30572.

102. Siegel, "Online Hate Speech," 68, 71.

103. Susan Benesch et al., "Dangerous Speech: A Practical Guide," *The Dangerous Speech Project*, August 4, 2020, www.dangerousspeech.org/wp-content/uploads/2020/08/Dangerous-Speech-A-Practical-Guide.pdf.

104. Andrea Scheffler, *The Inherent Danger of Hate Speech Legislation: A Case Study from Rwanda and Kenya on the Failure of a Preventative Measure* (Windhoek: Fesmedia Africa and Friedrich-Ebert-Stiftung, 2015).

105. Paul Mozur, "A Genocide Incited on Facebook, with Posts From Myanmar's Military," *New York Times*, October 15, 2018, https://nyti.ms/2QToYQA.

106. As discussed by scholars such as Eric Heinze, "Hate Speech and the Normative Foundations of Regulation," *International Journal of Law in Context* 9, no. 4 (2013): 599. For an overview of several positions regarding

harms of repression, see Jacob Mchangama, "How Censorship Crosses Borders," Cato Unbound, June 11, 2018, www.cato-unbound.org/2018/06/11/jacob-mchangama/how-censorship-crosses-borders.

107. Mchangama, "How Censorship Crosses Borders."

108. Lasse Eskildsen and Christian Bjørnskov, "Does Freedom of Expression Cause Less Terrorism?" *The Future of Free Speech*, April 5, 2020, https://futurefreespeech.com/wp-content/uploads/2020/06/Freedom-of-Expression-and-Terror-Apr-4.pdf.

109. Jacob Aaslund Ravndal, "Explaining Right-Wing Terrorism and Violence in Western Europe: Grievances, Opportunities, and Polarization," *European Journal of Political Research* 57, no. 4 (2017): 845–866.

110. Laura Jacobs and Joost van Spanje, "A Time-Series Analysis of Contextual-Level Effects on Hate Crime in The Netherlands," *Social Forces* (2020): 1–25.

111. Jason Murdock, "Donald Trump's Facebook Gains Almost 150,000 New Likes Since He Was Blocked 'Indefinitely,'" *Newsweek*, January 14, 2021, www.newsweek.com/donald-trump-facebook-page-new-likes-indefinite-social-media-block-1561526?utm_medium=Social&utm_source=Twitter#Echobox=1610696780.

112. Siegel, "Online Hate Speech," 72; Aleksandra Urman and Stefan Katz, "What They Do in the Shadows: Examining the Far-Right Net-Works in Telegram," *Information, Communication & Society* (2020): 1–20.

113. Tatyana Flegontova, "Telegram Downloads Soar as Trump Supporters Deplatformed," *Moscow Times*, January 12, 2021, www.themoscowtimes.com/2021/01/12/telegram-downloads-soar-as-trump-supporters-deplatformed-a72579.

114. Siegel, "Online Hate Speech," 74. See also, Gerrit De Vynck and Ellen Nakashima, "Far-Right Groups Move Online Conversations from Social Media to Chap Apps—and Out of View of Law Enforcement," *Washington Post*, January 18, 2021, www.washingtonpost.com/technology/2021/01/15/parler-telegram-chat-apps.

115. Katherine Eban, "The Lab-Leak Theory: Inside the Fight to Uncover COVID-19's Origins," *Vanity Fair*, June 3, 2021, www.vanityfair.com/news/2021/06/the-lab-leak-theory-inside-the-fight-to-uncover-covid-19s-origins; Cristiano Lima, "Facebook No Longer Treating 'Man-Made' Covid as a Crackpot Idea," *Politico*, May 26, 2021, www.politico.com/news/2021/05/26/facebook-ban-covid-man-made-491053.

116. Jennifer Allen et al., "Evaluating the Fake News Problem at the Scale of the Information Ecosystem," *Science Advances* 6, no. 14 (2020).

117. Andrew Guess, Jonathan Nagler, and Joshua Tucker, "Less Than You Think: Prevalence and Predictors of Fake News Dissemination on Facebook," *Science Advances* 5, no. 1 (2019): 1–8.

118. Jacob L. Nelson and Harsh Taneja, "The Small, Disloyal Fake News Audience: The Role of Audience Availability in Fake News Consumption," *New Media and Society* 20, no. 7 (2018): 1–18.

119. Christopher A. Bail et al., "Accessing the Russian Internet Research Agency's Impact on the Political Attitudes and Behaviors of American Twitter Users in Late 2017," *Proceedings of the National Academy of Sciences of the United States of America* 117, no. 1 (2020): 243–250.

120. Hunt Allcott and Matthew Gentzkow, "Social Media and Fake News in the 2016 Election," *Journal of Economic Perspectives* 31, no. 2 (2017): 232.

121. Andrew M. Guess and Benjamin A. Lyons, "Misinformation, Disinformation, and Online Propaganda," in Persily and Tucker, *Social Media and Democracy*, 26.

122. Matteo Cinelli et al., "The Limited Reach of Fake News on Twitter During 2019 European Elections," PLoS One, June 18, 2020, https://arxiv.org/abs/1911.12039

123. Bail et al., "Accessing the Russian Internet Research Agency's Impact."

124. Guess and Lyons, "Misinformation, Disinformation, and Online Propaganda"; Gordon Pennycook and David G. Rand, "Lazy, Not Biased: Susceptibility to Partisan Fake News Is Better Explained by Lack of Reasoning Than by Motivated Reasoning," *Cognition* 188 (2019): 39–50.

125. Guess et al., "Less Than You Think"; Allen et al., "Evaluating the Fake News Problem." See also, Vidya Narayanan et al., "Polarization, Partisanship and Junk News Consumption over Social Media in the US" (Oxford Internet Institute, 2018); and Nahema Marchal et al., "Polarization, Partisanship and Junk News Consumption on Social Media During the 2018 US Midterm Elections" (Oxford Internet Institute, 2018).

126. Paolo Barberá, "Social Media, Echo Chambers, and Political Polarization," in Persily and Tucker, *Social Media and Democracy*, 35.

127. Barberá, "Social Media, Echo Chambers, and Political Polarization," 45–48.

128. Hugo Mercier, *Not Born Yesterday: The Science of Who We Trust and What We Believe* (Princeton: Princeton University Press, 2020).

129. Nic Newman et al., *Reuters Institute Digital News Report 2020* (Reuters Institute for the Study of Journalism, 2020), 14, https://reutersinstitute.politics.ox.ac.uk/sites/default/files/2020-06/DNR_2020_FINAL.pdf.

130. Nomaan Merchant and Tim Sullivan, "Election Officials Worried by Threats and Protesters," *Associated Press*, November 6, 2020, https://apnews.com/article/arrests-vote-count-oregon-new-york-f92075a34ce8dd166ff17bbd9bedc49d.

131. Jonathan Easley, "Majority of Republicans Say 2020 Election Was Invalid: Poll," *The Hill*, February 25, 2021, https://thehill.com/homenews/campaign/540508-majority-of-republicans-say-2020-election-was-invalid-poll.

132. "If China Valued Free Speech, There Would Be No Coronavirus Crisis," *Guardian*, February 8, 2020, www.theguardian.com/world/2020/feb/08/if-china-valued-free-speech-there-would-be-no-coronavirus-crisis.

133. "How Belarus's Protesters Staged a Digital Revolution," *Financial Times*, February 24, 2021, www.ft.com/content/a68a1c28-fdd0-4800-9339-6ca1e81d456a; Sean Williams, "Belarus Has Torn Up the Protest Rulebook. Everyone Should Listen," *Wired*, August 18, 2020, www.wired.co.uk/article/belarus-protests-telegram.

134. Alexey Navalny, "Putin's Palace. History of World's Largest Bribe," January 19, 2021, YouTube video, www.youtube.com/watch?v=ipAnwilMncI.

135. Repucci, *Freedom and the Media 2019*, 25.

136. Shahbaz and Funk, *Freedom on the Net 2019*, 11.

137. Luke Harding, "'A Chain of Stupidity': The Skripal Case and the Decline of Russia's Spy Agencies," *Guardian*, June 23, 2020, www.theguardian.com/world/2020/jun/23/skripal-salisbury-poisoning-decline-of-russia-spy-agencies-gru.

138. Matthew Hill et al., "Their Goal Is to Destroy Everyone: Uighur Camp Detainees Allege Systematic Rape," *BBC*, February 2, 2021, www.bbc.com/news/world-asia-china-55794071; John Sudworth, "China Uighurs: A Model's Video Gives a Rare Glimpse Inside Internment," *BBC*, August 4, 2020, www.bbc.com/news/world-asia-china-53650246.

139. Janis Wong, "Protests Decentralised: How Technology Enabled Civil Disobedience by Hong Kong Anti-extradition Bill Protesters," (paper, 8th Asian Privacy Scholars Network Conference 2020).

140. Jen Kirby, "'Black Lives Matter' Has Become a Global Rallying Cry Against Racism and Police Brutality," *Vox*, June 12, 2020, www.vox.com/2020/6/12/21285244/black-lives-matter-global-protests-george-floyd-uk-belgium.

141. Jane Hu, "The Second Act of Social-Media Activism," *New Yorker*, August 3, 2020, www.newyorker.com/culture/cultural-comment/the-second-act-of-social-media-activism.

142. Ted Hesson, Mimi Dwyer, and Andy Sullivan, "Videos of Alleged Police Misconduct Went Viral. Then What Happened?" Reuters Graphics, June 23, 2020, https://graphics.reuters.com/MINNEAPOLIS-POLICE/PROTESTS-VIDEOS/oakveazawvr.

143. "As More Gay People Come Out, Tolerance Will Spread," *Economist*, August 6, 2020, www.economist.com/leaders/2020/08/06/as-more-gay-people-come-out-tolerance-will-spread.

144. Savannah Vickery, "Queer Connections: Social Media as a Versatile Tool of the Marginalized Moroccan LGBT," *Independent Study Project (ISP) Collection* (2016); Nick Duffy, "Kenya's Censorship Chief Claims Western Charities Pay Kids £22,000 Each to Become Gay," *Pink News*, May 6, 2018,

www.pinknews.co.uk/2018/05/06/kenya-censorship-chief-charities-bribe-kids-20000-to-be-gay.

145. Ideas Beyond Borders, www.ideasbeyondborders.org. Numbers as of June 2021.

146. "Big and Bold Move: India Lifts Tax over Sanitary Napkins," She the People, July 21, 2018, www.shethepeople.tv/news/big-and-bold-move-india-lifts-tax-over-sanitary-napkins.

147. T.N. Hari, "Opinion: If Not Closure, #MeToo Movements Has Given Women Freedom from Fear," *Mint*, September 18, 2019, www.livemint.com/mint-lounge/business-of-life/opinion-if-not-closure-metoo-movement-has-given-women-freedom-from-fear-1568802815416.html.

148. Carl Miller, "Taiwan's Crowdsourced Democracy Shows Us How to Fix Social Media," We Are Not Divided, Reasons to be Cheerful, September 27, 2020, https://wearenotdivided.reasonstobecheerful.world/taiwan-gov-hackers-technology-digital-democracy.

149. Carl Miller, "How Taiwan's 'Civic Hackers' Helped Find a New Way to Run the Country," *Guardian*, September 27, 2020, www.theguardian.com/world/2020/sep/27/taiwan-civic-hackers-polis-consensus-social-media-platform.

150. Jacob Mchangama and Jonas Parello-Plesner, "Taiwan's Disinformation Solution," *American Interest*, February 6, 2020, www.the-american-interest.com/2020/02/06/taiwans-disinformation-solution.

151. "Cofacts," Gov, https://cofacts.gov.tw.

152. Carl Miller, "Taiwan Is Making Democracy Work Again. It's Time We Paid Attention," *Wired*, November 26, 2019, www.wired.co.uk/article/taiwan-democracy-social-media; Carl Miller, "How Taiwan's 'Civic Hackers' Helped Find a New Way to Run the Country."

153. Chelsea Barabas, "Decentralized Social Networks Sound Great. Too Bad They'll Never Work," *Wired*, August 9, 2017, www.wired.com/story/decentralized-social-networks-sound-great-too-bad-theyll-never-work.

154. Nicholas Thompson, "Tim Wu Explains Why He Thinks Facebook Should Be Broken Up," *Wired*, July 5, 2019, www.wired.com/story/tim-wu-explains-why-facebook-broken-up.

155. Mike Masnick, "Protocols, Not Platforms: A Technological Approach to Free Speech," Knight First Amendment Institute, August 21, 2019, https://knightcolumbia.org/content/protocols-not-platforms-a-technological-approach-to-free-speech.

156. See, for example, ARTICLE 19, *Blockchain and Freedom of Expression* (London, 2019), https://article19.org/wp-content/uploads/2019/07/Blockchain-and-FOE-v4.pdf; and Jeff Kaplan, "Locking the Web Open: A Call for a Decentralized Web," *Brewster Kahle's Blog*, http://brewster.kahle.org/2015/08/11/locking-the-web-open-a-call-for-a-distributed-web-2.

157. Jack Dorsey (@jack), "Twitter is funding a small independent team of up to five open source architects, engineers, and designers [. . .]," Twitter, December 11, 2019, 6:13 a.m., https://twitter.com/jack/status/1204766078468911106. See also, Oslo Freedom Forum, "Jack Dorsey Discusses Disinformation, Bitcoin, and the Open Internet. 2020 Oslo Freedom Forum," September 25, 2020, YouTube video, www.youtube.com/watch?v=L8aG_ekh6EQ.

158. ARTICLE 19, *Blockchain and Freedom of Expression*, 20–23; Barabas, "Decentralized Social Networks Sound Great."

159. "Tim Berners-Lee: 'Stop Web's Downward Plunge to Dysfunctional Future,'" *BBC*, March 11, 2019, www.bbc.com/news/technology-47524474.

160. Katrina Brooker, "Exclusive: Tim Berners-Lee Tells Us His Radical New Plan to Upend the World Wide Web," *Fast Company*, September 29, 2018, www.fastcompany.com/90243936/exclusive-tim-berners-lee-tells-us-his-radical-new-plan-to-upend-the-world-wide-web.

Conclusion

1. L. M. Sacasas, "The Analog City and the Digital City," *New Atlantis*, Winter 2020, www.thenewatlantis.com/publications/the-analog-city-and-the-digital-city.

2. James Madison, *The Report of 1800*, January 7, 1800, in *The Papers of James Madison*, vol. 17, ed. David B. Mattern et al. (Charlottesville: University Press of Virginia, 1991), 303–351.

Index

493

Jacob Mchangama is the founder and executive director of the Danish think tank Justitia and the host of the podcast *Clear and Present Danger: A History of Free Speech*. His writing and commentary on free speech have appeared in the *Economist*, the *Washington Post*, *Foreign Policy*, and other outlets. From 2018 to 2020 he was a visiting fellow at the Foundation for Individual Rights in Education (FIRE), and in 2018 he was a visiting scholar at Columbia's Global Freedom of Expression Center in New York. He lives in Copenhagen, Denmark.